New Supply Side Economics

Lin Xiao

New Supply Side Economics

The Structural Reform on Supply Side and Sustainable Growth

格致出版社
Truth & Wisdom Press

Springer

Lin Xiao
Shanghai Municipal Archives
Shanghai
China

Translated by Xiao Weiqing, Tang Yichen, Du Lei and Li Yan
Reviewed by Zhou Shixun, Tan Min

ISBN 978-981-10-4638-4 ISBN 978-981-10-4639-1 (eBook)
DOI 10.1007/978-981-10-4639-1

Jointly published with Truth and Wisdom Press

The print edition is not for sale in China Mainland. Customers from China Mainland please order the print book from: Truth and Wisdom Press.

Library of Congress Control Number: 2017944289

Printed on acid-free paper

This Springer imprint is published by Springer Nature
The registered company is Springer Nature Singapore Pte Ltd.
The registered company address is: 152 Beach Road, #21-01/04 Gateway East, Singapore 189721, Singapore

Contents

Chapter 1
Theoretical Comparison of Supply Side Economics and Demand Side Economics

The supply or demand economics discussed in this book refers to theories focusing the economic analysis and policies on the supply side or the demand side. The so called "supply economics" and "demand economics" may not be as popular as other terms in economics, but they are used as a basis of the methods and terminology in the following research into "structural reform on the supply side". In this chapter, we briefly review the theories of both supply and demand economics as well as the development of their branches, aiming to form the theoretical foundation and methodology for the new supply side economics in China. Since the subject of research is "structural reform on the supply side", this chapter does not cover all that belong to supply and demand economics but the relevant theories and researches, including: (1) supply and demand in market mechanism; (2) basic theories of supply side economics and demand side economics; (3) reflection and transcendence of supply side economics and demand side economics; (4) the studies and discussions in the Chinese economic academia.

1.1 Supply and Demand in Market Mechanism

Supply and demand are two basic terms in modern economics, on which the basic analytic framework and a series of important theories are based. The idea of automatic market mechanism under this framework dominates those theories.

1.1.1 The Origin of Supply and Demand

The concept of supply and demand was formed long before the classical economics (from Adam Smith to the school of subjective value) with the initial meaning being a little bit different from the modern one. "Supply" referred specifically to the fiscal

L. Xiao, *New Supply Side Economics*, DOI 10.1007/978-981-10-4639-1_1

chartered supply and the military logistical support, while "demand" carried a broader meaning of undertaking and utility. The two terms were rarely put together since there is no obvious correspondence.

The rise of the classical economics revolutionized the concept of supply and demand. The former has been widened, indicating the general supply of goods and services, while the latter has been narrowed down to the specific goods-and-service utility correlated with consumers' income. In the classical economics, the quantity demanded refers to the corresponding need in situations with varying prices for different goods or services (Groenewegen 1973). Supply and demand were first used as a coupled term in the book *On the Principles of Political Economy and Taxation* written by David Ricardo. It was also in the book that market, price, supply and demand were first jointly analyzed and the framework of market studies was formed. As for Marx's economic theory, supply and demand is not its core. However, Marx was one of the earliest German economists discussing the concept, whose interpretation of supply was much closer to the modern definition than other classical economists.[1] What's more, the two terms were also linked in his theory.

1.1.2 The Theoretical Framework of Supply and Demand

The concept of supply and demand forms the theoretical foundation for theories regarding how the market works and for different economic policies.

1.1.2.1 Supply and Demand in Microeconomics

Both based on the theoretical framework of supply and demand, supply side economics and demand side economics have different theories and policies at different stages, however. The market mechanism theory in modern economics is concluded in the following paragraphs.

In microeconomics, supply refers to the particular goods or service producers want to sell; demand refers to the particular goods consumers want to buy. The supply function presents the quantity supplied at different prices based on the seller's marginal cost of producing that product. The quantity supplied is proportional to the price. The demand function, on the other hand, shows the buyer's demand for a certain product when the benefit he receives reaches the top according to its price and budgets. And the quantity demanded is inversely proportional to the price.

Market mechanism means the adjustments between price, supply and demand. In private markets for goods and services, prices, quantity supplied and quantity demanded tend to automatically gravitate toward market equilibrium, overcoming

---

[1]For instance, Marx did not use the German term "Angebot" (offer) but "Zufuhr" (supply).

excess supply or excess demand. Furthermore, after the adjustments in private markets, there appears a new supply and demand relationship among those markets. They will also automatically adjust the price and quantity so that there is no more excess supply or excess demand in the end and the General Equilibrium (or Walrasian Equilibrium) is achieved.

1.1.2.2 Supply and Demand in Macroeconomics

In macroeconomics models, aggregate supply stands for the total supply at a specific employment level. Other factors such as labor, capital, land and technology are sometimes taken into account as well. Influenced by all those factors, the aggregate supply function shows the relationship between the overall level of output and the general price. Unlike the supply function in microeconomics, an individual product's marginal productivity and other influential factors are no longer significant at the macro level. Aggregate demand is formed based on the demand for goods, services, capital and money in the actual market. It is also related to the general price. However, the benefits and favoritism of individual demanders are not as significant as those in microeconomics. In markets for commodity, factors of production and labor with the ideal automatic adjustment between price, demand and supply, market equilibrium with full employment can be achieved on a macro level.

Economics theories based on the idea of a free market (supply side economics) hold that the above ideal market mechanism does exist on both micro and macro levels; while those opposing to it (demand side economics) argue that there are certain defects in the market on micro or macro levels which block its automatic gravitation towards equilibrium.

1.1.2.3 Say's Law

Jean-Baptiste Say introduced his idea of supply and demand in his work *A Treatise on Political Economy* (Traité d'économie politique). He demonstrated the above automatic adjustment in the market and his ideas were later called the Say's Law.

Three main principles of the Say's Law include: (1) the value of products (the cost of production) equals the consumers' purchasing power (2) supply creates demand (the purchasing power of one commodity comes from the selling of another) (3) money is a mere medium, which cannot change the current situation of supply and demand. In the original *A Treatise on Political Economy* (Chap. 15), those principles are elaborated as follows: (1) the production and purchase of a product consist of "other values of other products, likewise the fruits of industry, capital and land." (2) "a product is no sooner created, than it, from that instant, affords a market for other products to the full extent of its own value"; "all produce…is ultimately converted into other produce", "in no other places are the sole means of purchase created, that is, values"; "commodities be exchanged for another", "the commodity … appears to" be "the end and object of all transactions"; "all produce naturally gravitates to that place where it is most in demand", "it is production which opens a demand for products." (3) money's "whole utility has consisted in conveying to your hands the value of the commodities, which your customer has sold, for the purpose of buying again from you", "it is products that you want, and not money", "money is but the agent of the transfer of values"; "Sales cannot be said to be dull because money is scarce, but because other products are so."

The "supply creates demand" rule in the Say's Law demonstrates the automatic market mechanism. Generally, supply side economics conforms to the Say's Law, advocating the view that a market, at its full employment level, can automatically gravitate towards equilibrium. Conversely, in demand side economics, a market does not have the ability to automatically reach equilibrium. Due to the different bases, supply side economics argues that there should be no or less government regulation so that the market mechanism works best; demand side economics holds that the government, for the purpose of maintaining full employment and market equilibrium with steady economic growth, must take a series of measures to increase demand and regulate the market through either direct or indirect ways.

1.2 Basic Theories of Supply Side Economics and Demand Side Economics

Relevant theories and policies in supply and demand economics are to be summarized based on the above framework.

1.2.1 Demand Economics with Its Core "Three Carriages"

It was probably mercantilism that first opposed the idea of automatic equilibrium. Criticized by classical economists such as Adam Smith, demand economics was a challenge to the mainstream economics and was then suppressed for a long time. Unlike the mainstream economics, its earlier points of views had been much more distinctive.

1.2.1.1 The Classical Theory of Insufficient Effective Demand

At first, the Say's law was criticized by the classical economists, such as Malthus and Sismondi, from various aspects based on their observation of the economic depression and the collapse of small producers after the French Revolution and the Napoleonic wars. Their criticism, however, is now believed to be the result of misinterpretation. Nevertheless, the concept of insufficient effective demand has been mentioned, which is the origin of relevant concepts and theories in modern economics.

One of the earliest critics of the Say's Law was Malthus, the significant classical economist then. His theory can be divided into four parts: (1) Demand decides supply. According to Malthus, effective demand is people's natural demand, which is both a necessity and a guarantee of supply. Consequently, unlike the relationship described in Say's Law, demand serves as the premise of supply. (2) There exists insufficient effective demand. The situation can be further divided into two types. One refers to the situation of excessive savings, and the other refers to relative demand insufficiency compared with supply. The former, like putting one's income into the cellar, can cause insufficient investment. This denies the equivalence between savings and investment proposed by Smith. The latter type of situation, on the other hand, refers to inadequate consumption. In his correspondence with Ricardo, Malthus elaborated on this second type, holding the view that the savings of workers were transformed to investment, which expanded the capacity of supply and thus caused inadequate consumption. Malthus emphasized it was a kind of long-term effect of the transformation from savings to investment. The problem lies in the fact that the workers' demand is not expanded despite their growing capacity of consumption. (3) Money has the storage function. In his argument against the Say's Law, Malthus held that money was not only a medium for exchange, but could be stored as well. The storage function of money can possibly store people's purchasing power too. (4) The demand side policies. Malthus has put up several policies to solve the problem of effective demand insufficiency, such as the expansion of government expenditure on public utilities. What's more, it is suggested, which is also the target of criticism, that there should a special social class who consume products only, but never produce them (e.g. landlords, officials, ministers etc.) so that the excessive supply can be consumed.

The above points of demand economics were opposed by Ricardo. And they received little attention during the later golden period of Britain in the mid-19th century. The main stream of economics was still the supply economics with a belief of free market.

1.2.1.2 The Keynesian Economics

During the Great Depression in the 1930s, John Maynard Keynes published *The General Theory of Employment, Interest, and Money*, in which he formed his own theory of insufficient effective demand based on that of Malthus.

According to Keynes, the effective demand is the demand at the point of intersection of the total supply and total demand. In other words, the total supply and total demand are balanced. The effective demand determines the social employment, which is not necessarily at the full employment level. Effective demand is composed of consumption and investment. Since the marginal propensity to consume is less than 1, the gap between income and consumption will continue to widen and needs to be filled. Keynes disagrees with the classical economics in the opinion that the savings can be transformed into investment. What insufficient effective demand implies is not only the lack of consumption, but also the lack of investment, which had not been emphasized by Malthus. Investment depends on the uncertain expected rate of return on investment and the current market rate of interest. In the process of capital accumulation, investment shortage with the decline in profits makes it difficult to automatically fill the gap of the savings. Keynes also criticizes the Say's law in that it regards currency as a mere medium of exchange, which is neutral and only affects the nominal GDP and the general level of prices. Keynes points out that money or value storage means that money also affects the actual production and income. In this condition, the value supplied can be temporarily "cached" in case it is "absorbed" by the demand. Keynes puts forward the theory of liquidity preference of interest. He believes in the existence of a kind of "liquidity trap" since the decline in the interest rate of money is slower than that of other assets. The automatic regulation of interest rate, which maintains the equal investment and savings in classical economics, is also negated. As for the wage, it cannot be adjusted automatically to achieve full employment. Keynes thus proposes that the government should take measures on the demand side such as intervening the market, boosting investment and increasing its expenditure in the consumption of public facilities.

1.2.1.3 The Dynamic Keynesian Economics in the Long Run

Originally, the Keynesian economics concerns the short-term employment problems in the depression. During the period from the 1950s to 1970s, it expanded its scope of study, involving the discussion of long-term full employment and sustainable development. The Harrod–Domar model, also called the model of economic growth, was developed.

In *Economic Dynamics*, Roy Harrod further discusses the relationship between savings and investment. He believes that the balanced economic growth is achieved when the savings rate equals the investment rate. In an economic system with elements of labor and capital, the equal relationship also means the synchronous growth of the savings rate, the capital output ratio and the labor growth rate ($s = vn$, "s" refers to savings rate, "v" capital output ratio, "n" the labor growth rate). Harold further points out that there will be excess or insufficient supply capacity with corresponding economic boom (full employment) and recession (unemployment) if the savings rate is higher or lower than the investment rate. This point of view is later accepted by the Solow Growth Model. Harrod also considers the savings rate, capital output ratio and the labor growth rate to be independent of each other. The equal relationship is just accidental. According to Evsey Domar, once the economy has deviated from this equivalence, the rising or recession of the economy will be accumulated due to the short-term and long-term influence of investment on demand and supply (the investment will influence the demand in the short run and will influence the supply in the long run).

According to Harrod and Domar, the capital output ratio and the labor growth rate depend on the technological progress and the natural population growth. Hence, the government has scarcely to do with keeping economic growth balanced. The only desirable way is to adjust savings and consumption-investment structure (profit-wage structure) on the demand side.

1.2.1.4 The Economic Growth Theory of "Three Carriages" on the Demand Side

Keynes and his followers have consequently developed the demand economics with theories on the demand side. To maintain stable economic growth and full employment, the demand management is highlighted from three aspects: consumption, investment and export. These form the renowned theory of "Three Carriages". In short, the first carriage is to encourage consumption. The government can promote the distribution and redistribution of property and income system (including the progressive tax and the legacy duty so that the uneven distribution can be avoided) as well as strengthen the social welfare and security to protect private consumption and increase the propensity to consume. The second is to encourage investment. Apart from a series of tax policies to encourage private investment, the government also invests directly in the infrastructure and public sector to form a strong state-owned economy in the industrial field. The third is to encourage exports, meaning to encourage processing trade to form external demand and promote export-oriented economy by relying on the country's peculiar resources (such as the cheap labor). Although policies to encourage export are not involved in Keynesian economics, they have been successfully widespread from the early 1960s to the 21st century among such countries as Japan, China and the "Four Asian Tigers".

1.2.2 Relevant Theories on the Demand Side

There are also some social theories on the demand side other than the Keynesian economics and "Three Carriages". Some of those theories elaborate on the social background for economic policies and others explore the value of demand side.

1.2.2.1 The Theory of Regulation

In his theories, Keynes puts forward the demand management to achieve full employment and stable growth. Effective demand management is based on specific systems. In the 1970s, French economic sociologists, such as Michel Aglietta, Alain Lipietz and Robert Boyer, proposed the regulation theories and built a theoretical framework for the demand economics.

The regulation school of economics opposes the idea that the market can attain the balance between supply and demand through the "invisible hand". It is believed that capitalism needs three kinds of coordinating systems to achieve economic expansion at different developing stages. Namely, the production paradigm, the accumulation system and the adjustment mechanism. The production paradigm refers to the micro production operating mode (such as the division of labor). The accumulation system is a system of macro resources and income distribution that maintains consumption and keeps the balance between supply and demand. The adjustment mechanism guarantees the constant production and accumulation through adjustment of marketing, economics, finance, society, ideology, media action and the world order (in micro and macro areas). The appropriate adjustment mechanism is the basis for the production paradigm and the accumulation system.

The regulation school divides the postwar western society into two stages. The first is the period before the 1980s, when capitalism took a paradigm of massive and standardized production with corresponding accumulation system of massive and standardized consumption, which formed the adjustment mechanism with lawful union wage negotiations and populist democracy. The second is the period after the 1980s, when, with the development of modern communication technology, there appeared small-scale, customized production mode and flexible accumulation system with innovation and financial features. The corresponding adjustment mechanism has also been developed with wage dispersion negotiation, equity stimulation, regulation relaxation, the new public management, etc.

1.2.2.2 The "General Economy"

The theory of Georges Bataille is one of the origins of the contemporary Western ideas. Bataille argues that economists only consider economy per se. In his *The Accursed Share*, what he discusses is the general economy.

According to Georges Bataille, an economy with vitality absorbs more resources (supply) than what is needed to maintain its survival (i.e. the demand reproduced). The excess resources (savings) are used for economic growth (investment in expanded reproduction). But there is a surplus, which must be consumed without the restriction of economic interests. Bataille calls this part of surplus the "cursed part". And since the accumulation of economic interest is always limited, the "cursed part" is inevitable. If the community does not take the initiative to consume this part by ways of luxury, games, art, abnormal sexual behavior, it will be consumed in the end through a kind of "catastrophic consumption" (such as war). The specific way of consumption varies from society to society. And in economic and social evolution, development and transformation, this part of consumption is necessary.

Thus, from the perspective of the supply and demand, Bataille's objective demand is similar to the effective demand, which cannot completely consume the supply in a normal economy. It is necessary to find special approaches to consume the supply which have no specific objectives so that the economy and the society can be transformed and the society can be operated and managed soundly.

1.2.3 *Supply Economics with Its Core Theory of "Four Factors"*

Generally speaking, the classical economics holds the idea of a free market. It is considered to be a normal state of the economy to be automatically adjusted to reach equilibrium. A variety of economic analyses are also carried out on this premise. These ideas of classical economics are basically consistent with the so-called supply economics. In other words, supply economics is classical economics. But after the World War II, economic theories advocating the demand management of the government has dominated the field. And the term "supply side economics" is used by the school of free market to distinguish itself from the theories and policies of the demand economics.

1.2.3.1 The Classical Economics of Free Market

Classical economists such as Adam Smith and David Ricardo can all be grouped in the school of supply economics. Here we regard Ricardo as the representative of supply economics in the classical period, for he inherited the theory of "invisible hand" from Smith and his ideas also corresponded with the Say's law. What's more, he made an original, accurate and profound conclusion of Say's law in his discussion with Malthus.

Adhering to the free market theories of general classical economics, Ricardo, comparing with the demand economics of Malthus, also clarified three points of supply economics. First of all, it is a temporary phenomenon that the supply surpasses the demand, which will occur only under the condition of coordination failure, miscalculation and imbalance. Therefore, it is not a universal and long-term problem and thus cannot be classified as systematic and structural problems. Nevertheless, Ricardo showed no objections to the government's intervention of certain temporary imbalances. Secondly, Ricardo denies Malthus's generalized insufficient effective demand. Ricardo argues it is almost impossible for massive insufficient consumption to appear. Malthus discusses insufficient consumption in a peculiar situation when the consumption structure changes. However, the long-term supply structure (investment or accumulation) is not affected by the short-term consumption structure. And the supply structure will be adjusted correspondingly according to the consumption structure. Thirdly, with the accumulation of capital, the consumption structure and the investment structure tend to overlap with each other.[2] These views advocate the regulation mechanism of full employment, economic growth and the automatic balance between supply and demand. In the

[2]However, Ricardo also admits one special case: the rising wage (due to the rising rent) reduces the rate of profit, causing the deficiency in capital competition and investment demand (*Principles of Political Economy and Taxation*, Chap. 21). In this case, he opposes the idea of equal savings and investment by Adam Smith (another case of the Say's law). Therefore, Ricardo is opposed to

mid-1810s, Ricardo actively advocated the repeal of the Corn Laws, insisting the implementation of free trade policies to promote the development of capitalism.

After Ricardo, the theory of free market remained the mainstream of economics. Although classical economics and the framework of supply and demand evolved after the 1870s, the opinion of free market has not changed and has been even stronger than before.

1.2.3.2 The Opinions of the Automatic Adjustment of Market

During the Great Depression in the 1930s, the rise of the Keynesian economics ended the dominance of the classical supply economics. During the 30 years after the World War II, the mainstream of economics was the demand economics. However, one can find the ideas of supply economics in the demand economics as well. The combination of the Keynesian economics and the free market theory formed a new classical synthesis theory, providing the foundation for the later revival of the supply economics.

There are mainly two models related to supply economics: (1) the IS-LM model, which applies the general theory of equilibrium and thus corresponds with free market theories; (2) the AS-AD model (based on the concept of the aggregate production function on the supply side), which is an important framework for the discussion of economic growth and inflation in demand economics.

Influenced by these models, the Keynesian economics has become a special short-term case of the market economy in depression, while the free market has become the general theory in economics.

1.2.3.3 The Endogenous Growth Theory

In macroeconomics, the aggregate supply is a function of the number of jobs. Representatives of neoclassical growth theory and the later endogenous growth theory such as Robert Solow, Paul Romer, and Robert Lucas have studied the economic growth. In their models, the aggregate supply capacity on the supply side is classified into four factors: labor, capital, land (natural resources) and technologies. Following the Theory of the Firm, the aggregation of labor, capital and land form the function of aggregate production.[3]

These growth theories discuss the contribution of labor, capital, land and other factors to the supply side. The fourth element (technology) is analyzed from two special perspectives. It is firstly looked at as the remainder of the other three factors

(Footnote 2 continued)

Malthus's opinion of insufficient consumption, which is the starting point of his theory of insufficient effective demand.

[3]The general aggregate production function only includes two factors: labor and capital.

(called the Solow residual), which is the integrated contributions or "total factor productivity". Secondly, technology is regarded as the additional parts to labor, capital and land (e.g. education, training, operation, improvement, etc.). The supply side theory of four factors is thus formed.

After the 1980s, the endogenous growth theory was improved in the study of technical elements. Terms created by Schumpeter such as the "entrepreneur-spirit" and the "creative destruction" were brought into the framework. (Schumpeter is therefore improperly regarded as a supply economist.) That turned the attention of supply side economics to technological innovation, in sharp contrast to the demand economics.

1.2.4 Relevant Theories on the Supply Side

In addition to the four factors, other theories elaborating on the supply side economics include the theory of "Limits to Growth", the supply side economics and the shortage economy.

1.2.4.1 Resource Depletion

The Limits to Growth, commissioned by the Club of Rome, is a well-known report on the resource depletion in the long-term economic growth. A model of world development is developed in the report using the methods of the system dynamics. The report made pessimistic predictions for the future economic growth. With population explosion, food production, consumption of non-renewable resources, industrial pollution, environmental pollution and other issues becoming bottlenecks in the economic development, the economic growth would stop during the year 2000–2100 if people continued with the current developing mode. Accordingly, the report suggested controlling the growth so as to keep the balance between the population and capital.

The report is not based on the supply side economics, but the five questions raised relate directly to the problems of basic factors of supply (population, land and energy, etc.). The ideas in the report are not generally approved by economists. Supply-side economists might consider it impossible for the growth to stop. Since the market mechanism can be automatically adjusted, resource prices will zoom before the depletion, turning other resources into substitutes.

1.2.4.2 Supply Side Economics

In the 1980s, theories of supply side economics emerged in the U.S. and Britain. Although there was no theoretical framework of four factors, those theories were consistent with the supply economics, providing relevant policies and advocating the idea of a free market.

Representatives of supply side economics include George Gilder and Arthur Laffer. Gilder provides the theoretical background, holding the idea that wealth and poverty is linked to the efficiency and fairness in the modern society. Keynesian economics emphasizes equity and the cause and effect relationship of supply and demand is reversed. He agrees with the idea of "supply creates demand" stated in the Say's Law. Laffer proposes a "Laffer curve", in which the number of tax, with the increase in tax rates, will rise at first but gradually fall after reaching the maximum. The rising of tax rates implies more leisure in place of production, reducing the income and the tax base. Therefore, Laffer proposes that the government cut the tax and limit the welfare so that the market can play its role and the supply capacity can be increased.

Supply-side economics is indeed a reflection of postwar European economic policies. Its theoretical value is limited. Economists such as Robert Mundell and Steven Cheung even have sympathy for the school.[4]

1.2.4.3 The Revolutionary Theories of Socialist Countries

The socialist countries started their revolution in the 1980s as well. A majority of theories and policies were put forward by economists from Eastern Europe. Among them, János Kornai and his shortage economy were among the most important, significant for the economic development and revolution.

Kornai proposes three possible restraints of enterprises from the perspective of the supply side: resources, demand and budget. In capitalist enterprises, the restraint of budget is effective, forming the effective demand restraint. What is prevalent in the economy is the insufficient effective demand. However, in socialist economies, production factor and the distribution of products are planned. The budget and demand restraints are relatively invalid.[5] The shortage or lack of supply is widespread in the economy due to massive production, hoard and lack of investment. In addition, enterprises in the socialist economy tend to reduce output and change the product mix in the face of resource restraints, further exacerbating the shortage economy. Kornai traces the invalid budget restraints to the paternalism of the government. Therefore, he proposes a reform of the socialist ownership and its decision-making mechanisms to resolve the problem of shortage.

[4]In the early 1970s, Robert Mundell criticized from the supply side perspective the Nixon administration for curbing inflation through high tax. However, he had not made contribution to the school and was not an active advocator.

[5]Invalid budget restraints include: (1) the flexible planned price. Most companies can raise the price in disguised form to shift losses. (2) The flexible tax system (3) the appropriation from the State (4) the flexible credit system (5) the flexible conditions for investment.

1.3 Reflection and Transcendence of Supply Side Economics and Demand Side Economics

1.3.1 Reflection on Division of Economy into Supply and Demand

According to Kornai's economics theory, it is the soft constraints of demand side that have caused the shortage in the supply side of the socialist economy, which forms the cause and effect relationship between supply and demand. This will naturally trigger some problems in terms of the reliability and inevitability of the division of economy into supply and demand, the feasibility of policy practice, and the possible transcendence of this "dichotomy".

1.3.1.1 Three Viewpoints in Terms of the Dichotomy

Currently, there are three attitudes towards the dichotomy of economy.

The first holds the opinion that the economy has potentials and sustainability. Supply economics is concerned with the productivity and long-term economic development. Therefore, the supply side policy will affect the potential growth rate for the long-term institutional and structural problems. Demand economics, on the other hand, focuses on short-term problems, especially during a depression. Demand-side policies may be effective in the short term by enforcing short-term management policies but they may also be invalid for the long-term systematic problems. Many economists, especially those from China, agree on this point. Therefore, the government is supposed to pay attention to long-term systematic problems and promote the establishment and improvement of market order, acting as the market guardian.

The second view acknowledges the law of economic development, holding that the productivity depends on the level of development in the long run. However, it is also the productivity that raises the potential of economic development or growth to a certain height. It does not mean that the economy will forever stay at that level. The government's short-term management policies of demand may be incapable of changing this potential height, but they can and they must influence the economy so that it will maintain at this level or at least not deviate too far. The role of the government is not just to make orders and act merely as the guardian of the market, but to actively intervene the market and be a participant in it. This view has been prevailing the economics field for a long time.

Economists holding the third type of view don't even admit the long-term problems which do not depend on short-term ones (such long-term problems may only exist in situations after "we are all dead", described by Keynes). The long-term potential level of economic development and growth is based on short-term policies. Management policies of demand have impact not only on the short-term level but the long-term as well. The economy will demonstrate the long-term potential by effecting one short-term policy after another.

The divergence between the first two is whether the long-term or the short-term economic development and growth is normal. The third point of view puts forward ways of how to distinguish and connect the short-term and long-term and how to transform from short-term to long-term in the mechanism.

1.3.1.2 Two Sides of One Coin—Supply and Demand

Other theories apart from the dichotomy of economy describe supply and demand as the two sides of one coin.

For instance, Steven N.S. Cheung, in his interpretation of the Say's law, points out that the supply side is the opposite of demand side and the supply of a commodity is actually its demand as well. (1) The quantity of a commodity a person is willing to give up means, on the other hand, the quantity of such goods he is willing to hold. (2) In the absence of fixed production and trading, the marginal cost equals the marginal utility. (3) Considering the possibility of production and investment, the choice to produce (invest) or not to depends on the evaluation of utility. In other words, whether to produce or not, or how much goods should be produced are reactions to the utility. Therefore, the supply and demand form a kind of "mirror image", which is fundamentally one thing. Supply and demand curves are also the same curve and the equilibrium always exists. Savings, according to Cheung, seems to be voluntary with no investment or profitless investment.

However, Cheung does separate supply and demand in his correction of the Say's Law. The Law holds that supply does not create demand. Rather it aims for demand. But Cheung thinks that there exists a cause and effect relationship between supply and demand. The former is the cause while the latter is the effect.

1.3.1.3 The Result of Social Division

Based on the inframarginal economic analysis, Yang Xiaokai provides a good way of thinking in terms of the division of supply and demand. According to him, the structure of the supplier (enterprise) and the demander (consumer) in the new classical economics is exogenously determined. Therefore, people's supply and demand is not related to their choices. However, in reality, the distinction between supply and demand shows the professional level of performance. It is the final decision made by people based on transaction costs. In the completely self-sufficient economy, the division becomes clear with the decline of the transaction costs, and the economic benefit of division begins to rise, promoting the economic evolution and finally leading to the specialization of the economy. For the same kind of product, some people are specialized in the production and supply, while some others are specialized in demand. Therefore, the separation of supply and demand is related to the specific transaction costs.

We can infer from Yang's discussion that the policies of reducing transaction cost may change the structure of both supply and demand. It is difficult to distinguish between supply side policies and demand side ones. There is no such necessity. The key lies in the transaction cost, social division and specialization.

1.3.1.4 Convergence of Research Approaches

In theoretical researches of economic growth, full employment and economic cycle, there exists no distinction between the supply side and the demand side. And the two are also converging. One of the main causes of this integration is the micro research in macroeconomics.

Macroeconomics (such as the new classical economics) has long been regarded as theories lack of micro foundation and established on mere statistical phenomena. The traditional microeconomic behavior is considered to be affected by the market price adjustment, which can reach balance by itself. In the 1980s, influenced by theories of free market and policy economics (such as the school of rational expectation), macroeconomics is explored in a micro way to provide a systematic and comprehensive basis for requirement administrative policies.

In this respect, the new Keynesian economics is an important theory. It holds the opinion that uncoordinated behavior and asymmetric information are the micro foundation for the fact that people can not automatically adjust to the market equilibrium. Since the 1990s, economists of this school, such as George Akerlof, Janet Yellen, Joseph Stiglitz, have been arguing that these short-term factors and the demand side policies in response to these factors have long-term supply side effects on economic structure. Stiglitz studies the interaction between supply side factors and demand, as well as the influence of demand on technological progress (total supply power). The beginning of the 21st century witnessed the proposition of the theory of dynamic stochastic general equilibrium (DSGE), which brought the imperfect competition assumption (prices and wages are not fully adjusted) to new Keynesian economics in replace of that of perfect competition. The rational decision-making is also synthesized to dynamic general equilibrium. Therefore, in general, these ideas converge the approaches of research on both the supply side and the demand side.

1.3.2 Evaluation of Supply Side and Demand Side Policies

In addition to the discussion of theories, it is also significant to assess the actual effects of supply side and demand side policies. In fact, it is also hard to completely distinguish between the effects of the two. We are going to look at the them from two aspects: policy simulation and practical implementation.

1.3.2.1 Results of Stimulation of Supply Side and Demand Side Policies

Giovanni Dosi and others (Dosi, Fagiolo, and Roventini 2010, hereinafter referred to as DFR) evaluated the effects of policies on both the supply side and the demand side through simulation. Their three research questions are (1) the supply side problems ('Schumpeterian' problems), which deals with the influence of technological innovation on full employment and long-term sustainable growth; (2) the demand side problems ('Keynesian' problems), which deals with the interaction between the supply side technology innovation and demand side consumption, investment and other areas; (3) the influence of demand side conditions on the long-term growth, or whether it is supply side (technical innovation and other factors) or demand side (consumption and investment) that fuels the long-term economic growth. DFR simulated the policies in various systems with different demand side conditions (the result is displayed in Table 1.1).

According to the result, DFR have found that in the long run, in terms of the economic growth momentum, easier market access, higher technological opportunities, strong anti-monopoly policies and higher technology searching competence

Table 1.1 Stimulation of policies on the supply side and the demand side in different market conditions

Market environment	GDP growth rate (%)	GDP instability	Unemployment rate (%)
General situation	2.54	8.09	10.72
Fewer opportunities for technological innovation	1.95	7.94	*13.57*
More opportunities for technological innovation	*3.15*	*8.28*	10.25
Lower capabilities to do technological researches	2.31	*8.25*	11.76
Higher capabilities to do technological researches	*2.68*	7.75	10.31
With no imitation	2.54	6.93	10.49
Narrow patent (esp. for particular technology)	2.42	7.61	11.32
Broad patent (esp. for proximity technology)	1.63	*6.31*	13.29
Difficult market entry (weak competitors)	1.83	7.98	*14.02*
Easy market entry (strong competitors)	*3.76*	6.97	*8.53*
Weak anti-monopoly	2.65	6.98	10.36
Strong anti-monopoly	*2.73*	*5.08*	*8.37*
Supply-side policies without demand management policies	1.11	155.11	78.55

(1) The supply side policies in the table include policies for technological innovation policy or Schumpeterian policy;
(2) GDP instability is the standard deviation*100 in standard condition

are the most powerful impetus of long-term economic growth. In terms of the economic stability, more technological innovation opportunities and less technology sourcing can increase economic instability, but a strong anti-monopoly and generalized patent system can reduce the instability. In terms of employment, strong anti-monopoly and easier access to the market can increase the employment, and fewer technological innovation opportunities and more difficult market access can largely reduce employment.

DFR also think that the Schumpeterian supply side technological innovation policies without any demand management policies will reduce the level of economic growth and break the stability of growth, causing sudden increase in unemployment. Demand management policies of the Keynesian economics help to slow down the economic decline. It also has a long-term impact on the supply side, especially long-term productivity and growth. Schumpeterian technical innovation policies per se cannot maintain a high-level growth for a long time. Nor can they reduce the volatility of the economic cycle and reduce the unemployment rate. In situations with low income, low R&D and low investment, there is no demand management policy. And it is impossible for the economy to grow at a fast speed with supply side policies. After reaching a certain point, financial measures can no longer change the long-term level of average growth. However, the fluctuations of growth can be reduced and the state of full employment can also last.

Additionally, DFR have further studied the effect of the demand management policies in different labor market systems. They have found that the effect of the demand side fiscal policies has nothing to do with the wage adjustment mechanism, no matter it is average productivity based, consumption index based or unemployment growth based. Especially in the unemployment growth based mechanism (or other mechanism added this basis), the promotion of economic recovery and growth by the self-adjustment of wage and price, stated by classical economists, will not naturally occur. Demand management policies are thus necessary and effective. After all, there exists no wage adjustment mechanism which can restore economic growth and the demand side policies of Keynesian economics play a role in the maintenance of long-term growth.

To conclude, the supply side and demand side policies coexist and complement each other. Therefore, they cannot be completely effective when discussed alone.

1.3.2.2 Practice of Supply Side and Demand Side Policies

Since 1940s, countries around the world have implemented demand side or supply side economic policies in different periods. However, there has been no conclusive evaluation of the actual effects of these policies.

Generally, western countries implemented demand management policies from the 1950s to the 1970s, bringing a stable golden period of development lasting over two decades. But the long-term demand management policies caused the later stagflation, and this implementation was further proved to be ineffective by supply economists, who advocate the free market. Even so, demand management policies remain standing measures for countries in the later recessions after the 1980s (such as the Asian financial crisis in the late 1990s and the economic and financial crisis since 2008). In socialist countries and some non-socialist developing countries, although many of their policies cannot be easily classified, but their plans and management policies often possessed the characteristics of the demand management, which is regarded on one hand as the foundation for the rapid development within a specific period of time, but on the other hand the cause of long-term economic or vitality shortage.

Since the 1980s, during the reign of Reagan and Thatcher, most western countries have implemented the free-market policies of supply side economics for more than 20 years, resisting excessive government intervention through large-scale privatization, deregulation and competition. Some countries had even followed the complete supply side economic policies for a period of time. It is generally believed that these supply side policies have revitalized the economy. But some also think that those policies should be responsible for the failure of regulation, income gap, bubble economy, and especially the world economic crisis since 2008. Although many countries, after the crisis, have readopted regulatory measures to control the market, so far they have had no intention to return to the early extent of intervention. In countries transferring from planned economy to market economy, such as China, there is no desire to return to the planned economy either. Furthermore, almost all big countries are taking efforts to improve their market competition system (e.g. innovation) to restore long-term growth, and the supply side policies are often involved in this process.

Therefore, in terms of practice, the demand economics might be effective during depression, while the supply economics might be more concerned with the development of productivity and the long-term economic vitality. However, this kind of argument might be right only in a narrow sense.

1.3.3 Economic Theories Beyond Supply and Demand

The supply and demand is the basic analytic framework in modern economics, from which policies and theories based on different sides are formed. There are also many economic theories with no direct connection to supply and demand but economic structures of certain types. These theories, though mostly not mature, can provide different perspectives for the reflection of the framework.

1.3.3.1 Structural Problems in Supply and Demand

The structural problems in economics are long-term problems to a large extent. Even in supply economics, the short-term imbalance between supply and demand is inevitable. For instance, in Ricardo's discussion with Malthus, they also admitted that supply might surpass the demand when there occurred coordination failure, calculation error and proportion imbalance. In their opinion, however, the imbalance was just a short-term problem. In the long run, supply and demand would be balanced with no structural problems. Therefore, the short-term imbalance is not attached importance to by economists holding the view of a free market. Those against free market, on the other hand, contend that there are some long-term structural problems. To put it in a simpler way, there is no possible equilibrium state in the long term.

1.3.3.2 The Circulation of Reproduction

The macroeconomic process is the circulation in different sectors. From this perspective, supply and demand are input and output between different sectors. The terminology of aggregate supply and aggregate demand is not necessarily quoted here. The economy means a kind of structural relation and dynamic process. The balance between different sectors must be maintained so that the economy and the production can be sustainable and keep developing.

Francois Quesnay, the French leading economist of the physiocratic school, made his "Tableau économique", a diagram presenting the circulation of national production and the distribution of products in different classes under the condition of constant prices, simple reproduction and closed economy. In his analysis of social reproduction, Marx has extended Quesnay's idea and further analyzed value and expanded reproduction. Marx does not directly use the concept of "aggregate social supply" and "aggregate social demand". He divides the total value of social product into three parts: c, v and m. Social production includes the production of consumption and the production of capital. And the structural relations in social production is analyzed with the reproduction of social capital added, which further forms the theory of balance between aggregate supply and aggregate demand. This is the balance of reproduction, value and price, which is also a kind of balance between the total amount and structure, between the plan and result, and also between the value and quantity. Based on Quesnay and Marx, Wassily Leontief developed his analysis of input and output during the period from the 1940s to the 1970s. His methodology provides a tool for the systematic analysis of the complicated supply-demand relations in different industries and sectors. It is commonly used in national economic planning and is thus considered to be closely related to the planned economy. However it is neglected by many economists in that it can hardly be applied to detailed analysis of the market and the policies.

1.3.3.3 Economics of Structuralism

Economics of structuralism was formed during the period from the 1950s to the 1970s (economists of this school include Rosenstein-Rodin, Hollis Chenery, Ragnar Nurkse etc.) It provides methods for analyzing the structure and system of supply and demand in developing countries where long-term economic problems prevail.

Generally speaking, the supply and demand in structural economics is the relation between production sectors, factor markets and systems. In developing countries, there exist two mutually associated 'circulation chains': a supply side circulation chain of "low income—low savings—lack of capital—low productivity—low income" and a demand side circulation chain of "low income—low consumption—lack of investment—low capital using rate—low productivity—low income".[6] Due to the effect of the two chains, there is a systematic fracture and imbalance in long-term supply and demand. As a result, it is often difficult for developing countries to achieve market equilibrium and to develop sustainably. They are mired in poverty in the long run. Meanwhile, the failure of market and price regulation between the supply and demand lies in the incomplete markets in developing countries, with the indivisibility and complementarily behind the supply and demand, which leads to the lack of marginal effect and the ability to substitute.[7] And these factors can be accumulated, leading to the market's further deviation from equilibrium, blocking the long-term development in supply and demand. Therefore, for developing countries, it is suggested by structural economics that the industries and tax system should be reformed structurally and large-scale centralized industrialization should be promoted.

The policies advocated by structural economics have not achieved great success due to its neglect of market effect. Nevertheless, structural economics provides a new aspect for economic analysis of developing countries.

1.3.3.4 Theory of Innovation and Development

In the mainstream economics analysis, the concept of technical or commercial innovation is discussed according to the Solow Residual of the aggregate production function. However, Schumpeter's innovation theory is more profound than that.

The innovation theory (*The Theory of Economic Development*, 1912; *Business cycles: a theoretical, historical, and statistical analysis of the capitalist process*, 1939) is part of Schumpeter's theory of development, which is based on the idea of economic circulation or structural theory. He believes that the future can be predicted according to the economy providing the condition of circulation does not change. In this economy, mere factory owners, rather than real entrepreneurs, consist of the main body of production. And their daily business practice is just a formality. Savings is zero in this economic form, as it is fully predictable.

---

[6]Structural economics argues that capital accumulation (formation) or investment is a hub to connect the two 'circulation chains', and capital accumulation is not only the allocation problem of the capital market itself, but the problem of both the capital and the consumption, involving factors such as the system, culture, market size and structure, international trade and so on.

[7]Inseparability: non-continuous subdivision in production factors or variables, the mode of production or production function, demand and other aspects. Complementarily: the correlation between industries and their lack of independence.

Circulated economy is one that tends to be balanced or sustainable.[8] Schumpeter believes that innovation can enter the economy once it is approaching the state of equilibrium. In this respect, innovation can be technological innovation, or more extensive business innovation and system innovation, which stops the original trend towards balance by completely changing the conditions for economic circulation. And this is the start of the new economy. Schumpeter believes that entrepreneurs are those who innovate, and they are not common business owners. Entrepreneurs do not belong to a fixed class. They "float" in the market forever.

Schumpeter does not deal with economic growth, but its dynamic nature. Innovation, through investment, spreads in the economy, changing the structure of industries and of supply and demand. The theory extends to a broader area than general economic analysis.

1.4 Study and Discussion in the Chinese Economic Academia

During the period from the 1950s to the 1980s, the purpose of the socialist production was to meet the needs of the people's increasing social demand. The planned economy, therefore, put more emphasis on the guarantee of supply. In terms of the economic theory, the research focus was also on supply. China started its reform and opening-up in the 1980s. The purpose was to liberate the productivity from the planned economic system. Therefore, a lot of reforming theories were attributed to the supply side. Most Chinese economic theories had focused on the reform of supply system for more than 30 years. With the establishment of the market economy system, the supply market in China has been gradually transforming to the demand market since the mid-1990s. The economic growth was increasingly dependent on demand. Under this condition, the economists drew their attention to the policy factors of the demand management, bringing a large number of theoretical discussions about demand. Meanwhile, economists also paid special attention to systematic problems involved in the study of demand. Since the reform has been implemented in the economy with an unbalanced structure, the reform itself is also unbalanced in most cases. As a result, a lot of structural problems have been studied as well.

The main foundation for the theory of supply side structural reform is the theory of socialist market economy of China and researches on the supply side, demand side and structure. Here we make a brief review of these theories and researches.[9]

---

[8]Therefore, in a specific aggregate production function, if there is a repeated residual, as an innovation factor, is close to the equilibrium state according to Schumpeter.

[9]The discussion follows the problems involved rather than the order of general theoretical structure.

1.4.1 The Formation and Development of the Theory of Socialist Market Economy

Since the reform and opening-up of China, the theory of socialist market economy has been the mainstream of economics in the country, forming the supply side theories related to structural reform. We will analyze the major market reform and the effect of the government and the market, and our discussion will be divided into four parts.

1.4.1.1 Market Adjustment

In 1978, with its reform and opening-up, China aimed at managing the problems of planning and market combination by obeying economic rules and focusing on the value. In 1982, during the twelfth national congress, the effect of the market on economy was confirmed and it was put forward that the country should focus on planned economy assisted by the adjustment of the market. Therefore, planning was in the dominant position during this period, while market was still supplementary. However, on the other hand, the market has been legalized since then, which is a starting point for China's exploration of the theories of the socialist market economy.

1.4.1.2 Commodity Economy

In 1984, the theory of the commodity economy was put forward during the Third Plenary Session of the Twelfth Central Committee. The development of the commodity economy was described then as an inevitable stage in social development. During the thirteenth national congress in 1987, the theory of the primary stage of socialism was formulated, the aim of which was to expand various areas of the economy in the public-owned system and to encourage entrepreneurs, despite the scarcity of this group, to make a fortune. The commodity economy became the key component. The concept then was vague since it did not elaborate on the definition of "commodity", but it nevertheless foreshadowed the subsequent market economic theory.

1.4.1.3 Market as the Foundation

During the fourteenth national congress in 1992, it was suggested that the market should serve as a foundation for the allocation of resources. That became a goal of the socialist market economy in 1993 and was specified and systemized during the Fourteenth Central Committee. The fundamental effect of the market was emphasized repeatedly during the subsequent years in the fifteenth to eighteenth national congresses from 1997 to 2012. During the sixteenth congress, the goal of the modern market system was defined. During the seventeenth congress, a macroeconomic control system was the new objective. And during the eighteenth congress, the goal set was a good relationship between the government and the market. Those goals and the operation followed help to perfect the theories of the socialist market economy.

1.4.1.4 Market as a Decisive Factor

During the Third Plenary Session of the 18th CPC Central Committee in 2013, comprehensive economic reform was the core of the systematic economic reform. The key issue was to deal with the relationship between the government and the market so that the market could play a decisive role in the allocation of resources. The economy with mixed ownership was also proposed, which marked a new stage in the development of the socialist market economy theories. The Fourth Plenary Session of the 18th CPC Central Committee in the next year further noted the promotion of the economic and peaceful development. In 2015, adherence to scientific development and revolution was emphasized in the Fifth Plenary Session. All the above proposals and objectives have formed the foundation for the supply side structural reform.

1.4.2 Economic Researches on the Supply Side and Demand Side in China

1.4.2.1 Researches on the Supply Side

The Chinese economists have conducted a lot of researches on the socialist market economic theory. The efficiency of factor supply further provides foundation for the sustainable development theory. Therefore, researches nowadays are factor-supply oriented. The system and revolution of factor supply have become the main subject in the discussion of the sustainable development theory. Supply economics is a revolutionized field to a large extent.

Wang (2000) first studies the impact of capital, labor and resources on the economic growth, basically consistent with the general studies of the four factors. The subsequent studies have shifted their focus to the market-oriented reform, industrial restructuring and their respective effect on technological progress and economic growth. Wei and Hou (2007) assess the value of factors such as labor and capital. According to Michael Porter's four stages of economic growth, they argue that that the economy of China is still at the investment stage with dependence on factor supply, extensive growth and intensive capital. In their study, technological innovation and the systematic reform of factor input are regarded as the foundation for a successful transformation.

The studies of the factor supply system and its reform focus on ownership, property rights, modern enterprise system, the efficiency of factor supply and the role of the government.

In terms of the reform of ownership, Dong (1994) suggests a variety of public ownership systems followed by various non-public ones. Xiao (1996) and Fan (1998) propose the collaboration, integration and conversion of public and private ownership. The structure of ownership is closely related to supply side matters such as the efficiency of factor allocation and the issue of equity. According to Dong (2002) and Gao (2005), the non-public economy tend to be more efficient. Chang (2006), based on the efficiency standards, also puts forward the problems of organization and structuring for the state-owned economy. Liu and Zhang (2008) propose the "anti-efficient allocation" of the state-owned economy that exists among the secondary and tertiary industries. These studies present the reform towards privatization through fierce competition and new regulations among monopoly industries (including service industries) (Wang 2001; Wang et al. 2013; Chang 2001).

The studies on modern enterprise system, with the supply system as the core, include the study of property right and its form, governance structure and other aspects. It is basically agreed that the key to the reform of state enterprises lies in the independence and distinction of property rights as well as the diversification of investment subjects (Wu et al. 1994; Zhou 2000; Liu 1998). The shareholding system reform of state enterprises is an effective way to improve the efficiency of capital factors (Gao 1998; Wei 2008).[10] It is also believed that the capital market IPO of state enterprises can improve the internal governance structure of state enterprises, prevent short-term opportunistic behavior and establish a modern enterprise system (Zhang and Zhou 1997). After 2010, as state enterprises have gradually dominated the market, there have appeared new researches on issues of system and supply efficiency such as the relationship between the state enterprises and the government, improvement of the market order etc. (Jin 2010). State enterprises are proposed to attract more private capital investment so that the subjects can be diversified.

In terms of the labor factor in discussions about the efficiency of production factor supply, it was put forward at the beginning of the reform and opening-up that the labor market was a necessity in the socialist market economic system (Wang 1994; Xing 1994). Subsequent researches shifted their topics to issues of labor factor efficiency such as human capital, education (Cai 1999; Yang et al. 2003) and aging population (Wang 2010; Liu et al. 2013). There are also a majority of researches dealing with the effect of labor transfer on the structure, economic

[10]Zou (1997) proposes three stages in the realization public ownership: public ownership dominant, state-owned economy dominant and the asset organization of public ownership. The shareholding system belongs to the third stage.

growth and the efficiency of labor factors in the process of industrialization, urbanization and marketization (Li and Yin 2005; Cai 2012). Pan and Wei (2013), Wan and Li (2013) further study the institutional barriers such as the mobility of labor factors and the reform of household register system. In terms of the capital factor, Lin and Liu (2003) as well as the research group of economic growth and macro stability (2010) link the contribution of capital to developing mode and strategies. It is also pointed out by the research group that, like most developing countries, the economy in China is transforming from the planned economy to the market economy. After the rapid capitalization of the economic resource stock, the forging ahead of the economy and the efficiency improvement have a positive effect on economic growth. In terms of the land factors, the input of land factors contributes to the rapid economic growth. However, the low efficiency is also the cause of the unsustainability of economic growth. Economists have paid attention to the effect of low efficiency on fiscal and land systems (Jiang 2014). The studies of technological innovation factors have calculated the contribution of technological progress to economic growth. Liu and Zhang (2008) also believe that, with marketization, the contribution of technological progress tends to surpass that of industrial structure and market changes. On the other hand, the research group of economic growth and macro stability (2010) thinks that the capitalization in China might restrain technological innovation, so the technological progress contribute little to the economic growth. Economists have also studied the total factor productivity, which depends on reform and structural bonus to a large extent (Zhang et al. 2009). Researches also trace the problems of supply efficiency with low total factor productivity to the incompleteness of reforms. Hence, complete reform is a solution to the problem of total factor supply efficiency (Wu 2008).

As for the role of government, economists have proposed specific ways of reform and development models. In the discussion of the supply system and its development, many researches put emphasis on the relationship between the central government and the local one. Xu (2011) thinks that China has adopted a decentralized local authority system. Qian (1996) concludes that the fiscal system of China follows a special The Chinese-style federalism. These studies emphasize the important role the local government has on factor supply and arrangement. The decentralization of competition among local governments and the unification of growth target, welfare and interests lay the foundation for rapid economic growth.

1.4.2.2 Researches on the Demand Side

There have been researches on the demand side as well in China since the formation of basic market economy system. In the implementation of macroeconomic demand management policies, the “Three Carriages” (investment, consumption, exports) are the general measures. Lin (1998) put forward the idea of “Three Carriages”. He thinks that individuals can make the most of the “Three Carriages” in the demand constraint economy so that the constraint can be overcome and the economic growth sustains. In order to maintain the scale of demand and investment, he also proposes the diversification of investors and the institutional reform of finance, foreign investment and social funds. The demand side theories also attach importance to the reforms.

Between the 1990s and the 2010s, in addition to researches of the contribution of consumption, investment and export [e.g. the study of consumption by Hu and Guo (2012); the study of investment by Wu (2002); the study of export by Shen and Wu (2003) as well as Lin and Li (2003)], studies of the "Three Carriages" focused on problems in the income distribution system, capital markets, foreign exchange markets comparative advantages and the role of the government.

The income distribution system has long been taken into consideration. Gao (1993) and He (1998) consider the distribution according to work to be no longer applicable in the market economy. Distribution according to production factors is the new principle, which means the workers get their wages based on the contribution of the labor factor. However, even in state enterprises or other public-owned enterprises, unjust income distribution still exists due to monopoly (Xia et al. 2012; Chen et al. 2010). According to the results of many studies on the impact of income distribution on demand, with the reform of the market economy, the income imbalance in the primary distribution caused by monopoly (Yue et al. 2010), imperfect social welfare system in the redistribution (Zhu 2010) and off-the-books income existing in the whole process (Wang 2010) have widened the income gap and weakened the effect of the demand (consumption) policies on economic growth. Lu et al. (2005) further point out that a huge income gap will directly impact economic growth.

In terms of capital markets and foreign exchange control, the studies of the effect of the capital market system on investment and economic growth started in the 1990s. The investment and economic growth are generally connected to particular monetary and financial policies (the research group of economic growth and macro stability, 2007; Liu et al. 2002; Wang et al. 2009). The innovation of the capital market system expands the scope of monetary and fiscal policies, which promotes investment and economic growth (Liu et al. 2012). Some studies focus on the effects of the foreign exchange control on investment (Wan et al. 2004).

As for the role of the government, economists have studied the administrative monopoly, check and acceptance and their connection with the stimulating policies of macro investment (Yu and Zhang 2010). Lin (2010) studies the "tide phenomenon" of the investment and overcapacity, pointing out the significant role played by the government in investment. Even the investment impulse is the result of the local government's distortion of the market mechanism (Ba 2004; Guo and Jia 2006).

Studies of the opening up and comparative advantages in the 1990s concentrate on the systems in special administrative regions and development zones (Ge 1995; Liu et al. 2015). The recent researches shift their focus to new systems such as that in the free trade zones (Shi 2015). Lin Yifu and other economists suggest working out development strategies based on comparative advantages, in that the rapid economic growth in China is ascribed to the reform and opening-up policy. With two resource origins and two markets, the efficiency of resource allocation increases due to comparative advantages, which further expands employment and promotes economic growth. For the future development, it is encouraged to allocate resources worldwide and to increase the total factor productivity so as to create a long-term beneficial external environment (Lin et al. 1999; Lin et al. 2004; Jiang 2008).

1.4.2.3 Researches of the Structure

Economists in China generally study the supply side and the demand side from a structural perspective. According to the view of structural dynamics, the urbanization and changes in the labor structure will impact the economic growth (the research group form the Development Research Center of the State Council 2010). The gradual adjustment of the relative price system promotes capital accumulation and further stimulates economic growth (Liu et al. 2008). Studies also include the influence of the banking structure on economic growth (Lin and Sun 2008) and the approaches of structural transition such as the value of the double-track price system (Zhang 1996). Liu (2004) studies the structural macro-control policies and summarizes the feature of the macro-control policies in China—structural adjustment in various aspects such as exchange rate policies, industrial policies, fiscal policies, monetary policies etc. Studies also show the various stages of the implementation of the structural policies. For instance, the mode of structural dynamics and adjustment lies in the profit limitation stage. And the economic growth and adjustment will shift from the government-oriented stage and the middle-proliferation stage to the demand-derivative stage (Yang 1998).

1.4.3 Structural Reform Theories on the Supply Side

Based on the current achievements of the socialist market economic theories and practice in China, the decisive role of the market in both the resource allocation and the law-based governance was emphasized in several plenary sessions of the 18th CPC Central Committee. That has represented the research orientation for reform and development in the future as well. Some significant theoretical ideas are proposed as the economy enters the stage of New Normal, encountering the challenges brought by the "three-stage overlap".

1.4.3.1 New Structural Economics

Lin (2012) proposes his theory of the "new structural economics", and applies the international trade theories to the national development strategies. He thinks that the developing countries have late-developing advantages. They can form and develop industries with comparative advantages based on the factor endowment to promote economic growth. As a result of the economic reform, the factor endowment with comparative advantages is dependent on the market. And promoted by the investment policies, industries with comparative advantages are formed in the market. The supply side system reform, as the foundation of Lin's theory, is consistent with the emphasis on the decisive role of market in the resource allocation. And the rule of comparative advantage that focuses on the structural adjustment is a specific approach to the government's management and development of the economy.

1.4.3.2 Discussions About Supply Economics

The theory of "new supply economics" is proposed by Jia (2013, 2015) and other economists. The idea derives from the supply side theories of Reagan and Thatcher and later specifically focuses on China's economic theories and its over-thirty- year reform. Yet there has been no systematic framework.

According to this new theory, there are two weak points in the mainstream economics: the first is neglect of supply side problems in the hypothesis of supply side environment and the second is the insufficiency of researches and inconsistency of practice. Therefore, the new supply side economics aims at further analysis and cognition of the supply side so that the basic theories can be more efficiently applied. Various economic entities (e.g. market, government, non-profit organization) can thus better serve their functions. It is also proposed that the aggregate demand management is less necessary, since the new supply can automatically create the new demand.

1.5 Proposal of China's Structural Reform on the Supply Side

The reform and opening-up of China, the theories of socialist market-oriented economics and the researches on the supply side and demand side reforms have laid the theoretical foundation for the supply side structural reform.

In November, 2015, the significance of supply side reform of the central government of China was emphasized by several meetings. The "supply side reform" and the "supply side structural reform" were also mentioned by President Xi Jinping on various occasions. He pointed out that the problems of the world economy could not be solved by monetary stimulus but the economic structural reform that could make the supply system fit for the changes occurring in the demand structure. In addition, with the moderate expansion of the aggregate demand, the reform could improve the quality and efficiency of the supply system, making the economic growth sustained. In December, 2015, the idea of the supply side reform was proposed by the Central Economic Work Conference to achieve sustainable and sound economic growth. During the 12th meeting of the Central

Committee's Leading Group for Financial and Economic Affairs in January 2016, President Xi set the reform as the fundamental objective in the development of social productivity.

Subsequently, a relatively complete interpretation was offered based on the framework of "supply side + structural + reform", "which means starting from elevating the supply quality, then restructuring the economy, reallocating resources and expanding effective supply".[11] The reform is people-oriented, with five objectives: innovation, coordination, green, open and sharing. "The decisive role of the market should be better utilized in resource allocation" so that the former excessive administrative allocation can be adjusted and the market can fully play its decisive role. The reform also aims at the limitation of the government's administrative power. There should be less government intervention independence is pursued. "The five major tasks include reducing production capacity, unloading inventory, de-leveraging, lowering cost and filling the short board of the economy." To conclude, the supply side structure is to be reformed and the equilibrium of supply and demand is reached at a higher level.

[11] Q&A with an 'authoritative insider' on China's supply side structural reform, *People's Daily*, Jan 4, 2016.

Chapter 2
Generation and Development of the Structural Reform on the Supply Side in the Global Perspective

In the 1970s, the global environmental changed and economic structural troubles brought major economies problems such as the economic stagnation, inflation, financial burden, budget imbalance, low productive efficiency, slow structural adjustment etc., which the Keynesian demand management could no longer handle. Since the late 1970s, with new leaders such as Thatcher, Reagan and Cole, those major economies had started their structural reforms on the supply side, confining the attention to the market and free competition. Economic growth became the primary goal and there were new relationships between the government and the market, the government and the enterprises, the government and the people, capital and labor, and unity and structure as well.

2.1 Historical Background of the Structural Reform on the Supply Side in Major Economies

Since the 1970s, the economic globalization and the new technological revolution had been the powerful impetus for frequent and convenient communication, trade, capital exchange and technology transfer among major economies. The structure of supply and demand was globalized. Global economy surpassed the borders, with factors of production allocated freely across the globe. Economy was gradually interconnected and unified among a majority of countries and regions. Technological innovation caused the shifts among major economies in terms of competitive advantage rotary, the expansion of market economic system and the surge in the quantity of multinational companies. All these greatly influenced the adjustment of the worldwide supply and demand.

L. Xiao, *New Supply Side Economics*, DOI 10.1007/978-981-10-4639-1_2

2.1.1 The Relationship of the Supply and Demand Broken by Globalization

Since the 1970s, economy had gradually been globalized. The closed supply and demand structure within a country had been broken and it was the new characteristic of the world economy that all countries depended on each other and developed together.

2.1.1.1 The Fierce International Competition Breaks Internal Structure of the Economy

The implementation of Marshall Plan after the Second World War brought about the US assistance to EU and Japan in the rebuilding of basic industries. By the 1970s, Western Europe and Japan had already become competitive economic opponents to the US. By the end of the 1970s, EU had surpassed the US in economy, and Japan had become the second economic giant among capitalist countries. The rise of the Western Europe and Japan stimulated the world trade. Statistics show that from 1964 to 2005, the export volume of international trade annually increased by 11.2%, while the average annual growth rate of the world GDP in the period was only 3.6%. The rapid growth of the global trade brought a large number of cheap goods to the US. And the steel and automobile industries in Western Europe and Japan became a real threat to the US manufacturing industry. The demand for domestic manufacturing products was gradually shrinking in the US, causing a decrease in production enthusiasm among enterprises. Since 1976, import had exceeded export in the US and the gap has kept widening, reaching $148.4 billion in 1985. By the end of the 1980s, US share of steel output in the world had fallen to more or less 10% (Fig. 2.1).

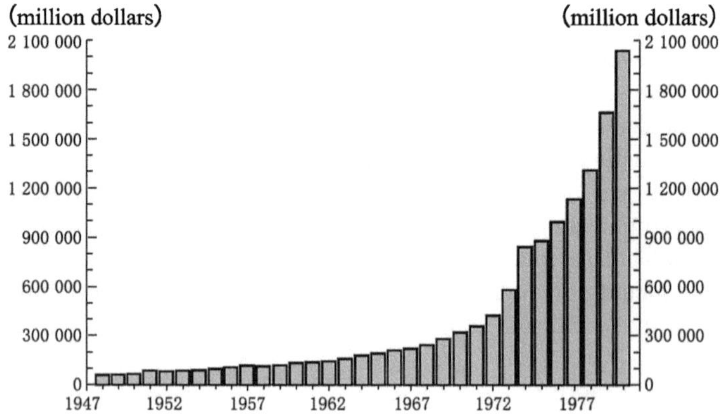

Fig. 2.1 Global exports from 1948 to 1980 (million dollars). *Source* Wind Info

2.1.1.2 Globalization Disturbs Macro Control Policies

Economic globalization synchronized the economic cycles of major economies. The domestic fiscal policies, monetary and other macroeconomic control policies were thus often seriously affected by other economies. Since the 1970s, trade and finance had been of top priority in global economy, and a multilateral trading system with free trade had been gradually formed. The monetary and capital markets in the world were interconnected through modern means of communication. There appeared growing number of financial services across borders in internationalized financial markets. All these added uncontrollable factors to one single economy, making it harder for domestic control policies to work when facing shocks from abroad.

2.1.1.3 The Impact of Price Fluctuation on Supply

After the World War II, oil had replaced coal as the main energy source in the world. From 1950 to 1975, the proportion of oil and natural gas consumption in the world increased from 37.5 to 64.5%. Major economies imported a large amount of oil, which to a large extent promoted the economic development. The demand for oil in developed countries grew at an average annual rate of 7.1%, which was much faster than the average annual growth rate of industrial production and GDP. In 1973, OPEC carried out the "war for oil", raising the price of oil from $1.71 per barrel (1950) to $5.11 (1973). The price reached $34 in October, 1981. The rise of oil price triggered a global supply shock by pushing up the price and reducing the consumers' demand, forcing major economies to adjust the internal economic structures. In Japan, for example, the oil crisis had a serious impact on a large number of energy consuming industries such as iron and steel, aluminum, petrochemical etc. These industries went into structural depression due to the over-dependence on oil import.

2.1.2 Advantages Brought by Technological Innovation in Competitions

Since the mid-19th century, enormous revolution in technology had taken place. The application of new technology had boosted the production and reduced the cost. Economies with advanced technology became powerful rivals for others.

2.1.2.1 Changes Brought by Technological Innovation on the Competition Structure

In the 1970s, technological innovation played a primary role in international competition. Innovation often took place in one economy and was then introduced to others, which resulted in huge technological gaps among different countries.

There appeared forerunners in various fields in the global competition. For instance, during the period from the 1950s to the 1960s, Japan made great efforts to introduce and implement advanced science and technology from the U.S. By the 1970s, the competitiveness of iron, steel and auto industries in Japan had indeed been a real pressure on the U.S. But in 1980, the U.S. exerted close control over technology transfer and information drain, leading to a sharp conversion in its competition with Japan and the Federal Republic of Germany. Due to its neglect of basic research and the lack of technical reserve, Japan encountered huge obstacles in its subsequent development and thus became less competitive with the United States. In 1980, Japan implemented a new development strategy by encouraging basic research and innovation to improve its science and technology.

2.1.2.2 Domestic Development Promoted by Technological Innovation

Since the 1970s, the industrial structure had been transformed due to the use of a wide range of innovative products such as computers, automation, jet engines, synthetic polymer materials, atomic power generation, ultra large scale integrated circuits, man-made satellites and so on. A series of new industries have emerged while the traditional ones are forced to change their industrial structures so as to transform from the labor-intensive type to the knowledge-and-technology-intensive one. Meanwhile, the transformation of industrial structures of major economies has further promoted the technological innovation. In 1982, the separation of AT&T was the starting point of the information revolution in the 1980s. Competition had since heated up in the telecommunications industry. In the U.S., for instance, the emerging network and mobile phone industries had recovered its economy.

2.1.2.3 International Industries and Resources Restructured by Technological Innovation

The invention, application and popularization of new technologies had reduced the cost and expanded the scope in terms of transaction. Take the computer as an example. With interconnected information terminals and the global network of communication and information, small, personalized computers had become increasingly popular, directly changing the mode of production and resource organization. These technologies were utilized multinationally to arrange production, operation and sales as well as to distribute surplus worldwide. Additionally, technological innovation had reduced the time for commodity circulation and the economic cycle. Major economies gradually followed the same economic cycle through business activities among transnational corporations, multinational banks and other institutions.

2.1.2.4 Opportunities for Capital Accumulation Created by Technological Innovation

Investment is essential for economic development while the accumulation of capital is the basis for investment. The accumulation of capital through the reduction of wage and the extension of working hours could no longer be accepted after the World War II. Major economies in the world were gradually relying on technological innovation, which helped to improve productivity and multiplies the surplus value so that the capital could be accumulated. After the war, the surplus value in Japan and the Federal Republic of Germany went up thanks to the rapidly rising productivity. From 1955 to 1970, the surplus value rate of Japanese manufacturing increased from 314 to 443%, leading to a huge amount of capital accumulation. From 1964 to 1973, the proportion of capital accumulation to gross national product in Japan and the Federal Republic of Germany were 38.4 and 27% respectively.

2.1.3 The Extension of Market Economy as the Foundation for the Global System of Supply and Demand

The extension of the market system is the essential foundation of economic globalization. Various kinds of modern systems such as the property system, contract system, monetary system, trade system, competition system etc. were extended with the globalization of production and circulation. The rules of the market became the rules of the global market.

2.1.3.1 The Market Economy System Expanded by Two Parallel Global Markets

In the 20th century, the world was divided into two: capitalism and socialism. The confrontation between the two worlds involved the confrontation of economy. In the late 1970s, China implemented the policy of the reform and opening-up and pursued the socialist market economy. In the early 1980s, Latin America suffered a debt crisis and was forced to take a free structural reform. In the 1990s, with the economic transition of former Soviet Union and socialist countries in Eastern Europe, the former two parallel markets gradually disappeared and a kind of economy oriented by the market became the first choice among a majority of countries in the world. The market economy had thus become the basis for global economy. And economic systems and rules in different countries were becoming consistent, gradually forming a unified economic and trading system without any barriers for cross-border transactions.

2.1.3.2 Establishment of Rules for Global Market Transaction

Under the leadership of the international economic organizations, international rules and regulations regarding monetary, financial, trade, investment and other aspects have been gradually established. Take the financial sector as a typical example. In 1988, the Basel Accords were issued by the committee on banking supervision of the Bank for International Settlements. The accords have played a positive role in regulating multinational banks, forming basic international rules and supervision standards in the field of finance. On the other hand, the settings, investment and strategies of multinational companies and regulations of global financial market are scarcely decided by one economy. The original adjustment and management within a single economy has to conform to the rules set by international organizations. In other words, the individual economy has lost its power in the global market.

2.1.3.3 The Establishment of Supranational Organizations and Their Roles

Since the 1970s, the influence of a series of supranational organizations of politics and economy has been exercised and expanded. These organizations include IMF, the World Bank, GATT, G7, OECD, EC and beyond. There are often contradictions regarding the concept of sovereignty in supranational organizations and traditional countries. The global capital flow is in need of a breakthrough in territory and sovereignty. Once the requirements of territory and sovereignty clash with those of global capital flow, supranational organizations will subordinate sovereignty to capital expansion. The growing impact of those organizations, especially on the politics and economy within a country, even surpasses boundaries between the sovereign states.

2.1.4 Multinational Corporations as the Leading Force in the Adjustment of Aggregate Supply and Demand

Multinational corporations, as the major carrier of global trade and investment, have directly influenced aggregate supply and demand in the world since the 1970s.

2.1.4.1 Capital Flow Propelled

In the 1970s, major economies in the world encouraged running companies in multiple countries. The number of multinational corporations has markedly increased ever since. In 1976, according to the statistics form the U.N., multinational companies with sales over $1 billion numbered 422, more than half of which were America-based. The total number of multinational corporations increased from about 11,000 in 1980 to 45,000 in 1997. The amount and stock of direct international investment have been increased to a large extent. According to the world investment report issued by UNCTAD in 2006, the global foreign direct investment reached $59 billion in 1982, and the investment stock was $600 billion and the total number of employees in the world reached 19 million. During the decade from 1986 to 1995, the foreign investment in the world maintained an average annual growth rate of 20%. During the latter 5 years in the 1990s, the growth rate reached 40%, far higher than the growth rate of GDP in the same period. At the same time, the foreign investment stock also grew at double-digit rates.

2.1.4.2 The Development of Corporations Promoted by Incorporation in Terms of Scale and Competitiveness

In the 1970s, the cooperation and even transnational merger and acquisitions of renowned multinational corporations became more and more popular. Most of the single M&A amount was over 1 billion dollars. Till 1990, the total M&A amount in the world had reached 160 billion dollars, which was about 7.8 times that in 1980 (18.3 billion). Incorporation can be both intra-industrial and inter-industrial. For instance, the inter-industrial Disney and ABC, the intra-industrial Daimler AG and Chrysler. Those strategic allies, take the Boeing and McDonnell-Donglas as examples, help the companies avoid fierce competition within the field and advance together.

2.1.4.3 Multinational Corporations as the Main Forces in Global Economy

Since the 1970s, multinational corporations have begun allocating resources globally in order to minimize the cost of transaction and to adapt to the complex market, the diverse products and different preference in varies regions. This is a change in the way of production, research and development within a single country. Investment, raw material purchasing, organization, production, business activities etc. are all globally distributed, forming a network to which every country belongs. In this situation, multinational corporations serve the main role of regulating and controlling the aggregate supply and demand in the world.

2.2 Development Dilemma of the Structural Reform on the Supply Side in Major Economies

After the World War II, there was a long period of economic growth in major economies which pursued the Keynesian theory of demand management. But with the oil crisis starting in the 1970s, major economies began to suffer economic stagnation and inflation. There were no more methods to promote economic growth. Problems of economy, society and other aspects began to emerge.

2.2.1 The Coexistence of Economic Stagnation and Inflation

Before the 1970s, short-term stimulation policies instead of macroeconomic ones were applied in the Keynesian demand management to eliminate the economic fluctuation. That resulted in a negative circulation in which the economy grew and stopped. The major economies had a kind of 'stagflation crisis' with economic stagnation, inflation and unemployment.

2.2.1.1 Slow and Negative Economic Growth

Economic growth gradually declined and even became negative. During the period from the 1970s to 1980s, the U.S. economy suffered "stagflation". Despite its adjustment policies, measures for income distribution and the government's macro adjustment gained from the great crisis in the 1930s, the country could not avoid the economic crisis. From the end of the World War II to the beginning of the 1980s, the U.S. had suffered eight economic crises in all. And from the year 1970 to 1980, the U.S. had suffered stagnation with an annual growth of GNP of about 3.8%, less than that during the first two decades after the war. Among all the crises, the eighth one, from July 1981 to November 1982, was the longest, during which industrial production had kept declining for 17 consecutive months. The GNP had dropped by 2.5%, and the unemployment rate had reached 10.8%. That crisis was subject to the second oil shock. Restrictive monetary policies were implemented in order to control inflation, resulting in high interest rates. Meanwhile, the slow production growth restricted the capacity to produce, making the industrial structure difficult to be adjusted (Table 2.1 and Fig. 2.2).

Britain's economy growth became negative. From 1964 to 1970 and 1974 to 1979, the British Labor Cabinet devoted considerable effort to create a wealthy working class and to establish an ideally socialistic society by following policies based on socialization and high welfare. The specific measures involved implementing a planned economy system (including nationalization of iron and steel, coal, railway, aviation, ports, postal services, telecommunications, automobile, shipbuilding, aerospace and other industries), raising taxes and cutting military spending (through disarmament, canceling new national defense research projects, raising the level of wages and benefits etc.) But the growth of GDP, against the good wishes of the Labor Party, became negative during its administration (Fig. 2.3).

Germany's economy was in trouble. After the World War II, the Federal Republic of Germany had been pursuing the theory of social market economy,

Table 2.1 US index of industrial production during the economic crisis after the war

Crisis period	Length	Decrease in industrial production (%)	Highest unemployment rate (%)	GNP growth rate (%)	Cause of crisis
1948.8–1949.10	15	10.1	8.3	0.02	The buying craze of consumers faded away with the interest rate growing and the ration system cancelled
1953.8–1954.4	9	9.4	3.2	−1.3	There appeared contractionary fiscal and financial policies and military expenditure were reduced after the Korean War
1957.4–1958.4	13	13.5	7.5	−0.7	The interest rate was increased and caused the monetary tightening
1960.2–1961.2	13	8.6	7.1	2.6	Deflationary monetary policies were adopted to restrain the increasing inflation
1969.11–1970.11	13	6.8	6.0	−0.3	Deflationary financial policies were adopted to restrain the monopoly caused by the Korean War
1973.12–1975.3	16	15.1	8.9	−1.8	The economy became worse due to the quadrupled oil price, deflationary financial and fiscal policies as well as the speculative add inventory in 1973
1980.1–1980.7	7	8.0	7.1	1.9	The second oil crisis begot the recession in 1980. President Carter further controlled the credit on March, 1980 and implemented the deflationary financial policies, which deteriorated the economy
1981.7–1982.11	17	12.4	10.8	−2.5	The low growth of production brought a large amount of underutilized manpower. And the interest rate grew rapidly due to the second oil crisis and the inflation-oriented policies

Resource Jonathan Hughes, Louis P. Cain. *American Economic History*. Shanghai: Truth and Wisdom Press, 2013

based on the Freiburg School, for a long time. A social market economy system was implemented and the ideas of free market were combined with that of social balance. Focus then was put on the social aspect of the market economy so that the market competition would exist together with a society in balance. Ludwig Erhard, the first Minister of Economics and the second Chancellor of the postwar Germany, described the system as a kind of conscientious capitalism that was different from the socialist planned economy and the autocratic Nazi economy. Germany was in its golden age during the 1960s to 1970s. But since the mid-1980s, the economic

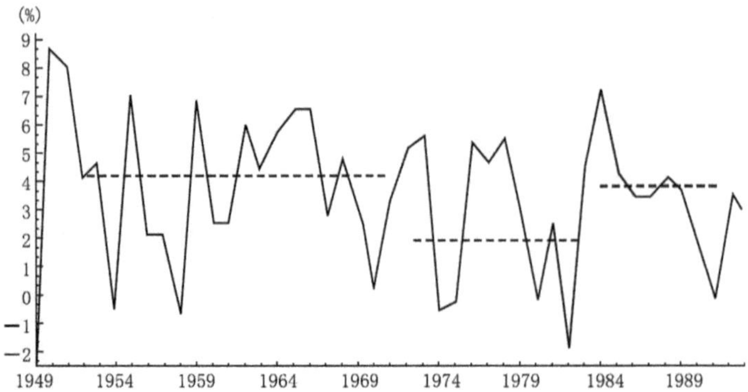

Fig. 2.2 Year-on-year growth of US GDP from 1949 to 1994. *Source* Wind Info

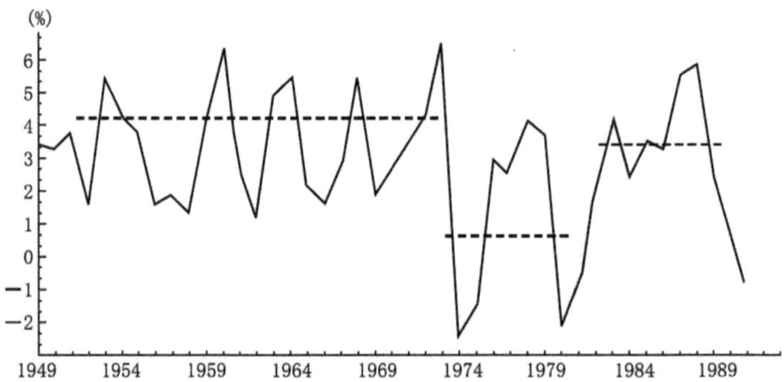

Fig. 2.3 Actual growth of British GDP from 1949 to 1990. *Source* Wind Info

growth had gradually slowed down. There emerged more conflicts and less innovation. In the early 1990s, despite the unification, the growth rate of the economy was only 1.95%, the lowest ever since the World War II (Table 2.2).

The Japan's economic growth was rapid at first but became slow thereafter. The economy had been growing fast in Japan since the mid-1950s and the growth rate in the 1960s remained over 10%. In the early 1970s, there appeared difficulties in export due to the appreciation of the yen. In addition, the oil crisis not only prevented the economy from growing at a high speed but also led to the most serious economic crisis after the World War II. The spectacular economic growth for two

Table 2.2 Annual economic growth of the Federal Republic of Germany

	1951–1960	1961–1970	1971–1980	1981–1990	1990–2000
Growth rate (%)	7.96	4.51	2.78	2.3	1.95

Source Institution of World Economy, Fudan University. *Institution Change and Structural Adjustment*. Shanxi: Shanxi Economic Publishing House, 2006

decades stopped and the growth has been sluggish ever since. The annual growth rate of 10% (from the 1950s to the 1960s) dropped to about 5% (from the 1970s to the 1980s). In the 1990s, the annual growth rate was close to 0.

2.2.1.2 Frequent Inflation

The 1970s witnessed a price spike concerning average goods and service. In the U.S., for example, the consumer price index rose fast in the late 1960s and even faster in the 1970s. The price doubled over a decade, from 38.8 in 1970 to 82.4 in 1980 (if we set 100 for the period from 1982 to 1984). In 1980, the inflation was close to 14% and the short-term interest rate surpassed 20%, the highest in its history (Figs. 2.4 and 2.5).

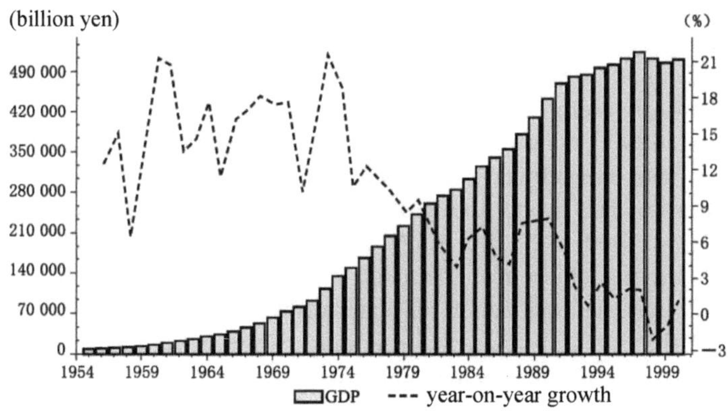

Fig. 2.4 GDP and its growth in Japan from 1954 to 2000. *Source* Wind Info

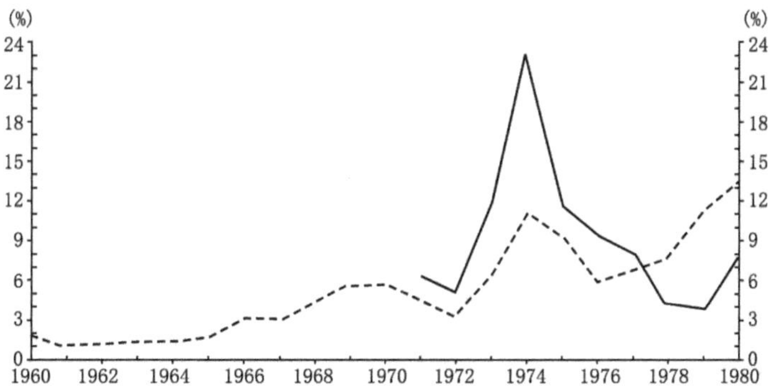

Fig. 2.5 CPI in Japan and US from 1960 to 1980. *Source* Wind Info

2.2.2 Imbalance Between Financial Revenue and Expenditure

Following Keynesian demand management, major economies generally implemented fiscal stimulus policies. Since the 1970s, the increasing social welfare, military expenditure and personnel cost in national agencies have increased fiscal burden and caused imbalance between income and expenses.

2.2.2.1 Fiscal Deficit

In the 1970s, fiscal deficit existed in major economies. In Germany, for instance, governments at all levels tried to make up the deficit through credit and issuance of bonds. The government debt in the 1970s, excluding certain years, maintained a double-digit growth rate. By the end of 1981, the total government debt had surpassed 240 billion Deutschmark, equivalent to the total fiscal expenditure in 1982. In the federal government budget in 1983, the interest payment for government bond amounted to 31 billion Deutschmark, accounting for 12.3% of the total budget as the third major expenditure in the country after the social expenditure and that of national defense. The proportion of the government debt in the total capital rose from 10.3% in 1969 to 37.6% in 1981. Government budget promoted risk-free investment, leaving alone other demands of enterprises and families. During the same period, the nationalization of enterprises, unification of salary and high welfare in Britain caused excessive spending of the government and worse relationship between financial revenue and expenditure.

2.2.2.2 Imbalance Between Global Revenue and Expenditure

In the 1970s, imbalance existed in all the major economies. There was negative trade balance in the U.S., Britain and Japan. Germany, with its manufacturing advantages, maintained a positive trade balance. But it was disturbed in the 1970s. From 1978 to 1980, Germany's foreign trade decreased and Deutschmark depreciated due to its loss of international confidence. In order to maintain the stability of the currency, the Federal Bank of Germany had to operate a tight monetary policy, which further limited the economic stimulation through the countercyclical monetary policies (Figs. 2.6, 2.7 and 2.8).

2.2.3 Slow Structural Adjustment Leads to Low Production Efficiency

The 1970s witnessed several declines in labor productivity among major economies in the world. Under the premise of full employment of Keynesian demand

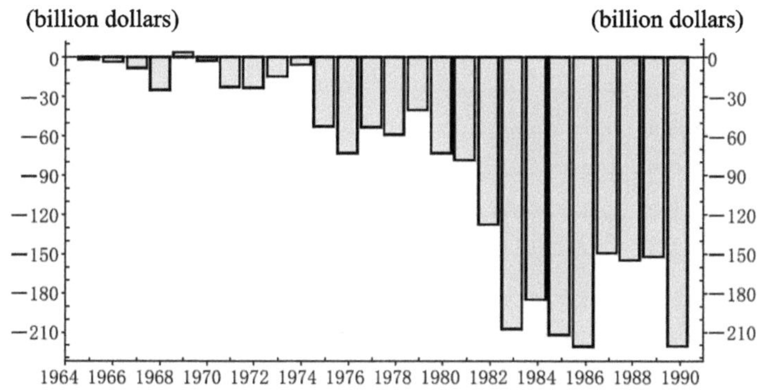

Fig. 2.6 US Federal Fiscal Surpluses from 1964 to 1990 (billion dollars). *Source* Wind Info

management, the real wage rate will be further increased if the labor productivity is low and the wage cost is high. And the cost for production of goods will be thus increased. At the same time, the traditional industries were confronted with overcapacity, tax burden and lack of vitality.

2.2.3.1 The Coexistence of "Stagflation" and Growth Decline in Labor Productivity

Take the U.S. as an example. The growth rate of labor productivity from the 1960s to the year 2005 was represented in a U-shaped curve. From the late 1960s to 1970s, there was a decline in growth rate along with the 'stagflation'. From 1975 to 1980, the annual growth rate of U.S. manufacturing industries was only 1.7%, and that of all its industries was only 1.2%, much lower than that during the postwar period and that of trade rivals in Europe and Asia. It was not until the 1990s that there appeared a rising trend (Fig. 2.9).

2.2.3.2 Overcapacity

In the 1970s, a number of industries in the U.S. were confronted with excess capacity, which caused a sharp decline in capacity utilization ratio. In the early 1980s, there was serious overcapacity. The utilization ratio had been less than 80% since June, 1980. It reached the lowest point of 72% in the first quarter of 1983. After the ratio rose slowly but did not surpass 80% until 1987. The problem of overcapacity lied mainly in traditional industries such as minerals, steel, wood, leather, automobile, furniture, etc., especially in the iron and steel industry and the automotive industry, the ratios of which were 50 and 52% respectively. As for Japan on the other hand, there was a rapid increase in equipment investment during

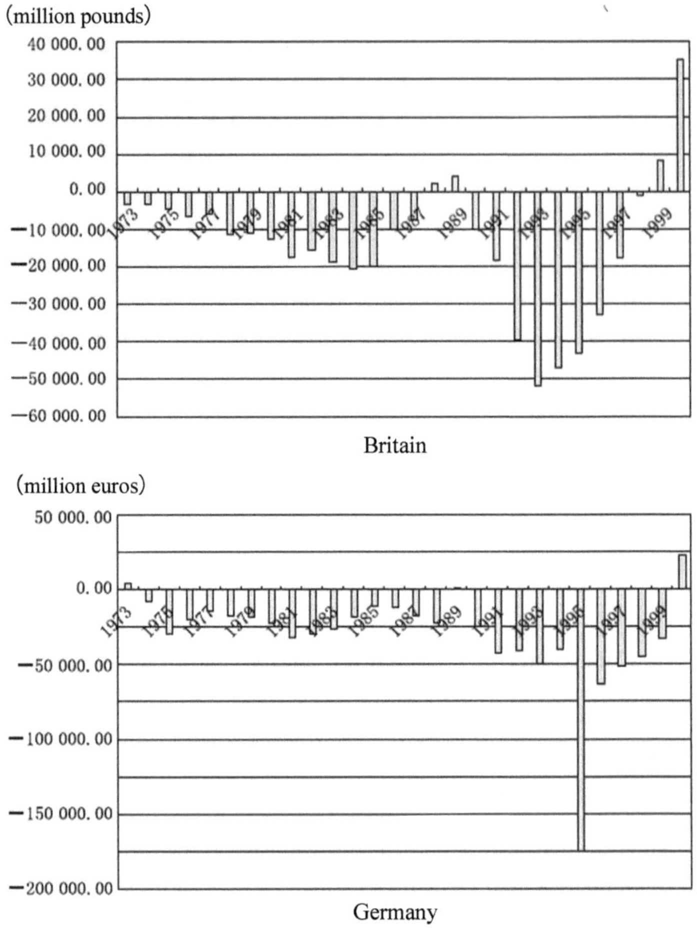

Fig. 2.7 Fiscal Surpluses in Britain and Germany from 1973 to 2000 [(Million pounds) Britain, (million euros) Germany]. *Source* Wind Info

the bubble era. Equipment investment in 1990 amounted to 88.7 trillion yen, accounting for 19.5% of GNP. It increased by 58.6% compared with that in 1986. Affected by the false prosperity of the bubble era, large-scale production lines have been launched. The rapid increase in investment also resulted in serious overcapacity (Table 2.3).

2.2.3.3 Scarce Technological and Industrial Innovation

Two-thirds of the research funding in Germany in the 1980s was from enterprises. Aiming at short-term interests, world leading enterprises of chemical, machinery

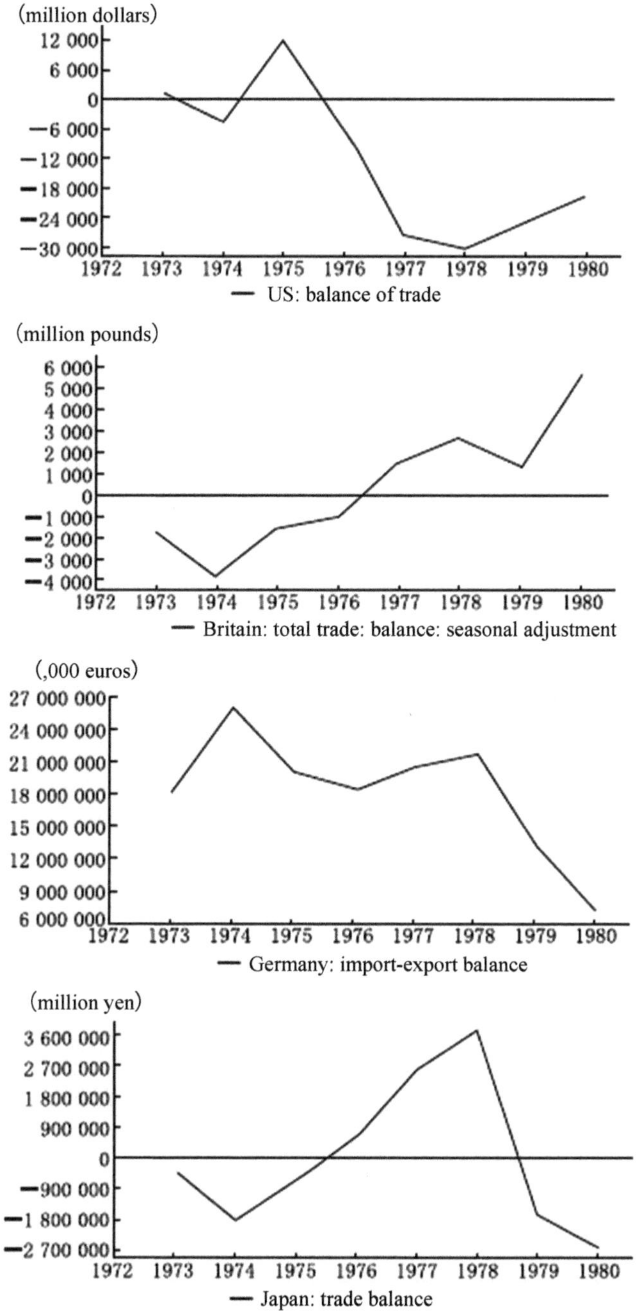

Fig. 2.8 Trade balance of major economies from 1972 to 1980 [(million dollars) US: balance of trade, (million pounds) Britain: total trade: balance: seasonal adjustment, (000 euros) Germany: import–export balance, (million yen) Japan: trade balance]. *Source* Wind Info

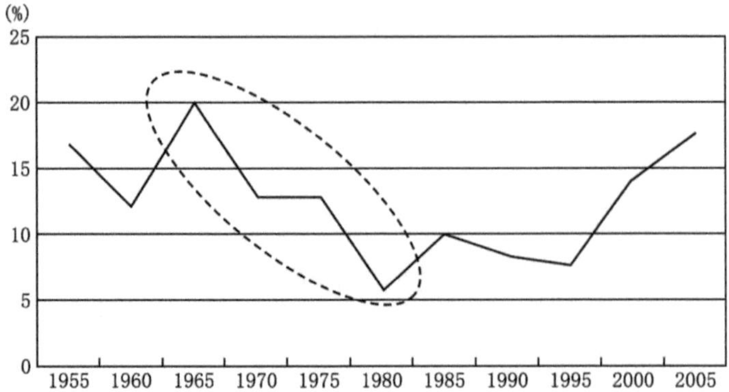

Fig. 2.9 The total labor productivity growth rate of the US Enterprises from 1955 to 2005. *Source* Jonathan Hughes, Louis P. Cain. *American Economic History*. Shanghai: Truth and Wisdom Press, 2013

Table 2.3 Productivity Index of US from 1950 to 2005

Year	All enterprises		Non-agricultural enterprises		Manufacturing business	
	Labor productivity	Growth (%)	Labor productivity	Growth (%)	Labor productivity	Growth (%)
1950	37.3		41.9		34	
1955	43.6	16.89	47.5	13.37	38.8	14.12
1960	48.9	12.16	51.9	9.26	41.8	7.73
1965	58.8	20.25	61.4	18.30	48.5	16.03
1970	66.3	12.76	68	10.75	54.2	11.75
1975	74.8	12.82	76.2	12.06	64.3	18.63
1980	79.1	5.75	80.6	5.77	70.1	9.02
1985	87.1	10.11	87.4	8.44	82.3	17.40
1990	94.5	8.50	94.5	8.12	92.9	12.88
1995	101.6	7.51	102.1	8.04	110	18.41
2000	116.1	14.27	115.6	13.22	134.4	22.18
2005	136.5	17.57	135.9	17.56	170.6	26.93

Labor productivity refers to the productivity within 1 h, which was 100 in 1992
Source Jonathan Hughes, Louis P. Cain. *American Economic History*. Shanghai: Truth and Wisdom Press 2013

manufacturing and automobile etc. focused their research on mature fields related to technical improvement. The lack of scientific research and innovation widened the gap between Germany and the U.S. in the field of information technology in the 1990s. During the first half of the 1990s, the proportion of German research

Fig. 2.10 The capacity utilization rate of US manufacturing business from 1976 to 1990. *Source* Wind Info

investment in GDP was less than 2%. Though the proportion had started to rise from 1996 and reached 2.15% in 2001, it rose rather slowly compared with other countries. In 2002, the research investment dropped to 1.75%, ranking seven in the world after Sweden, Finland, Japan, Switzerland, US, and South Korea (Figs. 2.10 and 2.11).

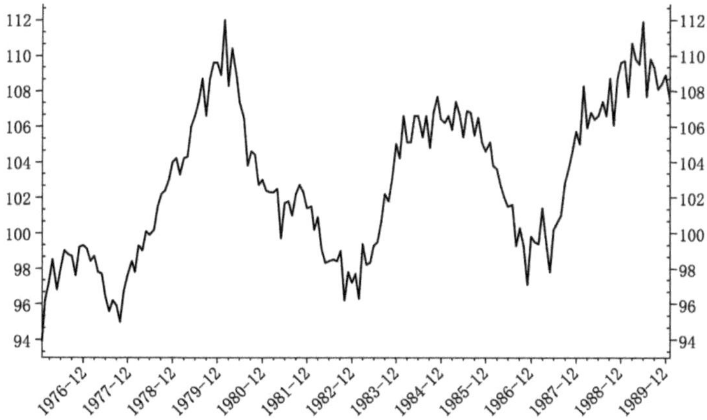

Fig. 2.11 The capacity utilization index of Japan from 1976 to 1990. *Source* Wind Info

2.2.3.4 Enterprises with a Lack of Vitality Due to Heavy Tax

In the 1970s, enterprises lost their vitality with the heavy tax burden. In Japan, for example, the corporate tax rate was 37.5% before 1998. But if the local tax and cost were taken into account, the actual tax rate went up to 49.98%, the highest among the developed countries. Large enterprises with good benefit accounted for less than 1% in the country and one-third among the rest 99% were efficient small and medium-sized enterprises (SMEs) which enjoyed the tax relief. As for the two-thirds, they were enterprises running at a loss and therefore they did not pay taxes.

2.2.4 Social Conflicts and Structural Problems

2.2.4.1 The Widening Gap Between Regions

After the World War II, the state intervention through regional policies was encouraged by the Keynesian demand management. State intervention was widely believed to narrow the gap of unemployment between regions. The unemployed labor force could also be used to develop the macro economy without inflation. Therefore, major economies frequently exercised fiscal and financial policies and even directly intervened in the administration of declining areas, encouraging large enterprises to assist those regions by investing and building factories to create job opportunities and those regions would keep up. But in the late 1970s, new problems and disputes occurred despite the existence of the older ones. In Britain, for example, before Thatcher's reign, the expansion of the "recipient" regions added financial burden to the government. The British government's spending on regional policies increased from 20 million pounds (from 1962 to 1963) to 324 million pounds (from 1969 to 1970). By the end of the 1970s, the annual spending had been as high as about 1 billion pounds. Unfortunately, government intervention did not realize the goal of recipient regional development. Worse still, it caused industry hollowing in the prosperous southern regions. "Inner crises" such as the urban environmental problems and deteriorating order were also becoming increasingly serious.

2.2.4.2 Deteriorating Labor and Capital Relationship

Trade unions, with their legal status affirmed after the World War II, were encouraged to participate in political and economic decision-making. In the 1970s, as the power of trade unions gradually grew, the labor market and capital investment was hindered by high salary and frequent strikes. Labor unions became the bottleneck in economic development and even led to political turmoils in major economies. In Britain, more and more people in the 1970s believed that the country was suffering from the unions' extortion. From 1978 to 1979, a series of strikes had broken out with growing dissatisfaction with the British government. In Germany, the power of trade unions was described as a mystery by the economic research center in Cologne. There was one in every five practitioners who belonged to trade unions in the country. Enterprises of all types had representatives of the trade union in both the executive committee and the business committee.

2.2.4.3 Welfare Systems as the Government Burden

The Keynesian theory, the theoretical basis of the social welfare systems, holds that the fundamental way to avoid the crisis is to take various measures to stimulate the effective demand of the society. Since there is no mechanism for the effective demand in capitalist economies, this should be realized by the government, which, through the establishment of public utilities and the development of the social welfare and relief systems, can improve the social consumption trends, increase effective demand, achieve full employment, as well as alleviate the economic crisis. But in the 1970s, the drawbacks of welfare systems gradually appeared. They reduced the labor efficiency and destroyed the economy. Especially for the donators, they lowered their enthusiasm since they fostered laziness and decreased personal savings. By 1988, the British national health system (NHS) had been implemented for 40 years, second only to the pension insurance. The proportion of its spending in GDP rose from 4.4% in 1970 to 6.1% in 1980. Patients received over treatment in that there was scarcely cost worries among the doctors, nurses or even the managers. It was not the main goal to pursue efficiency and innovation. Resources were thus easily wasted.

2.3 Implementation of the Structural Reform on the Supply Side in Major Economies

Since the 1980s, major economies have implemented structural reforms on the supply side. U.S. and Britain adjusted the macroeconomic management under the mode of market economy, transforming from the Keynesian demand management to the supply management, which focuses on market and free competition. In order to solve the problems exposed in the process of economic development, Germany also transformed to the supply management from the social market economy mode. It struggled to provide the economic basis for social welfare by limiting the government's intervention so that the market can develop freely. Japan launched a series of structural reforms on the supply side, trying to evolve into the market economy from the government dominated economy.

2.3.1 The "New Right" as the Theoretical Foundation for the Structural Reform on the Supply Side

To deal with different problems, various ideological trends emerged during the 1960s and the 1970s in the western society such as the New Left thoughts, radicalism, Neofascism etc. Among them, the most influential one was the "New Right", composed of the "new liberalism" and the "conservatism". The former had long emphasized market value while the latter social order. Although individualism in the new liberalism was often criticized by the conservatism, there was a tendency for the two to merge at the end of the 1970s. Both the British Thatcherism and the American Reagan economics manifested the 'New Right' trend. Germany also followed the trend and put focus on market and free competition.

2.3.1.1 New Liberalism

The new liberalism includes the monetarism school, the supply side school, the public choice school and the Austrian school. In addition, the new liberalism expands from the economic field to the field of politics and society. It has a system of its political views. New liberalism doesn't allow too much government intervention in the economy. Government activities are thus limited so that the market can restore its self-regulation function. Private property and the freedom of personal choice, completely destroyed by collectivism and socialism, are highly inviolable. The government should establish law and order to maintain freedom and market order.

2.3.1.2 Conservatism

Conservatism, involving philosophy, politics, economy, culture and other fields, has a significant impact on politics, economy and social life. It advocates tradition as the backbone of social order. When there is a threat to personal freedom and social operation with the country's gradual expansion, the conservatism will advocate freedom as a tradition that needs maintenance. Private property is also protected since the property right is linked to the family, whose reputation is manifested by the accumulation of property—savings. The social rank is regarded as a natural and necessary part to be maintained in the society while the hierarchy is bound to exist even in a family. An ideal government is one with strong but limited power so as to obtain both freedom and efficiency. The law and order are also emphasized. Additionally, reforms are not discouraged despite the respect for tradition.

2.3.1.3 The Merging of the New Liberalism and the Conservatism: The "New Right"

Based on the tradition, order, authority, legal, private property and other basic concepts of the conservatism, the "New Right" absorbs the limited government intervention of the new liberalism and maximizes the market mechanism and the vitality of enterprises. The government, whose role is limited but necessary, serves as a tool to achieve economic freedom. The government's macroeconomic control and management should be improved. The Keynesian effective demand management and full employment model are criticized. Individuals have the freedom to choose and the market has the freedom to automatically adjust itself and maintain its order under the legal system.

2.3.2 The Prelude to the Structural Reform on the Supply Side

2.3.2.1 President Reagan

The U.S. structural reform started in the Kennedy era, flourished under the Reagan administration and continued to the Clinton years. In as early as the year 1964, the government of Kennedy had already taken measures to cut tax. On January 20, 1981, Reagan became the forty-ninth president and he put forward his economic recovery plan to the Congress on February 18. The plan includes the reduction of the personal income tax rate and the reduction or exemption of enterprise tax to stimulate employment, savings and investment. Cuts in the civil expenditure, especially welfare, were also included. National defense expenditure was supposed to be increased and the expansion and investment of enterprises were encouraged by canceling or loosening the regulations. The plan also suggested a tightening monetary supply to control inflation.

2.3.2.2 Mrs. Thatcher as Prime Minister

The British structural reform had a significant turning point. After the World War II, the Labor Party and the Conservative Party agreed on the Keynesian demand management in order to restore the British economy. The year of 1979, when Mrs. Thatcher was elected Prime Minister, became the turning point for British macroeconomic management, for she advocated the structural reform on the supply side, bringing fundamental changes to all fields. Despite the economic and social ups and downs during the 11 years of her administration, what could not be denied was the fact that there was a distinct improvement on the previous economy with those reform policies, which were followed by the succeeding major government as well.

2.3.2.3 Kohl as Chancellor

The supply side structural reform in Germany began in 1982 when Helmut Kohl, the chairman of CDU, was elected the Chancellor. The reform had lasted for over 20 years until 2005, when Gerhard Schroder, SPD chairman, stood down. In October 1982, Kohl's political agenda indicated the new direction for the economic reform. The market economy was encouraged with less government intervention. Individuals were supposed to freely make achievements without any pressure from the group. The economic structure should be more flexible with the individual initiative and competitiveness. During the reform of over two decades, Germany aimed at stimulating the economy, increasing the employment and reducing the contribution rate of social insurance. It also struggled to reform the welfare system, emphasizing personal responsibility, reduction of benefits, stable contribution rate and cuts in cost. The investment of enterprises and individuals was promoted. Additionally, the policies of the labor market were adjusted so that more opportunities of employment, reemployment and entrepreneurship were created (Tables 2.4 and 2.5).

2.3.2.4 Reforms in Japan

Japan had long taken the mode of government-directed market economy. Hence, the government had intervened in the aggregate demand and aggregate supply for a long time. In 1978, Japan enacted a special law for the structural improvement of

Table 2.4 The macroeconomic management measures taken by the previous British governments from 1945 to 1997

Ruling period	Prime Minister	Party	Macroeconomic management measures
1945.07.26–1951.10.26	Clement Attlee	Labor	Keynesian effective demand management
1951.10.26–1955.04.06	Winston Churchill	Conservative	
1955.04.06–1957.01.10	Anthony Eden	Conservative	
1957.01.10–1963.10.19	Harold Macmillan	Conservative	
1963.10.19–1964.10.16	Douglas-Home	Conservative	
1964.10.16–1970.06.19	Harold Wilson	Labor	
1970.06.19–1974.03.04	Edward Heath	Conservative	
1974.03.04–1976.04.05	Harold Wilson	Labor	
1976.04.05–1979.05.04	James Callaghan	Labor	
1979.05.04–1990.11.28	Margaret Thatcher	Conservative	Supply management focusing on market and free competition
1990.11.28–1997.05.02	John Major	Conservative	

Table 2.5 The macroeconomic management measures of Germany before and after the supply side structural reform

Period	Development model	Economic system	Macroeconomic management measures	Ruling party	Chancellor
1948.9–1982.10	Rhineland capitalism	Social market economy of the Freibury school	Keynesian effective demand management	CDU	Konrad Adenauer
					Ludwig Wilhelm Erhard
					Kurt Georg Kiesinger
				SPD	Willy Brandt
					Helmut Schmidt
1982.10–2005.10	Rhineland Capitalism transforming to Anglo Saxon model	Social market economy transforming to free market economy	Supply management focusing on market and free competition	CDU	Helmut Kohl
				SPD	Gerhard Schroder

specified industries, classifying 14 industries as underdeveloped, including steel, aluminum refining, shipbuilding, ammonia manufacturing and textile industries. According to the government's plan, these industries should discard excess equipment. In the early 1980s, influenced by the second oil crisis, tax deficiency led to the budget deficit, which stimulated administrative and fiscal reforms. During the administrative meetings from 1981 to 1983, it was proposed that the three major state enterprises (Japanese National Railways, Nippon Telegraph and Telephone Public Corporation, Japan Tobacco and Salt Public Corporation) be privatized through tax increase, fiscal reconstruction and reduction of health care costs. In the 1990s, there were the financial reform and the tax reform, including the "Big Bang" reform carried out by Ryutaro Hashimoto through raising the consumption tax and reducing the personal income tax. In 2001, the structural reform was initiated by the Koizumi cabinet, merging the urban banks to solve the non-performing loans and to attempt postal privatization.

2.3.3 Goals of Structural Reform on the Supply Side

Keynesian demand management aims at full employment, while the main objective of the supply side structural reform is economic growth. Additional goals of the reform are related to the political power, regime stability, social order etc.

2.3.3.1 Economic Growth

Economic growth, conducive to democracy in the long term, has the top priority in the supply side structural reform. Tight-money policies are adopted to beat inflation and alleviate unemployment. The social conflicts are settled by providing the resources for reciprocal solution. The individuals, groups and governments will thus have surplus to support social welfare. Therefore, during the Reagan era, the primary goal of the supply side structural reform was to revitalize the U.S. economy, which was first presented in the Republican National Convention on July 15, 1980. The major goal was economic growth, with full employment but without inflation. In mid-1985, the British government also renounced its post-war goal—full employment.

2.3.3.2 Necessary Government Intervention

Deregulation is an effective way to promote economic growth in the supply side structural reform. The role of the government is thus changed so that it cannot intervene the market. However, on the other hand, deregulation is not absolute. The government formulates and implements all the economic policies, "intervening" the market in a way that it cannot intervene. It is the government that serves as the guarantee of the free market and trade. Therefore, the so-called "deregulation" is optional, which is not applied to all areas. The government intervenes where needs to. The balance between the economic freedom and the government intervention is thus achieved.

2.3.3.3 Regime Stability

Surely, the goal of the supply side structural reform is not mere economic growth. The stability of the government is also part of it. The British Conservative Thatcher, the US Republican Reagan or the German SPD Schroder, as the elected ones, their main objectives were to maintain the regime stability. The supply side structural reform is a perfect strategy to crack down on the competitive party. The ruling party which carries out the reform tends to be conservative, struggling to protect the private property as well as the existing social order. It hates and fears socialist reform and thus regards the labor movement and the labor union as the target to be banned.

2.3.4 Characteristics of Structural Reform on the Supply Side

As a whole, the practice of supply side structural reform is natural, systematic, comprehensive, flexible and progressive.

2.3.4.1 Naturalness

Since the 1970s, the economic globalization and technological innovation have had a huge impact on the economic and social structures of the major economies in the world, which motivates the supply side structural reform. The saturation of the market made it difficult for large-scale production to make profit. Flexible, scattered, technology-intensive and specialized production has replaced the large-scale one to meet the growing personalized demand. That has also promoted the transformation of industrial structures, the adjustment of hierarchical structures, the diversification of social values as well as the gradual integration of the neo-liberalism and neo-conservatism. The Keynesian demand management, which depends too much on authoritarian and conventions, is challenged. The supply side structural reform is thus considered to be a natural response to the adjustment and changes of economic and social structures.

2.3.4.2 Systematization

The tax reform of the Reagan administration has long been considered as tax cutting, while the reform of the Thatcher government is regarded as privatization. Notwithstanding, the measures taken have promoted the reform of the industrial restructuring, innovation system, financial system, multilateral trade, employee–employer relations, social security, streamlining administration, the government budget etc. These innovative and systematic measures have been implemented correspondingly, eliminating the structural and institutional barriers against the economic growth.

2.3.4.3 Comprehensiveness

Some of the economic problems, caused by external shocks and internal imbalances, are temporary, while others are long-term, triggered by the Keynesian demand management policies. One single theory, however perfect, can hardly solve them all. As a result, the theories, policies and measures in the supply side structural reform are like a hotchpotch. Some are based on supply economics and some are developed from monetarism. In fact, with the "New Right" ideology as the theoretical core, the reform applies various theories and policies to solve different economic problems, emphasizing the supply management and the function of the free market and competition as well as the theories of the Keynesian demand management.

2.3.4.4 Flexibility

Despite the explicit policies of the supply side structural reform, its actual implementation encounters obstacles in dealing with disputes among different parties. In addition, there are widespread concerns about the adverse effects. Hence, the major economies adjust, amend and supplement the policies and even compromise or make a concession according to the changes of international and domestic situations. The flexibility of the policies adds the probability of success and plays a positive role in the reform.

2.3.4.5 Progressiveness

The reform is also progressive with certain areas prioritized. Take the privatization reform undertaken by the Thatcher government as an example. During her three consecutive terms, the reform was carried out from the specific to the overall, from the superficial to the core. Generally, the trade reform was ahead of that of the financial system, since a large number of trade inflows would to some extent lower the voice against the financial reform. Then the reform of product markets and the deregulation of products were gradually carried out. In the late 1980s and the early 1990s, the civil aviation was opened earlier than telecommunications, and the reform of electricity and gas had just started.

2.4 Major Tactics of the Structural Reform on the Supply Side in Major Economies

All the economic policies of structural reforms on the supply side have been based on the "New Right" ideology since the 1970s. The ideas of the Keynesian demand management have been adjusted, and so have the relationships between the government and the market, the government and the enterprise, the government and the individuals, capital and labor, structure and the whole.

2.4.1 Readjustment of the Government-Market Relationship

In order to sustain the economic growth, one major part of structural reform is to adjust the relationship between the government and the market through market improvement, role exchange, power limitation, objective resetting etc.

2.4.1.1 Expansion of the Scope of Market Adjustment

The market adjustment is emphasized in the structural reform. The fluctuation of market price implies the changes in supply and demand, which can be further noticed by the producers and consumers in the market. The balance between the supply and demand can be achieved through the adjustment of the quantity. It is believed that economic turmoil is the result of wrong finance or financial policies, for the market can automatically reach equilibrium. Adequacy, fairness and effectiveness are the core qualities of competition and they can promote production, technology, management and efficiency. In competitions, the industrial structure can be adapted according to the consumers' demand and waste of resources can thus be avoided.

2.4.1.2 The New Role of the Government

The government is not only a "calm arbitrator" in the structural reform but also a guide for structural adjustment. On the one hand, the government is supposed to limit its control over micro economy and social life so as to restore the market mechanism, encourage competition, and to create a market with free social order. The loss of efficiency caused by market failure can be thus avoided. On the other hand, a powerful and efficient government can ensure the success of the reform by removing the "shackles" of the market economy and maintaining its overall order.

2.4.1.3 Reduction of the Government Intervention

In the structural reform, the bottleneck of economic growth is believed to be caused by the government intervention, which does not aim at the public interest but the benefit of some party or other. Therefore, the government intervention should be limited to the compensation of market efficiency loss only. The Thatcher administration, advocating the model of a "small government", made it extremely clear that the national borders should be put aside so that the economy and enterprises could develop freely. In his inaugural speech in January 1981, Reagan also pointed out that the government was not the solution of the problem but the problem itself. Reagan believed that the traditional excessive government intervention would affect the overall strength of the country and was therefore determined to limit it.

2.4.1.4 Adjustment of the Objective of Government Intervention

The objective of the government intervention is confirmed and is often limited within certain time and scope. In terms of time, the government will intervene only when the economic fluctuation range is large with recession so serious that the market itself can hardly recover. In terms of scope, the government is supposed to be involved in macroeconomic policies with limited intervention into micro economy and social life.

2.4.2 Readjustment of the Government-Enterprise Relationship

A strong government, according to the core ideas of the supply side structural reform, cannot solve the problems caused by market failure. Instead, it will waste resources excessively and supervise the extension of the enterprise development that adds impetus for the economic growth. Enterprises under the protection of the government gradually degenerate, losing the capability of innovation. Worse still, they will get used to lobbying and bribing to enjoy administrative protection and to avoid competition. Therefore, the relationship between the government and the enterprises is adjusted through reduction of burden and regulations so that the potential of enterprises can be exploited.

2.4.2.1 Less Burden

Major economies take comprehensive measures to relieve the burden on enterprises. Reducing the tax and the cost is one of the direct ways to stimulate the economy from the supply side. Social security systems with the largest expenditure and rising deficit, such as the pension system, the medical insurance systems and the welfare system, are reformed to reduce the cost of indirect wages and to avoid high tax rates. The burden is also eased through encouraging entrepreneurship by relaxing the dismissal protection requirements and lowering the standards for entrepreneurship. In addition, the increase in civil technology investment and the priority of civil technology development will reduce the research cost and improve the competitiveness of enterprises if the government cooperates more with the enterprises.

2.4.2.2 Deregulation

Deregulation is necessary in the reform since the resolution of economic problems lies not in the demand but the supply. The increase in the production efficiency, which is on the supply side, can improve the competitiveness of their products and expand the market. The major economies have cancelled the inflexible rules and regulations on competition and expiration. Companies with natural monopoly can also compete in the free market. The productivity can be further promoted with the enterprises throwing off their "shackles". Statistics show that the proportion of production over GDP was 17% in 1977 in the U.S., with industries under the control of regulations. It fell to 6.6% in 1988, with an average annual rate of nearly 1%. On the other hand, the relaxation of rules does not equal laissez faire. In specific fields, such as finance, the regulations are specially strengthened.

2.4.2.3 Maximization of Potential

In the Keynesian theory of demand management, the substitution of efficiency and equity promotes the growth of the public sectors at the expense of economic growth. As a result, one of the major strategies is privatization. Driven by the "New Right" ideology, privatization, as the main means of reducing the government intervention, shifts the public ownership to private ownership. The relationship between the government and the enterprises is thus changed. The outlook for entrepreneurship and private enterprises helps to inspire people's confidence in the free market economy.

2.4.3 Readjustment of the Government–Individual Relationship

If individuals depend too much on the government welfare, they will gradually become lazy. Therefore, it is necessary to readjust the relationship between the government and the individual by strengthening the individual's rights and responsibilities and reducing the excessive government spending.

2.4.3.1 Property Rights Protection

The amount of private property can more or less manifest the degree of concentration of the national power. And therefore the violations to personal freedom are avoided. If a market is established on private ownership and the pursuit of self-interest, it can benefit from the personal interest as a whole. Thus, the supply side structural reform focuses on property rights as the essential element to develop the supply side. The private property and the market mechanism are linked as the premise of market exchange. The protection of private property rights is the foundation of social stability.

2.4.3.2 Opposition Against Material Equality

Analyzing the substance of the supply side structural reforms of the major economies, one can easily find out that various types of policies, issued by the government of Thatcher or Reagan, are in favor of the equality in terms of politics and business opportunities but are strongly against the material equality. In a market economy, people at an advantageous position will become much richer. However, because of the balance between the rich and poor, it is almost impossible for the poorer people to become very rich. That is why the pursuit of material equality will inevitably lead to repression and coercion.

2.4.3.3 Welfare Cuts

High welfare often leads to negative results such as high cost, high debt, high taxes, low competitiveness, decline in exports, low profit, high bankruptcy rate, low consumption and low domestic investment. This will form a vicious cycle and ultimately affect the welfare. Besides, high welfare hampers the economic and social development seriously due to its characteristic of being easy to increase but difficult to decrease. The major economies have modified the post-war social welfare policies, which have generally caused inefficiency, bureaucracy and excessive centralization, for the social welfare system has formed a special culture of dependency, undermining the family ties and destroying personal responsibilities, creativity and work ethic.

2.4.4 Readjustment of the Labor-Capital Relationship

The labor-capital relationship, which is also termed labor relationship or employment relationship in some countries, is an important part of social relations. Labor ideas and policies, consistent with the mainstream economic ideas, depend entirely on the needs of the social and economic development. The labor-capital relationship generally has a negative influence on economic development and its readjustment is necessary.

2.4.4.1 Subject Clarification

Economic interests are the everlasting subject in employee–employer relations. In a capitalist society, the interest of employees and that of employers always diverge. The former expects a better working environment with higher wages and benefits, while the latter hopes for higher efficiency and lower labor costs so that the profits can be maximized. Economy is closely related to politics, therefore the employee–employer relations are not just an economic problem but also a political one. Political rights and status have also become important parts in the employer–employee game. Influenced by the "New Right" ideology, any intervention in economic freedom is opposed in the supply side structural reform. As for the relationship between employees and employers, in their negotiations, the subject should be limited to production and living conditions with neither political content nor threats or intervention of the government.

2.4.4.2 Establishment of Regulations and Laws

However, the government will intervene indirectly. Actually, the government depends more and more on laws, which have a stronger effect on the employee–employer relations. Unlike policies, laws have a long-term effect, which are also mandatory and authoritative. The government sets up laws and regulations to maintain social order and extend its power, which will affect the employers and employees as well as their relationship.

2.4.4.3 Limitation of the Power of Labor Union

Employers and employees are regarded as a unity in the supply side structural reform, which makes the labor union unnecessary. The role of labor union is not management. It is limited to the establishment of the employment clauses. Generally, the monopoly of the trade union in labor market can "distort" the price of labor, making it much higher than the market level, fix the mode of employment, investment and production, and hamper the adjustment and cause inflation and massive unemployment. It also obstructs job cuts and the adoption of labor-saving technologies, which impedes technological progress. Therefore, labor union is generally looked at as an obstacle against economic growth and its real power should be limited.

2.4.5 Readjustment of the Macro and Micro Structures

Strategies of the supply side structural reform include division of powers between the state and regions, the increasing of the efficiency of public services and the support of the real economy by the virtual economy.

2.4.5.1 Proper Division of Powers Between the State and Regions

Traditional regional policies are adjusted in the supply side structural reform. The market force substitutes the state intervention as one of the options to solve regional issues. Through encouraging self-sustaining development, the relevant policies, region-oriented rather than state-oriented, aim at equal employment opportunities among regions. The responsibilities and powers of public services are divided between the state and different regions. Fiscal transfer no longer takes place through specific appropriation but a special "incentive grant" to stimulate competition according to specific development goals.

2.4.5.2 The Efficiency of Public Services

It will be difficult to carry out the supply side structural reform if there is no reform in the government administrative system. Public sectors have great benefits with little open competition. The efficiency of public services is increased by joining the private sectors in competition. The competitions between public and private sectors and inter-sector competitions are encouraged and the results-oriented systems take the place of the traditional rule-based ones so that the potential of civil servants can be developed.

2.4.5.3 Real Economy Supported by Virtual Economy

The virtual economy, represented by finance, is reformed in order to support the real economy. For instance, the central bank's control of money is strengthened to guarantee the stabilization of price. To build a solid financial system, disintermediation is prevented and depository institutions (especially savings and loan associations) are developed. The interest rate liberalization, which provides the small depositors with equal interest, is also encouraged through flexible financial regulations along with efficient financial systems and depository institutions with a wider business scope.

Chapter 3
Policy and Assessment of Structural Reform on the Supply Side in the Global Perspective

Influenced by the "New Right" thoughts, the major economies carried out the structural reform on the supply side in succession to clear the development obstacles in the 1970s, resulting in the structural advantages that kept those countries at the leading position. Nevertheless, with the emphasis on the market and the free competition, the reform had negative effects as well. Therefore, China, having lately been conducting the reform following those countries, has been struggling to extend their success and to solve the possible problems.

3.1 Economic Policy of the Structural Reform on the Supply Side in Major Economies

Ever since the late 1970s, the major economies have frequently implemented policies of the aggregate, departments and enterprises to promote the reform.

3.1.1 The Aggregate Adjustment Policies

The aggregate adjustment policies include financial and tax policies and monetary ones.

3.1.1.1 Financial and Tax Policies

The major economies have reformed the public income system and expenditure system. The core of the former is the tax reform and that of the latter is the control of the total expenditure and the increase in the efficiency.

L. Xiao, *New Supply Side Economics*, DOI 10.1007/978-981-10-4639-1_3

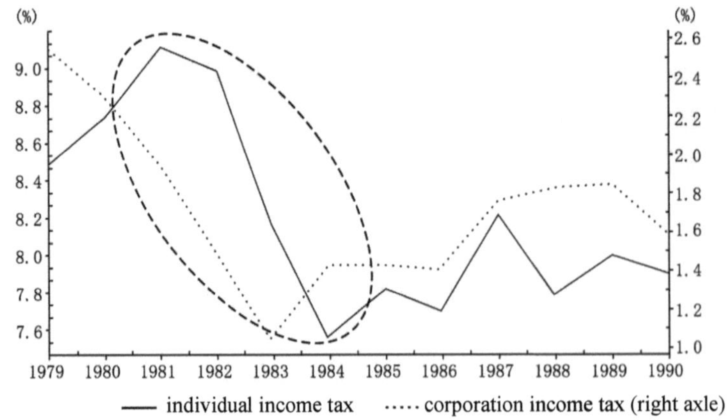

Fig. 3.1 The ratio of individual and corporation income tax to GDP in the US from 1979 to 1990. *Source* Wind Info

Take the U.S. as an example of the reformer of the public income system. President Reagan's message to the Congress on May 29, 1985 was a prelude to the large-scale tax reform in the Western countries and it led to a worldwide reform aiming at lower tax rate, larger tax base, simplified tax system and efficient tax collection. The tax system lasting over half a century was greatly adjusted, with the income tax rate of individuals and corporations minimized. The taxation scales, the marginal tax rate and the total tax were reduced through various measures (Fig. 3.1 and Table 3.1).

Since 1970, the U.S. and other western countries have been pushing ahead with the reform of the public expenditure system. The basic ways of budget analysis and setting have been reformed to realize the zero-based budgeting. The financial supervision has been enhanced and a single account has been set up to ensure the fair transfer, allocation and utilization of massive financial resources (Tables 3.2 and 3.3).

3.1.1.2 Monetary Policies

In the 1980s, the U.S. and other major economies set the monetary growth control as their major goal. Under the traditional micro control, there was less limitation to the credit. The competition was encouraged as well. One of the measures was to control the monetary and the credit base through the central bank. The Depository Institutions Deregulation and Monetary Control Act of 1980 (DIDMCA) standardized the regulations of the commercial banks, mutual saving banks, savings banks, savings and loans associations and credit unions which had accepted the Federal Deposit Insurance or were qualified to do so. Federal Reserve controlled all the monetary bases and credit bases in the financial activities of the U.S., providing the best conditions for the regulation of money circulation and interest rate.

Table 3.1 Measures taken by major economies to reduce income tax

Country	Measures
US	15 scales from 11 to 15% of the individual income tax was reduced to 2 scales, namely, 15 and 28%. The highest marginal tax rate dropped from 50 to 28%. And 5 scales from 15 to 46% of the corporation income tax was reduced to 3 scales, 15, 25 and 34%
UK	6 scales of the individual income tax was reduced to 2, 25 and 40%
Japan	5 scales of the progressive tax was reduced to 4. The highest tax rate was also reduced, from 50 to 37%. The tax threshold was raised and the tax base was narrowed. The corporate tax had been reduced for two straight years, and the tax rate was reduced from 37.5% in 1997 to 30% in 1999
Germany	The basic individual deductibles were set significantly high, which was increasing from 12,096 Deutschmark to 13,014 Deutschmark. Till 1998, the individual income tax range had been reduced from 25.9–53 to 22.5–39%
	In 1998, the rate of the corporation income tax on retained earnings had been reduced from 45 to 40%, on distributive earnings 30 to 28%. In 1999, the former had been further reduced to 35% and the latter 25%
	Schroder valued the function of enterprises. He implemented large-scale reform right after coming to power in October, 1998. Both the individual and corporation income tax was reduced within 4 years. The rate of the former was reduced from 25.9% in 1998 to 19.9% in 2002, with the highest tax rate reduced from 53 to 48.5% in 2000 and the tax threshold raised from 12,386 Deutschmark in 1998 to 14,100 Deutschmark in 2002. The child tax exemption per month was raised from 220 Deutschmark to 250 Deutschmark. As for the corporation income tax, the rate was reduced from 45 to 35% in 2002. From January 1, 2001, the sale of shares of another enterprise (be held for over 1 year) will not require tax. The highest special tax rate for corporation income was reduced from 47 to 45% and the tax rate for accumulated benefit was reduced from 45 to 40%

Source compiled

Meanwhile, a discount window was allowed among all the deposit institutions that set reserves for deposits. The Federal Reserve also announced new standards to measure the total amount of money, including new types of deposits and invoices derived from the financial innovation. Another measure was to coordinate with monetary and fiscal policies to control inflation. Since the early 1980s, the major economies had maintained the price stability, which was considered the main solution to serious inflation. The monetary fiscal policies were thus less efficient in the short term so that the central bank could beat inflation.

3.1.2 Adjustment Policies on Departments

Since the 1970s, major economies strengthened the reform of virtual and industrial departments to encourage competition and increase efficiency.

Table 3.2 Measures taken by Japan and Germany to indirectly reduce corporation and individual tax

Country	Measures
Japan	In the 1990s, Japan reduced and even froze the land-value tax to promote the real estate industry. The bourse transaction tax was also cancelled to attract the capital
Germany	1. The working capital tax, the main resource of local income, was abolished to expand the ownership capital. This was one of the policies adopted by Germany to insure the leading position of industry. The working capital tax, depending on the operating capital, would force a company with little operating capital or at a loss into bankruptcy, reducing the company's capacity to accumulate capital. For joint-stock companies, it caused double taxation on the ownership capital
	2. The rates of inheritance tax and gift tax were reduced and the tax allowance was increased. Despite the fact that inheritance and gifts belonged to private property, the business property of family enterprises took up the major part. The reduction of inheritance tax and gift tax could indirectly ease the burden and promote the development of family enterprises
	3. The abnormal depreciation allowance was increased from 240,000 Deutschmark to 400,000 Deutschmark. The normal depreciation rate was reduced. For companies applying progressive depreciation, the maximum deprecation rate was reduced from 30 to 25%. For those applying direct depreciation, the maximum deprecation rate was reduced from 4 to 3%
	4. Other measures included the extension of the tax rebate deadline, from 2 to 5 years. And the maximum tax rebate of each enterprise was increased from 300,000 Deutschmark to 600,000 Deutschmark
	5. The way of profit report was reformed as well, involving the evaluation of facilities and debt, the limitation of tax rebate for loss and deficit. Enterprises could thus calculate the profit objectively with less influence of investment in tax. From the perspective of cash rising, those measures could reduce the loss in income tax caused by tax reduction
	6. The conditions for tax of employees were reformed additionally. The limit of payroll tax expenditure was raised from 1200 Deutschmark per year and 1600 Deutschmark per year. The maximum wage of employers for whom the enterprise should pay insurance increased from 12,000 Deutschmark to 18,000 Deutschmark. The procedure and rules in the reduction of helpers' wage and social insurance were simplified to improve the outside environment of family enterprises

Source compiled

3.1.2.1 Policies to Reform the Virtual Departments

There have occurred great changes in the financial management of major economies. Since the 1930s, the initial competition limitation, security insurance and depositor protection have been replaced by competition, efficiency, investor and consumer oriented policies and measures. The financial supervision has even been globally opposed. In 1980, the U.S. announced the Depository Institutions Deregulation and Monetary Control Act. And in 1996, Ryutaro Hashimoto, the former prime minister of Japan, introduced the "Big Bang" reform. Other major economies also accelerated their reform by cancelling or releasing the control of virtual departments to encourage competition. The currency transformation between

Table 3.3 Measures taken by the US to reform the public expenditure system

Country	Measures
US	1. The basic analytical approach and the decision-making process of budgeting were reformed to realize zero-based budgeting, which started from a fresh budget and followed the new standards of calculation rather than the previous budgeting. The budget expenditure was more accurate without the shackles of budget base and disputable matters
	2. Financial supervision was enhanced through different measures. Cash budgeting was applied to control the total public expenditure and stabilize the macro economy. The power of management was transferred to lower levels so that the managers could take full use of the motivate mechanism. Additionally, each manager was supposed to assume the responsibilities of the accountant. Those measures helped to motivate the employers of public sectors and reinforced the fiscal administration, perfecting the public sector supervision of inner expenditure
	3. A single account, which was one of the features of the treasury system of the US, was set up in the central bank to control the public expenditure. This meant that neither the department in charge nor the department spending the fund had a bank account of their own. The fund would be transferred directly from the single account of the government to that of the suppliers once there was actual consumption

Source compiled

the credit receiver and the loaner became more efficient and the consumption became more convenient. Meanwhile, supervision of other fields was also enhanced so that the role of the market mechanism could be fully played.

3.1.2.2 The Reform Policies of Industrial Sectors

Since the 1980s, the adjustment of industrial policies made by various countries has been focusing on the promotion of technological development and high-tech industries, the modification or elimination of declining enterprises, as well as the adaptation of competition modes and the market structure (Tables 3.4 and 3.5).

The first subject of reform was the industrial policies on technology. In the early 1980s, the international competition between the major economies intensified with the change of the international conditions. America's steel, automobile and other industries were in trouble. By the mid-1980s, even the high-tech industries with absolute advantages in the U.S. were challenged in the international competition. It was then realized that the original models of technological innovation and policies on technology were not suitable for economic development any more. Consequently, the U.S. made adjustment to those policies. In the 1990s, almost at the same time, Japan and Germany also carried out reforms of industrial policies on technology by confirming national policy status, enhancing the role of the central government in the industrial and technological development, strengthening the macro-control of the industrialization of science and technology etc. Credit, tax incentives and government subsidies etc. were used to encourage and support the

Table 3.4 Measures taken by the US and Japan to encourage competition, deregulate among the virtual sectors

Country	Measures
US	1. Competition was encouraged to improve the efficiency of the transfer of funds between debtors and creditors. In terms of credit management, the Depository Institutions Deregulation and Monetary Control Act of 1980 allowed the negotiable orders of withdrawal across the country, expanding the source of funds for all depository institutions. Services of consumer credit (up to 20% of total assets), credit cards as well as trust services were also approved among savings and loan associations. Restriction on the interest rates of mortgage loans and other types of credits was cancelled or relaxed. In October 1982, the Garn-St Germain Depository Institutions Act was adopted to further diversify the roles of savings and loan associations by allowing the establishment of MMDA and Super NOW Account
	2. There were fewer or even no regulations for banks. Restrictions on deposit interest rates were abolished. As was stated in the Depository Institutions Deregulation and Monetary Control Act of 1980, Q regulations on savings and fixed deposit interest rates would be phased out by 1986. By April 1, 1986, the savings deposit interest rate ceiling had been completely abolished. More than 14,000 commercial banks and more than 3000 and 500 savings institutions could decide their own interest rates on deposits. It's only prohibited to pay interest to business checking account. Restrictions on international business were no longer rigid. Activities among financial institutions of different countries received fewer limitations, producing more opportunities for foreign institutions to enter the domestic market restrictions and the domestic ones to explore markets abroad. It was also freer to input and output funds since the foreign exchange was less controlled
Japan	1. Mixed business became the mainstream so that industries were interconnected in various facets, including insurance. The form of financial holding company had been introduced, through which financial institutions might engage in mixed business, thus providing an assortment of financial products or services and more or less activating Japan's financial markets
	2. The banking industry was reformed. The services of banks were greatly diversified, including securities, through flexibly adopting the form of financial holding company. Business related to investment trust, online banking, final accounting and so forth had been developed since December, 1998 with corresponding products sold at the counter. The introduction of the spending cap system after the closure of banks (10 million yen) left the choice to the depositors, who decided which bank to choose according to the operating efficiency of each bank. The banks checked their business according to the capital adequacy ratio. Once the ratio had declined, the financial supervision department would limit the scope of the bank's business or suspend its financial services and order it to take prompt measures
	3. The reform of securities industry was pushed. Firstly, the mode of the financial holding company was applied so that there was no difference of business between securities companies and their subsidiaries. Hence all the companies were forced to increase their efficiency and quality in this new competitive environment. Secondly, the service charge for trusted had been flexiblized. Ever since April, 1998, there had been no fixed service charge for trades with more than 50 million yen and so had been for those with small amounts since October, 1999. The competition had thus become ruthless in the securities industry with charges going down. To avert the decline in revenue, investment trust products were introduced and deals were

(continued)

Table 3.4 (continued)

Country	Measures
	always made online to avoid extra costs. Thirdly, the license system had been changed into a registration one since December, 1998, making it possible for other industries to participate and compete in the securities industry. And lastly, in April, 1999, the securities exchange tax was cancelled
	4. The insurance industry was reformed. Japan's insurance industry was specially protected and supervised by the "monopoly law". With financial liberalization, the revised law was issued in April, 1996. And in October, companies of life insurance and property insurance began to interoperable among their subsidiaries. By July 1998, property insurance premiums had been flexible, and foreign investment in Japan's insurance industry had also been accepted. This had fundamentally changed the competitive environment of the insurance industry, with more choices of insurance varieties, prices and services, which has improved operational as well
	5. The international financial transactions was reformed. Since April, 1998, the new "foreign exchange law" took effect. The notification system of large capital transactions had been abolished and the domestic and foreign capitals were transferred without restrictions. The specialized foreign exchange bank system was cancelled. Either individuals or corporations could set up their deposit accounts abroad and calculation service of foreign currency for domestic citizens is provided. Therefore, enterprises and individuals had an easier access to foreign securities investment. Chain stores could also engage in foreign exchange business, increasing the business opportunities to a large extent

Source compiled

Table 3.5 Measures taken by the US and Japan to supervise the virtual sectors

Country	Measures
US	The supervision focuses on certain areas. There were increasing bank failures at the beginning of the 1980s due to the economic downturn and the competition of interest rate after its deregulation. In 1981, ten banks went bankrupt, which was normal after the wars. However, the number reached 79 in 1984, 120 in 1985 and 150 in 1986, which caused the attention of relevant management departments. Regulations regarding some areas were tightened. In early 1986, the Federal Reserve Board, the Office of Comptroller of Currency and the Federal Deposit Insurance Corporation set the reserve requirements for risk loans at 9% of the bank assets (6% originally). The speculative high-yield securities were not allowed for the merger of enterprises. The Office of Comptroller of Currency and the Federal Deposit Insurance Corporation also explored ways to maintain the operation of those banks in trouble by providing funds for partial ownership. The supervision of the federal registered banks by the Office of Comptroller of Currency was strengthened and the number of bank closure orders, penalties on the heads and dismissal of bank officials was 5 times more than that in 1980. The number of inspectors of those two departments was increased as well. In 1985, 300 inspectors were added and there were additional 1200 employees in the liquidation team. One special full-time bank inspector was sent to each bank under the jurisdiction of Office of Comptroller of Currency, who was also responsible for the management of the Federal Home Loan Bank of 3500 savings and loan associations. In 1986, the increase of savings deposits and the types of investment were also severely restricted

(continued)

Table 3.5 (continued)

Country	Measures
Japan	The reform of financial administration has been initiated. Japan has made significant adjustments to the financial administrative systems in order to effectively supervise them. In June, 1998, the Financial Services Agency was established for the Prime Minister of Japan and His Cabinet, separating the roles of inspection and supervision of the Japanese Ministry of Treasury. Committees of inspection of securities trading and so forth were set up in the system reform in 1992 to prevent inner fraudulent practices of trading. But those committees belonged to the Japanese Ministry of Treasury and their power was thus limited. Consequently they were moved to the Financial Services Agency. The reorganization of the Japanese Ministry of Economy involved two stages. First, the department of finance and that of supervision were united in July, 2000, as the Financial Services Agency as a peripheral bureau of the Financial Reconstruction Commission. Next, in January, 2001, the Financial Reconstruction Commission was incorporated into the Financial Services Agency as a peripheral bureau of the cabinet and the Ministry of Treasury was renamed the Ministry of Finance

Source compiled

technological industrialization. Private enterprises were also encouraged to play a main role by the government through the combination of industries, officials and universities and the coordination of human, financial and material resources (Table 3.6).

The second subject of reform is the industrial policies on structure. The concept of industrial structure was popularized in Japan after World War II, when the economy was on the edge of collapse. The government thus defined goals of developing the industrial structures and outlined practical approaches. The "leading industries" of different periods were recognized and a series of policies were adopted to ensure that those industries dominate. In the 1980s, the United States, Japan and Germany introduced policies on industrial structure adjustment, emphasizing the significance of adjusting the structure through the development of new industries and the revolution of old ones in recession (Tables 3.7, 3.8 and 3.9).

The third subject is the policies on industrial organization. The rules, norms and market economic order are adjusted so that the competition between enterprises and market structure is modified to improve the industrial efficiency and the achievement. The policies are divided into two kinds: policies to maintain competition and those to limit competition. Since the 1980s, there has been differentiation in the reform of industrial policies on organization among major economies. The US and Japan chose different ways, the former gradually removed the limitation of monopoly, while the latter further promoted the anti-monopoly policies (Table 3.10).

Table 3.6 Measures taken by the major economies to reform the industrial policies on technology

Country	Measures
US	1. The research results achieved by the federal government is applied to the regulations on private enterprises, including those concerning transfer, diffusion and commerce based on the value of the investment in science and technology from the national defense after the World War II. The University Small Business Patent Procedures Act of 1980 allowed exclusive patent licensed by a majority of federal research laboratories to universities and enterprises so that private enterprises would put in more resources and the commercialization as well as the innovation of technologies were promoted. The Stevenson-Wydler Technology Innovation Act of 1980 elaborates on the multiple roles of the federal government in promoting business innovation. It had for the first time transferred the technologies of federal laboratories to private enterprises with special departments set up. The Federal Technology Transfer Act of 1986 further issued policies appreciating the business value of investment and development, authorizing cooperative research in agencies, enterprises, universities and non-profit research institutions
	2. Private enterprises were encouraged to conduct researches cooperatively. The obstructions caused by the antitrust law are removed to improve research abilities and international competitiveness. During this period, the US government aimed at improves the environment of economy, taxation and regulations. The National Cooperative Research Act of 1984 encouraged cooperative development and research between enterprises
	3. The government and enterprises were encouraged to cooperate to increase the long-term international competitiveness and to enhance the function of the federal government in the development of the industrial technology. The Omnibus Foreign Trade and Competitiveness Act of 1988 authorized the National Institute of Standards and Technology of the Department of Commerce to start two national programs, one of which was related to advanced technology and aimed at government-enterprise cooperation for future economic growth and employment opportunities, while the other of which concerned the cooperation of manufacturing industries, providing technical and management assistance for 380,000 SMEs
	4. The status of the national technological policies was further emphasized. The major mission of the federal government is to formulate and implement technological policies so as to improve the quality of life, to promote economic growth and to enhance the national security. In September, 1990, the Bush administration handed a document regarding the United States' technological policies to the Congress, which formally proposed the base, target, implementation and plans
Japan	1. The government's macro regulation and control of the development of science and technology and the industrialization of technologies was strengthened. In 1995, Japan reenacted the policies of science and technology, adding information, electronics, software, semiconductors, new materials, energy, life sciences, marine science, space science, earth environment and so forth as new focuses of research and development. In 1994, a ministry with the Prime Minister as its head, was set up to promote advanced information technology. In 1995, MITI initiated a plan of a high-tech society with specific policies and comprehensive planning. In November, 1995, the Japanese government issued the basic law of science and technology. And in June, 1996, the basic plan of science and technology was also formulated based on the law. The development of high technology and high-tech industries has thus been a matter of the national laws and regulations, moving Japan a further step into a new stage of technological industrialization with scientific structures
	2. The industrialization of technologies was encouraged and supported by credit, tax incentives, government subsidies and other means. According to the laws, private enterprises could obtain low interest loans for high tech research and development and repay the capital and interest according to the preferential terms if they succeed. Once they

(continued)

Table 3.6 (continued)

Country	Measures
	failed, they would only repay the capital. As for electronics, software, bio engineering, new materials and other high-tech products, there were additional tax incentives, special depreciation as well as government subsidies. The government was also responsible for the cost of researches with longer period and higher risks, such as the basic research and strategic technology research
	3. The government combined industries, officials, universities and human, financial or material resources to propel the high-tech industrialization, which was highly efficient considering the considerable cost and risks that might come about in the implementation of high-tech projects. For instance, ultra large scale integrated circuit, deep-sea exploration vessel, H2 rocket etc. were studied and developed cooperatively. Intermediary official agencies such as the basic research of biological technology development promotion center, research institutions, New Technology Corporation, new energy and industrial technology development organization and such were established to provide technical advices and research results to assist the private enterprises
	4. Private enterprises were encouraged to increase investment in research and development, to use new technology to upgrade traditional industries. Japanese enterprises had utilized foreign scientific and technological achievements, especially for automation and information, and the achievement is impressive
Germany	1. The German Center for Research and Innovation was set up to foresee and define scientific problems, determine the future direction and enact specific measures. The members were appointed by Chancellor Kohl. In March, 1995, the first 17 members were appointed, who came from relevant government departments, fields of science and technology, education, economy and influential trade unions. The Federal Minister of Education and Research as well as the Minister for Economic Affairs and Energy were the permanent representatives of the federal government
	2. The Federal Ministry for Education, Science, Research and Technology, was formed at the end of 1994, when the new federal government was formed and the former Federal Ministry of Research and Technology and the Federal Ministry of Education and Science merged. It was also called the "Ministry of Future" on many occasions because of its special mission of increasing the international competitiveness of Germany in the future. It was proved to be a successful integration because the new ministry was operated in a more coordinated, flexible and efficient way in line with the country's development of science and technology
	3. Policies were adjusted and optimized. The adjustment of policies on science and technology dealt with the integration of the world economy and high-tech challenges. The policies were adjusted to form proper social and economic structures. The specific measures included guiding and funding. The formal referred to legal, policy and planning guidance. And the latter referred to the assistance of contract research projects, commissioned research and technology consulting. The government provided indirect subsidies to the small and medium sized enterprises with technologies to be revolutionized and the participants of basic applied research projects which would cost a lot of time and money

Source compiled

3.1.3 Adjustment Policies on Enterprises

The policies on enterprises focus on the reform of state-owned ones, small and medium-sized ones and corporate governance, aiming to change people's negative

Table 3.7 The US and Japanese institutions and principles in the adjustment of industrial structures

Country	Institutions and principles
US	In 1983, President Reagan established the Commission on Industrial Competitiveness, which released a report entitled "Global Competition: the New Reality" 18 months later. It made clear that the aim of industrial structure adjustment was to improve the international competitiveness, to keep pace with other advanced countries, to regain the comparative advantage, and to expand the US market share in the world
Japan	In 1980, the Science and Technology Agency issued a white paper on science and technology, which was the main focus the nation's future development. Since the 1990s, industrial policies on creative and intensive knowledge have been formulated. Due to the bubble economy, the process was delayed. In October, 1995, the sub-committee of Japanese industrial structure put forward a plan on the structural reform of the twenty-first century. It was pointed out that international division would be inevitable and new industries would be developed. In terms of the old ones, it would be advisable to deregulate, revolutionize, and transfer to industries with higher added values. In 1998, MITI withdrew from the plan, creating a new industry in the face of the challenge of the global economic environment

Source compiled

Table 3.8 Measures taken by the US and Germany in the development of new industries

Country	Measures
US	A huge market was provided for new industries by military orders. Since the 1980s, the US military budget had increased significantly, most of which was the procurement of sophisticated weapons. According to the U.S. Energy Information Administration, the budget made by the US Department of Defense for the electronic industry was $42.2 billion in 1983 and it increased to $48.4 billion in 1984. The significance of electronic warfare had further expanded the market for the military products with electronic optical and microwave technologies. From 1985 to 1989, the government spent large sums money on sophisticated products including infrared and laser smoke detection apparatus. The military research on science and technology was focused on integrated circuits, artificial intelligence and automation tools, which is a driving force for development of the country's high technology industry
Germany	Emerging industries such as the electronics, nuclear power and aerospace were formed and developed. With the country's overall fiscal adjustment, the government's funding for researchers' grew at an annual rate of 4.1% from 1981 to 1985, which surpassed that of financial expenditure that was less than 3%. In addition, the government promoted the automation of production of automobile, textile and other industries. The utilization of manufacturing capacity increased from 75% in 1989 to nearly 90% in 1982

Source compiled

attitudes to private companies and entrepreneurial activities through promoting the competitiveness of enterprises, which are the core power in the supply side structural reform.

Table 3.9 Measures taken by the major economies in adjusting and assisting the declining industries

Country	Measures
US	1. Outdated industries were eliminated through restriction and mergers. For instance, the steel industries, leaving its dominant position, were merged in more than two decades in order to survive and compete. Through restructuring, the United States Steel, Nucor Corporation and Severstal became the leading steel enterprises in the US as well as the globe. Although the production is lower than that before the structural adjustment, these new steel giants have been significantly improved in terms of the company's health and technological innovation
	2. The bankruptcy proceedings were standardized. In order to reduce the destruction of excess capacity on the economy when a large number of enterprises close down, the US government also formulated policies to standardize bankruptcy. For example, enterprises could hang up debt repayment during their application of bankruptcy, and they must take certain responsibilities for the future jobs of the unemployed workers. These regulations created opportunities for those enterprises to seek assistance and relieve, and they can also reduce the impact of excess capacity
Japan	1. Having suffered from oil shocks twice, the Japanese government enacted the Special Law for the Structural Improvement of Specified Industries, the main content of which included the basic plans, specific credit funds and allowing cartel in depression. The main purpose was to scrap equipment and stop the operation. The ministers determined the amount of equipment scrapped in the plans and the debt was paid by credit fund. The unemployed workers as well as small and medium sized enterprises were assisted and provided with relief. Those who were fired because of the scrap of equipment caused guaranteed golden handshake by the information fund. In addition, the deadline of the employment insurance payment was extended and the scale of financial assistance was expanded. Through the Public Employment Security Office, new jobs, vocational training and guidance were offered. In a depressed area, public jobs were given priority to provide employment opportunities. Extra activity fees, training allowances etc. were supplied by the government. In terms of SMEs, interest loans became low while the credit insurance, refund tax, corporate tax and subsidies were increased. Credit for industry transference was allowed as well. Local enterprises could thus transfer and get investment from other regions
	2. The Special Law for the Structural Improvement of Specified Industries was overturned in April, 1983, when the Temporary Measures Law for the Structural Adjustment of Specific Industries was created, with the stipulation that the ministers of the industries develop the basic plans for structural improvement. The new investment plan for business cooperation and the development of technology was added. A special industrial credit fund was launched to guarantee the execution of those plans, and a variety of financial subsidies and preferential tax measures were offered and taken. To adapt to this new law, two other laws were adopted, adding measures dealing with unemployment. Business owners were to pay wages to employees in conversion training for 6 months, with average rate of subsidy being 2/3, and 3/4 for small and medium sized enterprises. When employees were introduced to new business owners, the old employer would give a 1-year wage subsidy with the general rate of 1/4, and 1/3 for small and medium enterprises. Financial assistance and preferential loans were also provided for enterprises developing new fields, markets, technologies and employee training. The maximum amount was 10 million yen, supplied by the county and the central

(continued)

Table 3.9 (continued)

Country	Measures
	government. The preferential loans were decided by the county magistrate and supplied by finance corporations of small businesses
Germany	1. For iron and steel, coal, shipbuilding, textile and other departments with "contraction" or "stagnation", financial subsidies were strictly controlled with production, personnel and equipment compressed so that they would be orderly adapted to the market
	2. For agriculture, coal mining and other departments with strategic needs, their core technology should be preserved on purpose

Source compiled

Table 3.10 Policies on industrial organization taken by the US and Japan

Country	Measures
US	Since the 1980s, the US had gradually relaxed the restrictions on monopoly. The anti-monopoly, anti-merger and anti-unfair-trading policies were implemented with different degrees in different periods. During the Reagan administration, anti-monopoly and anti-merger policies were the core. In 1982, the US government made a lot of changes to these regulations for horizontal mergers, cross-industry mergers as well as supply and marketing mergers. In 1984, the Clayton Antitrust Act was adjusted with a laissez faire attitude towards mergers, which marked the fourth wave of corporate mergers in the US
	Since the 1990s, the US policies on industrial organization have been encouraging mergers. In 1996, the Boeing Company incorporated McDonnell-Douglas Corporation with $13.3 billion, becoming the largest aircraft manufacturer in the world with $50 billion of assets and 200,000 employees, accounting for 75% of civil aircraft sales. In 1998, the Citibank and Travelers Group merged and the new Citigroup possessed the total asset of nearly $700 billion and the market capitalization of $166 billion
Japan	Since the 1980s, Japan had further promoted policies on the monopoly prohibition; due to the fact that, from the 1970s to the 1980s, the Japanese enterprises were accustomed to the market competition and large scale ones had developed to a higher level, resulting in the increasing restrict competition in the market. The government modified its anti-monopoly law. In 1980, the Japan Fair Trade Commission tightened its regulations concerning merger and revised the rules of application as well as the conditions. In 1983, MITI formulated specific laws to improve the industrial structure. Approval from the Commission should be obtained when taking measures of restrict monopoly such as Cattell and business cooperation as well as business intensification. On May 19, 1993, the Japanese Unfair Competition Prevention Law was further modified, focusing on the patent of trademarks and designs before registration and imposing punishment for the imitation of goods (especially toys, groceries, clothing, domestic appliances etc.) and fraudulent use of the trademarks. Three acts were added as unfair competition behaviors and the resolutions were enriched, which had since made the law comprehensive and almost perfect. This revision mainly covered the types of acts, resorts as well as the right to request restitution of credit

Source compiled

3.1.3.1 The Reform Policies on State Enterprises

Based on the "New Right" ideology, the privatization policy of the Thatcher government dominated the reform. The British mixed economy was transferred to market economy with less government intervention. People began to have faith in the free market economy since the economic and political structure had been fundamentally reformed.

The first step was to promote the privatization policy by stages. Since the 1980s, Britain had gone through three stages of the privatization, which was correlated with Thatcher's terms of office. The first was the tentative stage (from 1979 to 1983), when privatization was promoted in certain areas with limited conditions. The second was the promotion stage (from 1984 to 1987), covering state enterprises with natural monopoly and public services. The third was the further development stage (from 1987 to 1990), extending to state enterprises with serious loss, government institutions and social welfare etc. (Table 3.11).

The second step was to launch the privatization program using the legal system. In the process of privatization of state owned enterprises of major economies, complete legal procedures and plans were attached great importance to. Any program should comply with legislations and be authorized legal before implementation (Table 3.12).

The final step was to take a variety of ways to promote privatization, including the sale of public sector assets. In terms of those enterprises with losses and not yet ripe for the privatization, they were deregulated and the monopoly was broken to encourage competition. For those involving no transfer of property rights, the state enterprises were contracted to private enterprises through concession bidding so that the competition mechanism was also introduced. The private sectors provided supplementary services to the public ones (Table 3.13).

3.1.3.2 Policies to Support SMEs

Policies to support SMEs are part and parcel of the supply side structural reform. Since the 1980s, the major economies have made regulations to support the development of SMEs. Japan and Germany redefined the role played by those enterprises and expected them to be active, flexible and creative and become the driving force of economic growth. Policies and measures were also introduced to construct the environment of market competition and set up the new system of innovation and entrepreneurship so that SMEs could be developing in a stable way (Table 3.14).

3.1.3.3 Policies on Corporate Governance

Firstly, the new management concept is popularized. The concept of enterprise culture has been introduced after the 1980s, emphasizing the values, norms and

Table 3.11 Measures taken by Britain and Germany in the privatization of enterprises

Country	Measures
Britain	During the tentative stage (from 1979 to 1983), when privatization was promoted in certain areas with limited conditions, 25 enterprises were privatized, most of which were secondary profit-driven state-owned companies. Hotels of Amersham International and British Rail as well as branches of state-owned companies were sold. The share of Cable & Wireless was sold out in 1981 and 1983. For some companies, part of the property right was also transferred, generally with a government's share of less than 50%
	During the promotion stage (from 1984 to 1987), the privatization was further promoted due to the huge success of the first stage. The Tories, in their election manifesto in 1983, asserted their determination to privatize Bigger Thinking, Royal Dockyard, British Airways, Leyland Motors, British Steel (a large proportion), British Bus and most airports. During her second term, Prime Minister Thatcher set "Popular Capitalism" as a political goal. The government sold the cross channel ferry companies, Jaguar and British Telecom. Nearly 2 million people bought the share of British Telecom, which marked the first systematic privatization of state enterprises with natural monopoly and institutions of public service. British Telecom was not the monopoly in telecommunications even before its privatization, Through the introduction of Mercury as its major competitors, the company was first liberalized and then privatized, which served as a good example of opening up the market and promoting competition in the market
	During the further development stage (from 1987 to 1990), the policies of privatization were applied to state enterprises with enormous losses. In addition, the public services and natural monopoly industries were privatized to a larger extent, involving all aspects of government institutions and social welfare, such as the reform of education, security system, local government, etc. During the annual meeting of the Conservative Party in October, 1988, Mrs. Thatcher made it clear for the first time that there was no restricted area of privatization, which would be further expanded in natural monopoly industries of electricity, water and so on. The central bureau of electric power was split and lost its monopoly control of the state grid, which was jointly owned by 12 regional transmission companies. An effective competition mechanism was thus set up in replace of the original national monopoly
Germany	The scheme of the privatization of assets and share policies was approved by the federal government on March 26, 1985. It was proposed to reduce the government's share in eight large companies. For example, the share of Volkswagen was reduced from 20 to 14%, United Industry from 100 to 74%, Lufthansa from 79.9 to 55%. In 1982, there were 950 industrial enterprises with more than 25% of the federal government's share. The total investment was about 2.1 billion Deutschmark, accounting for 1.6% of all the shares of the industrial sectors and corporations limited. By 1992, after a decade of privatization, the number of companies with the federal government's shares and the total share had declined by half

Source compiled

goals among the staff. It is realized that the spiritual beliefs can influence the production efficiency to a large extent, and measures are consequently taken to meet the people's spiritual needs in terms of safety, respect and self-realization. An

Table 3.12 Stages of the privatization of state enterprises in Britain

Stages	Content
Policy-making	The feasibility of privatization was first studied among those state enterprises by neutral non-government research institutions, commercial banks and management consultants and then reported to the relevant departments of the government, which further made the decision based on the possibilities, approaches and conditions of privatization concluded in the research results
Law-making	One or several commercial banks were chosen as consultant through government's tender. Management and sales teams were formed to publicize privatization among the public and explain the specific scheme. Private sectors were responsible for the audit and relevant regulations were formulated. The privatization would be implemented after the approval of the relevant government departments of the final laws and administrative regulations
Implementation	Banks and enterprises signed the contract for the sale of shares and then officially listed the stock. The whole process was commercial, which was in essence not different from that of the private companies
Audit	Since privatization concerns the public interest, the National Audit Office was responsible for the audit before and after the privatization to ensure the fairness, openness and reasonability of the process and to prevent the loss of assets. A department was set up in the F Department to audit the performance of the privatization of state-owned assets

Source compiled

Table 3.13 The flexible measures taken by the UK in the privatization of state enterprises

Measures	Content
Partial sale	The Thatcher administration first sold part of the public assets to the private sectors in the form of shares through four approaches. The first was to offer shares publicly. The government's share in mixed enterprises was sold to private companies while that of wholly state-owned ones was reformed first and then listed. This approach was thorough and applicable to large-scale state enterprises. The second was to sell state enterprises to private enterprises as a whole, which was applicable to relatively small enterprises. For instance, Royal Ordnance was directly sold to the privatized British Aerospace Corporation in 1987. The third was to sell shares of the enterprise to the management personnel and the employees of enterprises. This approach was also applicable to small companies, especially those whose asset was controlled by the management staff or employees. The assets could be used by employees as mortgage when applying for loans in banks
Free competition	This measure was aimed at social welfare reform and those enterprises with losses but yet not mature to be privatized. Regulations were relaxed and the monopoly was broken to encourage competition. Private sectors were allowed to enter the field that was monopolized by the public services and was encouraged to compete with them. Besides, capitals were attracted to public companies by selling shares and inviting bids. State-owned corporations were reorganized as stock corporations. Meanwhile, the state enterprises were no longer encouraged to fulfill the traditional "social

(continued)

Table 3.13 (continued)

Measures	Content
	responsibility" but to focus on profitability. In 1980, the Parliament passed a law of competition, aiming to increase the competitiveness by making the state enterprises fulfill the economic indicators. Committees of monopoly and merger were specifically authorized to supervise and investigate the performance of state enterprises. During the Thatcher administration, many state enterprises were first liberalized and then completely privatized after the conditions of them were improved
Concession bidding	The transfer of property rights was not involved. Through concession bidding, the state enterprises were contracted by private enterprises the competitive mechanism was introduced even to those with less competitiveness. School meals, campus cleaning, park maintenance, garbage collection, road maintenance and so on were privatized. The role of the public sectors was limited while the private sectors' business was expanded
Labor service	Supplementary labor services were provided by the private sectors to the public sectors. In addition to private schools and hospitals, the establishment of private reformatories, prisons, mental hospitals, disability and retirement homes were promoted. Private sectors provide a wider and wider range of services due to its low cost

Source compiled

Table 3.14 Measures taken by Japan and Germany to support SMEs

Country	Measures
Japan	1. To create conditions for market competition. In order to prevent the market insufficiency of SMEs and enhance their competitiveness, the prevention of excessive competition, promotion of export and guarantee of tender were no longer the goals in new policies. Instead, the new policies emphasized the following points. (1) The capital was supplied through diversified ways. The financing guarantee system was reevaluated with additional non-financial indexes such as technology, market growth and the ability of managers. The capital market was improved with more credit liquidity and the issue of corporate bonds was readjusted with diversified interest rates, repayment period, etc. to meet various funding needs of these enterprises. (2) The management resources of enterprises were enriched. The diagnostic system of SMEs was examined. The venture capital companies were encouraged to be set up under the guidance of experts. The administrative institutions played various roles in the implementation of policies using competition principles. (3) Human resources were attached great importance to. The mobile environment of labor, pension and annuity system was reviewed to improve the welfare and pension of retired employees of the SMEs. The cost of the labor migration was reduced in the improvement of and the working conditions and improved. Companies could also flexibly hire those of other companies and personnel training became significant. (4) The functions of organizations were crucial and the management resources are to be shared. The central finance system of the SMEs group was evaluated with more emphasis on strategic alliance and the relationship between enterprises. Technological and institutional innovation was encouraged. (5) The fairness of trade was pursued. The cartel enterprises and those with direct administrative intervention were examined. (6) The tax system was

(continued)

Table 3.14 (continued)

Country	Measures
	reformed. Special measures of tax were taken to help SMEs to stabilize their business foundation and further develop in new areas
	2. A system to guide innovation and entrepreneurship for SMEs was set up. To make those enterprises independent and professional, the new policies no longer pursued the traditional goal of economic profits but projects such as business transformation, venture capital, innovation and technology development and strategic measures were taken to guide the entrepreneurs to discover and take opportunities of new business and transformation. The strategies of venture capital and innovation included policies of simple and open support to improve the investment environment of venture capital and regulations to improve the financing environment of risk investment and to promote over-the-counter markets and enterprises based on investment. The strategies of transformation included the expansion of the market with modern equipment, information technology investment, researches, and personnel training and so on. The strategies of technology development included the improvement of the infrastructure of technology development and the emphasis of the function of research institutions and the cooperation of the government, industries and universities with more budget, technology development achievements as career as well as flexible use of external resources
	An economic security system was built. With the globalization of economy, enterprises, especially small and medium-sized ones, were placed under greater pressure in the international competition. The establishment of the security system became one of the major goals of SME policies in the twenty-first century to soften the impact of global changes on those enterprises and to assist their transition and stable development. The mechanism was set up to respond to emergencies. There appeared credit guarantee and low-credit financing in financial businesses. The basis of operation is focused and the business activities are divided. The insurance system of risks was also developed. Private insurance institutions were often reluctant to accept insurance of SMEs because of their high risks and low income. Administrative support on insurance was thus provided. For example, a cooperation system was set up to prevent bankruptcy and regulate pensions. A bankruptcy mechanism was activated to evaluate and development relevant laws so that the procedures of reform and reestablishment could be simplified
Germany	1. The German government encouraged people to set up their own business. Colleges, universities and other institutions offered courses to impart relevant knowledge and skills and encourage the graduates to engage in economic activities independently. The spirit of independence was advocated through the country, which had also become the core of school education and vocational training. With the variety of specific funding provided by the government and banks and the professional information and consultation provided by federations and associations, 1.9 million people started their own business during the period between 1990 and 1995, 1.4 million from the west and 500,000 from the east. In the west part of the country, about 0.8% of the people who had the ability to work set up business by themselves every year, with 62% engaged in industry and commerce, 33% engaged in free occupation. 12–13% of these entrepreneurs were unemployed before the establishment of their own companies. In the east part of the country, about 1.2% of the people who had the ability to work set up business by themselves every year, with 71% engaged in industry and commerce, 26% engaged in free occupation.

(continued)

Table 3.14 (continued)

Country	Measures
	12–13% of these entrepreneurs were unemployed before the establishment of their own companies. The government not only encouraged those unemployed to set up independent business, but also encouraged those who were employed, being trained and idling to do so. Among the entrepreneurs in the west, 55% were employees while 31% were trainees and idle personnel's, and in the east, the corresponding figure was 74 and 13%
	2. In order to encourage entrepreneurship, a number of funding plans had been implemented by the government, such as the capital assistance plan, structural adjustment plans of federal and state government, loan plans of the KFW, new business plan for Ausgleichs bank and assistance plans under the labor assistance laws (e.g. the new enterprise provide new workers with subsidies). The federal government's capital assistance plan was carried out in 1979. According to the data from Munich Economic Research Institute, from 1987–1992, 46,164 people received the fund, and by the end of 1992, about 45,300 people "survived" and it was estimated that around 40,600 people would succeed in the end. For SMEs, funds were directly from the federal budget to supply the interest and compensate the loss. After the implementation of the new plan, the investment in the western region for those new companies was 1.5% of that from 1987 to 1992. There was an increase of about 4 billion Deutschmark in terms of the average annual output and there were 54,000–93,000 new jobs every year. 3 billion Deutschmark was saved for the national fiscal expenditure
	3. The government helped companies to raise capital. Financial institutions had always been important in Germany, which provide loans, interest subsidies and insurance for SMEs. Generally speaking, SMEs, especially small ones, rarely turn to large private commercial banks. Instead, they sought assistance from savings banks, cooperative banks and national banks, which were more likely to meet their needs. But those banks had to follow the principles of the market and profit management. Therefore, more direct loans were actually from the government. The funding was mainly provided by KFW, which is the Marshall Plan Assistance Fund. In addition, the government also provided interest subsidies for the bank loans in a range of 2–3% and guaranteed for the bank loans of up to 60% of the loss (in reality, the loss rate is only 1–2%). From 1950 to 1980, 75,000 government guaranteed were provided; the average loan of each was 145,000 Deutschmark. The German government had made great efforts to help raise capital in various aspects. For example, the German government was considering some suggestions from a panel of experts so that the new and existing SMEs could enter the capital market. Some new measures on the market were taken. Enterprises in need of valuable documents had an easier access to the securities market according to different levels of ownership capital, which would also activate the market. The listed investment companies were not required to repurchase a portion their issuing stocks so that they could invest more in SMEs. The equity market was activated so that companies would raise fund for new SMEs and those not listed. Measures of tax preference were taken to lessen the tax paid in exchanges and foreign funds and domestic funds were attached equal importance. Preferential measures were also taken in terms of property policies. The Federal Constitutional Court also allowed that SMEs could pay tax in lower rates on property inheritance. The laws of inheritance tax and gift tax would also take their needs into consideration. The government provided support for the replacement of managers as well

(continued)

Table 3.14 (continued)

Country	Measures
	4. Innovation was fostered. Germany's position in high technology competition was largely determined by the innovation of SMEs. Therefore, the German government implemented policies to support high-tech SMEs. In 1995, the federal government implemented a capital plan, in which 900 million Deutschmark was allocated before 2000 to address the risks. Funds from KFW were provided to promote the development of new products, craftsmanship and for services and marketing
	5. Training was strengthened. It was believed by the German government that training and retraining were particularly important. In order to enable professional personnel to promote so that they could independently engage in economic activities, the federal government put forward a drafted plan of funding the whole or part-time participation in training programs. If the trainees set up independent business later, they could be exempted from the returning the fund. Meanwhile, the traditional occupation training was also attached great importance to and is further improved in content and structure. The federal government, together with the trade unions, business organizations and other social partners aimed to create of new kinds of careers in order to help young people with poor abilities to master new skills needed by the enterprise. The vocational training was regulated. The general training should not exceed 2 years, while the special training should not exceed 1 year. The government, trade unions, employers and the actual executives (vocational schools and enterprises) should reach a consensus in terms of every aspect of the training

Source compiled

incentive mechanism is also established to cultivate and initiate employees' innovation. Through the encouragement and promotion of those concepts, the government manages to promote the capital-labor relationship and the development of enterprises.

Secondly, entrepreneurship is praised and encouraged, which is characterized by personal struggle, independency, aggression, hard work and perseverance. Those features are essential for enterprises and the lack of them will eventually impede the development of companies and the economy.

Finally, the concept of "customer first" is advocated, which requires each employee's awareness of customers. The enthusiasm for working is stimulated through the realization of the close relationship between the quality of products or services and the benefit for the enterprise and the individuals. Promoted by the government, the consciousness has been gradually raised. For example, in the first annual report of the British water company after its privatization in August, 1990, it reported that each employee had participated in a course specializing in the notion of "customer first". The British Gas Company has also published booklets entitled "to our customers", on the front page of which the president wrote: "to you, our customer, service is the most important task of our enterprise."

3.2 The Social Policies Conducted by Major Economies in the Supply Side Structural Reform

In the early stage of supply side structural reforms in major economies, influenced by the "New Right" ideology, the opportunities for individual development were reduced by government intervention. The welfare policies habituated those in need of help to turn to the government, rather than to their families, communities or even themselves. The policies also gave to vulnerable groups extra powers to challenge the traditional authority. Consequently, governments reestablished a role which is depicted as "a responsible father", reforming the social policies as well as the welfare system.

3.2.1 Policies Regarding the Reform of Trade Union

Trade union has become the target of the supply side structural reform. The government has taken a series of tough measures to limit, crack down and weaken the trade unions.

3.2.1.1 Restriction of the Power of Trade Unions Through Legislation and Administration

The major economies regulate and gradually control trade unions through a series of norms and bills. In 1980, 1982, 1988 and 1990, the British government promulgated a number of decrees regarding employment. In 1984, it also issued the trade union law, which compressed its power by legitimizing the scope, target, action and other aspects of strikes, political fund and the closed shop. A fundamental change had thus taken place in terms of the legal status and power of the trade unions and their members.

3.2.1.2 Tough on Strikes

In the initial stage of the supply side structural reform, the dissatisfaction of trade unions with the government gradually intensified with the latter's restriction on the former's power. Strikes were thus used as a means to force the government to yield, such as the Federal Aviation Administration strike in the US in 1981, the British coal miners' strike in 1984 and the pressmen's strike in 1986. The Reagan and the Thatcher Administration, however, did not compromise or concede. Fully prepared, they took a tough line on those strikes and finally managed to send the workers back to work.

3.2.1.3 Indirect Measures to Weaken the Power of Trade Unions

Inflation control, rather than full employment, was the top priority of the supply side structural reform in the early days. Consequently, the government no longer expanded the demand as in the past when unemployment rose. Instead, to curb inflation, the growth in demand was limited, causing a further increase of unemployment. The Thatcher administration made it clear that the economy should be reformed at the expense of high unemployment. Surely, this was a means to promote the economic growth, but an intention to weaken trade unions as well. The increase in unemployment could make the employees afraid to lose their jobs and thus not join the trade unions' strikes anymore. Meanwhile, the promotion of privatization has given birth to a large number of SMEs and the introduction of popular capitalism have turned traditional workers into self-employed ones who are basically not members of the union. The majority of workers own a certain number of stocks with the double identities of employee and shareholder. The trade unions thus become less influential since the personal interest and the fate of the enterprise are linked and employees will no longer care about themselves regardless of their companies.

3.2.2 Policies of Housing System Reform

Since the 1980s, political, economic and social changes have taken place in the major economies, changing the relationship between supply and demand of housing. Therefore, the housing policies and housing security system have become significantly important in the supply side structural reform.

3.2.2.1 The Government's Intervention in Housing Supply: From Direct to Indirect

Emphasizing on market and free competition, housing policies aim to reduce the central government's intervention in housing issues. Before the 1960s, the housing shortage was a major problem faced by the government, who directly established specialized agencies and provided operating funds to deal with the contradiction between housing supply and demand. From the 1970s and 1980s, the supply and demand had been balanced and the government's intervention had gradually turned from direct to indirect, providing preferential loans for ordinary housing developers and private residential construction investment (long-term low interest loans or soft loans) and relieving loans to support the nonprofit development of low cost, low rent housing. Through the function of the market, the indirect intervention helped to provide housing for low-income residents.

3.2.2.2 The Privatization of Property Rights

It is generally believed that those who own houses belong to the most stable class in the society. The privatization of public housing not only propels the social stability but also releases the government's pressure brought about by the direct intervention in the housing market. Therefore, from the early 1970s, there had appeared a trend of housing privatization among the major economies. The stock of public housing was reduced and public houses were sold. Public institutions took charge of the management of houses. As the representative of the housing reform, Britain had 1/2 total residential as public housing by the end of the 1970s. The rent then was very low, only 57% of the cost. Therefore, the government had to allocate large sums of money to rent subsidies, bringing great financial pressures. The Thatcher government reformed the housing security system, encouraging and supporting the residents to build or purchase houses. Houses were sold in large amounts and the housing market became free. In the process of reform, the idea of preemption was proposed, which gave the tenants priority to buy their rented houses at a better price. They would also get discounts according to their length of residence, the maximum of which was 60%. The worse the living condition and the longer the residence, the higher the discount.

3.2.2.3 Reform of Subsidies

The 1980s marks an important turning point for the U.S. housing subsidy policies, which were limited to low-income families, excluding those with low and middle income who previously received subsidies. Statistics show that from 1981 to 1987, the funding from the ministry of housing and urban development had fallen from $31.9 billion to $9.4 billion. The object of subsidies was no longer the suppliers but the demanders of houses. The tax was abandoned or reduced for purchasing houses among almost all of the residents, which encouraged personal housing, increased the rate of house ownership, and stimulated the demand for housing. Rent subsidies were given to the low-income group in order to help families with limited capacities to rent suitable houses. The major changes made by the Reagan administration were the cessation of basic housing subsidies. Apartments were again rented low, and low-income people were provided with the payment voucher (direct payments) by the government so that they had more choices in the market (Table 3.15).

3.2.3 Policies of Education Reform

In the 1980s, in order to cope with the fierce international competition, the major economies attached great importance to the reform of education as the main base for innovation, dissemination and application as well as the cradle for innovative spirits and elites.

Table 3.15 Rental allowance of major economies

	US	Japan	Germany	UK
Allowance	Construction + maintenance and repair	Construction + maintenance and repair	Interest	Interest + maintenance and repair
Rent/cost (%)	32% or lower	32% or lower	70%, but a decrease after 12 years	35–60%

Source Tian Donghai, Housing Policy: International Experience and China 's Practical Choice, Tsinghua University Press, 1998

3.2.3.1 More Emphasis on Education Reform

Since the 1980s, the major economies have issued a series of reports on education reform. In April, 1983, the high quality education committee in the US issued a special report describing the new crisis the country was in and the inevitability of education based on a large number of materials. On July 29, 1988, the education reform act was promulgated in Britain, which was the largest reform of primary and secondary education in the UK for half a century, completely changing the long-term laissez faire mode of management. In the 1990s, the former Japanese Prime Minister Nakasone proposed "the postwar politics always makes a final accounting" to make Japan's voice in the world louder and the education reform was also included in his proposal.

3.2.3.2 Reform of Educational Expenditure

The financial burden of the government is reduced in the first place. With the gradual introduction of the competition mechanism, resource collocation and the principle of "those benefit are to take the responsibility", the financial structure of universities have changed. The tuition and fees paid by the students are doubled and redoubled while fiscal burden of the government are reduced and reduced. In the 1990s, the proportion of fiscal appropriation of the Japanese government in the total revenue of higher education dropped to about 50%, while the part paid by the students increased from 20 to 50%. This has helped to popularize the higher education.

Secondly, the efficiency of educational appropriations is increased. In the field of basic education, the UK, based on its education reform act of 1988, set a policy of direct funding. Schools are directly funded by the education minister of science through central funding. The local education authorities, on the other hand, are responsible for the cost of infrastructure, traffic and welfare. In 1991, with the increase in the direct funding schools, the British government carried out a new reform of the primary and secondary education system and introduced a new law of education in 1993. The school fund is established to replace the direct funding from the Ministry of Education. It consists of 10–15 members, appointed by the Secretary of State, most of which come from the industrial and commercial sectors outside. As to higher education, the act also specified that the newly established university fund was to replace the university grants committee. And in 1992, the higher education foundation replaced the university fund committee with influential members from the industrial and commercial circles.

Thirdly, the private schools are encouraged to compete. Ever since 1970, the Japanese government has started assistance in private education through subsidies. An assistance act was also promulgated in 1975 to vitalize private education. With the rapid development of private education, the changes in national development strategy and the need of higher education reform, the proportion of financial subsidies from the government to private schools gradually decreased from 28.9% in

1981 to 12.2% in 2000. Private institutions are depending more on the market. Meanwhile, the government subsidies are no longer general but specific grants (special subsidies), following a mode of inclined allocation or balance allocation. After 1982, in order to improve the efficiency of the grant, the subsidy allocation has been further adjusted, putting more emphasis on special subsidies for private schools. Those with better education and research conditions are granted more, while those with worse operation and less efficiency receive a subsidy sanction of 5 years. Subsidies are used mainly to improve the quality of graduate education in private colleges, to promote academic research, to sponsor high-tech international activities, and to reform university education.

3.2.3.3 Reform of Curriculum

Curriculum is the key to the success in the education reform and therefore its reform is the core.

Firstly, the basic education curriculum pays more attention to students' basic skills. Importance has been attached to subjects such as science, mathematics and technology, which are compulsory for all children. Students use their imagination freely so that their personality, innovation and viability are gradually cultivated so that they can be competitive in the international society (Table 3.16).

Secondly, higher education courses should be connected with economic development. The major economies also readjust the setting of courses so that colleges can step out of their ivory towers and make positive contributions to the economy. In the 1980s, the Thatcher government issued a number of policies related to the reform of higher education, marking the beginning of governmental intervention in higher education. The reform in UK aimed to improve the quality and efficiency of education, to cultivate the students' capabilities and to strengthen the link between higher education and the industrial and commercial circles as well as between curriculum and career (Table 3.17).

3.2.4 Policies of Health Care Reform

3.2.4.1 Increasing the Efficiency of Medical Systems with Marketing Principles

The major economies have also reformed the medical systems which were initially free. Marketing principles have been introduced to improve the efficiency of the National Health Service. In the white paper on NHS reform in 1988, the Thatcher administration proposed to apply market operation in some non-private way with no increase in funding so that the financial crisis could be dealt with along with the

Table 3.16 Curriculum Reform for Basic Education in Major Economies

Country	Content
US	In 1985, together with 12 departments including the National Academy of Sciences and the Department of Education, the American Association for the Advancement of Science(AAAS), the prestigious civil scientific group, published a research report on science, mathematics and technology – "Project 2061: Science for all Americans". It showed in detail the plans, steps, goals and scientific theories for the comprehensive reform of elementary and secondary education, and later became a major project in the basic education reform in the US. The focus of Project 2061 was on the popularization of scientific knowledge in the 21st Century. The reform of primary and secondary school curriculum was representative of the reform of curriculum and basic education in the US. It was the year when Halley's comet approached the earth and the next time would be the year 2061. The project got its name from "2061", meaning that it would aim to adapt the current generation, the master of the 21st century, to the science and technology as well as the social life in the future. In the project, it was stated that the teenagers' knowledge for science and technology was still very poor and it was necessary for students throughout the country to acquire scientific literacy. For the education of science, mathematics and technology, basic standards should be set up. A new syllabus was made for the popularization of science and technology in school and kindergarten education so that the future generations would possess the basic knowledge. However, it was not encouraged to augment extra knowledge and information in teaching. Rather, the emphasis was on the basics and the effect of teaching. The core of the basic education should be the students' abilities and learning methods so that they can acquire knowledge with better comprehension abilities. The reform thus focused on a series of scientific skills; investigation; practice; the abilities to solve practical problems, to adapt to social changes and to study on one's own; as well as the ideology. To conclude, the major goal of education is to achieve self-realization and to cultivate scientific methods, attitudes and values, emphasizing the cultural and ethical functions of scientific knowledge.
UK	The main content of the Education Reform Act is the unification of the national curriculum in primary and secondary schools. For this reason, the government has formulated the National Curriculum as the basis for teaching in schools of different regions. It is pointed out in the act that the national curriculum should be balanced and comprehensive. The main goals include: (1) to promote the spiritual, moral, cultural, mental and physical development of the students; (2) to prepare for the opportunities, responsibilities and experiences in the future adult life. In terms of the subjects, 10 courses are required in addition to the traditional religious course in the compulsory education of the primary and secondary schools for students of 5 to 16 years of age. There are 3 core subjects (Mathematics, English, science) and 7 basic ones (history, geography, technology, music, art, sports, students at 12 are also required to learn a foreign language). The complete curriculum also involves other disciplines such as housekeeping, individual and social education, vocational education and instruction, classical language, economics and technology, etc. The act also reforms the examination system of the compulsory education. The additional national examinations for those at the age of 7, 11 and 14 are added, as well as the GCSE for the 16 year olds, which is the combination of the previous two. All those exams form the national examination system of the compulsory education. Only those who passed the GCSE are qualified to participate in the college entrance examination (A / LEVEL). English, mathematics and science are compulsory subjects in all the exams.

(continued)

Table 3.16 (continued)

Country	Content
Japan	In 1996, the Central Education Council of Japan announced a report of an outlook for the country's education in the 21st Century. The emphasis of education was put on students' basic qualities and abilities, in other words, the ability to LIVE. Major issues such as the curriculum reform policies, curriculum system and the content of education were discussed. A free style of education is encouraged. Through free imagination and the full display of personalities, the innovation, creativity and talents can be promoted to a large extent. And students can thus be more internationally competitive. In June, 1998, the Ministry of Education, according to the final report of the Council, revised the curriculum standards and issued the new guidance for primary and junior high school learning.

Resource compiled

Table 3.17 Curriculum Reform for Higher Education in UK

Country	Content
UK	(1) The Practice of the Enterprise in Higher Education. Motivated by the new public management, the former training office of the Department of Employment of UK started its practice of the Enterprise in Higher Education (EHE) in 1987. The objective was to cultivate entrepreneurship among those who seek higher education qualifications so that they could combine knowledge with business, recognize demands and gain some working experience. (2) Education for Capability Manifesto. In 1979, the Royal Society of Arts announced a manifesto named "Education for Capability", pointing out that "a well-balanced education … must also include the exercise of creative skills, the competence to undertake and complete tasks and the ability to cope with everyday life; and also doing all these things in co-operation with others". The main ideas of the education for capability include: a. to cultivate students' confidence in the following aspects: taking effective and appropriate action; explaining the action; living and working with others effectively; learning from others' experience; b. to make the students take effective and appropriate actions in an unfamiliar and changing environment, to make them confident in their judgment, assessment and risk response and let them learn from experience; c. to make the students take the responsibility for their continuous personal and professional development; d. to prepare the students for their role in life and working environment. (3) To strengthen the links among curriculum, working experience and employers. Many universities train students' skills by providing a direct working environment, including internship and "work-based learning".

Resource compiled

improvement of the quality and efficiency of NHS. Protect the interests of patients. In 1991, laws of the NHS and community nursing were issued, marking the formal operation of the new free medical care system with "internal market" and separated supply and demand. The NHS trust has been established and there have appeared competitions among suppliers.

3.2.4.2 Adjustment of the Management Mechanism

Health management departments play different roles in the reform, turning from the manager to the buyer. Medical service was purchased from public or private institutions through contracts. The original centralized management has been abandoned, and the power has been distributed among the 200 or so District Health Administrations (DHA), which are responsible for management, medical services, patient guidance and distribution of the government fund in order to enhance the local authorities' sense of responsibility and develop health care services within the little scope with unified plans, better projects and more efficiency. Meanwhile, the government also requires that the hospital should sign a contract with the local health authority's general practitioners and private medical institutions before gaining any profits. Only the hospitals with the status of "trustee" are qualified to manage their income and staff, and get 6% of the total profits.

3.2.4.3 Introduction of the Competition Mechanism

The market competition mechanism has been introduced. Medical institutions put forward their working and spending plans and compete with each other in accordance with the goals set by the government, who choose the preferred ones as the target of funding. A quasi market mechanism is formed in the welfare field, in which British citizens have the right to choose hospitals among those (including some private medical institutions) provided by local healthcare bureaus with medical expenses subsidized. This can solve the problem of overcrowding and long waiting hours in some hospitals. Patients can also choose those with more favorable conditions and better techniques. In the face of this kind of market competition, public hospitals have to work hard to improve their medical level as well as services in order to attract more patients.

3.2.5 Policies of the Reform of the Relief System

In terms of the social relief system, the major economies have taken various measures to reduce the government welfare spending, including the abolition of subsidies, spending cuts, delay of beneficiaries, limitation of the conditions and tax preference etc.

3.2.5.1 Subsidy Abolition

In 1982, the British government abolished all the income-related subsidies, such as additional subsidies for the patients, pregnant women, disabled and unemployed people, by freezing or postponing or partly pay the allowances. The allowances for children were frozen from 1981 to 1988. The growth rate of short-term subsidies from 1981 to 1983 was 5% lower than that of the price. The cut in subsidies would only return to normal level until the allowances were taxed, which would save 400 million pounds for the annual unemployment insurance expenses, accounting for 1/10 of the total unemployment subsidies. In 1986, death and maternity subsidies were also cancelled.

3.2.5.2 Cut in Spending

The supply side structural reform has adjusted the pension system, in which the pension is provided based on the highest rate of inflation and wage growth. In the British budget of 1980, the basic pension should not be linked to the wage but the price. The government thought that the wage growth rate was higher than inflation in the long run, the increase of social security spending could not exceed the growth rate of wage if the pension was provided according to the inflation. The real value of the allowance was thus reduced. From 1980 to 1992, the government saved 43 billion pound. During the Reagan administration, the social spending on day care, breeding, family planning and others was cut by about 22%. The community service was cancelled and social services for people with low income were mingled with other projects, cutting the fund by about 39%. The reform of the medical subsidy also reduced the federal subsidies to the states. In 1982, it was reduced by 3%; in 1983, 4%, and in 1984, 4.5%.

3.2.5.3 Payment Delay

For unemployed people in Britain, they could delay paying for 2 weeks in 1984, which saved around 8 million pounds. For those under age, the deadline of payment was extended to 4 weeks.

3.2.5.4 Minimization of the Benefit Group

According to the estimation of the US Congressional Budget Office, the Reagan government's adjustment of the welfare projects included the reform of the support of minor breeding. Parents with jobs were off the project. Among 450,000–500,000 families in the project, 50% families were cancelled and the other 40% got less allowance. As for food stamps, the increase due to inflation was cancelled in 1982. Those with income 130% higher than the poverty line could no longer get food stamps, except families with elderly or disabled members. And punishment was given if there were errors in the distribution.

3.2.5.5 Tax Preference

Before the reform, the German unemployment and disease benefits were tax-free. After the reform, the scope of tax preference was narrowed. Those for unemployment, sick leave etc. should pay 50% of the tax. The employer should pay 50% of the pension and the non-employer 30%. Subsidies and exemptions for the night holidays and full exemption due to war, military service or civilian retirement were cancelled.

3.3 Performance Measurement of the Structural Reform on the Supply Side in Major Economies

During the 1980s and the 1990s, the major economies carried out the supply side structural reform, which has reversed the Keynesian way of balanced development through and through. The slow economic growth had been stopped through structural adjustment. Depending on the structural advantages, the major economies maintained their dominant positions in the world. However, side-effects had also surfaced along with the reform, which emphasized the market and free competition.

3.3.1 Four Major Successes

The structural reform has overcome the drawbacks of the Keynesian demand management and has gradually balanced the aggregate demand and the aggregate supply.

3.3.1.1 Improvement of Macro Economy

Two to three years after the introduction of the structural reform, the aftermath of policies was coped with and the macro economy started revitalizing, growing stably in mid-long term. Meanwhile, inflation and unemployment were controlled.

(1) There appeared short-term downturn, mid-term increase and long-term differentiation in the economic growth. The economy grew slowly in the short term (2–3 years). Despite the relatively obvious effect of monetary policies brought by the reform, effects of other policies were not significant within a short period. The impact of the previous policies thus caused the continuous decline in economy. Generally, the supply side structural reform will take 2–3 years to fully come into effect policy and the economy would then gradually grow. Three years before the Thatcher Administration (1982–1979), the economy growth was still negative. The Reagan administration came up with a substantial tax cut plan and implemented a

tight monetary policy, focusing on short-term emergency measures. The growth rate of GDP fell from 2.6% in 1981 to 1.9% in 1982. 6–8 years after the initiation of the reform, its effects started to surface. There was a marked acceleration in the continuous economic growth during those years. The economy became dynamic and innovative again. Since 1982, the "miracle" of Thatcher had appeared and the economy had been steadily growing for 9 years. From 1982 to 1989, the GDP growth rate of UK surpassed 2%, and reached 5.55% in 1987 and 5.93% in 1988, which had been the highest since 1973 and was then distinct in the recession of Europe. In 1984, the U.S. GDP growth rate reached 7.3%, the highest since 1970. The economy remained stable during Reagan's second term of office (1985–1989) with the growth rate between 3.5 and 4.2%. Differentiation started in the long-term (10–20 years). Britain, the US, Germany and other countries still maintain sustainable economic growth, which is a good example of the endogenous driving force brought by the supply side structural reform. Take the US as a typical example. Its economy had kept growing since the 1990s for the longest period ever since the war. During the second half of the 1990s, especially, the economic growth accelerated with low unemployment and inflation, which was obviously the result of the supply side structural reform in the 1980s. Japan, however, did have a gradual recovery of the economy, with new competitive advantages for which the technological policies had laid foundation, but the growth rate decelerated in the 1990s. Japan might be over satisfied with its success achieved through the early supply side structural reform. Therefore, the subsequent alterations tended to be superficial with no substantial measures to deal with the deep contradictions in the economic and social development. The economic and social system thus gradually became rigid, making it harder to reform the system and leading Japan to the so-called "lost decade" (Figs. 3.2, 3.3 and 3.4).

Inflation had also been kept in check. The supply side structural reform emphasized the function of market and free competition rather than the Keynesian demand management. The policies taken aimed more at the reduction of inflation than full employment, with monetary control policies as the core, solving the inflation problem that had long troubled the major economies. British inflation rate

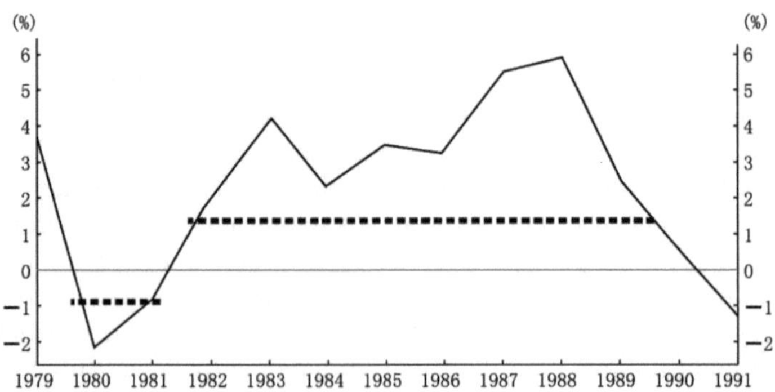

Fig. 3.2 GDP growth rate during the Thatcher's period from 1979 to 1990. *Source* Wind Info

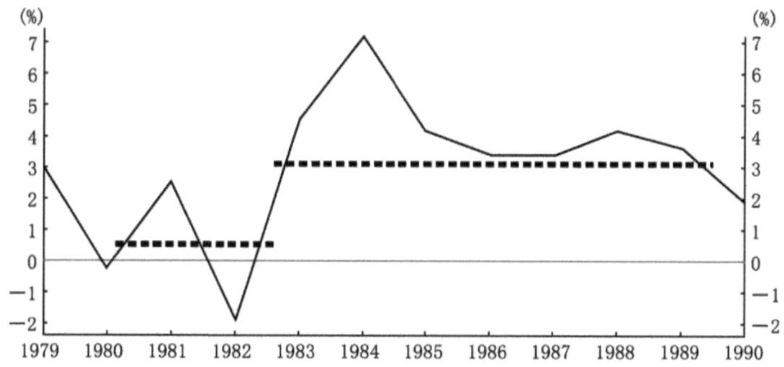

Fig. 3.3 GDP growth rate during the Reagan's period from 1981 to 1989. *Source* Wind Info

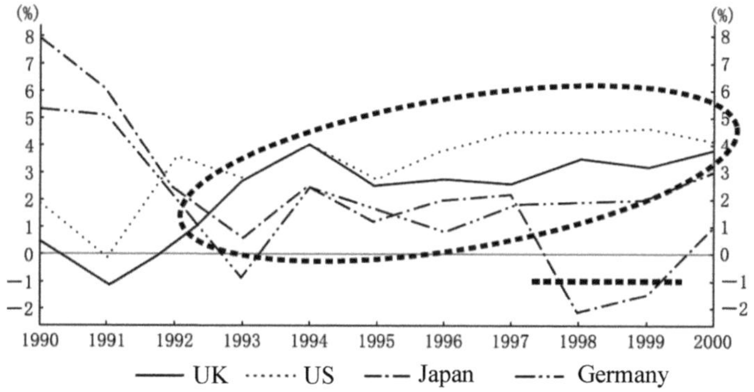

Fig. 3.4 Economic growth of the major economies after 10–20 years of the supply side structural reform. *Source* Wind Info

in 1980 was up to 19.7% but had remained through the 1980s at a low level since it was down to 7.7% in 1982. In 1981, when President Reagan entered the White House, the average inflation rate of America was 12% and the interest rate was up to 20%. But 8 years later, when Reagan retired, the inflation had slowed to 4.4%, and the interest rate fell below 10% (Fig. 3.5).

Unemployment rate declined after rising. In the initial stage of the supply side structural reform, inflation control prioritized full employment, which meant the government will no longer expand the demand as in the past when the unemployment rate rises, but would further limit the demand to curb inflation, thus causing the increase in unemployment. In terms of industries, those in recession such as iron and steel were amalgamated in the structure adjustment, resulting in the population growth of the unemployed. The emerging industries, however, were not able to employ enough people, which was also the cause of the further growth of the unemployment rate. With the gradual revelation of the middle and long term effect of the reform, more jobs appeared and the unemployment rate started to fall. For instance, the unemployment rate began to fall a year after the Reagan

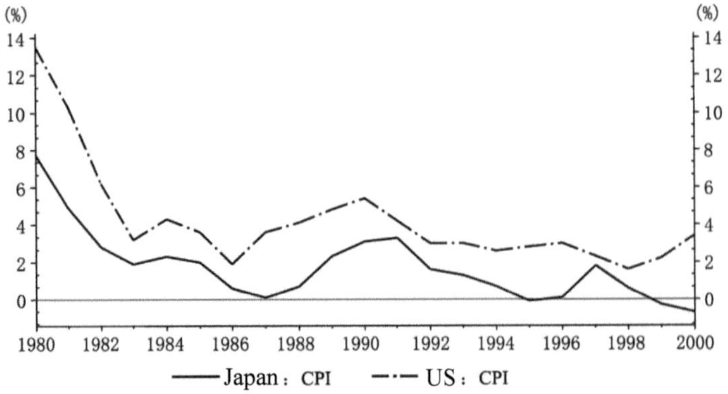

Fig. 3.5 Inflation of Japan and the US after the supply side structural reform. *Source* Wind Info

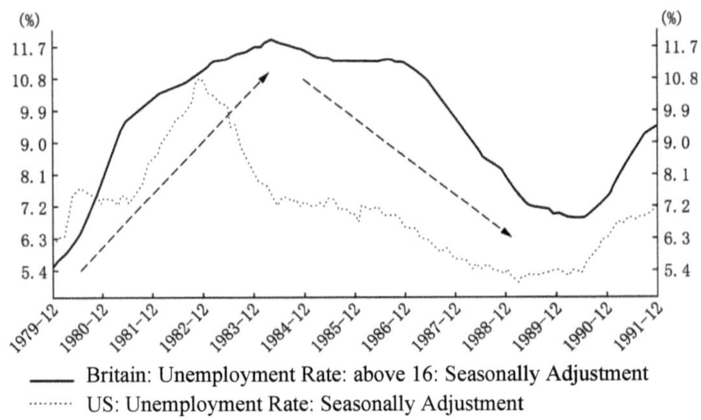

Fig. 3.6 Unemployment in Britain and the US after the supply side structural reform. *Source* Wind Info

administration. As for the Thatcher administration, though the unemployment rate maintained at a high level for some time, it was nevertheless stable. After 5 years, it also gradually reduced (Fig. 3.6).

3.3.1.2 Development of Industrial Structures

Besides the steady and sustainable economic growth, structures of industries were also developed in the supply side structural reform. International competitiveness was thus increased.

In the first place, the industry proportion was adjusted. For instance, in the US, the proportion of the primary industry declined more slowly in the 1980s, with that of output value and employment fell by 0.5 and 0.7 percentage points respectively. On the hand, the proportion of the secondary industry fell at a faster speed than that of the previous decades, with that of the industry and employment fell by 5.5 and 4.2 percentage points. The tertiary industry kept growing significantly. The proportion of the output value and employment increased by 6 and 4.9 percentage points respectively.

In the second place, dominant industries were gradually substituted by new ones. After the supply side structural reform, the high-tech industry with information technology as the core had rapid developed and gradually took the place of steel, shipbuilding, chemical and other traditional industries. Technologies of micro electronics, computer, software, information transmission (including the communication through microwave, optical fiber, satellite, Internet etc.), multimedia, database, digital compression emerged and integrated, coupled with the revolutionary progress of advanced technologies such as modern biology, nano manufacturing, artificial intelligence, new energy technology etc., increasing efficiency of the transmission, storage and processing of information. Leading the traditional manufacturing industries, those emerging industries had greatly stimulated the economic growth.

Finally, there appeared the integration of virtual sectors and the real sectors. The government' relaxation of regulations promoted the strategic complementary between industries and there emerged a variety of new industries. In the 1980s, the free pricing of financial products in the US generated innovation and internationalization as well as an assortment of deposit institutions. In Japan, the financial service industry and the information and communication industry mingled in a "strategic way". For example, supermarkets, through ATMs of their branches, started professional bank services of banking, life and property insurance, securities settlement etc. Manufacturing enterprises (such as SONY, TOYOTA, HITACHI, etc.) tried to develop a network of bank-based financial services and started business in the field of the automobiles, housing credit, credit card etc.

3.3.1.3 Revitalization of Enterprises

In the 1980s, enterprises of the major economies had far less output cost with more competitiveness owing to the reform of tax system and preferential policies in capital gains, inventory valuation and depreciation approaches.

There appeared an increasing amount of international mergers and acquisitions, especially in the late 1980s. By 1990, it had unprecedentedly reached $160 billion, almost 8.7 times that in 1980 ($18.3 billion, both domestic and cross-border). In 1991, it fell to $85.3 billion due to the global economic crisis and rose again after 1992, reaching $162.3 billion in 1993. Subsequently, the record of the number was refreshed repeatedly, exceeding $600 billion in 1998 and reaching $852.8 billion in 1999, which is roughly 5.3 times that in 1993.

Giant enterprises mushroomed. According to the UN statistics, there were 422 multinational companies in 1976, half of which belonged to the US, with sales of more than $1 billion. The number rose from 11 million in 1980 to nearly 4.5 million in 1997, which promoted the direct international investment and expanded the total investment stock with astonishing rapidity.

The number of high-tech enterprises increased enormously in the reform. Take the US as an example, Microsoft, IBM and other companies led the development of science, basic research facilities and large-scale researches. There were also other enterprises dominating fields of microelectronics, biotechnology, new materials, new energy, ocean development, laser, etc.

Additionally, there was a vast increase in the number of SMEs. All through the 1980s, there had been frequent registrations. In the UK, for example, the annual number of newly-registered small enterprises increased from 150,000 to 250,000. Between 1981 and 1989, the numbers of the Southeast, East Anglia and the Southwest were respectively 6.983 million, 759,000 and 1.535 million, the growth rates of which reached 96.1, 104.1 and 99.6%. In the North, Welsh, Scotland and Northern Ireland and other traditionally assisted regions, the numbers were 629,000, 759,000, 1.099 million and 319,000 respectively, with the growth rate of 56.1, 80.8, 54.9 and 63%.

3.3.1.4 The Steady Relationship Between Labor and Capital

As the core of the supply side structural reform, the employer–employee relationship has undergone radical changes.

First of all, the power of trade unions was limited. Major economies changed the legal status of trade unions and the members. Trade unions declined in importance, gradually losing their influence which had been extended after the World War II. Meanwhile, to increase efficiency, the reform also stopped the protection of the labor market and millions of low-income workers as well as non-union members so as to break trade union's monopoly of the labor market. In Britain, for example, there were significant changes in union members, the number of strikes and the working days lost by strikes in 1984. With the legal effect of relevant laws concerning labor-management relations, the abuse of trade union had been prevented and the leaders became more responsible for the members.

Secondly, the number of strikes fell. Several strikes took place in the major economies in the 1980s. Nevertheless, the total number of strikes, people and the lost working days kept dropping. According to the British employment bulletin, 2125 strikes took place in 1979, with 4.608 million workers involved and 29.477 million working days lost. In 1984, the number of strikes fell by nearly half to only 1221, involving 1.464 million workers and 27.135 million days (belonging mainly to the strikes of coal miners, while the number of lost working days in 1983 was only 3.754 million). In the year 1991, the number was reduced to 630, with 176,000 workers attending and 761,000 days lost. From 1987 to 1991, the number of strikes had fallen by 70% compared with that of the early period in the 1980s, which was also far below the average level of other countries in Western Europe.

Finally, there was an increase in the wages of workers. Take Britain as a typical representative. Although the unemployment rate during most of the time in the 1980s was relatively high, the workers' wages had been increased, and increase rate was higher than that of inflation growth. From 1979 to 1989, the net increase in wages had been 21%, with cash income growing faster, reaching 145% while the consumer price index of the same period had risen 103%.

3.3.2 *Six Major Problems*

The supply side structural reform carried out by the major economies put more emphasis on the market and free competition. With economic growth achieved by relevant measures, certain problems also cropped up. "Gaps" between various areas were widened.

3.3.2.1 International Adverse Balance of Payment

The ideal state of balance of payments is the equivalence of income and expenditure, which can be used to indicate a country's economic competitiveness. Take the US as a typical example. Before its supply side structural reform, the US was generally balanced with the adverse balance of payment in 1977 contributing only 0.7% of GDP. Since the administration of Reagan, the balance had been disturbed. In 1987, the adverse balance of payment accounted for 3.3% of GDP, with a current-account deficit of $160 billion. With the deterioration of international balance of payment and the widening trade deficit caused by the outflow of US dollars, the US could only depend on large-scale foreign bond to avoid the sharp decline in the dollar exchange rate (Fig. 3.7).

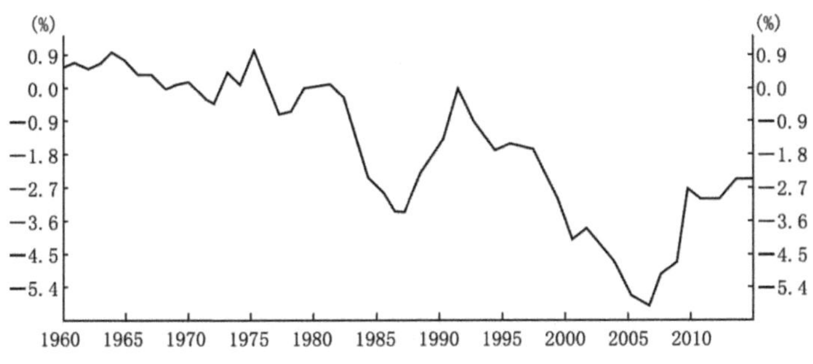

Fig. 3.7 The proportion of US current-account deficit in GDP. *Source* Wind Info

3.3.2.2 International Trade Friction

In the 1980s, the trade friction between Japan and the US became a major diplomatic problem. The US financial austerity policies taken in its supply side structural reform successfully curbed inflation but widened the fiscal deficit due to tax cuts and military expenditure. The high interest rates continued to attract overseas investment and increased the demand for dollar, which was appreciated higher and higher. The appreciation further increased the trade deficit, like a chain reaction, causing both fiscal and trade deficits. At that time, Japan's trade surplus was regarded by the US as the cause of its current-account deficit. The US thus asked Japan to reduce the current-balance surplus. Besides, Japan were demanded to take voluntary export restrictions and were criticized for all kinds of barriers to imports, which had made it difficult for American products to enter the Japanese market. Markets involved included those of beef, oranges and other agricultural and livestock products, auto parts, finance, telecommunications and so on.

3.3.2.3 The Wider Range of Public Debt

Before the supply side structural reform, the debt of domestic non-financial sectors of the major economies (including the central government, local government, enterprises and families) had a fairly stable relationship with GDP. For example, the debt of non-financial sectors in the US was generally 1.36–1.38 times the GDP. Ever since the 1980s, however, the debt had far exceeded GDP, the proportion of which in GDP rose from 138% in 1980 to 169% in 1985. The main factor was the rapid growth in the debt of the federal government. In the matter of Germany, the public debt rose year by year from 1991 to 2002, reaching 1.253195 trillion euros and increasing nearly 1.1 times. The proportion of debt in GDP was 60.8% in 2002, which was beyond the maximum of 60% set in the Growth Pact. In 2002, budget deficit of the German government accounted for 3.5% of its GDP, also surpassing 3%, the limitation imposed by the EU (Fig. 3.8).

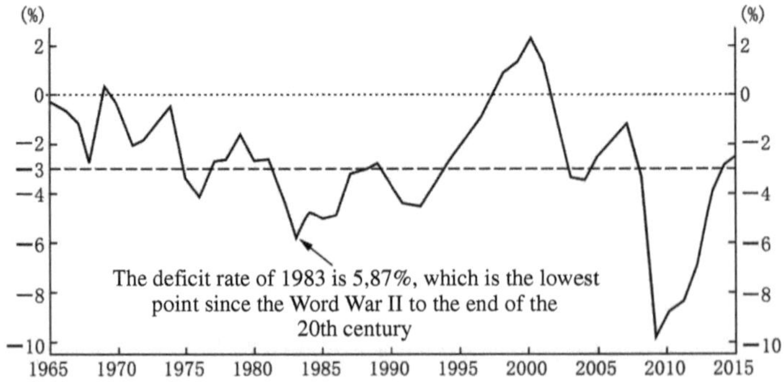

Fig. 3.8 The proportion of US Federal Financial Surplus in GDP from 1965 to 2015. *Source* Wind Info

3.3.2.4 Regional Development Gap

The reform challenged the traditional regional policy and depends on market forces rather than the government intervention to solve regional problems. The previous measures of intervention were replaced by those aiming at the exploration and maximization of regional potentials in order to realize the long-term sustainable development of recipient regions. There was no doubt that the gap between regions had been widened. For instance, in the mid-1980s, with the policy of industrialization implemented by the Thatcher administration, the southern England flourished. But, on the other hand, the limit of industrialization had triggered sharp recession of traditional industries such as mining, steel, shipping, manufacturing and so forth. Hence, the economy of the north part of the country suffered.

3.3.2.5 Financial Market Fluctuation

The relaxation of financial regulation, a major measure taken in the supply side reform, had promoted financial liberalization and innovation and expanded the scope and scale of the financially mixed operation as well. However, on the other hand, the financial supervision system was often rigid and out-of-date. The supervision system could hardly match the management system with rapid development and innovation, which was likely to lose control of financial innovation and thus increasing risks. As a result, the market fluctuates, eventually leading to financial crises. In the 1980s, the US gradually relaxed the regulation of financial markets and cut tax on the stock investment. This had brought huge capital into the stock market and the stock market crash in 1987, with further impact on the global financial market.

3.3.2.6 Gap Between Rich and Poor Widened

After the World War II, due to the income adjustment of the reformist policies, the gap between high and low income groups was narrowed, as the living conditions for workers and the poor were improved to some extent so that a social welfare safety system could be set up using the financial leverage. The income tax cut in the supply side structural reform, however, encouraged market economy and free competition, benefiting those with higher income more and widening the gap between rich and poor. Statistics show that in 1980, when Reagan took office, the rich accounted for 1% of the US population with the total wealth contributing 9% of GDP. In 2006, those 1% wealthy people possessed as many as 23% of the whole nation's wealth. From 1979 to 1987, the tax rate of those with half of the national average income in Britain rose from 13.9 to 16.1%, while that of people earning 5 times the average level declined from 51.5 to 43.1%, and to only 35% in 1992.

3.4 Lessons and Inspirations of the Structural Reform for Supply Side in Major Economies

The supply side structural reforms taken by the major economies were positive responses to external shocks and internal pressures, shifting from the traditional Keynes's demand management to the market and free competition. Although the current situation faced by China is not exactly the same with that of the major economies, the economic and social structural problems are similar to those in the 1970s and the 1980s. Therefore, as for the supply side structural reform carried out in China, experience should be gained from previous success and lessons learned from problems.

3.4.1 Three Insights in Terms of Ideas

The supply side structural reform follows the "New Right" trend, which is oriented toward market and free competition and is a breakthrough of Keynesian demand management.

3.4.1.1 The Historical Inevitability of the Reform

In the 1970s, economic globalization and technological innovation had a huge impact on the economic and social structure of major economies, which became the external driving force to promote the supply side structural reform. It was hard for mass production to maintain profitability in the increasingly saturated market. Specialized production, being flexible, decentralized, technological intensive, has substituted mass production to meet the increasingly personalized demands, leading to the transformation of industrial structure and the adjustment of hierarchical structure. Along with the change of social structure, social values also demonstrated unprecedented diversity. Neo-liberalism and neo-conservatism gradually intertwined, challenging reliance on the traditional Keynesian doctrines of demand management. In this context, the supply side structural reform, as a positive response to structural changes and adjustment in the society, is inevitable.

3.4.1.2 Demand Management Still Valid

In *The General Theory of Employment, Interest and Money*, Keynes repeatedly emphasizes the range of application of his economic theory, which is effective for the solution of short-term demand insufficiency. Subsequently, his framework had been extended to the analysis of long-term economic growth in works of Harold, Thomas etc. The supply side structural reform of the "New Right", with its focus on long-term growth, tries to adjust the structural adjustment of the economy and to reshape endogenous power so that the overall living standard of a country and its social welfare can be improved. Hence, there exists no either-or contradiction between the Keynesian demand management and the "New Right". The short-term macroeconomic management is equally important and the Keynesian framework is still valid in dealing with short-term economic fluctuations. But the theories and frameworks should not prevail the reform lest the government intervene economic fluctuations forever and the emphasis is put on public spending and investment rather the structural and systematic problems.

3.4.1.3 Supply Economics as Part of the Theoretical Basis

The economic problems in China involve temporary difficulties caused by internal or external imbalances, long-term problems in the implementation of the Keynesian policies, which is why one single theory cannot be the panacea. With the "New Right" ideology as its foundation, the supply side structural reform focuses on market and free competition, and is combined with the Keynesian demand management as well. The supply side structural reform in China will apply the theories from the supply economics, e.g. tax reduction in the field with heavy taxes, promotion of overcapacity clearing etc. Meanwhile, the reform will also critically judge some the supply economic theories such as comprehensive tax cuts and the reduction of the government intervention. The formulation of industrial policies should also accord with the situation and characteristics of the current China.

3.4.2 Six Insights in Terms of Measures

The specific measures taken in the supply side structural reform also focus on market economy and free competition so that the market can effectively play its role, its allocation efficiency can be increased, and various types of market competition can become fiercer. Along with the efficiency priority, fairness is also taken into account to prevent the differentiation.

3.4.2.1 Fiscal and Taxation Policies Stimulating the Market

With unique advantages in structural adjustment, fiscal and taxation policies play important roles in the supply side structural reform, especially in the short-term stimulation of enterprise and individual production as well as the market. In terms of the current situation of China, however, focus should be put more on the reform of the system. On one hand, a public revenue system with the tax system as its core is to be established to reduce the overall burden on individuals and enterprises. On the other hand, the reform of public expenditure system is to be carried out aiming at the total expenditure and the efficiency of expenditure. The public expenditure is to be strictly controlled so that there exist stable fiscal relationships between the government and the enterprises, the government and the individual, the central and local.

3.4.2.2 Suitable Monetary Policies

Firstly, monetary policies should not pursue short-term prosperity but fit the current situation. Those policies should not only focus on short-term economic growth but the long-term development as well. The implementation of loose policies in a blind pursuit of short-term prosperity can cause asset bubbles. Secondly, the reform of financial administration should be carried out with the coordination of financial liberalization and globalization. Under the protection of the government, institutions slow at management tend to expanding financing in the process of financial liberalization, resulting in the bubble economy and a large number of non-performing assets. Finally, the supervision of financial sectors should be adaptive and effective in the economic environment. Appropriate competitions can improve the efficiency of the allocation of funds. However, finance is a special area, with greater probability of the market failure. Therefore, it is of paramount importance to optimize the supervision and improve its adaptability and effectiveness in the reform.

3.4.2.3 Industrial Level Upgrades

Industrial stagnation is inevitable in economic development. The stagnation of specific industries is beneficial, since the influx of resources released will help those expanding and developing. But in resolving the production decline of stagnating industries, issues should be analyzed according to specific situations with the guide of the market. Government can deal with excess capacity by stimulating domestic demand, upgrading, transferring and adjusting industries. Technological innovation is the core for traditional industries to get out of the dilemma. The revival of the American semiconductor industry is in sharp contrast to that of the steel and automobile industries. In the supply side structural reform carried out in China, advanced, intelligent, green and service-oriented manufacturing industries are thus promoted. It also strives to foster the development of new industries, accelerate the development of quality and efficiency of the service industry.

3.4.2.4 Proper Measures for the Reform of State Enterprises

The measures taken to improve the efficiency can be used for reference. The operating efficiency of state enterprises can be boosted through breaking the original shackles and giving enough mandates. The wage should not be fixed so that employees can work more enthusiastically and fully demonstrate their abilities with the expectation of larger income and better welfare. The order of the reform, with perfect legal protection, should be settled as soon as possible, including decision-making, legislation, implementation, audit and other stages. Approaches are to be diversified to make the reform flexible in different situations, such as the sale of assets of public sectors, free competition for enterprises with a loss yet not ripe for privatization, franchise tender or assistance of public sectors by private ones to provide supplementary services etc.

3.4.2.5 Moderate Welfare

Through the observation of the supply side structural reform, it is obvious that the social security can be neither absent nor excessive. The relationship between income distribution and economic development should be handled well and the reform of the distribution system can promote economic development. Firstly, the reform of the housing system is supported. Currently, measures such as tax relief and subsidy offering are taken to benefit those in need of houses. Secondly, the education system is encouraged to reform through optimizing the investment and fiscal input as well as promoting market competition in order to increase the efficiency of educational funds. Thirdly, the medical system is also reformed. The efficiency of the existing medical system is enhanced by using the principle of marketing, exploring the revolution of medical management mechanism and introducing competition mechanism. Finally, assistance is reduced accordingly. Various ways to cut the welfare spending of the government are explored, including how to phase out subsidies, delay payments, limit the beneficiary population, reduce the tax benefits, etc.

3.4.2.6 The Prevention of the Intensification of Certain Problems

The supply side structural reform, on the other hand, aims to achieve the overall economic growth with inevitable “sacrifices”. Gradually exposed are the problems of the international balance of payments, international trade, public debt, regional development, financial markets, and disparity and so on. China, in its supply side structural reform, should develop emergency disposal scheme for potential emergencies to prevent the intensification of those problems and their adverse impact on the reform.

Chapter 4
Status Quo and Risks of Structural Reforms Under the New Normal

After more than 30 years' rapid economic growth, China's domestic and external conditions have both changed dramatically. Its economic growth is entering the New Normal with the growth rate shifting away from high to middle and high, growth model from inefficient one to the efficient one, and the structure reform from enhancing the industrial capacity to both optimizing and enhancing the existing industrial capacity, and the growth driving force from traditional growth points to the new ones. On the whole, China's economy remains sound in its fundamentals, but it still faces a lot of risks and difficulties. To be specific, it has serious problems in economic structure and in its supply and demand as well, and it has yet to step up structural reforms, rectify misallocation of resources, expand effective supply, improve the flexibility of supply, and boost comprehensive productivity to ensure the sustainable growth of economy.

4.1 Analysis on the Characteristics and Risks of China's Economy Under the New Normal

4.1.1 Characteristics of China's Economy Under the New Normal

4.1.1.1 Characteristics of World Economy Entering the New Normal

Firstly, the global governance is experiencing profound changes. Strength across countries becomes more balanced now with that of developing countries increasing over time and the core of global governance focusing more on formulating rules. To reform the global economic governance system and enhance international economic coordination are set as the common goal. As the key promoters of globalization, emerging economies are assuming more and more responsibilities.

L. Xiao, *New Supply Side Economics*, DOI 10.1007/978-981-10-4639-1_4

At the same time, the formulation of new rules for global trade and investment is stepping up. A total of 12 countries including the US and Japan have officially signed TPP (Trans-Pacific Partnership Agreement), while TTIP (Transatlantic Trade and Investment Partnership) has concluded its 11th round of negotiation and the negotiation of RCEP (Regional Comprehensive Economic Partnership) is accelerating. The target of this new round of global competition is shifting away from markets to a greater voice in the setting out global trade rules. New standards are being defined in areas like competition policies, state enterprises, environmental protection, intellectual property, labor treatment, competitiveness, business enhancement, transparency and anti-corruption so as to make global trade in goods easier and more convenient, leading to a new round of adjustments in both world trade landscape and the economic governance framework.

The global financial regulation is also improving. Since the financial crisis in 2008, the financial regulation reforms have been unfolding promptly. But, actually, many major reforms and regulations are yet to be put in place. Amid this new global financial turbulence, the international financial and monetary system needs a more rapid reform. In fields like short-term capital flow supervision, global financial market stability mechanism, and major multi-national financial institution supervision, the resource allocation should be more reasonable in order to lower the systemic risks.

Secondly, the world economic growth slows down, which can be evidenced in three aspects. Firstly, what with the ongoing restructuring of the post-crisis economy the world economy is expected to grow at a medium-low speed for a long time to come and the high growth rate will be something of the past. The adjustments will be with us for a long time with new growth points yet to emerge and the economy is yet to pick up with the faltering recovery. Secondly, developed countries and the developing ones face markedly different situations in economic growth with the former outperforming the latter. But the US, EU and Japan find their economic growth lower than expected. Emerging and developing economies suffer a bigger drop in growth rate and the economic performances are uneven among them. All emerging economies except India are in recession. Countries that rely on exporting energy and big commodities fell into crisis successively.

Thirdly, the global trade growth rate will remain low for a long time to come with weak external demand being normal. According to statistics from the WTO, the growth rate of global trade has been lower than 3% for 4 consecutive years. In the first half of 2015, the global trade in goods saw a 0.7% year-on-year decline, among which developed economies decreased by 0.2% and developing ones 1.9%. As economic growth slows and economic transformation unfolds, the global trade still has a long way to go before its recovery could pick up.

Thirdly, there are new trends in the reform of major economies. On the one hand, both developed and developing economies will deepen economic restructuring. Since the financial crisis, the advanced economies have been the first movers in starting comprehensive economic reforms and adjustments. They will be more cautious on easy monetary policies. Table 4.1 shows the global trade growth rate (%) from 2013 to 2016.

Table 4.1 The global trade growth rate (2013–2016) (%)

	2013	2014	2015	2016
The volume of global trade in goods	2.5	2.5	2.8	3.9
Export				
Developed countries	2.2	2.0	3.0	3.9
Developing countries	3.8	3.1	2.4	3.8
Import				
Developed countries	−0.1	2.9	3.1	3.2
Developing countries	5.2	1.8	2.5	5.2

Note The figures for 2015 and 2016 are predicted rates
Source WTO, *Trade Express*

Prudential policies to control the financial crisis are more likely to be put in place. Since the major economies are slow in their restructuring, structural reform will speed up to boost productivity and eradicate production bottleneck. On the other hand, the global technological revolution and industrial reform achieve new breakthroughs. The major economies are unveiling strategies to promote technological innovation and the development of emerging industries and to further digitize the manufacturing industry. More innovation will be engendered in areas like green and low carbon, artificial intelligence, life science, so the emerging industries will play an increasingly important role in the global industrial landscape. At the same time, technological revolution brings new technologies, techniques and philosophy, exerting huge pressure as well as giving an impetus to the upgrading of manufacturing industry. This fastens the transformation of industrial development mode and further integrates industrialization with informatization.

4.1.1.2 Characteristics of China's Economy Under the New Normal

Firstly, the growth has changed to low gear. As revealed by the data of National Bureau of Statistics, China's GDP for 2015 registered a total of 67,670.8 billion RMB Yuan, a year-on-year increase of 6.9%. It was the first time China's GDP growth had exceeded 7% for the past 16 years. As China's economy keeps going up, it's natural and reasonable for its economic growth rate to slow down. In the future, China's economy will be growing within the reasonable range for a long time. In the ensuing 5 years, the average minimum growth rate for the next 5 years will reach 6.5% if it is to achieve the goal of doubling the GDP and per capita income from the level of 2010, as was noted in the 13th Five-Year Plan. The quality of growth will be more emphasized. In the short term, the economic downward pressure will continue to weigh as China is now seeing a noticeable decrease in economic growth, the price of industrial goods, revenues of enterprises, fiscal revenue growth and dented market confidence. To worsen it, China's economy has yet to undergo market clearance and deleveraging. As a result, it's highly possible that the economy will operate under increasing downward pressure (Fig. 4.1).

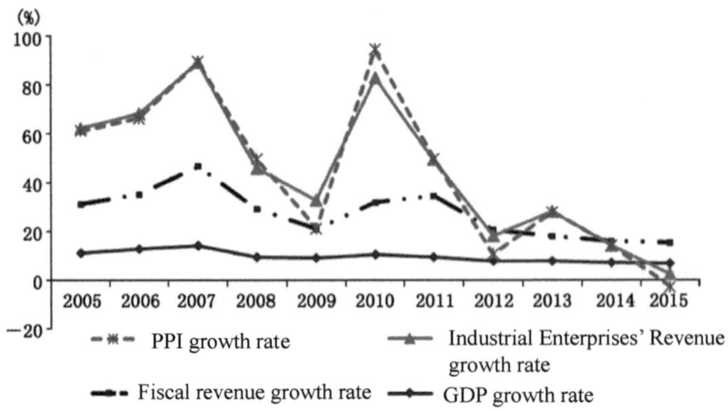

Fig. 4.1 China's GDP, fiscal revenue, enterprise profit and PPI growth in the recent decade. *Source* Wind Info

Secondly, the driving force for the economy has changed. In the aspect of demand, the economic transformation is shifting from the previous mode based on investment and export to a new one featuring the combination of consumption, investment and export. In 2015, consumption alone contributed 66.4% to the economic growth. Domestic demand is playing a bigger role in boosting the economy. In the aspect of driving force, the economy is transforming from a low resource and labor-cost-based model to an innovation-based one. So new technologies, new industries are contributing more to the economy. In the same year, the value-added of new and high-tech industries rose by 10.2% over the previous year and was 4.1% points higher than that of industrial enterprises. The tertiary industry featuring finance, IT services, tech-services, leasing, and commercial services have mushroomed, constituting the driving force for China's economic growth and structural upgrading, while capital, labor force and technology are

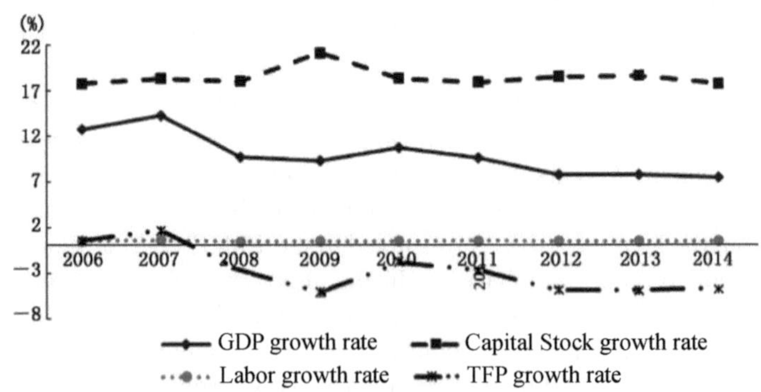

Fig. 4.2 Growth of capital, labor force and technology in China from 2006 to 2014. *Source* Wind Info

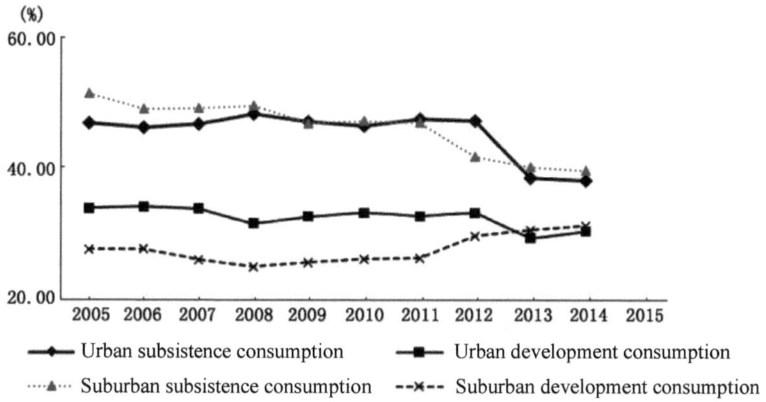

Fig. 4.3 The upgraded pattern of consumption of China's residents from 2005 to 2014. *Source* Wind Info

growing at a lower rate over the recent decade. This indicates that new growth drivers need to be fostered (Fig. 4.2).

Thirdly, the structural problems are pronounced. On the one hand, the traditional supply can hardly meet the new demand. In 1980s and 1990s, China's structural problems were represented by unreasonable industrial structure or the unbalance between input and output. At that time, the severe shortage of resources and basic industries restrains the flowing of its whole industrial chain and the even impedes the operation of the whole economy. Today, the structural problem today lies in the overcapacity in traditional industries coupled with the structural shortage, resulting in the lack of effective supply, especially in safe and quality products and medium-and high-end services, failing to meet the growing developmental consumption demand. On the other hand, new and old structural problems coexist. While dealing with the old structural problems including the high proportion of national income for the government and low one for the household are still with us, we are now facing some new problems, which encompass the huge influx of capital into the virtual economy and an underfunded real economy (Fig. 4.3).

Fourthly, risks are accumulating. On the one hand, with the global situation on constant changes, the world economy is still recovering from the financial crisis. This process is incubating new financial risks as external impacts may pose multiple risks to China's economy. On the other hand, China's economy is slowing down. Issues like high National Balance Sheet leveraging, accumulated inefficient industries and growing assets price bubble are looming large. In the next several years, risks in all aspects of China's economy may escalate and even show up together.

4.1.2 Risk Analysis of China's Economy Under the New Normal

4.1.2.1 The Analysis of External Risks

The risk analysis of geopolitical conflicts. Recently, there are increasing instability and uncertainties hovering around China's surroundings and the whole international community. Structural problems in international relations become more severe. Traditional and non-traditional security threats are interwoven. Geopolitical risks especially the disputes concerning China's territorial sovereignty occur more frequently, and the Sino-US relation face new challenges. With all these factors, China is under more pressure to maintain its economic growth.

The risk of global financial instability. The debt risks in Japan and Europe stay high. The euro-zone just bailed out of the recession is now still suffering the aftermath of its sovereign debt crisis. Peripheral countries in the region are under huge debt burden, and the medium and long term risk of this region's disintegration will persist. In Japan, the government debt is 243.2% of its GDP, the highest proportion in the world. With its unstable economic growth, Japan is quite likely to slip into another deflation. The chance of a sovereign debt default is good.

The financial risks of emerging markets. Just before and after the Federal Reserve raised the interest rate, these markets faced the threat of a massive outflow of cross-border capital and the currencies of each country suffered depreciations to different degrees. According to the statistics, from the rise of interest rate at the end of 2015 through the second half of January in 2016, exchange rates of Russian ruble, Mexican peso, South African rand, Brazilian real and Argentine peso to the US dollar depreciated respectively by 9.13, 7.66, 7.07, 4.29 and 3.69%. At the same time, South Korean won, Indian rupee and Philippine peso depreciated each by 2.09, 2.01 and 1.25%. Failure to proper handle this issue may lead to financial risks in the emerging markets and even the breaking-out of certain monetary crisis. Besides, the global deflation is on the rise. With less overall demand and declining inflation in the major economies, the euro-zone is on the brink of deflation. With both stalled economic recovery and deflation, the world economy may get stuck in a long-term deflation.

The security risks for world economy. Firstly, the Chinese companies are facing risks in its attempt of "going global". For instance, special economic policies in some countries will impact China's oversea investment and projects of China's business. The strengthened environmental protection and raised labor standards pose more risks and threats for Chinese companies to "go global". Secondly, the exchange rate fluctuation brings risks. Amid deepening financial fluctuation, the domestic currency of some countries may plummet in the short term, which hurts the oversea investment of these Chinese companies. Thirdly, China faces the new debt risks. The implementation of major projects like "the Belt and Road" and Asia Infrastructure and Investment Bank also involve risks especially those of the failure to reclaim the money invested. So efforts to enhance risk management should be intensified.

4.1.2.2 Analysis of Internal Risks

First, debt risks. The government debt ramps up with prominent structural risks. Since 2008, the ratio of central government's debt to its GDP in China has been rising rapidly, reaching 57.8% of its GDP by 2014, close to 60% commonly viewed as the alarming level by the international community. To worsen it, the risk of local government debt is also high. On the one hand, the ratio of local government debt to GDP is high. Towards the end of 2015, the local government debt registered 1.6 trillion RMB Yuan, and the ratio of this debt to its GDP was 23.6%, much higher than the highest local government debt-to-GDP ratio of 13–16% of the US. In Guizhou, Liaoning, Yunnan and Inner Mongolia, this ratio exceeds the alarming level. By January 22th, 2016, this ratio reached 120.2 and 197.47% respectively in Guizhou and Liaoning provinces, higher than the debt ratio upper limit of 100% set by the NPC Standing Committee. And the figures for Yunnan and Inner Mongolia were 111.23 and 104.7%, a little bit higher than the alarming level. On the other hand, the debt risk at the municipal level is also high. By the end of 2015, more than 100 cities and 400 counties saw their debt-to-GDP ratio higher than 100%. This issue needs more attention. Meanwhile, the leveraging of non-financial companies is also high. By the end of 2014, the debt for these non-financial companies had reached 94.94 trillion RMB Yuan, accounting for 149.1% of GDP. If the debt for the local government financing platform was deducted, the overall debt for these companies would be 78.33 trillion RMB Yuan, accounting for 123.1% of GDP, shedding light upon the high burden and risks now in the real economy. Table 4.2 shows the debt for China's real economy as of 2014 (Amounts in trillion RMB Yuan).

Secondly, financial risks. The credit risk in China is high. The non-performing loan (NPL) rate of commercial banks has been increasing for 16 quarters in a row. By the end of September in 2015, the NPL rate for these banks has stood at 1.59%. Now NPL is incurred by not only by small companies but also medium-and large-sized ones. The liquidity risk is also high. With easy monetary policies, the shadowing banks are expanding quickly, leading to problems like maturity mismatch and high leveraging, and risks in liquidity transfer, credit transfer. Meanwhile, the risk of ill-regulation is also high as the Internet finance and private lending lacks systemic supervision, with risks mounting considerably. As of November 2015, the unregulated peer-to-peer on-line lending platforms has increased to 82, an increase of 60.8% over the previous quarter, and 64 of these platforms witnessed their boss abandoning the platform and running away after collecting the money of the investors, an increase of 433% over the previous

Table 4.2 The debt for China's real economy as of 2014 (amounts in trillion RMB Yuan)

	Total debt	Debt to GDP ratio (%)	Growth rate (2008–2014) (%)
Government	36.8	57.8	17.8
Residents	23.2	36.4	18
Non-financial enterprises	94.93	149.1	51

Source Wind Info

Table 4.3 Some of the default cases in 2015

Name	Type	Main business	Bond name	Default time
Cloud Live Technology Group Co., Ltd	Private company	Cloud service platform	11 Print-Rite MTN2	April, 2015
Print-Rite group	Central enterprise	Energy	12 Xiangyue debt	April, 2015
Zhuhai zhongfu	Private company	Plastic products	12 Zhongfu 02	May, 2015
China National Erzhong Co.	Central enterprise	Equipment manufacturing	12 Erzhong group MTN1	September, 2015
Sino Steel	Central enterprise	Steel	10 Sino steel debt	October, 2015
Tian Wei Group	Affiliated to a central enterprise	Energy	10 Yingli MTN1	October, 2015
Shan Shui Group	Private enterprise	Cement	15 Shanshui SCP001	November, 2015
Nanjing Yu Run	Private company	Food	12 MTN	November, 2015
Si Chuan Sheng Da	Public company	Energy	12 Sheng da debt	December, 2015

Source Open data

quarter. There are altogether 1248 platforms reported to be unregulated nationwide, more than a third of the total. The Table 4.3 shows some of the default cases in 2015 alone.

Thirdly, the risk of real estate bubble. By October, 2015, the area of real estate in stock in China was 690 million m^2, 70.8 billion m^2 under construction. If the area of land converted for the property construction is added in, the whole area of property under construction is around 10 billion m^2. There is evidently too much property to sell. At the same time, the gap of housing prices among different cities continue to widen. The price in the first-tier cities remain stubbornly high, but these cities also face problems including surplus commercial housing and overheated real estate industry. The mid-western and third- and fourth-tier cities have also stored a huge quantity of unsold houses—an endemic plague. Even those houses are to be sold unstoppably at the current rate, but it will still take more than 20 months to clear up the inventory (as shown in Fig. 4.4). Heavy investment in real estate in regions with weak real economy and little flow of people and goods have erected many “death cities” and “ghost cities”. Such a bubble is much likely to bust.

Fourthly, the risk of overcapacity. On the one hand, overcapacity is seen in both the traditional industries including steel and building material and new industries like wind power equipment and photovoltaic. At present, now many local governments encompass new industries in their development plans, nearly 20 provinces announcing to establish themselves as a new energy foundation, leading to the overcapacity in this sector. On the other hand, heavy investment in some industries

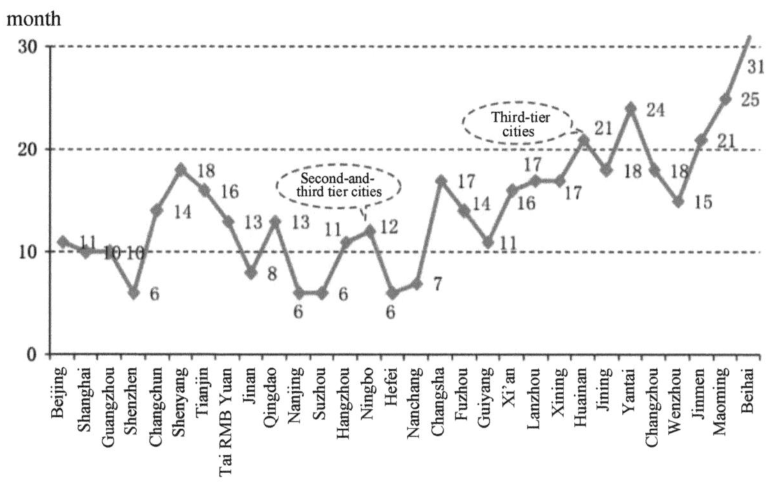

Fig. 4.4 The stock-to-sales ratio of 30 Chinese cities (as of Nov. 2015). *Source* Drawn from the Statistics by Yiju Real Estate Research Institute

incurred a serious overcapacity which is much higher than the peak consumption, giving rise to absolute and long-term surplus. This can profoundly affect the economy. Figure 4.4 shows the ratio between the newly built houses and sold ones in 30 cities.

Fifthly, the risk of deflation. Since 2015, the GDP deflator in China has been a negative number. The overall economy remains feeble with overall price level likely to fall into deflation. To be more specific, both the Producer Price Index and Purchasing Price Index were negative numbers for 45 months in a row. PMI had been below entrepreneurs' confidence threshold for 6 consecutive months. In January, 2016, PMI was 49.4, the lowest level since August 2012. The deflation in the industrial sectors is likely to escalate to the overall deflation. Although CPI has recovered a bit, the overall trend of decline may still occur. The impacts of weak demand can be more pronounced. The Import Price Index remains negative and the Export Price Index keeps hovering around 0 level, and the risk of deflation imported from other countries is still very high (Fig. 4.5).

4.1.2.3 Overall Assessment of Risks

Based on the analysis of risk transmission mechanism and eruption trend, China faces multiple risks under the New Normal. The real estate bubble risks, as well as the local government debt and overcapacity has created many risks which are transmitted and diffused through shadow banking and local financing platform, leading further to a series of risks that drive up company financing cost, cut their profits, increase debt burden, undermine the investment in the real economy and drag on the demand growth. Attention should be paid to the fact that as economic

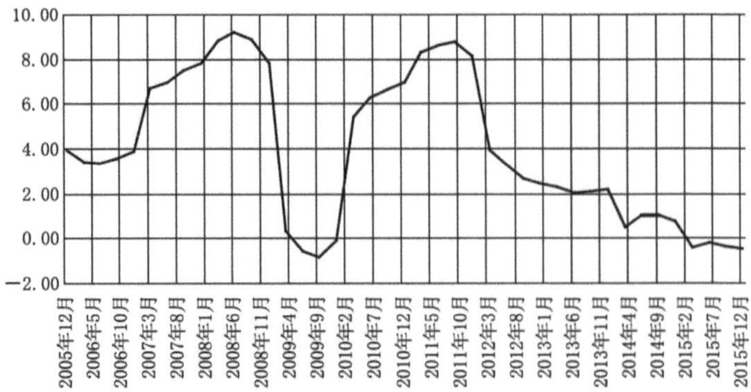

Fig. 4.5 The CPI deflator in China from December 2005 to December 2015. *Source* Data from *China Statistics Year Book*

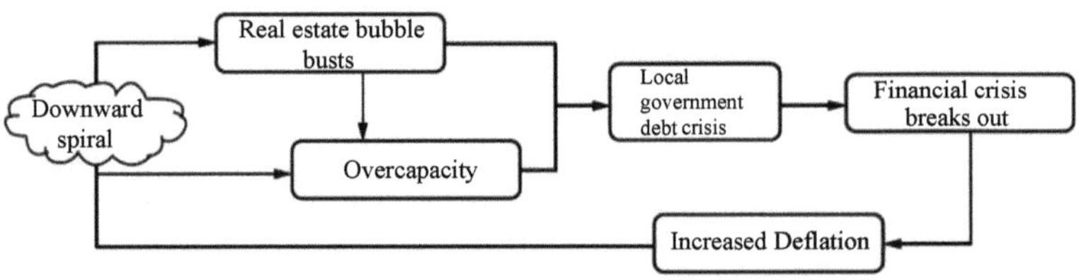

Fig. 4.6 Risk transmission mechanism

growth slows down, risks of all kinds occurred together. Now, there are many unprecedented difficulties for the third- and fourth-tier cities in the destocking of real estate industry. If not handled properly, it could trigger more risks. Once the real estate bubble goes bust, the increased over-capacity and lowered government revenue may provoke local government debt crisis, and impact the financial institutions. The multiple external risks can bring forth regional and systemic financial risks, further stoking the deflation, and accelerating the economic slowdown, assuming a downward spiral (as shown in Fig. 4.6).

According to the sketch of risk transmission, the risks are under control but need to be defused soon. China stresses adapting to and guiding the new economic normal, optimizing innovation macro-regulation, stepping up comprehensive reform and innovation-based development strategy, promoting structural reform in the supply and solving problems like high-leveraging and bubbles exposed. The risks under the New Normal are controllable, but we should be highly-alert to them especially to the risks of real estate bubble and over-capacity. Efforts should be made to improve the mechanism to defuse risks and deepen reforms of the supply. Reforms measures should be efficient to eliminate risks at their early stage and prevent small risks escalating into big ones, individual risks into complex ones, and regional risks into the regional or systemic ones.

4.2 Structural Problems of China's Economy Under the New Normal and the Analysis of Their Root Causes

Since the reform and opening-up 3 decades ago, China's economy has taken off. But the long-term inefficient economic growth has also created institutional and structural problems. As the economy enters the New Normal, there is growing downward pressure and systemic risks, which are attributed to the combination of cyclical and structural problems, among which the latter is fundamental. Those structural problems include the coexistence of lack of effective supply and low industrial capacity, that of the low fluidity in real economy and over-fluidity in virtual economy. All these problems combined restrain the further development under the new economic normal.

4.2.1 Structural Problems of China's Economy Under the New Normal

4.2.1.1 Imbalance in the Overall Demand

From the perspective of the overall demand, China's economy is moving away from investment and export to a combination of consumption, investment and export, and consumption is replacing investment to become the major driving force for economic growth. However, there are still structural problems, especially in sectors of investment and export.

Firstly, the investment pattern is not appropriate. Most of the investment goes to manufacturing, infrastructure and real estate. In 2015, the fixed assets investment in these three sectors accounts for more than 81% of the total social fixed assets investment, while the figure for social undertakings is only 5% and almost 0 for financial sector. The investment also favors the sectors high in waste and low in efficiency. Industries that are high in resource and energy consumption take up a lion's share of the investment with a lot of inefficient and ineffective projects. According to the National Audit Office's survey in August 2015 that checked the implementation of policies by 29 central government departments and 7 central enterprises to stabilize growth, deepen reform, adjust structure, improve livelihood and prevent risks in 29 provinces, autonomous regions, and cities under the direct control of the central government, around 23.7% of the projects fall short of their schedule, which involves an investment of a total of 286.862 billion RMB Yuan. Among the 333 railways under construction, 99 projects saw less than 50% of their annually-planned investments in place, involving an investment of 173.724 billion RMB Yuan, and 20 saw less than 10% of such investment in place. In 2015, the central government invested 12.433 billion RMB Yuan in the water-conserving agricultural projects in 29 provinces and by the end of July, only 708 million was

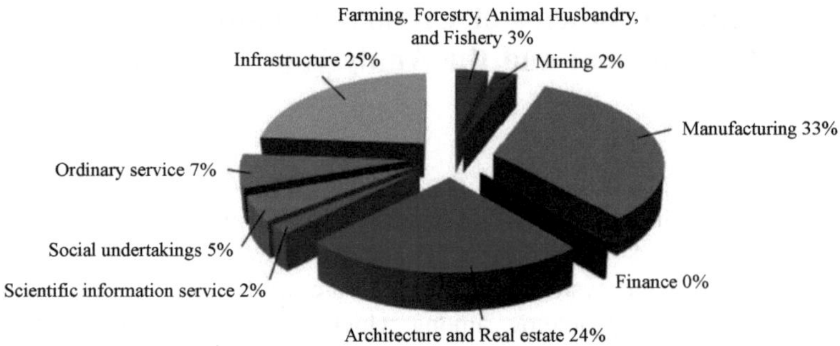

Fig. 4.7 The fixed assets investment in different industries. *Source* Wind Info

utilized. The over-investment also accounted for a high proportion. In the recent 2 years, the middle and west attracted a large share of the total investment. In 2014, the fixed assets investment in middle and west accounted for 53.3% of the overall investment, growing by more than 17%, and was 3% points higher than that in the east. There are development-zones everywhere and too many ineffective industrial zones (Fig. 4.7).

Secondly, the export pattern is not appropriate either. In spite of the fact that China has become the largest exporter of trade in goods, it still needs to catch up with others in terms of quality, efficiency of goods and services export. Firstly, the proportion of labor-intensive products is high in export. Now, most of China's export products are labor-intensive products, with only a few world-renowned brands. In 2015, the export of 7 major labor-intensive including textile, apparel, luggage, shoes, toys, furniture and plastic products took up 20.7% of the total export. While in the US, this proportion was no more than 1%. Secondly, most of the processing in China is the low-value-added. While the foreign-funded companies control the core technology and sales channel of the products, Chinese companies are only engaged in simple processing at the low end of the international specification chain. Some of the processing products are high in energy consumption, pollution and resource consumption. According to statistics, the share of electrical mechanics and new and hi-tech products in export are 57.7 and 32.6% respectively. But most of the core technologies are controlled by foreign companies. 60% of the electrical mechanics' products are produced by foreign-funded companies and more than 50% of them are just simply processed before then exported. Thirdly, the trade in service lies mainly in the traditional industries. The trade in service in China has not been developed until recently. Admittedly, this trade has been growing steadily, the service is low in technology and added value. The trade in service mainly available in transportation, tourism, architecture, and labor export has not been developing very fast in technology or knowledge-intensive sectors like consulting, insurance, finance, and information and postal. The service trade of which the export is quite small in amount and has yet to gain more competitive edge, is still in its infancy.

4.2.1.2 Imbalance in Key-Factor Supply

China's economy has long hinged upon the input of factors like capital and land while it enjoys much less inputs of high-level factors like talents and technology. What is noteworthy is that the supply of capital and labor force have structural problems that constrain the efficient utilization of production factors and the growth of productivity.

Firstly, the supply of labor element is not sufficient. Over the recent 5 years, the ratio of jobs to their candidates has been over 1, which exposed a structural problems characterized by the labor demand surpassing its supply. The first problem is the shortage of working labor force. According to China Human Resource Market Information Supervision Center, for the labor force aged over 45, the ratio of job demand to candidates is declining, indicating a labor surplus in this group of people. But for those aged between 25 and 44, the ratio has been increasing, indicating a bigger shortage in this age group. As China's population ages, the labor force shortage in the group of 25–44 will be more challenging. The second problem is the shortage of skilled labor. In China, the ratio of demand of skilled workers to their supply is higher than 1.45, much higher than the overall ratio of 1.06. Highly skilled engineers, technicians and advanced technicians are the most needed talents. The shortage of skilled workers is caused by the lagging-behind vocational educational system here. According to the Ministry of Education, in the past decade, the number of China's vocational schools has decreased by more than a third. However, this problem cannot be expected to be solved soon. The third problem is the coexistence of lack of low-educated labor force and difficulty in securing jobs for those holding high degrees. For those with only a high school or even middle school diploma, the ratios of job demand to candidates are 1.14 and 1.12 respectively, while the ratios for those who finished junior college, undergraduate and postgraduate education are all below 1. In particular, this figure for the undergraduate is only 0.85, signaling the surplus of labor force with a high diploma. These problems are caused by the face that China's industry is still at the middle and low end of the value chain, and the tertiary industry fails to provide sufficient jobs. Meanwhile, the low employment rates among those with a high diploma, in return, impedes the industrial upgrading and causes a vicious cycle.

Secondly, the effective supply of capital is insufficient. Now, China's economic growth slows down and the return of capital is declining with a growing real interest rate, leading to decreasing corporate profit and increasing debts. To be more specific, this problem is caused by two reasons. The first one is too much government capital support and a high market capital cost. In the economic structure of China, there are the state enterprises supported by the government, policy-based funds, the local financing platforms and the market. Since the financial crisis in 2008, the investment expansion led by the local government attracted a lot of capital to go into the companies supported by the government especially the big SOEs. The financial resources also favor those companies that have already got the capital support from the government, squeezing the space for market activities and making it more difficult especially for the markets of the small and medium-sized

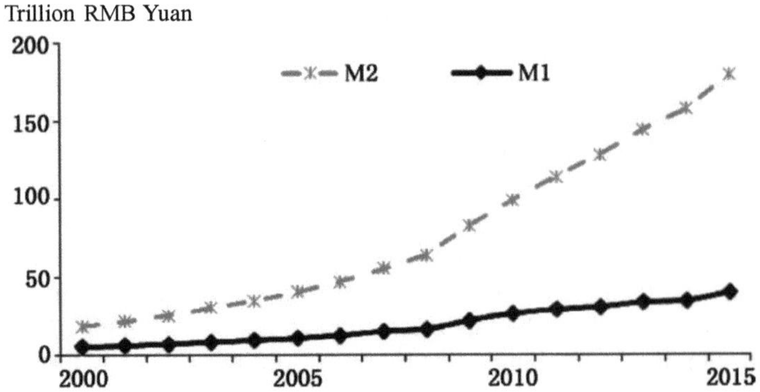

Fig. 4.8 M1, M2 growth from 2000 to 2015 (amounts in trillion RMB Yuan). *Source* Wind Info

and micro companies to solicit the capital. The second one is the low liquidity in the real economy and over-liquidity in the virtual economy. For instance, M2 increased its currency supply from 1.346 billion RMB Yuan in 2000 to 13.923 billion RMB Yuan in 2015, an increase of tenfold. However, M2 is growing increasingly faster than M1, indicating that less currency is required in the transaction and the capital is less effective. Instead of an influx into the real economy, a large share of the capital has gone otherwise to the stock market, financial products and Internet financing. For example, the two record highs in the stock market in 2014 and 2015 separately are indicators of the fact that the capital has bypassed the real economy, resulting in a serious shortage of capital in the real economy (Fig. 4.8).

Thirdly, the insufficient supply of technology. By and large, China only invests 1% of its GDP in technological research and development, much less than the proportion in developed countries (Sweden 3.4%, Japan 3.3%, US 2.7%). Moreover, what technology offers falls short of what the market expects. First, the technological investment does not catch up with the market demand. Now there is much governmental intervention in the resource allocation of technology and the market does not play a critical role. A major proof is that during the research plan and project organization, it is the government that has the final say over the technological research and development and project and product development that should have been up to the market. It leads to the mismatch between the research projects and market demand, so much so that the former cannot be translated into tangible products, and the resource is wasted. Second, the capability to transfer and apply technologies is weak. To promote the technological innovation and translate it into products, it takes concerted efforts on the parts of many technology service companies and institutions that offer R&D design, examination and accreditation, intellectual property right, start-up acceleration, and marketing. But China's technological innovation is constrained by its weak technological service. Most of the technology service providers are institutions affiliated to the government, with much unnecessary government intervention in operation. Some of these institutions even try to monopolize the market in the name of government and even practice administration approval, which limits the capability to transfer and translate technologies. Third, the management of technology resource is seriously inefficient. The current technology management system is over controlled, segmented and not systemic. The allocation of fund to technologies involves many departments and institutions, and every institution has set up too many technological projects, so the research projects are overlapped and the allocation of resource should be more proper and transparent.

4.2.1.3 Imbalance in the Industrial Pattern

By and large, China's first industry is waning, the second industry increasing before declining, whereas the tertiary industry continues to grow. In 2015, the ratio of increased value in these three industries was 9:40.5:50.5, which was in line with the rule of economic growth. But there are serious problems in all these industries, impeding the industrial upgrading.

In terms of the first industry, the development of modern agriculture is not fast, with both structural surplus and shortage. In recent years, the food production in China continue to rise and supply meets the demand, but there are still structural problems. The agriculture is large in scale but not strong enough, and the produce is diversified but of low quality. As a result, the production, stock and import of food all "rose together" in 2015, and the production of food in China sees an increase for 12 years in a row, hitting 1242.9 *jin*. Meanwhile, the crop import hits a new high and most of the domestically planted crop only goes to be stocked. Due to the mismatch between the agricultural productivity, market demand and resources, there is a curious coexistence of produce shortage and surplus. For instance, in spite of the periodical oversupply in the corn production, the bean is increasingly under-supplied. So the effective supply cannot meet the changing demand. There is also the shortage of quality produce and the surplus of low-quality produce. The produce in China still needs to catch up with those in the developed countries in its look, quality, nutrition content, safety standards, packaging, and the production and brand marketing of China's produce have yet to develop. The high-quality produce cannot meet the demands of the market. Quality and local special produce are under-supplied while the low-quality and unsafe produce are not rare. Thirdly, the coexistence of structural surplus and shortage in trade. That is to say, as China's grain output grows rapidly, its trade of produce sees net imports in all agricultural commodities, growing trade deficit, more fluctuation in the import prices and loss of momentum in the export of competitive produce, indicating China's insufficient agricultural production capability and effective supply, and lack of competitive edge in this field.

In the secondary industry, the manufacturing industry is large in scale but not strong. China is a large manufacturer with output making up one fifth of that of the world's total manufacturing industry, but it is by no means strong in this field. It is yet standing at the middle and low end of the global industrial chain. It faces both overcapacity and under-capacity in this industry. Its manufacturing industry and real economy have yet to increase their competitiveness. The first problem is the overcapacity in the traditional industry and under-capacity in the hi-tech industry. Take the steel industry as an example. There is both the overcapacity of low-quality steel such as the deformed steel bars, and the under-capacity of high-quality steel used in the express and aircraft carrier, which still rely on import. Another example is that although China produces a huge amount of chips for the electronic products, it still needs to import high-end chips used in mobiles phones and computers with 95% of universal chips imported. The second problem is that China has too much highly-polluting and too little green industries. Now China's manufacturing industry is highly-consuming and polluting with much emission. The oversupplied industries including the coal, steel, cement, electrolytic aluminum, and flat glass are all high in energy consumption with much pollution. However, little headway has been made in industrial upgrading. The heavy industry still accounts for more than 70% of the total industry. The third problem is the homogeneous industrial pattern and weak international competitiveness. Since the financial crisis, the increased investment from local governments leads to homogeneous industrial pattern with ineffective or inefficient overcapacity. Meanwhile, China's industrial foundation is weak with some basic materials and parts highly dependent on import. It serves as the assembly workshop of the global supply chain and fails to compete in the high-end market.

In the tertiary industry, the modern service industry is not well-developed, with the coexistence of growing service demand and insufficient effective service supply. In 2015, the service industry accounts for 50.5% of GDP in China, but this proportion is still considerably lower than the average level of 70.1% in the developed countries. In 2013, the figures for BRICK countries like Brazil, Russia, and India were 69.3, 60.3 and 57% respectively. In 2011 this proportion was 68.3% in South Africa. Over recent years, the internal structure of service industry in China has been upgraded, but this industry is still mainly composed of traditional storage and transportation sector, wholesale and retail, catering and accommodation, post and telecommunication. There is limited growth in the emerging service industry, and its supply can scarcely meet its demand. Therefore, this industry is constrained by the lagging-behind structure and slow growth. Firstly, the supply of productive service cannot meet the demands of economic transformation. For a long time, there has been little correlation between China's service industry and manufacturing industry. The production sectors mostly have their own accounting, market research, logistics and advertisement. In spite of the rising service outsourcing, the productive service sector is slow in its development with low specification. This growth is especially slow in capital and technology-intensive service like finance and insurance, information consulting, business service and so on. The support for the first and secondary industries are insufficient, making them hard to move the economy from manufacturing industry to service industry. Secondly, the supply of daily service does not meet the growing consumption demand of the residents. On the whole, the service industry here in China only meets the basic demand of

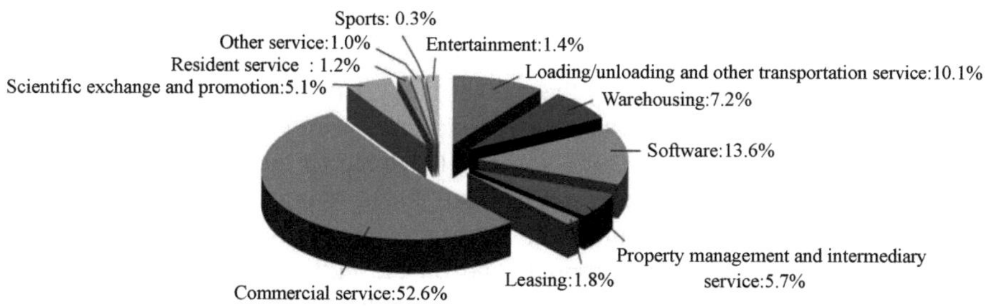

Fig. 4.9 Revenue of China's service industry by sectors. *Source* Wind Info

consumers with over-supply in the low-quality traditional service industry and undersupply in the high-quality service industry. The shortage is especially remarkable in the medicine, education and elderly-caring sectors (Fig. 4.9).

4.2.1.4 Inefficient Market Structure

After three decades of the reform and opening-up, China has made remarkable headway in developing the market economy, but there are many structural problems in the course of development. The market has to be further cultivated, the market competition facilitated and the resource allocation efficiency fostered.

On the marker side, the state enterprises are large in scale and low in efficiency while the private ones are high in efficiency and low in quality. The total assets of SOEs in China reaches 200 trillion RMB Yuan. As the SOEs become larger, they are not competitively robust. According to the statistics of China's top 500 companies in 2014, the year-on-year increase of private companies grows three times faster than that of the SOEs. Among the 500, 42 of the 43 companies that suffers loss are SOEs, with total loss reaching 72.66 billion RMB Yuan high. Besides, the local SOEs are getting lager in scale and lower in profits. The revenue of local companies grows faster than the central companies but the profit of the former is much lower than the latter, indicating that local SOEs are becoming larger in scale and lower in operation efficiency and profitability. Meanwhile, the private companies are flexible and efficient, but they still need to be further developed. In 2015, the private investment accounts for 65.2% of the total investment, much higher than the level of 30% a decade ago, but still lower than the level of 81.4% in developed countries. Most of the private companies are still engrossed in the low-tech and low-profit traditional heavy industries like metallurgy, architecture, non-ferrous metallurgy and calendaring processing. More private companies need to take part in the service industry, new and hi-tech industry and strategic emerging industry. The private capital only takes up 10% in the power generation, thermal industry and financial industry, and its share in the transportation, storage, post, water projects, environmental protection and public facility is even lower. The highly-lucrative industries like telecommunications, energy, and railway industries are all monopolized by the SOEs.

In terms of the market output, the market has yet to be specialized to optimize the product pattern. The domestic consumption has been growing at double digits for a span of many years. In 2015, the retail volume of consumer goods totalled 30.10 trillion RMB Yuan, the second largest in the world. People tend to focus more on the quality of consumption rather than quantity, on the service consumption rather than tangible products and on the individual consumption rather than mass consumption. Nevertheless, the supply of goods cannot meet the demands. The middle- and low-quality products are over-supplied and the high-quality ones are in short. The products become homogenous. There is little innovation in the products and the market is yet to be specified, especially those desired by the middle class, which results in its oversea purchase of the new products. According to the relevant reports, during 2015s National Day holiday (Oct. 1), around 400,000 Chinese tourists travelled in Japan and spent about more than 5 billion RMB Yuan there. They bought luxury goods, electric cookers, toilet seat covers, generic drugs and other daily goods.

In terms of the marker competition, industrial and regional monopoly are still pronounced problems. On the one hand, the monopoly in many industries is yet to be addressed. Since the reform and opening-up 30 years ago, the industrial monopoly has been very serious. The poorer the region is, the more serious the industrial monopoly gets. As a result, the market is not developed fully and competition is far from being sufficient. To be specific, the government monopoly covers such areas as oil exploration, military equipment, postal service, aviation fuel supply, tobacco, salt production, railway material purchasing and railway transportation. More efforts are needed to open the competitive industries and enable the markets to allocate the resources. There is also cartel in areas such as commercial banks, power, telecommunication and water and gas supply. The reform in separating the administration from the management, franchising, and government supervision has yet to be put in place. On the other hand, the regional monopoly is still with us. There is rising regional protectionism that blocks the free movement of key factors, so resources are not allocated well, impeding the formation of a unified market. Since the central government has announced to implement a holistic reform, it is focusing on regulating the regional monopoly. But the establishment of a unified market has just started and the rules and regulations to tackle the regional protectionism and unfair competition are yet to be put in place. Many local governments use their administration power to offer more benefits to the companies funded by the local investors than those by non-local ones. For instance, when promoting the new energy vehicles, apart from the cost and technological requirements, the local protectionism is one of the major barriers to this sector. Some provinces even ask the new energy automakers to set up local plants before allowing them to sale their cars in the local markets.

4.2.1.5 Inappropriate Wealth Distribution

A reasonable wealth distribution system is a must to adapt to the new economic normal. Since the reform and opening-up, the income gap has been widening. Although in recent years, the Gini Coefficient has dropped to some degree, it is still above the alarming level of 0.4. According to the statistics of National Bureau of Statistics, the Gini Coefficient of Chinese people's income in 2003 was 0.479. The figure peaked at 0.491 in 2008 and declined to 0.469 in 2014. In the beginning of 1980s, the Gini Coefficient of income gap was around 0.3. Only 10% of the countries in the world have their Gini coefficient higher than 0.5, which is a very high level, and this coefficient for the developed countries is usually between 0.24 and 0.36. Above all, the wealth distribution is not proper. The income for the labor is quite low while that for the government and enterprises is too high. There is also a big gap among residents, and between rural residents and urban ones, leading to many serious problems in the current economic operations.

In the primary stage of wealth distribution, most of the wealth goes to the non-labor elements. According to the relevant statistics, the share of labor in the national income is declining, lower than the world average of 50%. Meanwhile, the share of the government and enterprises in the national income is relatively big, and the specific share for the government is growing (Fig. 4.10).

In the secondary stage of wealth distribution, most of the wealth goes to the few people and the government. Due to the problems in the social security and tax systems, a majority of the wealth is in the possession of a small number of people and a majority of people are in possession of a tiny amount of wealth. Currently, the number of billionaires in China is only second to that of the US, and most of them are in the real estate industry. However, in China, around 150 million people are living under the poverty line. According to the relevant statistics, the income of the top 20% families is 20 times higher than that of the 20% family at the bottom.

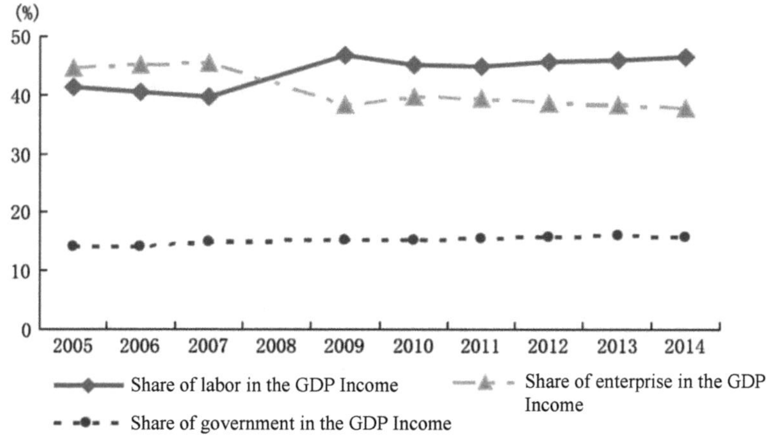

Fig. 4.10 China GDP income structure from 2005 to 2014. *Source* Wind Info

4.2.2 *The Roots of China's Structural Problems in the New Normal*

4.2.2.1 Flaws in Traditional Development Models

For the past 30-plus years, China's economy has been growing steadily and rapidly, and the government has accelerated economic restructuring. But it has not yet dropped extensive development mode. Generally, China has been moving forward with high costs and imbalance in different sectors, leading to an increasing number of structural problems. The following part analyzes the causes of these problems.

First, one cause that China's world's workshop-orientated development mode driven by foreign investment is deep-rooted. Many of China's capacity were generated during the golden period when the world economy soared. Worse still, many Chinese companies adopt the overdrawn mode, relying heavily upon investment of labor forces, land and capital rather than on technological innovation; they focused on quantity, instead of quality. The consequences of this type of production with high consumption and low efficiency are pressures form energy, resources and the environment. The country has gained surplus capacity in traditional and low-and-medium end sectors. Moreover, it lacks new effective supply, native brands and indigenous technologies, only stalemated at the low-to-middle range of the global value chain. And its real economy has been developing in the overdrawn mode with less and less investments flows into its industry capital. Therefore, driven by profits, surplus industry capitals flowed into virtual sectors and unprecedentedly vitalized the stock and property markets, making the prices in those markets exceedingly high. While creating financial bubbles, such trends deprived the real economy of the abilities to innovate and move on steadily.

Secondly, there has been an internal development mode of binary form. Binary economy represented by the separation of the market sector and sectors supported by the government, of urban and rural areas and of the coastal region and middle and western regions all serve to divide up the markets. Such differences give rise to barriers in market division and impede the flows of resources and production factors. They also lead to a market with much monopoly and inadequate competition. And increase in investments, a result of unwise actions of local governments, generated overloaded capacity. Due to the above binary differences, some problems even overlap and become interwoven, leading further to escalated structural problems.

4.2.2.2 Bottlenecks Within Current Systems and Mechanisms

Under the New Normal, China's economy is striving for a better form, more precise divisions and more reasonable structures. Current systems and mechanisms were established under traditional models, conflicting with new theories and practices. In essence, many structural problems in the New Normal are bottlenecks in current systems and mechanisms. If the Chinese government does not deepen its reform and improve systems and mechanisms, it is not likely to fix structural problems thoroughly. The following are five major bottlenecks.

First, the government has not totally transformed its role. The government has not yet clarified its relations with the market, and it interferes too much in some microeconomic activities. Its administrative approval system still needs to be improved. There are some examples. The government should have cancelled many examination and approval procedures. It has, in some cases, only cancelled minor procedures, while still keeping the major ones. It has also cancelled some procedures in form but kept them in reality. During the reform, the government lagged behind in reformulating examination and approval procedures and did not fulfill its responsibilities to regulate the reformulation. The market and the society need another round of stimulation. Besides, the government has been on default in some areas, especially in supplementing goods and services for the public, in governing the whole society and in monitoring some of its investment plans. To some extent, the previous system for evaluating and motivating local governments, based predominantly on GDP performance, motivated local authorities to spend money on credit, creating more risks.

Second, systems and mechanisms of the market are far from being perfect. Two mechanisms need to be set up: a charging mechanism for environment protection and a pricing mechanism for production factors that demonstrates the relations between supply and demand, resource scarcity and cost of environment pollution. The subjects in the market need to be improved, especially to be more professional, international and market-based. And greater market access is desired. Intangible barriers from market access exist in some sectors, and some access requirements are out of date. More importantly, private capital is restricted in some industries. So a great amount of private capital still concentrates on the markets of stock and property, reluctant to upgrade industries. A modern and divided market system is not well-developed, without full competition in various markets. Therefore, the government must strive for regional cooperation, market integration, more effective market regulation and a society with better creditability system.

Third, fiscal and taxation systems are problematic. The demarcation between central and local governments is not clear in terms of regularly-performed power and responsibilities on expenditures, and regularly-performed power and financial power within local governments are increasingly mismatched. Under the influences from the international financial crisis, local governments need, as the top priority, maintain growth. Therefore, their expenditures continue to expand and revenues don't, and consequently their debts have increased.

Besides, China shoulders a heavy macro-tax burden. According to standards issued by the World Bank, the most favorable macro-tax burdens for countries with low, low-medium, medium-high and high incomes stand at approximately 13%, 20%, 23%, and 30% respectively. In 2014, China's gross macro-tax burden was 37%, equalizing the level of developed countries when its income has not reached that level. China has levied a variety of taxes, including value-added tax, consumption tax, business tax, individual income tax, corporate income tax, resource tax, urban land utilization tax, increment tax on land value, building tax, city maintenance and construction tax, vehicle purchase tax, vehicle and vessel tax, stamp tax, deed tax, tax on the occupancy of cultivated land, tobacco tax, tariff and vessel tonnage tax, etc. It also levies duplicated taxes, so companies, especially small ones, are invariably burdened with taxation. If a company's ratio of taxation against profit is above 100%, its investments in equipment and technological innovation will be hindered. The structure of tax mix needs to be improved. There are more indirect tax and less direct tax than considered reasonable amounts, and system design for major taxes, such as consumption tax, business tax and agriculture tax, need to be bettered. Apart from taxation, there are substantial administrative charges difficult to count. Off-budget revenue of some local governments is about to equalize or even exceed the sum of taxation and fiscal revenue, and for some people, non-taxation payments are nearly equal to or even outweigh tax. It is not clear how governments establish criterion for calculating fiscal revenues. Therefore, their budgets must be more complete and transparent.

Fourth, systems and mechanisms for technological innovation need to be improved. At present, in transforming and upgrading Chinese economic structure, the biggest challenge comes from the technological sector, since the country lacks indigenous and core technologies in particular. And the challenge stems from the weaknesses in systems and mechanisms for technological innovation. Enterprises have not gained a leading role in innovation. Market-based incentives for innovation are far from being perfect, and mechanism of guiding the whole society to invest in technological innovation still leaves room for improvement. The model for Industry-University-Research collaboration cannot satisfy the needs of major technological innovations; cooperation in key technological sectors is insufficient; there is not a sound mechanism that protects intellectual property rights and profits gained from achievements in aspects of the common input, result sharing and risk sharing; the public technology platform and service system that boost the integration of industry, university and research need enhancing. Research management systems cannot satisfy the demands from innovation projects, so the pattern for managing scientific and technological projects need to be revised. Assessment standards and motivation in universities and scientific research institutions are mismatched, and, as a result, the transformation of scientific and technological achievements is badly managed. The collaboration of innovation programs among regions within China and between China and the rest of the world is inadequate, so the country's innovative mechanism has to be more open.

Fifth, the government must accelerate reforms in financial systems and mechanisms. China's M2/GDP rate is nearly at 200%, way exceeding that of other countries at 100 and 150%. This indicates that China's economic growth is fueled by credit, and the credit assets tend to be less efficient. The financial system and resource distribution are not efficient, with abundant capital in sectors with low efficiency, leading to low exchange rate of currency. Without a sound hierarchy of financial institutions, state-owned banks are the main source of funds for SOEs. As a result, SOEs are overwhelmingly dependent on state owned banks. Therefore, a huge amount of capital gets lost in the supply or subsidy for SOEs, an example of inefficiency in distribution.

There are problems in financing mechanisms, with heavy imbalance between direct and indirect financing. Most demands for long-term capital are satisfied in indirect ways by commercial banks, the capital of which, nevertheless, comes predominantly from short-term deposited capital. This makes the liquidity suffer as the problem of short-term deposits and long-term loans arises, while risks the financial system tend to be transmitted to banks only. In China, loans from banks remain to be the major method to turn deposits into investment. Firms of security industry overlap in their businesses and the services they offer are identical and limited. The insurance industry is in embryonic stage, with quite a limited ability to realize capital expansion and to raise capital through the market. Therefore, a considerable amount of capital, yet to be turned into fund conducive to production, remains marooned in the state of sedimentary money in financial institutions such as state owned banks.

4.2.2.3 Previous Strong Stimulation Is Yet to Be Digested

After the international financial crisis broke out in 2008, China, to tackle the periodic fluctuation of economy, adopted a series of short-term macro control policies, including the proactive fiscal policy, prudent monetary policy and government investment policies and so on. It put forward an economic stimulus plan of up to 4 trillion RMB which did stabilize the economic growth. Yet, the marginal effects of these policies are evidently declining; GDP growth is going downward consistently; and the structural problems brought forth by the stimulation package of policies are increasingly pronounced.

First, macro-economic policies are overused. After the financial crisis, the government focused on stimulating demand. Since the fourth quarter of 2008, it comprehensively eased its fiscal policy and monetary policy. And in 2009, it put forward the "4 + 10", namely to add 4 trillion investments through the expansion of fiscal policy and to increase about 10 trillion credit expenditure through monetary stimulation. In 2009, the fiscal deficit reached a record high of 950 billion, accounting for 2% of the GDP. The growth of currency supply surpassed 27%. And in 2010, it continued the strong stimulus macro policy until October of 2010 when it declared to drop the comprehensive expansion policy. Admittedly, the demand-oriented stimulus policy has successfully cushioned the impacts of the crisis, it also incurred high costs and required a prolonged period to be digested. The monetary stock soared. The ratio of M2 and GDP way exceeded out of the appropriate range. The prices of all production factors rose. Speculative capital bubbles grew and the potential for the issued additional currency to turn into inflation is greater.

Second, industrial policies are overused. From the beginning of 2007 to the first half of 2008, the national industrial policies are primarily concerned with energy conservation and emission reduction and structural adjustment. From the end of 2008 to the end of 2009, the industrial policies are targeted at securing growth and revitalizing industries. China issued a package plan to adjust and revitalize key industries. The original intention of the government is to support enterprises in seeking new comparative advantages and growth point to boost sustainable economic development. Yet, in practice, to secure growth became the priority and the choice of value. Industrial policies turned into short-term methods to stimulate demand; supportive polices got rid of their limitations; investors and enterprises flooded in, to the ignorance of comparative advantages, their competitive edge and market demand. The results are that excessive production capacity got worsened, economic bubble of low level expansion grew and the problem of over capacity has expanded from manufactured consumer goods to industrial investment goods, from traditional industries to emerging ones. In some sectors, the relative over-capacity has changed into absolute over-capacity, adding to the difficulty of reducing over-capacity during the after-crisis recovery and adjustment period.

Third, regional supportive policies are overused. The central and western regions have relative small economic aggregate, extensive production mode and weak self-readjustment ability. To cushion the impact of the financial crisis, China has put forward regional development strategies and supportive policies that are aimed at the central and western regions and regions with limited recourses. For this, the government has strengthened especially the construction of infrastructure to maintain the sound growth there. However, under certain regional policies, a large amount of capital has flowed into enterprises with outdated capacity and no competitive edge or into sectors with low productivities. The leverage ratio of real economy keeps rising, hampering the long-term economic growth.

4.3 Difference Analysis on the Structural Reforms of China and Other Main Countries in the World

China's supply side structural reform represents a major innovation in adapting to and leading the new economic norm, it is a proactive choice of China to adjust to the new situation of post-crisis national strength competition. It differs from the reforms carried out by the Regan Administration or the Thatcher Administration in the 1980s in aspects of theory, background, and problems targeted. Thus, in lieu of simply copying other countries' examples, it is essential for China to lay a substantial foundation by exploring new areas for a sustainable and healthy economic growth in the medium to long term, on the basis of its national conditions and structural problems arising from the new norm.

4.3.1 China's Reform Is Based on a Different Theory

4.3.1.1 Socialist Political Economy with Chinese Characteristics

In the 1970s, amid the western circle of economics, there was a heated discussion with regard to the supply side reform, giving birth to the well-known subject of supply side economics. The western supply side economics is representative of a combination of a series of policy ideas without strong scientific doctrines to support it, built upon an economic analytical framework of individual and enterprise incentives. By contrast, China's supply side structural reform is based upon its theory of social political economy with Chinese characteristics, the successful practice of China's reform and opening-up, and it focuses on studying the new problems and challenges under the New Norm, putting emphasis on tackling the increasingly prominent structural problems of economic development. Essentially, it seeks to readjust and improve the socialist production mode, representing China's epoch-making theoretical exploration of new supply side economics through practices.

4.3.1.2 Paying Equal Attention to the Supply Side and the Demand Side

The supply side reform of America and Britain mainly focuses on improving micro efficiency to increase effective supply. It changed the old way of making macro policies based on Keynesianism and is basically a reform on the management of demand side. However, China's supply side structural reform does not negate the demand side. Rather, it shifts from its previous focus from demand management to an equal stress on supply management and demand management. By equally strengthening the supply and the demand side, it improves the supply and demand mechanism to release the potential of demand and to invigorate new growth drivers through supply innovation. The Central Economic Working Conference specified that it would speed up supply side structural reform on the basis of appropriated expansion of demand. And it puts forward five guiding policies that function as pillars: macro-level policy should be stable; industrial policy precise, micro-level policy dynamic, reform policy substantial, social policy supportive that ensures the basic livelihood. To sum up, it will stress upon striking a balance between economic growth and structural readjustment by moderately expanding demand to sustain economic growth and to safeguard supply side economic reform.

4.3.2 China's Supply Side Reform Confronts Formidable Difficulties

4.3.2.1 A Fierce International Environment

In the 1980s, developed countries relied too much on crude oil imported from the Middle East. After the second round of impact from oil price soaring, the US realized that it must formulate a new energy pattern and enhance energy efficiency. To cope with the severe inflation and slack domestic demands, it implemented new policies on the supply side. The US enjoyed a good environment for investment and a stable political situation with a high trade deficit, which means that it confronts few risks from the outside. In contrast, China faces a complicated international environment for its supply side reform against the background of synchronized global technological, economic and systemic changes. The system of global economic governance is disintegrating and a new one has yet not been established. Many advocate small-scale regional development under the game theory of stock. The global economy has not fully recovered and quantitative easing policies in many countries failed. The last round of technological innovation cannot further increase the efficiency of industries. There are no more bonuses from cross-border capacity transfer and globalization whereas difficulties arise from both economic and political sides.

4.3.2.2 A Complicated Domestic Environment

Compared with well-developed market economies, China's market economic systems have not yet matured. Most of China's structural problems come into being as a result of its planned economy and extensive development model. For supply side reforms in countries like the US and the UK, they did face minor structural problems, but the main objectives of such projects were improving the efficiency of resource distribution. For instance, the marginal taxation rate of personal income in the US was up to 70% and that of enterprises 46%, discouraging investments in market and production. By contrast, China faces a more complicated domestic environment. There are difficulties from the cycles of globalization and of investments in fixed assets. China also needs to deal simultaneously with the slowdown in economic growth, make difficult structural adjustments, and absorb the effects of the previous economic stimulus policies. Thus, here emerge problems such as great local debts, huge real estate inventory and structure-inflicted surplus capacity, etc. Moreover, China is an enormous economy with distinct differences between rural and urban areas and among regions, and SOEs account for too much a part of its economy. Therefore, under the New Normal, it is more demanding to solve structural problems. The reform is not only a plan for quick fixes, but also, more importantly, a project for restructuring, requiring patience and resilience.

4.3.3 *China's Plan Boasts Huge Potentials*

4.3.3.1 Globally, China Has Opportunities for Upgrading Technologies

After the international financial crisis, the global economy has been in recession. It is now looking for opportunities for innovation and technological breakthroughs. That is why major economies are in recent years promoting technological innovations, including technologies of the Internet, shale gas, robotics, artificial intelligence, 3-D printing and new materials. It's obvious that the world is experiencing a new round of technology revolution, presenting chances for China to drive its economy by innovation. Meanwhile, the industrial division based on global value chain is evolving, generating enormous flows of goods, information and capital. This also offers China golden opportunities to go global and move to higher positions in the global value chain.

4.3.3.2 Domestically, China's Economy Is Resilient

After years of unrelenting efforts, China has been stronger in economy, science and technology, national defense, and has greater international clout. Indeed, China's economy needs to address many challenges, including economic headwind, unsuitable development approach, unreasonable economic structure, and unsustainable utilization of resources and the environment. Nevertheless, it enjoys not a few favorable conditions. China, with a promising overall economic situation, is carrying out new industrialization, informatization, urbanization and the modernization of agriculture. Middle income group and tertiary industry of the country are growing. Domestic demand and the potential market are enormous, and its economy is resilient. These all pave way for China's supply side reform.

China is still in the primary stage of capital accumulation. It has a high deposit rate and enough funds for capital deepening. Compared with the US and the UK in the 1980s, China has the highest deposit rate, great prospect for urbanization and big room for macro-economic control. These lay a solid basis for China's supply side reform.

4.4 Difficulties for China in Implementing Its Supply Side Reform

Supply side reform is universally acknowledged as a difficult mission and China's reform is carried out under a unique background and has distinctive rules and features. Thus, it is in a more demanding situation and needs to address more tough issues, especially those in maintaining a tempo for reform, dealing with relations and preventing risks. The government must be confident about and determined upon the scheme and be persistent and resilient during the process. In this way, it is able to orchestrate the reform and solve the problems with precision.

4.4.1 Maintaining Good Tempo of the Reform

On one hand, China should capture the opportune moment. As the country is undergoing a transition from deflation to inflation, it is on a perfect occasion for reform. During this period, it should reduce overloaded capacity, restructure its economy, improve the profitability of real economy, eliminate capital bubbles and increase the efficiency of capital distribution. By doing these, China's economy is able to welcome a soft landing.

However, on the other hand, China should not be too hasty in undertaking the reform. China has been developing in an extensive way for such a long time that it structures of industries and income distribution have already become fixed. Therefore, it is impossible to solve all the problems that have haunted China for a dozen years only in a short term. Acting blindly for long term goals will incur hazards. For this reason, the government should take into account the following issues: the cost of transition, the tempo and the width of the reform, the relation between the reform and economic development, the bottom-line of the reform. Moreover, the government should particularly coordinate reforms in different sectors because they are at different layers and have different objectives. Only by doing this, the reform is likely to take effects.

4.4.2 Deal with Relations Within the Framework of Reform

4.4.2.1 Deal with the Relation Between Strengthening Supply and Increasing Demand

Supply and demand are not contradictory with either of them able to turn into the other. In supply side reform, a stable environment is necessary. When it is impossible to boost total demand in a short term, the government must avoid blind stimulating policies and prevent a cyclic deflation from happening. It should put forward a positive fiscal policy and a prudent monetary policy, focusing on effective investments. These measures are particularly necessary especially in the sense that the current monetary policy does not function sufficiently well. Therefore, the government should maintain the flow of currency and stabilize the markets of stock and foreign exchange, creating a favorable economic environment for reform.

4.4.2.2 Deal with the Relation Between Administrative Interference and Market Operation

At present, surplus capacity is mainly concentrated in sectors invested by local capital, such as local SOEs and investing and financing platforms. Measures of the reform, like capacity reduction, de-inventory and de-leverage, have hurt and will hurt interests of local governments. And it is hard to cut surplus capacity and boost inadequate capacity, to balance the interests, equities among local fiscal and taxation agents restructure debt in debt restructuring. In performing these roles, the government runs the risk of over-interference and causing new market distortion. Therefore, the reform requires the government to play a navigating role and transform its functions. And more importantly, the market should be given full play to take the dominant role in the reform and the state should propel the reform through market-based measures.

4.4.2.3 Deal with the Relation Between New Development Models and Traditional Ones

China's supply side reform is an innovation in which new views, new technologies, new organizations and new trends in industries rise and, inevitably, challenge traditional ones. So it is necessary to reduce the friction, coming from traditional development models. Meanwhile, the reform applies a new distribution approach and rearranges vested interests, which will be the biggest obstacle for the reform. Therefore, the government should solicit the biggest common divisor of recognition and support for the project and should, in sectors with rigid frameworks, establish new rules that underline innovation and efficiency.

4.4.3 Prevent Risks Brought by Reform

4.4.3.1 Prevent a Gap Between New and Old Growth

According to economic principles, restructuring will slow down growth in a short term and lead to an unequal development among industries. Besides, China's economy is not yet fully driven by innovation. Without a formal new model for economic development, China still mainly relies on traditional industries. If China goes too far in fostering new sectors, it probably will create new surplus capacity and economic bubbles, lacking sustained impetus for growth. And during economic downturn, reforms cannot instantly boost efficiency of the economy. When some of the above risks emerge simultaneously, it is likely that China's economy will run the risk of going downward during the reform.

4.4.3.2 Prevent the Society from Destabilizing

At present, most companies with surplus capacity are big-sized SOEs, which are major employers in their cities. The reform will lay off many workers and increase unemployment rate. If China fails to provide effective supporting policies and social security for them, social conflicts will escalate and the society will be destabilized.

4.4.3.3 Prevent a Hyperinflation

Although China's CPI is generally stable, it is likely to undergo inflation. While decreasing capacity surplus and economic bubbles, China may let a slack monetary policy govern too much in real economy and the sector of consumption commodities. This will lead to a craze for commodities driven by capital and even a new round of inflation. Therefore, China should prevent this from happening.

4.4.3.4 Prevent Being Locked on Low-End Industries in International Capacity Export

Exporting is a major channel for China to deal with capacity surplus. In this respect, "the Belt and Road" plays a significant role. But when exporting, China may, to some extent, incorrectly stimulate the unhealthy growth of the low-end industries, therefore covertly locked on them, which in turn will backfire on the reform and upgrade of industries.

Chapter 5
Theories and Practices of Supply Side Reform Under New Normal

China is building a well-off society in an all-around way and its economy is in New Normal. Against this backdrop, the Chinese government plans to reform the supply side and to transform its growth model and regain economic momentum through the reform. In contrast with supply side reforms in developed countries and regions, China plans to reform in a different development phase and under a different background. Therefore, China's initiative should have its own features, theories, practices and foci.

5.1 The Background of China's Supply Side Reform

China's supply side reform is a systemic project against a special background. To fully understand the reform and its tasks and objectives, the government needs to analyze the background as well as the current perspectives and viewpoints centering on it. This can make the government definite about the orientation and the requirements it needs to fulfil for the reform, laying a solid basis for the government to understand it accurately and to carry it out.

5.1.1 The Background Under Which China Plans to Reform the Supply Side

Since the reform and opening-up, China has been building a socialist market economy and striving to reform SOEs, factor markets and the private sectors. Thanks to such efforts, China has been rapidly developing its economy and has improved its overall economic strength. But in the 21st century, especially after the global financial crisis, China's economic growth has stepped into a challenging

L. Xiao, *New Supply Side Economics*, DOI 10.1007/978-981-10-4639-1_5

period, in which its economy slows down and lacks driving force. "The Three Period Superimposed" is the country's biggest challenge, indicating that the structure and internal momentum of its economy are changing. Under such a background, Chinese government plans to reform its supply side, which is logic and reasonable in consideration of the overall situation.

5.1.1.1 Slowdown in Economic Growth Indicates Diminishing Internal Momentum

After years of rapid growth, China's economy growth rate is markedly on the decline. China's economy grew at an annual average rate of 11.6% from 2003 to 2007 and at 9.6% from 2008 to 2011. Since 2012, the growth rate has dropped to about 7%. There are two reasons for this gear shift. First, China's economic output kept growing over the last decades. As the scale of an economy increases, the base of its growth will become larger accordingly. Even if the economy continues to expand, its growth rate will slow down as investment that goes into factors such as labor, capital, and technology and economic output maintain the same. Second, China's economic impetus dwindles when its supply method, based on low-end production factors, cannot provide any more power. As globalization deepens, China has become more open to the outside. After it won WTO membership, China has been more closely connected with the supply and demand of the world economy. Chinese companies became part of the base of the global value chain, which turned China into the "World Factory". After going global, China's economy benefited from low-cost and labor-intensive manufacturing and assembly which require few advanced technologies. So its economy expanded considerably. Over the past few decades, China's economy depended on gradient supply of its manufacturing, which gave it a fixed position in the global value chain and a fixed growth model. In recent years, however, Chinese currency has appreciated, the cost of production factors ramped up, and its environment become more fragile, Moreover, India, African countries and other countries with huge populations take over the low-end global division of labor. And the global consumption structure has been upgraded. All these make it more and more difficult for China to grow its economy only by relying on low-end products and low-end production capacity. Against the backdrop, China's traditional supply method, based on low-end production factors, has reached its "peak" and entered its bottleneck stage, thus unable to provide any impetus. So its economy is experiencing hardships and lacks power for sustainable growth.

According to the above analysis, the reason why China's economic growth shifts its gear is that with the traditional supply method, its internal driving force wanes and is unable to achieve sustainable growth. Indeed, China's technologies and labor forces improved in global competition. But such changes only took place in quantity, not in quality. As the nature of its supply side has yet not transformed, it can only boost China's economy to a very limited extent.

5.1.1.2 Economy Slows in Restructuring Means It Faces Severe Structural Problems

From its transition from a planned economy to a socialist market economy, China's economy has been confronting structural problems. Before the reform and opening-up, China utilized the "scissors gap" between the prices of products and produce, which served to boost the industries but led to an imbalance between the first and second industries as well as an imbalance between rural and urban areas. Since its 9th "Five Year Plan", China has made up its mind to restructure its economy and accelerate the transformation of growth model. But as its economic output and national strength increase, the structural problems have not been solved, and worse still, some has escalated. At the moment, China faces severe structural problems and they must be solved. Nevertheless, these problems have become unprecedentedly complex. The first reason is that China needs to address both new and old structural problems. In its economic development, China carried out stock development and reform on the basis of incremental development and reform, which presented the country with both new and old structural problems. On one hand, old problems still persist. In terms of income, governments claim a lion's share while non-governmental individuals, not favored in the allocation of national revenue, only touch upon a small fraction; consumption merely accounts for a small part in the demand side. On the other hand, new problems keep propping up. Trade of goods way surpassed that of services. There are more low- and medium-end products than medium- and high-end products. Real economy gets more funds than virtual economy. And the list goes on and on. The second reason is that structural problems cross borders of different sectors. Apart from structural problems in economy, China faces structural problems in regional development and public services. Structural problems in different sectors related to one another, which made them still harder to tackle. Given the situation, the structural problems of China's economy are increasingly challenging. The Chinese government must conduct an overall analysis and solve them in a systematic and orderly manner.

According to economic theory of growth, economic growth is the outcome of growth in all sectors. Growth is not only the increase of economic output, but also, more importantly, it could be the result of the transformation of structures in different sectors. The general structure of supply and demand sides and the internal structures of each side are key to a balanced and coordinated increase of an economy. Therefore, when its market scheme is not mature, China's production structure, relying on the supply of production factors and the allocation of national revenue, will lose its balance. Consequently, the unsolved structural problems persist to interweave while getting more complicated.

5.1.1.3 Absorbing the Effects of Previous Stimulus Policies Means Traditional Growth Model Must Be Replaced

Since the reform and opening-up, China has been focusing on stimulating demand side and promoting guiding policies on this side. Through policies governing demand side and supporting measures of macro-control, China has expanded its economy, withstood fluctuations and weakened cyclic volatility. With the stimulus of such policies, China's economy had been burgeoning for decades and its aggregate output soared, putting China in the second place in the world. However, due to its focus on governance of the demand side for so long, China has been stuck in low-end development, growing more in quantity than in quality. At present, China's traditional growth model faces serial problems, unable to support sustainable growth.

The first problem is that owing to an extensive development model, different regions have similar industrial structures, resulting in overloaded capacity. After the reform and opening-up, Chinese government focused on the governance of demand side, which played a major role in its transition from a planned economy to a market-based one and helped it acquire impetus for rapid growth. But it focused on demand side for a long term. As a result, China got acclimated to an extensive development model, with over-focus on quantity. It means that China's growth was mainly powered by the increase of investment, and its technologies only advanced slowly. There are a few examples. In the second half of 1980s, the country constructed basic industries and infrastructure, and in the second half of the 1990s, its heavy industries grew faster. Thanks to projects in the two periods, investments in fixed assets in China have been soaring. After over 30 years of the reform and opening-up, China's increase rate in this area is about 13.5%, fairly higher than that of other emerging markets. While the central government was focusing on demand side, local authorities, based on the needs of local taxation and development, took even more advantage of demand side governance. With the support of local authorities, there sprang up a large amount of general manufacturing industries with short investment cycles and quick returns as well as heavy chemical industries capable of motivating related industries. But this led to duplication of low level construction and similar structures of product and industries in different areas, intensifying the pressure from surplus capacity.

The second problem is the "troika" on demand side, namely investment, consumption and export, has weakened in driving economic growth. After China has developed in an extensive model of high investment and high consumption for a long time, the "troika" representing "three forces" of its demand side are losing power to push growth. On one hand, the marginal utility of investments shrinks due to high investments and consumption. Here is an example of this kind. During the period of its 6th "Five Year" plan, China needed to invest 180 million CNY in fixed assets to generate GDP of 100 million CNY. And during the 7th and the 10th "Five Year" plans, the amount of needed investment increased to 215 million CNY and

499 million CNY respectively. On the other hand, the "troika" causes the Crowding-Out-Effect, abating the overall effect of driving growth. In China's economic development, investment is the most effective way to stimulate growth and increases at the highest possible rate. However, when the amount of demand is certain, investment growing too fast will impede consumption, because income will be allocated disproportionately if investment grows too fast. Generally, capital holders will get considerably more income than ordinary workers. Therefore, fast-growing investment does not mean that people's income will rise greatly on a par with each other. Rather, it makes it very hard to give full play to the potential of the whole society.

The third problem is that policies on demand side amplify structural problems in China's economy. With sustained stimulation from policies on demand side, resources are not evenly distributed among the society, worsening the structural problems. Such problems include unreasonable income allocation, unreasonable capital distribution, unequal development among regions, etc, will slow down China's economy when they become more severe.

It is fair to conclude that governance on demand side greatly contributed to China's economic development. But, in the meantime, continuous policies on demand side in too many sectors constrained the transformation of its economic growth and the quality of its growth. According to theories of neoclassical economics, governance on demand side is only short-term stimulus that can expand aggregate output in a short period. The flexibility of policies on demand side is relevant to supply side. Fiscal and monetary policies that support policies on demand side cannot directly influence factors like productivity of the society, economic system and resources, which are the origins of economic growth. And these factors are, in fact, on the supply side. Therefore, without the support from supply side governance, policies on demand side always overlook technological and systemic innovation, generating only ineffective supply. The consequence will be that policies on demand side will fail to stimulate supply, and aggravate the mismatch of production factors. And this will further cause structural problems slowing down economic growth and imbalance between supply and demand, suppressing the increase of overall demand.

Given the above picture, China needs to deal with many hurdles at the same time. The numerous structural problems, the power shrinkage of traditional growth model and the limitations on its development have taken a heavy toll on its economy. The main reason for its predicament is that governance on supply side lags behind that on demand side and the two don't go hand in hand. And the root is that the building of systems on production side is slow in a socialist market economy. Therefore, under New Normal, if China wants to regain momentum and improve the quality of growth, it must inaugurate supply side reform as soon as possible.

5.1.2 Analysis of and Review on Opinions About Supply Side Reform

Many Chinese scholars have studied and interpreted China's supply side reform and have provided some guidelines and approaches for the reform. Generally speaking, understandings vary from scholar to scholar without any consensus. Theoretical construction is yet to come. The following are views on it from different perspectives.

5.1.2.1 From the Perspective of Governance on Supply Side

Many experts and scholars have tried to understand supply side reform from the perspective of governance on supply side. Their principal opinion is that supply side reform should focus on production side, improve the system and efficiency of supply so as to enhance its quality and effectiveness. Their opinion includes the following three aspects. First, the reform should focus on the effective supply of products or services and the core of the reform is to improve the effective investment in labor forces, the talents of entrepreneurs, administration, resources and lands. If the authority can adjust the approach and the structure of investment as well as transform low-end products and services, it will achieve adequate effective investment. Second, the reform should focus on the quality of supply of goods and services and the top priority of the reform is to restructure the mechanism of production and services. If the authority can improve the allocation of resources, boost productivity and encourage technological innovation of companies, it will enhance the core competitiveness of industries and efficiency of its economy. Third, the reform should focus on the vitality of companies, and the major objective of the reform is to reduce companies' costs from the administrative system. Such costs include taxations, transaction cost, financing cost, and social security for their employees, etc. The authority should provide an incentive system and environment for entrepreneurs to innovate and initiate start-ups. In this way, companies will be able to enjoy a free environment so as to create values and tap their potential in innovation and creation, which will foster a sustained power for economic growth of China.

5.1.2.2 From the Perspective of Restructuring

Some experts and scholars understand the reform from the perspective of restructuring. Their principal view is that supply side reform, aiming to improve the overall structure of the economy, should, through adjusting supply and demand, strike a balance within investments, productions and industries so as to improve the efficiency of the market and enable it to develop sustainably. Their restructuring-based understanding includes the following three points. First, the government should focus on optimizing the structure of supply and demand, and the major task in the structural reform on supply side is to "reduce supply" by getting rid of overloaded capacity and to eliminate unproductive companies. By doing this, the government will match supply side with demand side, stabilize the prices of goods and services and enable companies to regain profits. Second, policymakers should upgrade the structure of product supply and understand that the supply of low-, medium- and high-end products is imbalanced. While boosting total demand, China should deal with the structural problem of low-end product surplus and high-end product shortage. In the meantime, it should, through innovation on supply side, change the consumption structure of nationals and improve the quality of the whole supply system. Third, the authority should understand that resources are unevenly distributed among industries, regions, corporations and sectors and the authorities should improve the structure of resource allocation. The objective of supply side reform is to rearrange stock resources and to improve the structure and efficiency of resource allocation by guaranteeing optimal flows of resources among fields.

5.1.2.3 From the Perspective of Systemic Reform

Systemic innovation is the fundamental standpoint of many scholars' views on supply side reform. Their main viewpoint is that supply side reform should be innovative in administration and macro-control. It should pay more attention to high quality systemic supply for medium and long term and start the transformation of administration from supply side. There are 5 sub-points.

First, the project should include systemic reform that enhances the efficiency and quality of production factor supply. The objectives of structural reform on supply side include building a market system that reasonably allocates and prices production factors, and guaranteeing the sound flow of resources and exploring their values. For example, the government can reform the system of land-using and form a turnover system of land crossing urban and rural areas. Besides, the state should reform its financial system and take initiatives to get rid of "financial suppression" so that the financial sector can support the real economy. Meanwhile, the reform should adjust the system boosting the quality of resources. For instance, it can adjust policies on population control and educational system that improves the quality of labor forces.

Second, the plan should change the system that vitalizes companies. The goals of the reform are invigorating companies, empowering small market entities and building a fair and equal market economy. For instance, the government should break off monopoly and restrictions of market access. It should foster an environment that encourages entrepreneurship and innovation. It should build a system that motivates entrepreneurs and protect intellectual properties. It should reform SOEs and corporations with mixed ownership.

Third, the plan should focus on systemic reform that boosts innovation. The government should formulate policies specific for new industries, companies of new technologies and new trends in different industries. It should be innovative in systems that increase companies' investment in R&D so that they can improve core technologies and indigenous brands.

Fourth, the reform should focus on system of public services. The government is the provider of public services. And it should, in structural reform of supply side, accelerate reforms on social security and revenue distribution. The government should also transform its functions as soon as possible.

Fifth, the government should focus on innovation of macro-control and implement reforms through the coordination of fiscal and monetary policies.

The above understandings and explanations have an in-depth analysis on supply side reform from various perspectives. Despite this, such studies have the following shortcomings.

First, they forgot to consider China's local conditions in supply side reform. Many studies discussed the theories, tools and experience of supply from the supply side economics and their significance to China's reform, and identified major directions and tasks of the reform. Such studies focused too much on the mechanism of economic development and were based on an assumption that China has similar economic systems with other countries and is at a similar development stage. As globalization deepens, China, as an emerging economy that is transforming itself, is building a sound socialist market economy with Chinese features. Its development is unique and its supply side reform is also distinctive in various facets. Therefore, the theories, tools and experience of supply from the supply side economics should be localized when applied to China.

Second, their discussions are short of analysis on the overall situation of China's supply side reform. Many experts eyed on the directions and major tasks of the reform, and they identified the main approaches and sectors that deserve greater reform. But they tended to focus on short-term effects and minor issues of the reform and did not suggest how to build a medium- to long-term system and on how to build a system for structural reform on supply side. In effect, supply side reform is a systemic task. It should generate effects in a short term, but it also has features of a medium- or long-term project. It attaches importance to short-term regulation, dealing with urgent problems. Besides, it requires reform and construction of a medium and even long span, which should be carried out on the basis of a thorough analysis of the supply side reform system.

Third, their understandings are not based on the analysis of the background of China's supply side reform in details. Many scholars studied the key areas, pointed out the main objectives and the approaches of the reform in different phases, and they suggested on policies. But their analysis was based on the reform itself and highlighted how to carry out the reform and how to forward it at the next step. Though some of them took into consideration of the environment of China's supply side reform, they were inclined to concentrate on the economic situation and future trends. In fact, however, China needs to deal simultaneously with the slowdown in economic growth, make difficult structural adjustments, and absorb the effects of the previous economic stimulus policies. It is in this phase the economic New Normal that the reform is put forward. It means that the reform is closely related with changes of its background. Therefore, the analysis of the reform should be based on its background and it should be guided in accordance with China's new normal.

5.2 Understanding China's Supply Side Reform

To understand the reform, we should, on the basis of the background of China's supply side reform, consider the interpretations from the central government and the analysis based on classical economics and opinions from Chinese experts and scholars. After thinking over the above, we can find that the first objective of the reform is achieving sustained and rapid growth of the economy. And the other objective is, with the cooperation between market and government, supplying production factors effectively, improving the quality of the supply and distributing factors efficiently. To realize the above goals, Chinese government should supply resources through the market, reform the distribution system and provide systemic guarantee. It should improve the supply and production method of production resources. It should also coordinate supply side with demand side and deal with structural problems in its economy so that it can boost productivity and achieve sustainable economic and social progress.

5.2.1 Foci of China's Supply Side Reform

The foci of China's supply side reform include three parts, namely "supply side", "structure" and "reform". "Supply side" means that the reform should focus on regulating supply side and production side and building relevant systems. That is to say, the government should regulate the investing structure and investing methods of factors like labor, capital, and technologies and should regulate the costs and methods of production. It should also construct a market in which production factors are effectively supplied and efficiently distributed, a market that improves the quality of production factors. "Structure" means that it should optimize structures. The Chinese government should, while gaining a foothold by effectively distributing resources and matching supply and demand, improve the structure of production, industries, income allocation and regional development. By doing this, it is able to take advantage of misdistributed resources, improve the efficiency of distribution and achieve coordinated development of the economy and the society. "Reform" means to reform old systems and set up new systems. To optimize structures and to realize effective supply and efficient allocation, the government should overhaul old systems that hinder effective supply, market-based allocation and structural improvement. It should provide systemic guarantee conducive to productivity increase.

The analysis above includes the three foci of China's supply side reform, which are interlocked and complementary to. Governance on supply side and systemic reform are the foundation of supply side reform. The two are able to accelerate adjustment of structure and reform of relevant systems. They also help identify objectives of structure improvement and systemic reform. Thus, they can create a market-led force that helps adjust structures. Structure improvement is a key part of the reform. Through the method, supply and demand can be matched, mis-distributed resources can be utilized and resources can be effectively assigned. It helps improve the quality of factor supply and identify the fundamental missions of systemic innovation and the reform. Reform is the objective of the whole plan. By transforming existing systems that impede productivity and building new systems that boost socialist market economy, the government is able to promote governance on supply side and create an environment favorable for sustained economic and social progress.

5.2.2 *The Significant Objective of China's Supply Side Reform*

The fundamental objectives of the reform are to enhance the quality and efficiency of the supply and allocation of resources and, by boosting productivity, to realize sound and sustained economic development. The quality and efficiency of the supply and allocation of resources refer to the returns that investments in production factors yield in various sectors at a certain technological level. There are four approaches to achieving the above objectives.

First, the government should, by building a market of production factors and supportive systems, explore the values of resources and supply them in an effective way. Second, the government should, by restructuring, promote the flow of resources to sectors with higher efficiency, which means to distribute them reasonably. Third, the government should invigorate enterprises and coordinate supply and demand sides so as to effectively supply production factors. Fourth, the government should build effective supply system of factors and innovative supporting systems, and as a result, improve the quality of the supply of production factors.

5.2.3 *Driving Forces of China's Supply Side Reform*

There are forces, coming from the market and the government, which drive the reform. On one hand, the market should make full use of its decisive role in distributing resources as market-led driving forces are internal powers of China's supply side reform. Chinese government should set up a market system and regulate the prices of resources through market so that the authorities can supply resources effectively and distribute them efficiently. On the other hand, the government should promote the reform and support it through macro-control. In this way, it can restructure the supply of resources and improve the quality of it. The government should change its role and be innovative in administration as government's actions are external forces that drive the reform. By doing so, the government can establish a market and supporting systems, which are conducive to effective supply of resources and efficient distribution. Instead of directly interfering in, it should adjust resource supply and distribution through market-based measures.

5.3 Theoretical System of Political Economics of Chinese Socialism

The proposition of reform in supply side is a signal of the development of political economics of Chinese socialism. In terms of the connotation of structural reform of supply side, it is different from the reform advocated by Western schools of supply economics and different from reforms suggested by structuralism economics. However, it is a comprehensive integrated innovation of Chinese reform practices based on the current development of Chinese economy, and is also an exploratory reform and adjustment of Chinese economy in the new era. In this context, the theoretical basis of structural reform of Chinese supply side belongs to political economics of Chinese socialism.

5.3.1 The Formation and Development of the Political Economics of Chinese Socialism

The political economics of Chinese socialism is a product of the incorporation of Marxist political economics and the practices of Chinese economic development. The Marxist political economics, by profoundly analyzing the law of social conflicts movement and tendency of production mode of capitalism, has revealed the fundamental feature of socialism economic relationships. The political economics of Chinese socialism enriches the theoretical practices of Marxist political economics, and is considered as a Chinese version of Marxist political economics. It is formed as the development of Chinese socialism and will evolve as Chinese socialism develops.

After the foundation of the People's Republic of China, the Communist Party of China (CPC) developed the Socialist Transformation and economic recovery with the help of the basic principles of Marxist political economics. It explored the development method of socialist economy suitable for its national conditions. Basing itself upon exploration, introspection and summary, it put forward a series of unique theories of its own to navigate the development of socialist economy.

Those theories played crucial roles when they were used as guidelines for Chinese economic construction in the past and laid substantial foundations for the political economics of Chinese socialism. For instance, understanding the objective law of the development of the socialist economy requires us to review our successes and failures during the construction of socialism, and requires us to deal with various questions according to the objective law of economy. The only goal of socialist economy is to meet people's demands regarding to materials and culture. To ensure this, the socialist economy should develop continuously. The level of productive forces of socialism determines that the socialist economy is bound to be commodity economy, and the public ownership of the means of production stipulates socialist nature for commodity economy. The exploration of development method of national economy requires joint development of industry and agriculture. Besides, contradictions such as the relationship between major industries and minor industries and the balance and unbalance of national economy should be duly handled.

Since the reform and opening-up policy, CPC has combined the fundamental principles of Marxist political economics with the new practices of the reform and opening-up, continuously enriching and developing the Marxist political economics. It has also established and developed the political economics of Chinese socialism. In October, 1984, the approval of the "Central Committee of the Communist Party of China's Decision on Economic System Reform" officially kicked off the construction of theoretical system of the political economics of Chinese socialism. Deng Xiaoping, then the topmost leader, commented that the decision "reads like the draft of a textbook on political economy that integrated the fundamental tenets of Marxism with the practice of socialism in China".[1] The reform and opening-up policy, coming into effect over the last 30 years, has enriched and developed the theoretical structure of the political economics of Chinese socialism. For example, based on "what is socialism, how to construct socialism", the nature of socialism was put forward to; based on "productive relations must be adapted to the nature of the productivity", reforms of management systems and methods of national economy, which were unsuitable for the development of social productivity, were carried out, and gradually reform theory of economic system was formed. On the basis of the development of open economy, continuous opening up to the outside, implementation of "attracting foreign investment" and "going global" and establishment of system of open economy, the theory of opening to the outside gradually came into being. With socialist economy construction, economy system reform, corporation system reform and reform of income distribution, the socialist market economy theory was optimized step by step.

Since the 18th CPC National Congress, the CPC central committee, led by General Secretary Xi Jinping, has proposed a package of significant strategic thoughts and important theories based on the requirements of practices and focusing

---

[1] *Selected Works of Deng Xiaoping*, Volume Three, Page 83, People's Publishing House, 1993. Originally in Chinese, translated into English by Foreign Language Press.

on propelling the construction of socialist economy with Chinese characteristics. These thoughts and theories have further enriched and optimized the political economics theory of Chinese socialism, and pushed forward the theoretical development of the Chinese political economics into a new stage. For instance, it is a significant feature of the Chinese socialist market economy system to adhere to the leadership of the CPC and empower the Party to play its role in terms of overall planning and coordinating every aspect. For instance, let the government should play its role and enable the market to play its role in resource allocation. For instance, the basic economy system, which takes the public ownership as the main form and allows diverse forms of ownership to develop side by side, is a pillar for Chinese socialist system and is the foundation of the socialist market economy system. For instance, we should fasten the development of open economy and develop it into a higher level and pay more attention to the structural reform of supply side.

Therefore, political economics of Chinese socialism is an economy theory that benefited from continuous optimization as the construction of Chinese socialist economy, and is suitable for Chinese national conditions and characteristics of the time. It has insisted upon the basic principles of the Marxist political economics, and also endowed it with abundant practices. It has not only furnished guidelines for the development of Chinese economy, but also enriched the Marxist political economics and the treasure house of human thoughts.

5.3.2 Theoretical Framework of Socialist Political Economics with Chinese Characteristics

The political economics with Chinese characteristics has been enriched and improved during China's construction of socialist economy, and has become systematic. At present, though China is still in its primary stage of socialism, the construction of socialist economy has entered into a new stage: building moderately prosperous society and propelling the socialist modernization. The theoretical system of the Chinese political economics consists of the following eight aspects:

5.3.2.1 Theory of Developing the Productive Forces: Focus on Adhering to the Emancipation and Development of Productivity to the Largest Extent in Order to Promote Sustainable and Effective Development of Economy

To emancipate and develop the productive forces is the essential requirements and task of socialism. Its core is to improve the resource allocation efficiency, total factor productivity and people's welfare level constantly. The construction of socialist market economy centers on economical construction, taking the scientific outlook on development as the theme, promoting comprehensive, coordinative and sustainable development of economy, realizing effective synergetic development of economic, political, cultural, social and ecological construction. In order to enhance the efficiency and level of labor force, capital and technology, the government should emancipate and develop productivity continuously to furthest fulfil people's ever-growing requirements of materials and culture.

5.3.2.2 Economic System Theory: Focus on Adhering to the Basic Economic System that Upholds the Public Ownership as the Mainstay and Allows Multiple Forms of Ownership to Develop Side by Side

The socialist market economy takes the public ownership as the mainstay and allows the multiple forms of ownership to develop side by side, rather than taking private ownership as its basis. Therefore, public ownership economy should be enhanced and developed unswervingly, and the development of public ownership economy should be encouraged, supported and guided unswervingly. The insistence upon the status of the public ownership and state-owned economy is realized through the development of socialist market economy, which guarantees state enterprises' vital roles in the process of national modernization and safeguards people's common interests. It takes the mixed ownership economy, which develops state-owned capital, collective capital and non-public-owned capital, as its basic economic system.

5.3.2.3 Distribution System Theory: Focus on Adhering to the Basic Distribution System that Sticks to Distribution According to Work as the Mainstay and Allows Diverse Forms of Distribution Coexist

It is the basic requirement for the economic construction of socialist market economy to stick to distribution according to work as the mainstay and allow diverse forms of distribution coexist. The advanced group should be encouraged to advocate efficiency; reasonable income gap should be allowed to arouse everyone's enthusiasm to build up fortune. Also, income polarization should be prevented and social equity should be maintained so as to realize common prosperity step by step and enable people to enjoy benefits of economic development. Distribution according to work as the mainstay should be the major principle while distributing benefits of economic development, and other distribution methods should be employed as a supplement. Efficiency and equity should both be considered in the first and second round of distribution but more attention should be paid to equity in the second round of distribution.

5.3.2.4 Reform Theory: Focus on Adhering to the Optimization of Socialist System Through Reforms and Innovations

Reform is the self-improvement remedy of socialist system and is the impetus to promoting the development of socialism market economy. In conformity with the overall direction of optimizing and developing Chinese socialist system, the government should make efforts to change aspects of productive relationships and superstructure that are unsuitable for productivity development so as to adapt productive relationships and superstructure to the economic foundation and to bring mature, fixed and dynamic economic system. Reforms should be guided by the CPC and the government in a planned way, carried out in steps and in order, so as to realize the self-improvement and development of the socialist system.

5.3.2.5 Open-to-Outside Theory: Focus on Adhering to the Basic National Policy—Opening to the Outside so as to Make Strategy Open and Integrate into Globalization

Opening-to-outside is an importance mechanism and driver for the transformation and development of Chinese economy, and is the inner feature of socialist system. Opening up to the outside is the route that must be taken for the development of socialism. The government should be proactive in opening to the outside and deeply explore the comparative advantages of Chinese economic development in order to coordinate the domestic and international situations. It should take good advantage of domestic and international markets and resources so as to push the development of open economy to a higher level. It should also participate in global governance, promoting the international order to be equal and just, cooperative and win–win. At the same time, efforts should be made to persist in independence, take precautions against various risks and safeguard the national economy.

5.3.2.6 Developing Theory: Focus on Adhering to the Development as the Overriding Principle and Persisting in Development Philosophy of Innovation, Coordination, Green, Open and Sharing

China is still in the primary stage of socialism and its basic contradictions determined that development is the top priority and the overriding principle for its development. The CPC, adhering to focusing on problems, put forward to innovative, coordinative, green, open and sharing development philosophy, which reflects the CPC's new recognition for the law of Chinese socialist development. Innovation comes first in leading development, coordination is the inner requirement of sustainable and sound development, green is the necessity for everlasting development and people's pursuit for better life, opening to the outside is the route that must be taken for national prosperity and sharing is the essential request of Chinese socialism. These five development ideas are regarded respectively as a new understanding of socialist development dynamic law, strategic law, quality law, tactic law and functional law.

5.3.2.7 Methodology: Focus on Adhering to a Developing Road with Chinese Characteristics of New Industrialization, Information-Based, Urbanization and Agricultural Modernization

In this new stage of socialist economic development, China should focus on economic construction, fasten the scientific development, and stick to the road with Chinese characteristics of new industrialization, information-based, urbanization, agricultural modernization. It should also promote the deep integration of information and industry, try to bring positive interaction between industrialization and urbanization, and coordinate the urbanization with agricultural modernization. It should also try to bring synergetic development for industrialization, information, urbanization and agricultural modernization, amplify the development mechanism of urban-rural integration, and to bring new urban-rural relationship. Efforts should also be made to promote agriculture through industry, develop rural places through agriculture, and advocate mutual benefit of industry and agriculture. By doing so, the broad masses of people can be exposed to modernization and enjoy the fruits of its achievements.

5.3.2.8 Theory of Combination of Socialism with Market Economy: Focus on Adhering to Combining the Socialist Market Economy with Basic Institutions of Socialism

The socialist market economy should reflect the features and requirements of basic institutions of socialism. In order to stick to the reform direction of socialist market economy, China should concentrate its efforts on the integration of basic institutions of socialism with market economy and exploit their advantages to the full. To make sure that the market plays the determining role during resource allocation and make sure that the government plays its role in a better way, are two strategies forming an organic unity instead of mutually negative. Thus, efforts should be expended to ensure the organic unity of the functions of both the market and the government so as to create a mutually complementing, coordinating and promoting.

5.4 The Political Economics of Chinese Socialism and Reform of the Supply Side

The political economics of Chinese socialism came into being and developed through Chinese practices of socialist economic development. In reviewing those practices and the theoretical development of the political economics, it is not hard to find that during the construction of Chinese socialist market economy, reforms concerning the supply side were an integral part of Chinese socialist political economics. And China has been exploring reforms of the supply side ever since it advocated market economy.

5.4.1 Reform of the Supply Side Regarding Productive Factors

Since the reform and opening-up, China has been putting more efforts on reforms regarding land, labor force and technology innovation of the supply side.

5.4.1.1 Reform Regarding the Factor of Land

The household contract responsibility system with remuneration linked to output, an agrarian reform introduced since the 1970s, is a major sign of Chinese reforms regarding the factor of land, other signs include the formation of dual system of land system, land transfer and reform of land circulation system. In 1979, China began to explore and implement the rural land contract system, which served to promote the reform of rural land system. The system features the practice where the land was contracted out to individual households responsible for operation and management, representing the core of the basic managing system in rural area. Ever since then, the central government has passed laws, regulations and policies to stabilize contracting relationship. On the premise of retaining collective ownership of land, it has specified that the land use of contractors is protected by laws, which has kindled farmers' enthusiasm for production. In 1982, China established the dual system of land for urban and rural areas by stipulating that land in the urban area was owned by the state and land in rural and suburban area was owned collectively. In 1990, state-owned land in urban area was allowed to be transferred and circulated. From 1993 onwards, China has been experimenting step by step on the paid transfer of land contract.

5.4.1.2 Reform Regarding the Factor of Labor

The objective of the reform regarding to labor force in China was to loosen the tight control over the labor force in the period of planned economy, giving it full play in resource allocation, so as to improve economic quality and market efficiency and strengthen the protection of the rights of laborers. The main components of reform regarding the factor of labor are labor force training, employment, social security and income distribution etc. Since 1979, China has loosened its control over the flow of new labor force, which gave birth to the labor force market. In 1993, China implemented labor contract system with great efforts. All economic organizations, including state enterprises put labor contract system into practice, leading to constantly improvement of marketization of labor force in China. At the same time, to solve problems of laid-off employees due to market allocation of labor, China has gradually established the social security system for labor, and introduced policies which encouraged re-employment, such as career training and setting up service center for re-employment. Since 2002, China has seen more frequent flow of labor force, and it has carried out effective practices of labor force market reform and issued employment promotion policy, which combined to bring out a better labor force market mechanism.

5.4.1.3 Reform Regarding the Factor of Technology

Since the reform and opening-up, China has been putting more and more attention on technology innovation. Policies to promote technology innovation became more specified and clear-cut with its focus on the construction of an environment favorable for innovation. They also advocated the industrialization of science and technology and the ability of independent innovation. For instance, since 1985, taking science and technology system as the focus of technological innovation, China has provided the institutional and social environment for technology innovation; in 1986, the State Scientific and Technological Commission promulgated the mid- and long-term program, highlighting the requirements that science and technology must serve economic development, the technological innovation system must be set up, and, and we should tighten the relationship between science and production on the basis of funding more in scientific research; in 2006, China has taken the promotion of self-innovative ability as the core step for structure adjustment, method transformation and competitiveness improvement. With enterprises being the mainstay and synergy of production, study, research and practice being the feature of technology innovation, the national innovative system is now taking shape.

5.4.1.4 Reform Regarding the Factor of Capital

Reform regarding the factor of capital in China mainly focuses on interest rate marketization. Since January 1st, 1994, China has put foreign exchange settlement into practice and abolished the system of foreign exchange earnings sharing. It has also carried out banking foreign exchange sales system and rescinded dual foreign exchange rate. It merged listed RMB rate of exchange and price of foreign exchange swap market, allowed RMB to be exchanged in current account. China established inter-bank foreign exchange market, improved mechanism of foreign exchange formation and maintained reasonable and stable RMB exchange rate.

5.4.2 Supply Side Reform Aimed at Enterprise Production

While carrying out reforms of productive resources, China is equally engaged in reforms of enterprises.

5.4.2.1 Reform Regarding State Enterprises

Reforms of state enterprises can be divided into two phases. Prior to the 14th National Congress of the CPC, the first phase focusing on the adjustment of policies, dealt with the decentralization of powers and transfer of profits, the system of contracted responsibility and separation of two powers[2]; The second phase was after the 14th National Congress of the CPC. The approval of *Decision*[3] in the third plenary session of the 14th Central Committee of the CPC marked the beginning of the property right reform of the state enterprises reform. Since 2013 when the *Decision of the Central Committee of the CPC on Several Major Issues concerning Comprehensively Deepening Reforms* proposed that reforms of state enterprises would focus on "the development of mixed-ownership economy" in the next step. In the above *Decision*, all kinds of capitals were encouraged to participate in the mixed ownership reform of state enterprises. Besides, it also made specific arrangements on perfecting the mechanisms of enterprise governance, establishing operating rules in compliance with laws and regulations and building favorable environment and organizations.

5.4.2.2 Reform Regarding Enterprise Income Tax

In 1983, state enterprises carried out a two-step reform of "tax payments instead of profit deliveries to the state". The State charged state enterprises for income tax and charged medium and large state enterprises for regulatory taxes. In the 1990s, China

---

[2]The two powers refer to the ownership and control.

[3]The *Decision* refers to *Decision of the Central Committee of the Communist Party of China on Some Issues concerning the Establishment of the Socialist Market Economy.*

launched consolidated tax system for domestic and foreign capital enterprises. The unified tax system and generally reduced burden level of income tax greatly generated the investment enthusiasm. Preliminary results were achieved right in the year when the policy was introduced. In 1994, China launched a reform on enterprise income tax through replacing the enterprise income tax, the income tax of collective enterprises and the income tax of private enterprises with the unified income tax of domestic capital enterprise. Since China used to implement different taxes and tax rates for enterprises with different ownerships, the situation got changed after that. In 2011, China began piloting in some regions "the added-value tax to substitute the business tax" for transportation industry and modern service industry. This reduced the enterprise tax burden. In August, 2013, China began to charge the added-value tax instead of business tax nationwide.

Thus, it can be seen that reforms on supply side in the course of establishing market economy system in China are an integral part of the theory of political economics of socialism with Chinese characteristics. They also represent China's great explorations in attempting to transform the planned economy system into Chinese socialist market economy system. To attain this goal, the reforms have been encouraging growth increment and sporadic, only focusing on building resource elements markets of labor force, capital and technology etc. and constructing the mechanism of parts of resource allocation. However, we need to put more overall and systematic consideration into the institutional reforms on finance and taxation, enterprise system and social security system.

5.5 Theoretical Logic of Chinese New Supply Economics Theory

Based on the comprehensive analysis of the long period of world economy and phase characteristics of Chinese development and their interactions, the Central Committee of the CPC, led by the General Secretary Xi Jinping, has put forward a strategic thought which is to strengthen structural reforms regarding the supply side. Compared to previous supply side reform launched in the construction of China's socialist market economic system, they are more systematic and comprehensive, targeted at the overall performance. Considered as theoretical innovations, supply side structural reforms present a theoretical framework in the context of Chinese New Normal. Innovations and practices of China's new supply economy is an exploratory reform and adjustment in the new phase of China's socialist economy construction and is an important component of the political economics of socialism with Chinese characteristics.

5.5.1 *The Goal of Structural Reform of Supply Side Is to Realize Efficient and Sustainable Growth*

In the sight of the theoretical basis of structural reforms of supply side, the goal of the reform is to emancipate and develop productive force to the largest possible extent, to improve the quality and efficiency of economic growth and to enhance the continuous driving force on the premise of stabilizing and expanding total social demand. The goal of the reform can be divided into different aspects. First, to release potential and vitality of economic growth. Seen from theory, economic growth generally refers to the increase of products and total amount of labor which is equal to the increment of social wealth. To release the potential of economic growth requires efficient supply of labor force, capital, institution and innovation and giving these resource elements full play. Moreover, we need to promote the value conversion efficiency of productive factors. With a view to releasing economic growth vitality we need to strengthen the liberation of development impetus of market players such as enterprises. With the help of loosening control of start-up businesses, reducing tax cost, we could strengthen the enterprises' market competitiveness and profitability. Second, to improve the quality and efficiency of economy development. To improve the quality and efficiency, we need to promote the high efficiency and sharing of economy development. With effective supply, we could fulfil people's increasing material and cultural needs and meet with the people's upgrading consumption requirements so as to realize the effective match between supply and demand. Third, to realize the harmonious development and sustainable growth. On basis of the adjustment and optimization of productive structure, we could promote the coordination between industrial development and regional development; By virtue of technological innovation, we could boost the efficiency of economic development. By means of transforming development modes, we could release the social effects of achievements scored in economic development, so as to benefit people's livelihood; Through the coordination between human and nature, we could realize sustainable development of economy, society, ecology and environment.

5.5.2 *The Realization of Efficient and Sustainable Growth Calls for the Synergy of Structural Reform of Supply Side and Management of Demand Side*

The structural reform of supply side can be seen as a process. Basing itself on the old system rather than overturning it, it sets off to reform crucial systems, the defects of which have given rise to severe economic problems or crises. That is to say, the reform aims at upgrading the structure of the present system.

It is noteworthy that with its emphasis laid on a medium and long term construction of system, the reform will restructure the old system so as to bring out a sound development of economy. On the account of its nature of medium and long term, the reform should be pushed through in synergy with the management of the demand side. On one hand, we should give full play to the demand side for its effects of stabilizing and expanding total demand, specifically for its positive role in speeding up economic recovery, stabilizing employment and ameliorating people's livelihood so that to create opportunities for structural reform of the supply side. On the other hand, the management of demand side can serve as a locomotive for the reform of supply side. For instance, through optimizing the consumption environment and speeding up the consumer market and consumption system reform, the government will be able to promote the consumption upgrading so as to stimulate consumption needs, encourage the innovation of supply and form an efficient match between new demand and new supply; on the basis of the system reform of investment and financing, the government can improve the investment efficiency and make up for social weaknesses for the purpose of stimulating and creating more space for the supply of product or service.

5.5.3 Endogenous Variables of Structural Reform of the Supply Side Serves as the Inner Motive for Continuous Growth; The Mechanism Is to Realize the Maximum Efficiency of Production Factors

Endogenous variables of structural reform of the supply side refer to those variables directly pushing forward the liberation and the development of productive as well as realizing a new supply of elements. The reform of supply side requires the reinforcement of productivity of elements, the improvement of efficiency of resource allocation and the optimization of element resource efficiency.

5.5.3.1 The Promotion of Total Factor Productivity

The promotion of total factor productivity refers to the improvement of output efficiency of productive factors such as labor force, capital and technology. The improvement of output efficiency of labor force, capital and technology serve as the locomotive and baseline for the structural reform of the supply side as well as the foundation to liberate and develop productive forces. Major approaches to improving the output efficiency of labor force, capital and technology include: first, to optimize factor market system and establish factor market function, and to speed up the opening of various factors market so as to found set up a unified market system; second, to establish law-oriented, regulation-oriented and clear management system in order to improve participation rate of labor force, saving ratio and improve the structure of labor force and capital allocation; third, to improve technology and activate the growth potential of resource factors; fourth, to implement the strategy of facilitate development by innovation so as to promote the supply quality of labor force, capital and technology and to push the industrial stride forward from medium and low end to medium and high end.

5.5.3.2 The Promotion of Resource Allocation Efficiency

The promotion of resource allocation efficiency is achieved by promoting the rational flow of resource elements in different production areas, by adopting a scientific configuration and by improving the output efficiency of resources. This is an important embodiment of the decisive role of the market in allocating resources in the supply side structural reform. It is also the source of fully exploring resources and utilization efficiency, of releasing the vitality of economic development, and of maintaining the development of sustainable economy. The major approaches are: promoting the adjustment of production structure, strengthening the release of internal resources of different industrial structure and reconfiguration, and realizing re-exploration of resources value, for example to impel the "survival of the fittest" mechanism in industry with excessive production capacity; promoting the primary role of the enterprise in market to realize the autonomous management of enterprise, lower down system transaction costs, and make the enterprise flow in and out in a more convenient and more efficient manner. The case in point would be the lower-down of the threshold for enterprises' market entry and the removal of the barriers to exit.

5.5.4 With Their Mechanism to Seek for the Maximum Efficiency of Economic Development, Exogenous Variables (Institution, Structure and New Supply of Policy) of Structural Reform of the Supply Side Are the External Locomotive of Continuous Growth

Exogenous variables of structural reform of the supply side denote the institutional, structural, and policy-based arrangements that serve to guarantee, promote, liberate and develop productivity. Structure reform of the supply side needs the realization of new supply in terms of institution, structure and policy, so as to safeguard effective supply of resource factors and optimize the allocation of market, and further to realize continuous improvement of economic growth efficiency.

5.5.4.1 New Supply of Institution

The steady implementation of structural reform of the supply side requires the promotion of government function transformation, as well as the promotion of the reform of administrative system. To achieve this, we have to throw off the shackles that impede the display of market function or system and eradicate the mechanism that distorts the structure. Rather, we should strengthen the structural reform and implement the related institutional arrangement. It is mainly reflected in the following three aspects: first, to improve the system of market that can effectively supply resource elements, promote the free flow of resource elements, reasonable pricing, fair trade, and the rights and interests' protection system of the market. Second, to perfect the market system that effectively allocate the resource elements namely, to strengthen enterprise's main body status in the resource allocation, enhance the enterprise's vitality of competition, and to release the enterprise innovation power of the market system. Third, to remove the original institutional barriers that restrict the resources market supply and allocation, to improve the support of the construction of market economic system, and to strengthen the innovation in the management mode and concept. A case in point would be the promotion of the household registration system in the construction of labor factor market, and the reform of the social security system; meanwhile, efforts should be made to promote the reform of land system in the construction of the land factor market etc.

5.5.4.2 New Supply of Structure

Structural reform is a reform which is oriented towards throwing off the shackles of the structural and institutional contradiction that hinder the economic transformation and upgrading. Actually, it is the key to boosting economic transformation and upgrading. Structure optimization adjustment is an important part of the supply side structural reform. It also creates space for supply side structural reforms. In its course of long-term development, China has spawned various structural contradictions that exist between investment and consumption, between investment and economic growth impetus, and between investment and the lagging-behind of service industry and structural problems faced by the substantial economy. There are three reasons for these structural contradictions. First, the market fragmentation of resource factors leads to price mechanism failure of resource factors market, which in turn makes the mismatch of resource factors. Second, the slow pace of China's transformation leads to the low level of resource allocation and difficulty in effectively improving the supply quality. Third, unbalanced industrial development leads to out-of-balance of productivity allocation in different industrial areas, which makes it hard for resource factors supply to drive the demand. Structure supply, by aiming at resolving various structural contradictions in the current economic and social development, focuses on releasing the value of mismatched resource factors through structure optimization and increasing the dragging force of the demand of resource supply so as to further promote the effective supply of resource factors and improve the allocation efficiency.

5.5.4.3 New Supply of Policy

In order to ensure the supply side structural reform's role in resolving the short-term problems, adjusting and optimizing the long-term structure and system construction. We need to form an overall coordination, carry out policies in an orderly and reciprocal manner. To achieve it, it is essential to provide policy support for the structural reform of the supply side from the macro, meso and micro level and social level. First, in terms of macro level, with the help of the formation of scientific fiscal policy and monetary policy, we need to promote the basic stability of the social total supply and total demand and provide loose environment for supply side structural reforms. Second, in terms of the meso level, we need to strengthen the guide of industrial development and structural adjustment and to enhance the organic conversion between the increment and stock. Third, in terms of the micro level, we need to strengthen the enterprise market main body status and to reduce the enterprise production and operation cost and market transaction cost, encourage innovation, and stimulate enterprises to create new supply. Fourth, as for the social level, we need to strengthen the subject status of the government in public service supply, enhance and assure people's livelihood, intensify our efforts to construct public service platform and our support of the market rules. Fifth, we need to carry out a policy to tackle the prominent contradictions and the key problems present in the structural reform of the supply side in order to guard against risks. Meanwhile, efforts should also be expanded to strengthen the policy supply, dissolve the risks and respond to the challenges facing the reform.

5.5.5 The Structural Reform of the Supply Side Should Be Based on New Development Ideas, and Give Decisive Play to Market and Allow the Government to Play Its Role Better

Five major ideas, namely innovation, harmony, green, open, and sharing are CPC's new understanding of the law governing socialist development. China's socialist economic construction needs the correct understanding and accurate grasp and abide by the laws of development. The basic method to realize efficient and sustainable growth is to improve the efficiency of resource factors and efficiency of economic development, to guard against various risks at the same time. In so doing so, we need to make sure that the market plays a decisive role and give better play to the government in its role of performing various functions.

The problems that the structural reform of the supply side needs to resolve are intertwined and correlative, thus are complex in nature. It is need to strengthen the guidance of five development ideas. First, seen from the perspective of innovation, innovation represents the core of the structural reform of the supply side, whether it concerns the institutional reform, structural optimization or the upgrading of factors, is innovation. The economic development should shift its focus from the increase of material consumption to the improvement of science and technology and factor efficiency. Second, in sight of coordination, supply side structural reform is a systematic project. We need to coordinate fiscal and taxation reform, state enterprise reform, financial reform, the household registration reform and other reforms. Efforts should also be made to coordinate the relationship between expanding aggregate demand and reducing excessive capacity and inventory, deleveraging, cost reduction, and the compensation of drawbacks. Third, in light of concept of green environment, we need to implement an economic development model which focuses on the low carbon cycle and reduction. We need to be aware that this practice is helpful in redressing the distorted allocation of the ecological environment, improving the allocation efficiency of capital, labor and other factors, digesting excessive capacity, and establishing a virtuous circle of supply and demand. Fourth, in view of the idea of opening-up, the reform of the supply side based on the open idea will establish a new pattern of reform development, improve international trades and make better investment rules. In so doing can we establish a supply system which enables Chinese economy to integrate with the world economy and create a win–win situation. Fifth, from the perspective of the idea of sharing, the structural reform of the supply side will pay more attention to the equity of institution supply, better the distribution and social security systems, enhance the sharing mechanism and offer people an opportunity to the access to the material achievements scored in economic and social development (Fig. 5.1).

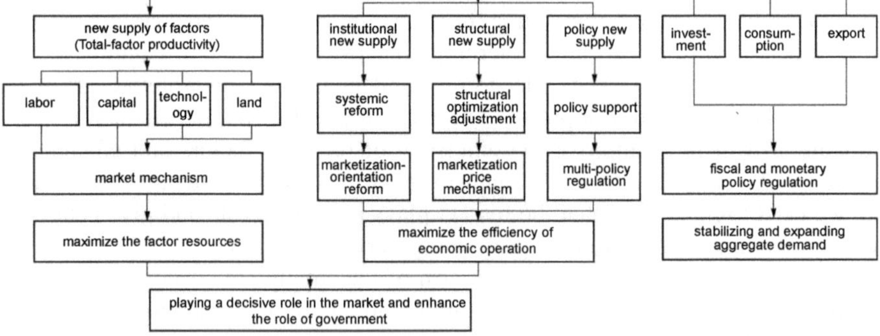

Fig. 5.1 The Logic and Theory of China's New Supply-Side Reform

5.6 Strategic Approach of Chinese Structural Reform of the Supply Side

On the basis of the theoretical and logic thinking of China's structural reform which is a systematic project, it is needed to account for all the possible risks and challenges. In order to choose the right strategic path, we need to proceed to make overall considerations, focus our efforts upon key issues, and forge ahead in an orderly manner.

5.6.1 The Method of the Structural Reform of the Supply Side

Three pairs of relations should be correctly dealt with during the process of structural reform, for they are important bases for China's implementation of the reform.

5.6.1.1 The Relation Between Development, Reform and Stability

The objective of the supply side structural reform is to resolve the problems arising during the economic development, enhance economic development dynamism and vitality. Therefore, the structural reform of supply side should not be carried out for the reform per se. Rather, it should take the economic development as the top priority. The liberation and development of the productive forces should be considered as important criteria against which reform measures and results are judged. At the same time, the supply side structural reform will inevitably lead to structural adjustment, resulting in the value revaluation and flow of resource factors. All these will lead to a series of problems such as unemployment, corporate restructuring, and further bring certain impacts upon economic and social stability. Therefore, the supply side structural reform must be supported by corresponding social security system construction, and place stability in the foremost position. We should also strengthen the policy in its role of underpinning, maintain the stability of the society and economy, so as to create a stable economic and social environment favorable for the supply side structural reform.

5.6.1.2 The Relation Between Government and Market Functions

Supply side structural reform, as an integral part of the political economy of socialism with Chinese characteristics, must further strengthen the construction of market mechanism, give full play to the market in its determining role of efficiently supplying resource elements, improving quality and allocating resources in an efficient manner. At the same time, in carrying out the structural reform of the supply side, we also need to strengthen the government's role in the reform of the system, improve the government's supporting and safeguarding function in institutional reform and macro-control, so as to promote the efficiency of the market mechanism. We maintain that to enhance the propelling role of the government and the driving role of the market is not only the inherent nature of the political economy of socialism with Chinese characteristics, but also an objective need for pushing forward the structural reform of the supply side. Therefore, it is needed to deal with the relationship between the government promotion and market driving duly. The government's push cannot directly replace the market allocation. Instead, the government power should be regulated in accordance with the market economy rule and the direction of the market-oriented reform so as to strengthen the transformation of government function and administrative management method. The promoting or regulating policies of government reform should be applied to elements, enterprises and other market main bodies, so that we can realize the organic integration of indirect guiding function of the government and direct market-driven function.

5.6.1.3 The Relation Between Short-Term Policy Regulation and Medium and Long-Term Institutional Innovation

The supply side structural reform emphasizes a long-term system innovation process. But the reform will not overturn the original system. On the contrary, it will be based on the original system. On the basis of reforms on key institutional defects of the original system which has led to serious economic problems or crisis, we aim to carry out related system construction and improvement step by step. In addition, we need to establish institutional system which is conducive both to releasing the economic development dynamism and vigor and to promoting sustainable economic growth. Therefore, supply side structural reform represents a process. It needs to focus on policy guidance which is problem-oriented, to provide policy supply guarantee for reform, and to win time and pave the way for the medium and long term structural reform. Meanwhile, we need to highlight the medium and long term system construction which is innovation system-oriented, and to set up the system of social market economy with Chinese characteristics. Such short-term policy and long-term reform should complement each other to the extent that the guidance of short-term policies should be incorporated into the basic requirements of the construction of the medium and long term system while the medium and long term system construction should in turn pay attention to the immediate effect of short-term policies.

5.6.2 *Strategic Path of Chinese Structural Reform of the Supply Side*

Based on the connotation of structural reform of the supply side and in accordance with the theoretical logic and idea of the supply side structural reform, the Chinese supply side structural reform should be implemented in terms of maximizing the efficiency of resources allocation and economic efficiency.

5.6.2.1 To Improve the Total Factor Productivity Through New Supply of Factors and Transform the Factor-Driven Mode to the Innovation-Driven One

The promotion of productivity of labor, capital, technology and other production resource factors is the locomotive of the supply side structural reform. Supply side structural reform should be focused on improving supply efficiency and quality of productive resources, giving full play to the role of innovation in promoting resource productivity. First, to promote the transformation of demographic dividend to talent dividend and to improve China's personnel capital advantage. By building a unified labor market, we can reduce the free movement cost of labor, promote the workforce flows in an orderly way in urban and rural areas, between enterprises, universities and research institutions so as to explore supply potential of labor force. We should shift the strategy of population from growth control to optimizing population quality, strengthen the education training and improve labor quality steadily. Second, to kindle innovation vigor, and promote the innovation of technology supply. We should proactively promote the "double innovation" in an effort to stimulate the microeconomic innovation and entrepreneurship activities. We should build the environment and incentive mechanism for science and technology innovation, speed up developing innovative culture, and establish a social atmosphere that is conducive to innovation. Third, to speed up the implementation of the financial sector reforms and improve capital efficiency. We should accelerate the establishment of multi-level financial system, diversified organizational system and three-dimensional service system which match with the real economy and realize effective integration of various financial resources. We should make efforts to accelerate the reform of the financial market and reduce the cost of capital. Fourth, to steadily push forward the land reform and to establish reasonable and efficient land circulation system.

5.6.2.2 To Deepen the Reform of Market Economic System Through New Supply of Institution, and Transform the Mode from Government Regulation to Market Allocation

To realize effective supply of resources, improve the quality and allocate resources with high efficiency, we need to give market its prevailing role in resource allocation. The government function transformation should also be strengthened. The reform of the administrative system should be deepened and reduce the government's intervention of market mechanism should be kept down. First, the reform of the market mechanism should go deeper. A new system with activating function for the market should be put in place. Market barriers should be removed, and a market environment which is conducive to the development of innovation should be created. So should be the market mechanism which is conducive to the enterprise independent operation and the fair competition, and a modern market system which is advantageous to the free flow and equal exchange of commodities and factors. Second, to speed up the transformation of government function, optimize the distribution of the functions of government institutions, increase the efficiency of the government and stimulate the market vitality and social creativity. Third, to promote the reform of state enterprises and to develop a mixed sector of the economy. We should improve the management system for state-owned assets and encourage private capital to participate in state enterprise reform. The modern enterprise system should be bettered to promote property rights protection under the rule of law, so as to regulate the operation, to foster fair competition and to enhance the vitality of enterprises. Fourth, to improve the system of open environment and to promote the market mechanism to be in line with international standards. With the help of opening-up, the government can impel the market mechanism reform, and with the help of open system reform, it can also develop the international market of product.

5.6.2.3 To Conduct Economic Structure Adjustment Through New Supply of Structure so as to Transform the Extensive Economic Mode to Intensive Economic One

The industrial structure which takes productivity configuration as the core, to a certain extent, affects the factor supply structure, regional development structure and energy utilization structure. Therefore, supply side structural reform should strengthen the adjustment of industrial structure, so as to develop new economic drivers and expand the effective supply and supply of medium and high-end through industrial restructuring. Meanwhile, we should advance the adjustment of inventory, reduce and eliminate invalid supply and low-end supplies, transform and upgrade traditional industries of comparative advantages. First, to speed up the development of emerging industries. Based on the reform of monopoly areas, the government will break mechanism constraints of service systems. By means of technical innovation and business model innovation, it can speed up the growth of emerging industry. Second, to accelerate the technology transformation, upgrade the traditional industry, and promote product innovation so as to accord the traditional products the quality to meet with the requirements of consumption upgrade trend. Third, to promote reasonable layout of industry in different areas, and promote urban and rural structure and regional structure optimization. For example, we can conduct territory development planning for the main body function and guide a rational layout of industry in different regions. Fourth, to promote the transformation of industrial production mode of industry so as to achieve a low carbon, green and clean development and to build a circular economy and green economy.

5.6.2.4 To Resolve Prominent Contradictions and Key Problems During the Development, Through New Supply of Policy so as to Create a Development Environment for the Supply Side Structural Reform

Supply side structural reform is a medium and long term process, but the emergence of prominent contradictions and key problems in the short-term economic development pose challenges and risks for the supply side structural reform to a certain extent, can even hamper the implementation of the reform. Therefore, we need to focus our efforts upon resolving the problems and addressing the conflicts that occur during the short-term economic development in order to expand space and build a favorable environment for the implementation of the reform. For instance, efforts should be made to tackle particularly the excessive capacity, promote the enterprise merger and reorganization, and release the mismatched production resource factors. The inventories of the unsold homes should be destocked effectively to secure a sound development of the real estate industry; the negative impact of the fluctuation of real estate industry upon the economy should be cushioned; the financial risks should be defused effectively, while the risks incurred by the local government debt, such as bad bank loans and enterprises' high debt risk should be warded off as well in an effort to prevent the systemic risks from happening.

5.6.2.5 To Strengthen the Effective Synergy and Comprehensive Employment of Reform of the Supply Side and Demand Side so as to Win Strategic Opportunity for the Supply Side Structural Reform

Supply side structural reforms should not just be carried out for the sole purpose of solving the problem of insufficient supply, more importantly, it should solve the problem of mismatch between supply and demand. Thus, supply side structural reform needs to be undertaken on "both the sides of supply and demand". Through effective demand side management, we can realize the moderate expansion of economic growth, ensure the overall stability of the economy and employment situation so as to provide a tolerant and easy environment for the supply side structural reform, and to bring forth a period of strategic opportunities. At the same time, through the improvement of consumption environment, we will be able to accelerate the reform of the consumer market and consumption system, to promote consumption upgrading and enable effective release for new consumer demands, so as to boost supply innovation and make the new demand and supply match effectively. Through the investment and financing system reform, investment efficiency can be elevated, a greater supply space for product or service will be activated and built. Through the foreign trade structure optimization, we can make breakthroughs in the production and investment of new supply products. In general, it is essential to strengthen the effective synergy between the reform of the supply side and the demand management, so as to protect and promote the structural reform of the supply side with a high efficiency.

Chapter 6
Structural Reform of the Supply Side and Endogenous Variables (New Supply of Factors)

The purpose of the supply side structural reform is to redress the mismatch between supply structure and demand structure and to correct the distorted factors allocation. It can further solve the problem that arises as the effective supply cannot adapt itself to changes of market demand, striking an balance between the supply and demand side on a higher level; To attain it, we need to assure the decisive role of the market in resources allocation, revitalize the excessive labor, capital, land and other production factors due to the excessive capacity so as to channel the latter from low efficient industries to high efficient ones, from excess industry to industries in high market demand. Our objective is to realize the resource optimization and reallocation, to improve the total factor productivity and to achieve a long-term sustainable economic growth.

6.1 Total Factor Productivity and Economic Growth

Macroeconomics research deals primarily with the analysis of the economic growth source. Since China's reform and opening-up, it has experienced a rapid growth phase, with its average annual growth rate standing at 9.9%, and its economic aggregate reached 40 trillion RMB Yuan in 2010 when it exceeded Japan to have become the world's second largest economic entity. At present, China's economic development has stepped into New Normal, with its gear of growth shifted. The result shows that the traditional source of power, which has served to support the growth over a long span has been weakened. From the point of the world economic history, rapid economic growth is known to be one of the "catching-up" phenomena of a particular stage. In 2014, for example, against the backdrop of the world economy's average growth rate of 2.5% of, the growth rate of countries with low-income stood at 6.3%, whereas for countries with upper middle income, the rate was 4.5% and merely 1.7% for high income countries. For countries still in the lower stage of development, the gap with advanced countries in technology and

L. Xiao, *New Supply Side Economics*, DOI 10.1007/978-981-10-4639-1_6

productivity entails late-development advantages. Unlike the latter, the former can rely on capital, land and labor input to gain the desired economic growth. This has been the case for China's long-term growth. For countries in higher stage of economic development, the economic growth must be achieved by the improvement of total factor productivity. So, stepping into the new phase of development, China has to be keenly aware that the economic growth can no longer rely upon the past practice of injecting inputs. Instead, it has to increase its total factor productivity rate as a major contributor to its economic growth, if it is to achieve a sustained and rapid economic growth in the next stage.

6.1.1 Evaluation of Total Factor Productivity

As an important tool to analyze the source of economic growth, total factor productivity is also an important standard against which the government formulates the policy for the future long-term sustainable growth. First, the evaluation of the total factor productivity is conducive to the economic growth source analysis. That is to say, it can be used to analyze various factors' contrition (inputs growth, technological progress and capacity realization, etc.) to economic growth. Thus, it allows the government to distinguish between input-type growth and efficiency-type growth, further confirming the sustainability of economic growth. Second, the evaluation of total factor productivity is the foundation of policy formulation and evaluation of long-term sustainable growth. Specifically, through the comparison of the contribution of the total factor productivity with that of the factor inputs to the economic growth, the government can make sure whether the economic policy should set as the priority the increase of total demand or the adjustment of the economic structure with the promotion of technological progress.

6.1.1.1 Measurement Method

Solow put forward the concept of total factor productivity (TFP), the measurement of total factor productivity has been developed and expanded continuously. Moreover, As Krugman called into question the so-called "East Asian growth miracle" and the breakout of Southeast Asian economic crisis in 1997, total factor productivity and sustainable economic growth have provoked a heated study and debate among the domestic scholars. At present, the measurement methods of the total factor productivity generally fall into two categories: parameter method and nonparametric method. The former includes the Solow's Residual method, Latent variable Approach and Frontier Production Function method.

Solow's residual method is used here. The equation below (in Cobb–Douglas form) represents total output (Y_t) as a function of total-factor productivity (A), capital input (K_t), labor input (L_t), and the two inputs' respective shares of output (α and β are the capital input share of contribution for K and L respectively):

$$Y_t = AK_t^{\alpha} L_t \beta_t$$

Take the natural logarithm on both sides:

$$\ln(Y_t) = \ln(A) + \alpha\ln(K_t) + \beta\ln(L_t) + \varepsilon_t \quad (6.1)$$

where ε is error term. This formulation assumes that returns to scale are invariable, which means α + β = 1. The regression equation is as follows

$$\ln(Y_t/L_t) = \ln(A) + \alpha\ln(K_t/L_t) + \varepsilon_t \quad (6.2)$$

Using OLS (ordinary least squares), we can estimate the respective values of α and β. Substituting them into the above equation, we can get the growth rate of total factor productivity can be concluded.

6.1.1.2 Variables Selection

(1) Capital stock. Capital stock is produced by using the perpetual inventory method (PIM). The equation is as follows:

$$K_t = (1 - \delta)\, K_{t-1} + I_t \quad (6.3)$$

The following four key variables need to be identified when the perpetual inventory method is used: capital stock of the base period, for which we select the year of 1978 capital stock as period's starting point; fixed capital investment, which is derived from *China Statistical Yearbook* providing us with the whole society fixed capital investment; price index, for which we use the fixed asset prices in 1978 as the base year; and depreciation rate, for which we use Guo Qingwang's (2005) calculating method.

(2) Labor force. Our labor force data is taken from *China Statistical Yearbook.* We use the number of total employment labor to measure labor inputs (Fig. 6.1).

It can be seen from the above Table 6.1 that since the reform and opening-up, capital stock growth is increasing very fast from 2000 to 2010, which conforms to China's investment-driven growth strategy. The growth of labor factors is relatively stable, since the result is produced simply by computation.

6.1.1.3 Results Analysis

By means of the above-mentioned method, we measured China's total factor productivity growth rate since 1978, and compare it with the findings of Guo

Fig. 6.1 Analysis of the growth rate of China's factor input and real output from 1978 to 2014

Qingwang and Jia Junxue (2005). As shown in Table 6.2, our result is analogous to those of other scholars. We put forward the following points after examining the growth rate of total factor productivity in different years:

(1) Generally, before 1993, China's factor productivity growth rate rises and falls alternatively with high and frequent amplitude of fluctuation. The reason for it is that China's economic system and market before 1993 underwent drastic and frequent changes, which inevitably led to the same effects in total factor productivity growth. A case in point would be the early period of the reform and opening-up (1979–1984) when the household contract responsibility system and state enterprises' decentralization of power and transfer of profits made the productivity gain great liberation and promoted the rapid growth of total factor productivity. But with the acceleration of the reform and opening-up, some deep contradictions of institutions appeared gradually, and brought limits for the total factor productivity growth.
(2) Since 1993, China's total factor productivity growth rate has shown a downward trend year by year. This decline trend did not cease until 2000 when it began going upward on a yearly basis. The reason for it is that since 1993, with the gradually cooling of macro-economy and the deflation breakout in 1998, there has appeared in the Chinese economy excessive production capacity. The state enterprises' staff downsizing and over deepening of capital exacerbated the problem of low level use of the labor force. To worsen it, the long-term low level of public spending on education and scientific research expenditure and the intensified social conflicts combined to lead to the continuous decline of total factor productivity growth rate. The year 2000 marked the turning point when the government put in place an active fiscal policy, and the state began to reap benefits from its previous expenditure on the construction of infrastructure and public education. With the macro economy gradually faring well, the total factor productivity growth has been on the rise year by year (Fig. 6.2).

Table 6.1 Population by educational attainment and region

Region	No schooling (%)	Primary school (%)	Junior secondary school (%)	Senior secondary school (%)	College and higher level (%)
China	2.09	15.27	34.47	24.84	23.33
Beijing	1.06	7.76	25.71	21.90	43.56
Tianjin	2.23	12.39	31.89	26.56	26.92
Hebei	2.29	18.05	39.84	22.76	17.07
Shanxi	1.25	13.35	32.72	31.72	20.96
Inner Mongolia	1.64	14.08	36.26	26.54	21.48
Liaoning	1.20	11.44	36.55	20.00	30.80
Jilin	1.19	10.13	37.19	32.38	19.08
Heilongjiang	1.27	12.21	40.42	26.31	19.78
Shanghai	2.05	10.77	37.16	22.60	27.43
Jiangsu	3.17	15.81	32.72	23.18	25.12
Zhejiang	2.67	17.74	31.59	20.20	27.80
Anhui	2.86	14.25	29.02	22.23	31.64
Fujian	3.01	22.25	38.08	23.84	12.81
Jiangxi	1.87	15.49	30.16	28.13	24.38
Shandong	2.64	16.30	33.35	24.36	23.36
Henan	1.45	14.50	32.20	27.64	24.20
Hubei	2.42	12.17	28.46	31.63	25.31
Hunan	2.81	18.71	32.58	27.79	18.09
Guangdong	1.30	14.84	41.40	25.74	16.72
Guangxi	1.43	18.48	36.61	23.28	20.19
Hainan	1.51	12.90	30.07	32.05	23.41
Chongqing	2.02	19.50	33.69	24.83	19.96
Sichuan	2.15	20.31	33.29	24.50	19.76
Guizhou	2.61	19.78	34.70	21.84	21.05
Yunnan	3.21	22.40	35.60	21.39	17.40
Tibet	14.38	35.12	19.06	12.71	19.06
Shaanxi	2.47	11.73	35.51	30.22	20.06
Gansu	3.33	17.64	32.00	27.46	19.55
Qinghai	3.41	20.47	34.65	20.12	21.26
Ningxia	2.83	21.68	37.28	17.63	20.46
Xinjiang	1.30	21.37	29.91	22.85	24.58

Source China Population and Employment Statistics Yearbook 2012

Table 6.2 The distort situation of Chinese capital factor from 1990 to 2010

Year	Y/L	K/L	MP	Distort
1990	0.29	1.35	0.83	8.14
1991	0.33	1.45	0.88	10.18
1992	0.42	1.55	1	11.59
1993	0.59	1.68	1.24	12.24
1994	0.86	1.83	1.6	15.79
1995	1.01	2.01	1.64	14.97
1996	1.08	2.2	1.53	14.56
1997	1.13	2.38	1.41	16.27
1998	1.15	2.57	1.27	17.95
1999	1.2	2.77	1.18	20.18
2000	1.34	2.98	1.17	20.01
2001	1.47	3.2	1.13	19.39
2002	1.57	3.76	0.92	17.3
2003	1.79	4.46	0.77	14.19
2004	2.14	5.34	0.65	22.88
2005	2.39	6.32	0.5	23.24
2006	2.73	7.43	0.39	26.5
2007	3.4	8.81	0.3	30.31
2008	3.99	10.49	0.18	28.84
2009	4.14	13.2	0.03	42.57
2010	4.65	14.28	0.31	47.24

Source Chinese Statistical Yearbook, Chinese Finance Yearbook

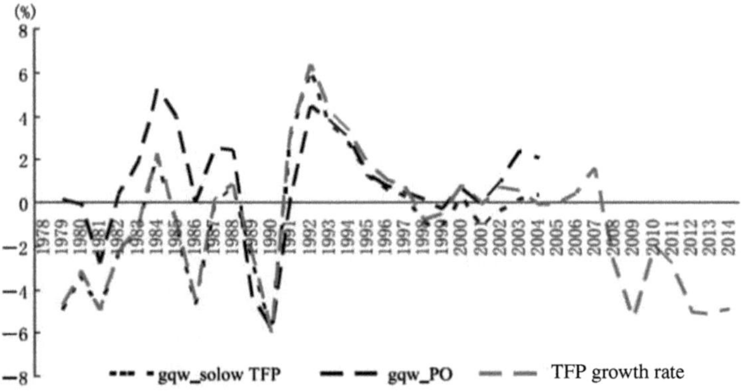

Fig. 6.2 Growth rate of China's total factor productivity from 1978 to 2014. *Note* gqw solow TFP and gqw PO TFP refer to the trends of growth rate of total factor productivity which was measured by Guo Qingwang in 2005 by employing Solow residual method and potential output method

(3) Since 2007, China's total factor productivity growth rate showed a downward trend, which is closely related to the impact of the financial crisis upon the real economy. The original growth balance was broken whereas the new balance has yet to be established, and the discrepancy between the system and mechanism became increasingly apparent. Those factors all contributed to the fall of total factor productivity growth rate. Therefore, the main factors influencing China's total factor productivity growth rate lie in China's economic system reform and the change of macro-economic policy.

6.1.2 *Analysis of Source of Total Factor Productivity and Economic Growth*

6.1.2.1 The Contribution of Total Factor Productivity to Economic Growth

With the foregoing calculation, we can estimate the contribution of the factor input and total factor productivity to economic growth respectively. The average contribution rate of total factor productivity to economic growth from 1979 to 2014 remains at 9.87%, which is a low level. In contrast, the contribution of factor input' to economic growth is as high as 90.13%. This implies that, on the one hand, China's economic growth mainly depends on factor input, and is a kind of typical input growth mode; on the other hand, it also demonstrates that in the future, there will still be considerable latitude for the total factor productivity to perform a larger role in contributing to economic growth.

At the same time, we cannot fail to notice that the total factor productivity presents a "low volatility" since the reform and opening-up. The two kinds of input factors of capital and labor have different effects on China's total factor productivity. The labor productivity is the main force to promote total factor productivity growth, while the capital productivity significantly inhibited further rise. It means that as China's economic development has taken full advantage of labor resources, the capital productivity is yet to be improved. As China's advantage of labor resource is gradually worn out, China face the huge challenge of how to improve and consolidate the capital productivity. Furthermore, China should realize that there is still a great room of improvement for its capital productivity. On the condition that we can enhance the productivity of capital in a steady manner in the future, we can maintain a high efficiency of economic growth in the coming decades.

6.1.2.2 Decomposition of Total Factor Productivity

Since the total factor productivity represents the aggregate contribution of all factors that can promote economic growth, after deducting the capital input and labor input, we can better identify the main factors influencing the economic growth after decomposing the total factor productivity. These factors include: the technology progress, resource allocation efficiency, market structure, and the opening level, etc., and they can be summarized as two aspects: the technology and the system/mechanism.

In terms of the technological progress, the improvement of knowledge, education, technical training, scale economy, and the organizational management can all bring economic growth. In sight of the systems/mechanism that has a bearing on the allocation efficiency, the contributors refer to a better and closer relationship between government and market, the development of non-state economy, the enhancement of openness opening to the outside world and market cultivation.

Within the total factor productivity growth, the average technical progressive rate registers a 0.954% high during 1979–2014 with its average contribution rate to economic growth reaching 10.13%. In contrast, the capacity enlargement driven by system/mechanism improvement is a negative of −0.063% with the negative contribution rate of −0.26%, which means that the system/mechanism served to hinder the economic growth. We can safely conclude that the reason of the low contribution of China's total factor productivity to economic growth lies in its low technical progressive rate on the one hand and the unreasonable resource allocation due to system/mechanism on the other. The above two factors incur a low level of capacity utilization. So, in the process of structural reforms to boost the supply side, we should make all-out efforts to remove the system/mechanism barriers that impair the allocation efficiency so as to foster the total factor productivity and achieve the long-term economic growth.

6.1.3 Major Problems Restricting Factor Allocation Efficiency

There are two major ways to improve the total factor productivity. We can either achieve increased production efficiency through technological progress or through the reorganization of production factors, which leads to the increased allocation efficiency. The two methods find expressions in practices such as the increased input of production factors, technological progress, system optimization, and better organizational management. From the micro level, the enterprises' practices of adopting new technology, expanding new markets, developing new products, improving management and reforming system can serve to stimulate the staff's enthusiasm and improve the total factor productivity. From the macroscopic level, through resource reconfiguration, practices such as the flowing of labor force from the low productivity agricultural sector to high productivity sector, the total factor productivity can be improved as well.

6.1.3.1 The Evolution of the Factor Market Reform

The traditional planned economy system denies the commodity attribute of production factors such as labor, land, capital and other factors, and put these factors under very strict restriction and planning. The consensus reached then was that the public ownership of productive factor is one of the fundamental features of the socialist economic system, and the private ownership of productive factors belongs to one of the fundamental features of the capitalist economic system.

After the 1990s, the Chinese residents' consumption has basically realized marketization and the marketization of productive factors started to be raised on the agenda. But is admitting that the labor force is commodity equal to repudiating the workers' master position? Whether to admit land, capital and other factors of production are commodity means to deny the public ownership of productive materials? These arguments became the shackles of marketization of productive factors until the third plenary session of the 14th Central Committee of the CPC in 1993 when the building of socialist market economic system framework was specified, and the affirmation for commodity attribute of productive factors such as land, labor and capital was made clear. These major decisions became the key steps in the liberation of productive forces.

But even today, the reform of the Chinese factor market still lags behind, affecting the overall economic development of the country. Over the recent years, China's economic growth is slowing down, for which most researchers habitually seek reasons and countermeasures from the demand level, that is to say, from investment, consumption and net export. If the issue is analyzed from the supply level, it will not be hard to find that there is still a very serious problem of "double-track system", which means that the planning and market are still going halves in the domain of productive factors. The presence of such a system deprives the factor price of its ability to reflect the relations between supply and demand or the resource scarcity flexibly, and there is a general rising trend for factor price, which reduces the efficiency of resource allocation and makes the rent-seeking activities rampant, inhibiting the vitality of the major productive factors, and reducing to a great extent the international competitiveness of China's economy. It is the deep cause of China's economic growth slowing-down.

6.1.3.2 Major Problems of Factor Supply Reform

Labor force. China's household registration system hindered the labor's cross-regional, cross-trade and cross department flow. Public goods provided by the government to different households such as education, health care, social security and price subsidies are not equal. Some cities, by means of carrying out regulations of discrimination against migrant workers, strengthen the protection of the local labor market. Workers in different areas, different departments, and different enterprises, though paying equal efforts, are not entitled to the same remuneration. These institutional arrangements reduce the labor factor allocation efficiency. In recent years, with the implementation of certain laws and regulations, labor costs have risen sharply. China's rate of social security (five social insurances and one housing fund) has increased to 40% plus. That is to say, if a worker's pre-tax income is 10,000 RMB Yuan, the enterprise should spend at least 14,000 RMB Yuan for employment. In addition, there are minimum wage growth and other rules on a regular basis. It is necessary to protect the lawful rights and interests of workers, but the actual economic development stage and the enterprises' bearing ability should be accounted for as well. At present China's rising labor costs does not rise relative to the natural pick-up of the labor productivity.

Capital. State enterprises are still rigidly depended upon state-owned banks, and private borrowing and lending costs are far higher than national bank loan rates. Enterprises with different ownerships encounter different degrees of difficulties as they gain credit capital, which gives rise to the serious capital price distortion. Besides, there are still many controlling measures in China's financial system that restrict capital and financial markets, such as interest rate control, credit control, restrictions on private enterprise in founding a bank, administrative examination and approval for stock issuance and the restrictions of the rising and falling limit-up, to name but a few. Those inappropriate restrictions on capital market end up distorting the capital price as well. However, as a country with the highest foreign exchange reserve and the highest domestic savings, China's interest rates are relatively high in the world.

Technology. In terms of scientific and technological innovation, China has not yet formed an effective mechanism for the transformation of scientific and technological achievements into real productive forces; There are indeed a lot of policies to promote the development of private investment, non-public ownership economy, but there are still some counter-measures that could be depicted as "the glass door", "the swing door" and "the revolving door". Not only do they run contrary to the entrepreneur spirit of innovation and check the development of private economy, they also discourage the momentum of SMEs. As a result, science and technology innovation are underpowered, mechanism inflexible and innovation abilities weak.

Land. During the 1989s national "two sessions", the amendments to the constitution were passed, announcing the separation of land ownership and management rights. It accords the land use right the commodity attribute. The Property Law passed in 2007 has stipulated the usufruct of land use. However, the marketization of China land has not fulfilled completely. The government still maintained its complete control of primary market of the land, charging differently for land used for real estate, commerce and industry. The land is sold by the government at a low price for attracting investment and business whereas the real estate developer bid against each other in securing the land, making the land price exorbitant. The state has strengthened its control over the supply of land since 2004. Although the planned supply of land is large, the actual market demand has run out of the supply for several consecutive years, verifying the economic law that "it is just the plan management that causes the shortage". And the more severe the shortage is, the more likely the land price will rise, and further promote the rise of real estate price. As a productive factor, the land's price has been seriously distorted.

Therefore, it is clear that almost all factors of production which can drive the economic growth, have serious bottlenecks in system. The crux of the problem lies in the absence of a market-oriented reform. Fundamentally, since the government fails to distinguish demarcation between the its administrative role of management and the market activities. The state interferes too much on microeconomic activities to the extent that the "macro management turns out to be micro", and "approval takes the place of the management". To make it even worse, the cross-functions of some departments and unreasonable setup of institutions and low-efficiency administration have greatly inhibited the contributions of all kinds of productive factors on economic growth.

6.1.3.3 Improvement of Factor Allocation Efficiency and Structural Reform of the Supply Side

To speed up the marketization reform in the field of productive factors is conducive to substantially reducing the government's direct allocation of resources, promoting the allocation of resources in following the market rules, and realizing the maximization of benefit and efficiency. Furthermore, a full competition in the field of productive factors is helpful to reducing factor costs, improving factor supply ability, and enhancing the international competitiveness of the industry.

In terms of the labor market, we should step up our efforts to further explore the potential supply of labor factors. Through moderately improving the fertility rate, carrying out a flexible retirement policy, and gradually strengthening the migrant policy, we can improve the demographic structure and increase the labor force participation rate (LFPR). In deepening the reform of the education system, supporting the enterprises in their role of cultivating innovative talents, establishing and improving the innovation intellectual property system, we could bring out an optimized human capital investment and raise the quality of labor supply. The system of innovation should be built and the equality of the labor market regulation system and operation mechanism should be set up. To be specific, we should: develop the rural social security mechanism; establish a rational urban and rural social security system; enhance the labor market intermediary organizations; produce a unified urban and rural employment system; coordinate our efforts in developing the urban and rural education and training resources; incorporate the urban and rural human resources development system; perfect labor market management; build a good labor market operation order and environment; speed up the building of urban and rural integration of the labor force factor market; improve the labor factor decision mechanism of compensation; further optimize the salary distribution system and structure; promote the scientific employer-employee relations; and protect workers' lawful rights and interests.

In terms of the capital markets, efforts should be devoted to further improving the capital allocation efficiency. To attain the goal, first, we should accelerate the interest rate marketization, improve the marketization of exchange rate formation mechanism, develop the capital account opening step by step, and establish the basic market price benchmark. Secondly, efforts should also be made to establish and perfect the multi-level equity market system, develop multi-level bond market, develop multi-channels to promote equity financing, give play to the futures market in its role of discovering price and managing risk, encourage financial innovation, and enrich the levels of financial markets and the diversity of products so as to establish a better multi-level capital market. Thirdly, the new investment and financing pattern should be adopted proactively and the innovation of structural finance should be utilized to liquidize the stock of fixed assets. We should improve the return rate of investment of the departments of enterprises, and innovate long-term capital supply mechanism. Last but not least, it is essential to further improve the efficiency of financial services, create a sound monetary and financial environment, strengthen the supportive role of the capital market and insurance market in the real economy, and raise people's security consciousness to prevent possible financial risks.

6.2 Factor Allocation Efficiency and the Supply of Labor, Capital and Technology

We should improve total factor productivity by new supply of factors, so as to realize the shift from the factors-driven mode to the innovation-driven one. The promotion of productivity of labor, capital, technology and other productive factors is the power source of the supply side structural reform. In carrying out the supply side structural reform, we will need to improve production efficiency of resources supply and supply quality, and give full play to the role of innovation in the production of resources.

6.2.1 Potential of the Supply of the Demographic Dividend and Labor Force

China's high-speed economic growth throughout the past 30 years is largely ascribed to the demographic dividend characterized by the cheap labor supply and high ratio of labor force in its population. Nevertheless, China's population size and demographic structure have changed as the state steps into New Normal. Having supported China in its 30-year plus of rapid economic growth, the demographic dividends start fading out. On one hand, the long-term implementation of population policy has led not only to a decline of China's labor force participation rate (LFPR), but also a drop-off in proportion of the working-age population. This has further caused the problem of low labor force allocation efficiency and made the potential labor force suffer under the negative influence of the falling birth rate. On the other, China's social welfare system is yet immature. The insufficiency particularly in education and the endowment insurance has escalated family's financial burden of child-raising, education and old-age supporting, limiting the human capital investment. To make it even worse, the regional differences in education resources distribution and personnel training all serve to engender a huge gap in the quality of Chinese population factor. As a consequence, the talents for China's industrial structure upgrading is in short supply. The labor market segmentation caused by institutional factors further exacerbated the structural shortage of the labor force in different industrial sectors. Therefore, the supply potential of labor force needs further taping in an effort to remove the discrepancy between its supply and demand faced by China's current economic growth.

6.2.1.1 The Evolution of Chinese Population and Labor Capital Since the Reform and Opening-up

At the beginning of the reform and opening-up in 1978, China's demographic transition has basically been completed, with death and birth rate kept at a very low level. Under the one-child policy, the average age of marriage for women in the 20th century rose from the age of 19.7–22.8 years, the total fertility rate from the average 5.7 children per woman in 1970 to 2.8 in 1979. Against the backdrop of family planning policy strictly implemented, China's population rose mildly from 960 million in 1978 to 1.37 billion in 2014, with an average annual growth rate of 0.98%. The rate of population growth has been in the state of steady decline since 1986 (Fig. 6.3).

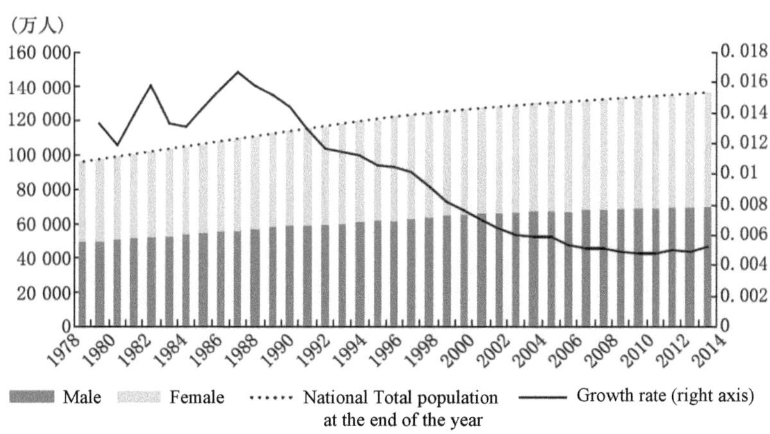

Fig. 6.3 China's total population by year (1978–2014). *Source* China's Population Statistics Yearbook

Along with China's reform and opening-up, industrialization and urbanization have been steadily pushed forward with a large number of labor force transferred from the agricultural sector to non-agricultural sectors. Many people changed their identity from farmers to industrial workers. Viewed from the angle of total employment, the working population achieved a fluctuating growth over the span from 1978 to 1990, which was attributed to the robust development of private economy and township enterprises during the period.

Since 1991, the employed population growth rate has registered a decline. In contrast to the rate of 3% in the 1980s, the average growth rate dropped to around 0.5%. This downward trend that began in 1980 was a reasonable response to the family planning policy. From the employment volume, the first industry employment declined steadily from absorbing 70% of the entire population in 1978 to 30% in 2014; the second industry practitioners accounted for 17% of the population in 1978 to about 30% in 2014, and stabilized approximately to the percentage of 30%; a bigger change took place in the tertiary industry whereby its practitioners accounted for less than 12% in 1978 but more than 40% in 2014. This means that a large quantity of labor force has been transferred from agricultural sector into the services sectors (Fig. 6.4).

In sight of human capital, some changes have taken place in China's education since the reform and opening-up. At the outset of the reform and opening-up, people who did not attend even the primary school accounted for more than 70% of the total population aged above 6 years old. By 2012 that figure dropped to only 2%. The change is the result of economic and social development on the one hand, and the efforts in popularizing the nine-year compulsory education and the implementation of the strategy of invigorating the country through science, technology and education on the other. At present, about 50% of the population have received an education of senior secondary school. Those are the people who will bring great demographic dividends and provide a powerful support for China's economic and social transformation.

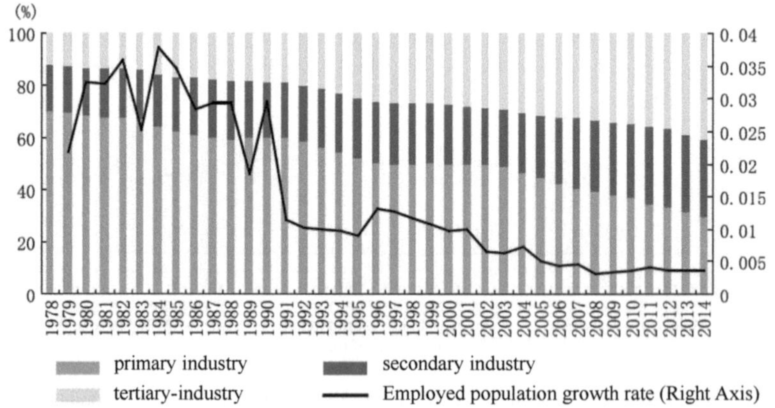

Fig. 6.4 Employed persons by year (1978–2014). *Source* China's Population Statistics Yearbook

6.2.1.2 Population Policy and the Improvement of Labor Force Participate Rate

Under the background of a rapid economic growth and mode-transformation, the 30 plus years' implementation of a strict birth control policy has brought China an accelerating aging population and a low fertility rate as the country steps into the New Normal l. From now onward, China will face the coexistence of an aging working population and a low fertility and will enjoy less and less demographic dividends. It is the task of the government to make forecasts about the trend and carry out policies to optimize the population structure. The policy should be formulated in such a way as to bring up the Labor Force Participation Rate and to effect a higher efficiency of labor force supply.

The fifth Plenary Session of the 18th CPC Central Committee put forward, "to promote balanced development of population, adhere to the basic state policy of family planning, perfect the population development strategy, and comprehensively implement the policy of 'one couple, two children'." This new policy will serve as the guideline for our reform of labor factor in the future. In addition to further releasing the fertility potential, it increases the labor supply to alleviate the pressure from the aging population, replenishing the quantity-based demographic dividends. On the side of the government, relevant policies and measures should be updated and revised, the services and management of family planning be innovated, the policy consistency be enhanced, the newly-born population monitoring and risk control and prevention be strengthened. In a bid to provide support and lower down the procreation cost, the central and local governments at all levels may cut taxes, offer social welfare and support women in being reemployed after giving birth. By means of issuing childbirth allowance, child-raising, kindergarten and other education subsidies, tax exempting or reduction, the government can give families further economic support in bringing up the extra child. On the part of the employers, they can encourage birth by endorsing a paid maternity leave, a paid parental leave, and a flexible working time and location option for their employees, especially for the women staffs who wish to have more time for their households. To lend more help, more kindergartens and schools of compulsory education should be set up, and a good prenatal and postnatal care, welfare and other public service system should be in place to ease the family's economic burden. In one word, we should strive to build up a social climate and formulate policies to encourage more couples to have the second child.

China currently adopts a unified system for the age of retirement. The so-called "one size fits all" approach not only causes a serious waste of human capital, making the potential human resources quit the labor market before they can give full play, but also increases the payment pressure of pension. So in face of the insufficient supply of labor factor incurred by the aging population, it is necessary to set up a flexible retirement system. The government should progressively extend the retirement age. The relevant policies should be carried out with perfect timing and in accordance with China's aging population and state of labor force. However, the mandatory age can only be "raised by small steps and reached in a progressive way". The age should be set in consideration of the legal maximum working age and the biological limitations. The unity of the fairness and efficiency should be achieved on the basis of making full use of the labor force. The auxiliary policies should be framed to support the employment of senior citizens. The organizations of volunteer activities should be given full play. The methods of tax exemption and reduction, administrative rewards, and endorsement simplification should take into effect to help the elderly with employment. Through strict examination and approval process, setting retirement age for special industries and special type of work, building corresponding incentive and constraint mechanism, we can promote the progressive extension of retirement age. A flexible pension system of rewards and punishments should be established. The pensions for the workers who continue to work after retirement should be specified. As for the rewards and punishments system of pension, we can operate it in light of China's realities and the experience of other countries and regions. For example, we could set pension as the benchmark. Those workers who choose to retire one year later would touch a remuneration relatively larger than his pension. On the contrary, if they retire one year earlier, their income will be docked and thus less than the pension.

6.2.1.3 Education Reform and the Optimization of Human Capital Investment

As the demographic dividends fade out and play a lesser role, China's long-term economic growth becomes more dependent upon the human resource dividends. Therefore, we should focus on solving the current mismatch of human capital in economic growth, making sure that economic structure and the human capital structure compatible with each other in respect of quality, and are in proportional relations. On the one hand, as a response to the industrial upgrading, the demand of the knowledge capital in the form of the human resource and research requires that more inputs should go into the human resource capital. Thus, we need to optimize the structure of education and invest more in it. In so doing can we combine the education and economic development to produce more innovative talents in a more rapid way. On the other hand, to achieve the upgrading of the structure of labor supply, and cater for the needs of transformation and upgrading of industrial structure and economic structure adjustment, it is essential to improve the quality the workforce. Meanwhile, we should perfect the system in a bid to attract more innovative talents. And in the process of creating human resource dividends, efforts should be made as well to bring about a better system that can facilitate the introduction, selection and employment of those talents.

We should deepen the reform of education system. Through an increased investment in education, its resources can be amplified, its allocation optimized and its system optimized. Emphasis should be laid on employment for graduates, and the need of industrial upgrading. With a view to improving the overall quality of the labor force and step up the accumulation of human capital, it is essential to conduct reforms in talent cultivation mechanism and provide more input and support to the secondary vocational and technical school. By doing so we can generate more "talent dividends" and "knowledge dividend" for economic growth and transform the traditional quantitative demographic dividend into qualitative human capital dividends. By means of the innovating the educational system, we can cultivate high-quality talents, and combine the education innovation with technological innovation so as to accelerate our supply side reform in higher education. The school should be set up with a proper management system and a good layout structure, run in multi-forms and provide students with a wide range of disciplines. While achieving economies of scale, the school should attach greater importance to the educational quality, the needs of the socialist market economy and the its role in China's modernization drive. A dynamic adjustment mechanism should be in place in a bid to optimize the structure of higher education in a continuous manner, optimize professions, disciplines, and structure, promote multidisciplinary overlapping and fusion, focus on cultivating talents with applied, interdisciplinary, skilled-oriented knowledge. By this, we can satisfy the needs of national, regional economic and social development. Meanwhile, reforms should be undertaken in the cultivation of teachers at vocational education tier. In turn, vocational education should also closely meet the requirements for the national economic development by strengthening reform of collegiate majors by means of optimizing the structure of majors and the system of management. The supply side reform in cultivating talents of vocational education should be put into practice in a vigorously way in order to provide high-quality human resource for national economic development. By adjusting the collegiate major in response to the requirements of both industries and professions, we can adapt the structure of majors to industrial upgrading and emerging professions. It is essential to plan and optimize the major layout so as to enhance the students' knowledge, abilities and qualities in accordance to the changes in regional industrial structure. Only in this way can we promote the seamless joint between talents supply chain and economic industry chain, break down the specialties barriers, cultivate compound talents with one specialty but multi-skills, reform the mechanism governing the setting-up of majors and open up the dynamic system of major construction. The supply side reform in vocational education should be market-need-orientated and take the construction and optimization of majors as the foundation and focus of the reform in enhancing talents cultivation.

Besides, in order to eliminate the flowing barriers between urban and rural labor factors, we need to build a unified labor factor market characterized by the integration of urban and rural areas. The migration policy with regard to the Registered Permanent Residence needs to be further adjusted. Restrictions on getting a residency permit in towns and small cities should be repealed. Medium sized cities should have an orderly opening-up for their residency permit. As for the large cities, the requirements for getting a residency permit should be rationally defined and their population size should be under strict control so as to solve the major problems arising from the transference of Registered Permanent Residence. Population management should be innovated and a unified urban and rural household registration system should be created. A sound residence permit system and an effective population information management system should be set up. Moreover, we should endeavor to ensure that all permanent urban residents have access to basic urban public services and cover all the farmers with permanent residency under the urban housing and social welfare system. For those residents, we have to make sure that the rural pension insurance and medical insurance they are previously entitled to are properly transferred to urban social welfare system. And a fiscal transfer payment mechanism should be introduced to facilitate the population urbanization.

6.2.2 *Monetary Capital Market Reform and Capital Allocation Efficiency*

Since the reform and opening-up, the relatively low factor cost and separation of rights have given rise to the competition between the governments, resulting in a high structural saving and investment in China's economic growth. Those advantages have brought China huge capital dividends.

6.2.2.1 Supply Efficiency of China's Capital Factor Since the Reform and Opening-up

The investment rate of China in 1978 was only 38.2%, and was close to 50% in 2015. The growth of investment rate suggests that the economic growth in China in the past years are mainly due to low labor cost, high saving, large investment and high capital. But with the global economic crisis and the negative impacts on the supply side, changes have occurred in China's capital dividends: firstly, the "depression of investment cost" comprised by low labor cost, financing cost and land cost have become less reliable and high investment relying on low factor prices is something of the past; secondly, the competition between the governments in high investments have resulted in low-efficiency questions such as vanity projects and repetitive constructions. This situation will have to change as we deepen our reform. In light of the foregoing, we can conclude that the growth mode characterized by high investment has become unsustainable, and the capital dividends produced by China's economic growth are gradually fading away.

At the same time, the market of factors especially that of the finance has merely achieved a low level of marketization. The monopoly of state-owned capital remains unsolved and the problem of state-owned financial institutions only providing services for state enterprises still persist. Government control is still stringent and the capital flow is still subject to the administrative instructions. It is clear that here are impediments for capital to flow, and the coexistence of regional or industrial capital congestion and rarity indicates that factors are seriously mismatched. Because of financial capital controls and its subjectivity to the government administrative instructions and its nature of serving only the state enterprises have not been fundamentally changed, the capital demand from the private enterprises and emerging industries can't be effectively met, and there are even different economic obstacles for capital flows between the individual and industry. This has led to capital price distortions and mismatch, causing the loss of total factor productivity.

We can determine distortions of capital factors by comparing the marginal output of capital with its price. The degree of distortions equals the marginal output of capital divided by capital price. The equation is:

$$Distort = \frac{MP_K}{w_K} \tag{6.4}$$

If Distort is more than 1, it suggests that the price of capital factor is underestimated, and the capital factor price has been distorted negatively. If Distort is less than 1, it means the price of capital factor is overestimated, and the capital factor price has been distorted positively. And if Distort equals 1, that indicates that the capital factor price has not been distorted. The value of Distort can tell the distorted degree of Chinese capital factor price.

Cobb–Douglas production function is adopted in the specific evaluation: $Y_t = AK_t^{\alpha}L_t^{\beta}$, where Y_t is the real output, L_t refers to the labor input, and K_t the capital stock. α and β denote the average capital output share and average labor output share respectively. The MP_K practical marginal output of capital factor can be figured out by applying the production function. If w_K is replaced by the basic interest rate of enterprise loan from 6 months to 12 in that year, we can get the distorted degree of Chinese capital factor. Seen from the Table 6.2, it can be concluded that there is a negative distort in the Chinese capital factor price, that is to say the capital price is relative low compared with marginal output. From 1990 to 2010, the degree has augmented to have reached its peak in 1999, the highest level over the recent ten years. The degree has been falling year by year since 1999, from the 20.18 times in 1999 to as low as 14.19 times registered in 2003. However, after 2004, the distorted degree has worsened, reaching 47.24 times in 2010.

On one hand, capital factor price distortions can be ascribed to the incomplete progressive reform that spawned institutional obstacles and path dependence. The market reform lags behind the market reform and the administrative power still determines the production prices of factors. On the other, unclear property rights system also serves to hinder the market-oriented reform process of the capital elements. In view of the above reasons, we need to redress the mismatch of capital elements to give full play to factor and make up for the loss of total factor productivity. Macro policies should be carried out in a bid to guide the industrial flow of the incremental capital investment (Fig. 6.5).

Through industrial policy, approval and examination system for the new investment projects, and the project management plan, we can facilitate the flowing of limited incremental capital into the industries in short supply, and reduce the degree of capital mismatch. we need to optimize the allocation of capital stock, improve its service efficiency, promote pricing mechanism of the capital factor and

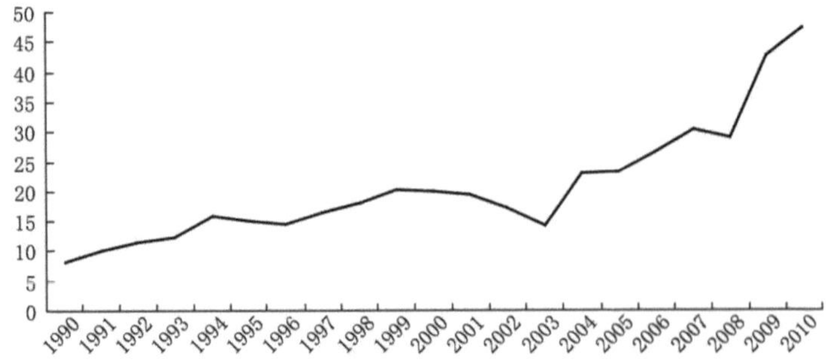

Fig. 6.5 Distorted degree of Chinese capital factor price and mismatch level of low capital from 1990 to 2010

break down the barriers that impede capital flowing, and promote efficiency of capital allocation. The government should phase out its administrative role of pricing, make capital allocation function transfer to the market and give the market the liberty to determine the price of productive factors in order to make factor prices consistent with factor productivity, reduce capital price distortion, promote the free flow of capital, and bolster the efficiency of capital allocation. We should deepen the reform of financial marketization and give full play to its capital allocation function. Moreover, efforts should also be made to speed up the market-oriented interest rate reform, proactively foster the access of private capital to the financial sector, get rid of the monopoly pattern in financial sector, solve financing difficulties facing the SMEs and emerging industries, and improve the utilization efficiency of capital.

6.2.2.2 The Amendment of Distorted Capital Factor Price

Redressing the capital factor price distortions calls for the promotion of the marketization reform of financial factors, and the formation of the market price benchmark. We should concentrate our efforts on marketizing the interest rate and exchange rate, forming market-oriented financial benchmark prices, offer sound price signals for the financial organization and markets, provide guidance for the efficient allocation of financial resources, supplying accurate information for the Central Bank to exercise macro-control and adopt effective methods. To attain this goal, we have to fulfill the following:

Firstly, to accelerate the marketization of interest rate. The interest rate should be taken as the price factor of financial market and should be utilized to allocate the resources effectively. We should ensure the decisive role of market in forming the interest rate price mechanism. Therefore, the marketization of interest rate has become the most top priority of China's financial reform. On the one hand, we should endeavor to loosen the control of deposit interest rate. Nowadays, the upper limit control of deposit interest rate has become the biggest obstacle to China's market-oriented interest rate reform, which means that to liberate the bank deposit interest rate control is significant in improving the efficiency of allocating the capital factor. To enact the deposit insurance system legislation as soon as possible and liberate the role of commercial banks in directly pricing the risks of deposits or create a bigger space for the fluctuation of the interest rate and make commercial banks the real risk-takers and offer more diversified financial choices for both the residents and enterprises. On the other hand, we should rebuild the system of benchmark rate and change the practice of the Central Bank docking the risk pricing directly with the commercial banks in setting the legal deposit benchmark interest to that of Central Bank setting the legal benchmark interest rate to indirectly influence the property price in financial markets. Reforms should be implemented in the design of the pattern of benchmark interest rate to ensure that the benchmark interest rate can more accurately and truthfully reflect the current state of the economy and the market interest rate level, reduce and eliminate the influencing factors of price distortion and conflicts of interest. Only in this way can we establish a scientific, systematic and comprehensive system to accommodate the domestic market benchmark interest rate.

Secondly, to perfect the formation mechanism of exchange marketization. We should push the reform of formation mechanism of RMB exchange rate in overall balance. Under the New Normal, we should coordinate the domestic and international situations by promoting the reform of formation mechanism of exchange rate and making the exchange rate more flexible. Those are the two measures that allow us to strike a balance between the internal and external, tap both the national and international resources, stabilize the growth and adjust the structure. The implementation of reform of exchange rate formation mechanism requires that we pay attention not only to the balanced relation between economic development strategy and current account, but also to the U.S.A.'s economic and policy trend and the international capital flow's effect on Chinese economy and monetary policy. On the basis of the principle of self-initiative, controllability and progressiveness, we should improve the RMB exchange rate formation mechanism, adhering to the supply and demand of the market as the main indicator, take a basket of currencies as the reference for adjustments, make increase the flexibility of the RMB exchange rate. The RMB exchange rate have fallen and risen, which is a two-way floating aimed at keeping the RMB exchange rate at a reasonable and balanced level. Only by doing so can we enhance the scientific nature, imitativeness and effectiveness of macroeconomic regulation and control. For financial markets and product innovation, efforts should be expended to give full play to the offshore market functions in free trade zone, to form local RMB financial center, and strengthen the internationalization of the RMB circulation ability. We should popularize the successful experience of promoting free trade area of Shanghai financial mechanism, promote the development of the free trade area construction, give full play to the financial mechanism and function of free trade, and expand the scale of the related businesses of RMB within the area.

Thirdly, we should make concerted efforts in advancing progressive capital project. The opening of capital market, marketization of interest rate and the exchange rate fluctuation are core contents of the Chinese financing system reform and the opening up of capital market to the outside. It is also vital to the internationalization of RMB. For the strategy of opening up the capital market, we should endeavor to seize its pace, carry it out in an orderly manner and in accordance with the procedure. Synergy should be gained between opening the capital project and the reform of interest rate and exchange rate. To open up the capital projects hinges upon the marketization of interest rate and the regulated fluctuation of exchange rate. It also requires a healthy interaction between the two. should be established. Moreover, we should coordinate the opening of capital project, interest rate marketization and the reform of exchange rate liberalization. To attain this objective, firstly we need to improve the coordination of the domestic and international financing policies; secondly, we need to create an excellent domestic economic and financial environment. Last but not least, we should strive to adjust the economic structure and optimize the foreign trade structure, transform the low-end value chain and production method of processing trade so as to export products of the medium-end and import the products of high added value and products with an extended chain value.

6.2.2.3 Construction of a Multi-level Capital Market

After years of development of direct financing, China's finance remains predominantly interbank financing in structure. In such a financial structure as is mainly composed of indirect financing and characterized by insufficient interbank competition, the investment and financing channel are narrow for enterprises and citizens. When negotiating with banks, they are short of needed skills. Simply relaxing the regulation of lending rates and deposit interest rate brings no efficiency. Therefore, the priority should be given to developing a multi-level capital market so as to increase the proportion of direct financing, optimize the structure of the financial system and respond to the demands of diversification of investment and financing. Only by doing so can we better serve the real economy, especially the small and micro businesses. To be specific, it is essential that we fulfil the following:

Firstly, to establish a better multi-level equity market system. We should develop a multi-level equity market to help the enterprises solve the problem of high leverage ratio. We should strengthen the mainboard, SME board market, carry out reforms in the GEM (Growth Enterprise Market), and speed up the share transfer system for national SMEs. We should integrate the regional equity markets into multi-level capital market system by means of checking-up and rectification in an effort to accelerate the construction of multi-level equity market. Reforms of stock issuing and registration system should be promoted. A stock issuance system centering around the information disclosure should be set up. Meanwhile, a delisting system should be built in accordance with China's actual conditions. Thus, we can protect the investors and gradually form a virtuous circle whereby companies can access and quit the market in an orderly manner while the markets can transfer the boards smoothly. The market should be clearly separated into the sections of issuing market and trade market. The register system of stock issuance should be available. The rules governing the transaction in Shanghai Stock Exchange and Shenzhen Stock Exchanges should be stipulated respectively so that the single nature of the A share market can be changed. In formulating clear-cut rules in regard to listing, accounting information disclosure, transaction and delisting, a new stock exchange taking the network system of the securities companies as the platform and the agents as the main players will come into being.

Secondly, to proactively develop and regulate multi-level bond market. Under the New Normal, the structural reform on the supply side set out new requirements for the development of the bond market. Over a long run, there are many problems of distortion in China's economy and finance with the bank financing still playing the dominant role. It has led to an accumulation of risks in the banking system. The banks start facing increasing pressure as they are occupied with liquidizing the assets and replenishing capital. The commercial banks perceive a mounting resistance in their course of transformation. They are in lack of a proper market financing system in their support of urbanization and they can barely hedge off the debt risks of local government. Thus, for a long time, difficulties and high cost present themselves as the SMEs (SMEs) are striving to finance. To solve these deep-seated problems, we should take full advantage of the fledgling bond market and its important role in recent years. To deepen the financial reform in a vigorous manner, we should enhance the bond market, adjust the financing structure, prevent and try to minimize the relevant risks. We should act in line with the market trend, create and develop a well-functioning multi-level bond market.

Furthermore, efforts should be devoted to introducing municipal bonds so as to solve financing problem in urbanization. We should proactively utilize the bond market to provide financing for urbanization construction and to prevent against the debt risk and financial risks for local governments. In promoting the issuance of the municipal bonds progressively, we will be able to put in place a standardized and transparent market for investment and financing. We should coordinate the internationalization of RMB with the opening of bond market in our support of "the Belt and Road".

By means of allowing more domestically-based institutions to issue bonds overseas and simplifying the procedures for issuing bonds in offshore RMB market, we will be able attract more international investors who invest in RMB-denominated financial instruments. Thus, types of institutional investors will become more diversified. We should enhance the collaboration between offshore market, monetary authorities, supervision departments and financing institutions, and lower down the management and transaction costs of market players of RMB, and boost RMB's attraction and confidence in international community.

Thirdly, to encourage the employment of multi-channels in developing equity financing. We can foster the equity financing through private-equity fund (PE), government guiding funds, insurance funds and pension funds and so on according to China's current situation and the experiences drawn from foreign countries. In the meantime, efforts should be made to standardize and develop the equity investment. As is known to all, amongst the various methods of equity investment, equity investment fund has the highest degree of marketization, hence an important organizational way to promote equity investment. Usually, for fund managers, the criteria for investment is to select the enterprises with greatest potential for growth and highest efficiency.

Through perfecting the related laws and policies, market system, we should establish an equity exit mechanism of diversification, make clear for equity funds' industrial policy objectives and developmental plan, guide and optimize the allocation of capital factors. The government guiding fund should be set up. The evaluation system which combines the economic and social benefits should be available. Efforts should be made as well in coordinating different objectives and providing risk-prevention. The duties of the government should be clearly defined and the supervision and management should be intensified to prevent the principal-agent risk. An open and transparent information disclosure system should be built to avoid the risk of moral hazard and prevent the rent-seeking behaviors.

Fourthly, to give full play to the functions of the futures market in price discovery and risk management. In terms of commodity futures, we should continue to launch bulk commodity futures, develop commodity options, commodity index and carbon emissions rights which are considered as trading tools. In terms of financial futures, it is necessary to carry out reforms of mechanism in collaboration with the interest rate marketization and RMB exchange rate formation so as to address the needs of capital market risk management and develop financial derivatives in a steady and orderly manner. We should gradually enrich the varieties of stock index futures, index options and stock options, develop bond futures, improve the Treasury Bond Yield Curve as the indicator of market supply and demand.

Fifthly, to encourage financing innovations, add varieties to the products and layers of the financial market. In order to secure a sustained growth for China's economy under the New Normal, we need to set up an "unified and open" financial system with orderly competition, which means that the market is eclectic and competitive. It is essential to further open the financial system, and encourage the financial industry to conduct integrated businesses and innovation activities such as Internet finance on the condition of moderate regulation. Based on the management of negative list and enhancement of supervision, we can speed up the development of medium and small financing institutions, establish various ownerships, and set up a financial system with diversified business models and the coexistence of large, medium and small institutions.

We should encourage the development of Internet finance, micro-credit organizations and other forms of financial innovations. As the Internet develops, Internet finance is growing rapidly, such as P2P financing platform, the third party payment and "crowd-funding" equity financing. The development of small loan companies, NGO micro finance and fund cooperation society are quite fast. These innovative financing organizations and businesses have all played a certain role in terms of optimizing small enterprises' financing services. Under the guidance of classified regulation, appropriate regulation, coordinative regulation and innovative regulation, we should concentrate our efforts in bringing out a healthy development of these new financing business models. In addition, we should develop various forms of consumer finance and green finance.

6.2.3 *Supply of Technology Factors and National Innovative System Construction*

It is true that technology progress can vigorously promote a country's economic growth and industrial structure change, and it has been verified in the path of most developed countries' economic growth. China, to catch up with the developed countries which is a long-term goal of industrialization, is also in need of the support from the technological innovation. At present, China is still in middle and late stage of industrialization. On one hand, the previous round of intensive input of capital and labor factors has made its marginal cost uplift rapidly and caught in bottlenecks. On the other hand, the "market-changing technology" of China in the 30 years has helped China gain rapid headways with regard to industrial technology, which is based on the import and absorption of foreign technology. However, China is yet far behind the world's leading level in terms of many core technologies. "Passive innovation lock" and "error of technological path selection" remain two major risks unavoidable as we are preoccupied with technological catching-up. Whether China can surmount the "middle-income trap" successfully is still dependent upon the improvement of innovative abilities and the upgrading of industry technology. Therefore, it is very paramount to gain progress in technological innovation for the structural reform on the supply side.

6.2.3.1 Change in Supply of Technology Factors Since the Reform and Opening-up

From 1978 when China started the reform and opening-up, with the popularization of education, the increase of colleges and universities and the acceleration of technology transfer speed, the contribution of China's technological factors to the economic growth has continuously increased. Between 1998 and 2003, the contribution rate of scientific and technological progress to GDP reached 39.7%; The 5 years between 2007 and 2012 saw that figure rise to 52.2%. Within 10 years, the share of contribution of scientific and technological progress to the total output has increased by 1.3 times (Fig. 6.6).

Technology factor supply is inextricably connected with the establishment of the technology factor market. As one of the important production factor markets, the technology factor market is an integral part of China's socialist market economic system, an important component of the national innovation system, and a significant part of science and technology intermediary service system. The development

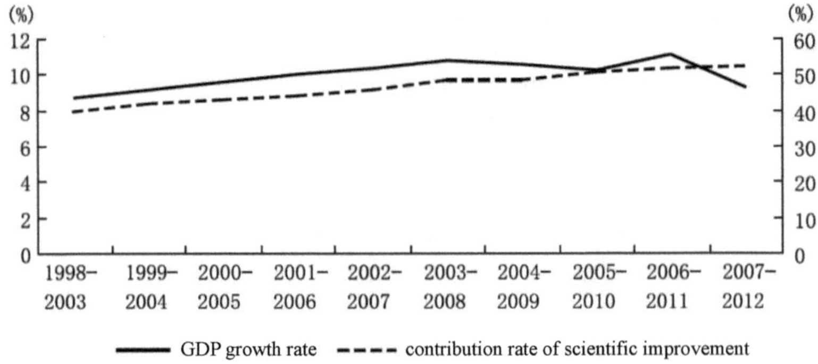

Fig. 6.6 The change of output contribution rate of scientific improvement from 1998 to 2012. *Source* Statistical Yearbook of Chinese Science and technology

of market and the price formation mechanism of China's technology factor has gone through four different phases: the first is embryonic stage (from the late 1970s to the beginning of the 1980s), during which the prototype of technology trading came into being; the second is the rising-up period (from the mid and late 1980s to the beginning of the 1990s), when the concept of "technology market is an integral part of Chinese socialist commodity market" was spelled out; the third is the preliminary formation stage (from the late 1990s to China's accession to the WTO). In October 2000, the second China Hi-Tech Fair held in Shenzhen marked the initial shape of the technology factor market; the fourth stage is the primary developmental stage (after China's entry into the WTO), when the operation mechanism of technical trade was gradually adapting itself to fulfil the requirements of the development of market economy. Reviewing the development of technology factor market, we found that the technology market turnover has risen steadily since 1995 with the growth rate fluctuating basically between 10 and 30%, and the trading volume, up from 26.8 billion RMB Yuan in 1995 to 857.7 billion RMB Yuan in 1995, 30 times amount of increase (Fig. 6.7).

Seen from the scientific investment, the fund of China's R&D increased from 56 million RMB Yuan in 1952 to 1422 billion RMB Yuan in 2015, and the average annual growth rate after 2000 stood at 21%. The proportion percentage of China's R&D input tripled from 1998s 0.65% of GDP to 2012s 1.98%. However, compared with major developed countries such as the U.S.A., Japan, German and France, China still has a long way to go (Fig. 6.8 and Table 6.3).

6.2.3.2 To Strengthen the Supply Efficiency of Technology in the Short-Term

The key to the reform that changes the mode of production of technology factors on the supply side is to improve the supply efficiency of technology factors, while sticking to macro-environment factor of technology production. A favorable innovation environment can serve to stimulate the innovation dynamism of the main

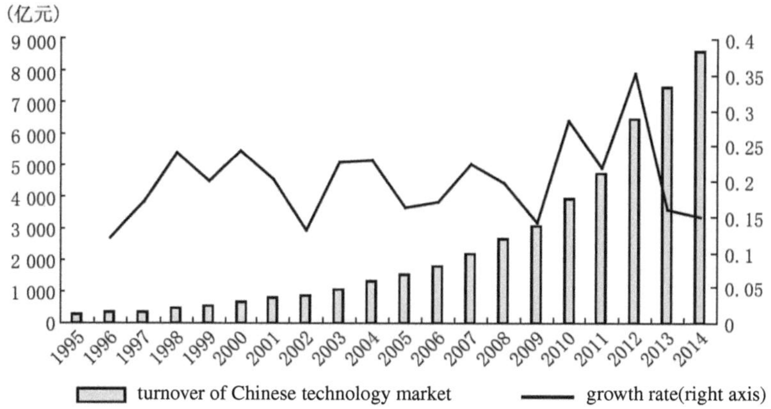

Fig. 6.7 The changing situation of turnover of Chinese technology market from 1995 to 2014. *Source* Chinese Science Statistical Yearbook

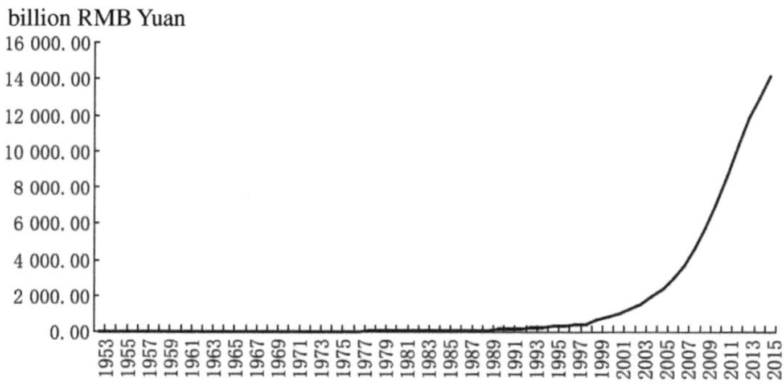

Fig. 6.8 China's R&D input situation from 1953 to 2015. *Source* Wind Info

body, and ensure the supply of emerging technologies. Besides, in face of China's periodical and overall economic downturn, we have to firmly seize the trend of the technology revolution, and set off to achieve technological breakthroughs in key areas which can represent the future development. By doing so can we address the current supply problem hovering over the production in the most effective way.

We should make solid efforts to press ahead with "mass entrepreneurship and innovation". To achieve this, on one hand, it is necessary to implement the structural reform by fulfilling the important task of "cutting down the redundant capacity", and provide guidance for the traditional industry to adapt to fast-paced, innovation-centered and modern production atmosphere. We should offer the traditional areas more incentives to allow them to apply innovative technology, and encourage more and more front-line technicians to innovate. On the other hand, we should adhere to the principle that knowledge of innovation should serve economic

Table 6.3 The R&D fund and its proportion in GDP of China and other countries

Country	R&D/GDP														
	1998	1999	2000	2001	2002	2003	2004	2005	2006	2007	2008	2009	2010	2011	2012
China	0.65	0.76	0.9	0.95	1.07	1.13	1.23	1.32	1.39	1.4	1.47	1.7	1.76	1.84	1.98
The U.S.A.	2.62	2.66	2.74	2.76	2.66	2.66	2.59	2.62	2.64	2.7	2.84	2.9	2.83	2.77	2.79
Japan	3	3.02	3.04	3.12	3.17	3.2	3.17	3.32	3.41	3.46	3.47	3.36	3.26	3.39	3.35
The U.K.	1.79	1.86	1.85	1.82	1.82	1.78	1.71	1.76	1.75	1.78	1.79	1.86	1.76	1.78	1.73
France	2.14	2.16	2.15	2.2	2.23	2.17	2.15	2.1	2.11	2.08	2.12	2.26	2.25	2.25	2.29
German	2.27	2.4	2.45	2.46	2.49	2.52	2.49	2.48	2.54	2.53	2.69	2.82	2.82	2.88	2.98

Source Chinese Science Statistical Yearbook

production and respond to the different requirements of the knowledge-intensive and industry-intensive areas by supplementing innovative supporters of various layers and types. Encouragements should also go to enterprises and social capital wishing to participate more in the construction of innovative supporters such as GIS (Group Innovation Space) and entrepreneur incubator.

We should step up the reform of the scientific research system innovation. Breakthroughs should be made in the traditional organization and management system to get researchers deeply involved in the R&D (Research & Development) of the demand side. We have to ensure the organic integration of the knowledge economy and industrial economy, continue to promote the pilot transformation state-owned research institutes, and establish new research institutes that are industry-oriented and service-economy-oriented; we should advocate the classified management of the research institutions and boost the initiatives and enthusiasm of different types of research personnel. Meanwhile, we should adopt a flexible management system for scientific research funds and try to satisfy the needs pf research personnel.

Furthermore, it is necessary as well to perfect the national policies concerning science and technology in an all-around way. We should review all the innovation policy baskets to avoid the possible policy overlapping or conflicts in a bid to make national macroscopic innovation policies that are standardized, unified and easy to operate. Our government should endeavor to provide guidance for the innovation system to develop in a healthy and orderly way. In this regard, efforts should be made to change the mode of stimulation for innovation policy, improve technical factor supply quality in a precise manner, and promote proactively the pilot innovation policy by "replacing the subsidy with input". The government's innovation policies in support of the strategic foci should be strengthened to enable the state-owned assets to perform the role of indicator. Moreover, we should strengthen the policies in order to better support those main service providers of science and technology. Our aim is to enhance the supply of the whole system and forestall the innovation drawbacks.

The government should improve the environment to allow scientists and researchers to be fully devoted to their work. On one hand, we should expend solid efforts to press ahead with "de-administration" in colleges, universities and research institutions, establish a full set of scientific and standard evaluation of peer review mechanism in order to minimize the administrative interference with academy. Only in this way can we achieve the purity of research environment for our researchers to carry out their work. On the other hand, the government should bring up the social service supply, grant the researchers a basic guarantee that tolerates failure to free them of the "worries". That is an important method effective to reduce the "non-research loss" for the entire society.

We should take the *Made in China 2025*[1] as the blueprint and seek breakthroughs in industrial technology. *Made in China 2025* calls for a subversive leap

[1]*Made in China 2025* was a plan unveiled in 2015 by the Chinese government as the roadmap for the future manufacturing. The plan regards the development for new information technology high-end numerically-controlled machine tools and robotics, biological medicine etc. (translator).

of manufacturing technology in ten key areas. To make such a leap, the success lies in whether we could have an asymmetric advantage in advanced manufacture over the western countries. With the help of vibrant industrial technologies, we will be able to remodel those industries excessive in capacity and re-digest the redundant capacity. In terms of massive industries such as steel, energy and chemical engineering, we should focus our efforts on digest the capacity and remodel the industry by means of modern technological revolution; it is well-know that currently manufactures are moving upwards the chain to be high-ended products with high added-value. We should work in tune with such a convergence trend and provide the industry with revolutionary and upgraded technology so as to promote the upgrading of the traditional manufacturing industry.

We should attach importance to productive supply of multi-disciplinary and general technology, and promote the integration of cross-disciplinary technologies. The prerequisite of enhancing the R&D of GT (Generic Technology) consists in the state-level transmission and sharing of those technologies of major strategic values; thus, it is necessary to build a general technology sharing platform to promote the basic technologies open source and the technology platform integration; we should strengthen the open innovation cooperation and facilitate the breakthrough in industrial technology.

6.2.3.3 To Develop Efficient National Innovative System in the Long Run

In light of the current supply side structural reform, China should, on the basis of fully implementing *National Strategy of Innovation-driven Development*[2] and *the 13th Five-Year Plan for Economic and Social Development* (the 13th Five-Year Plan), be more devoted to constructing a flexible and efficient state innovative system with Chinese characteristics. By adopting a balanced market approach and guiding policies, we can promote the efficient and reasonable allocation of technological factors. The National Knowledge Innovation Project should be carried out profoundly. We should continue to give full play to the pivotal role of national research institutions, since they represent the state's knowledge innovation power to tackle the key issues concerning basic subject, strategy and prospects. The construction of scientific centers at different levels calls for a faster pace in order that economies of scale can shape up; we should try to build as soon as possible a batch of professional scientific centers able to deal with a wide range of problems across different subjects and issues. Those centers will serve as the base for the world's first-class research team to launch major scientific projects. It is our objective that we can form the economies of scale in several areas of basic science.

[2]The 18th CPC National Congress proposed the *strategy of innovation-driven development* and stressed that scientific and technological innovation is a strategic pillar for boosting social productivity and comprehensive national strength and therefore must be placed at the heart of the country's development (translator).

We should emphasize the three balances in talent cultivation. Firstly, a balance should be struck between introducing high-end talent and cultivating local talent. We can serve the technological innovation continuously and perpetually only if an advanced talent cultivation system is set up. The second balance should be maintained between the cultivation of masters and that of key young researchers. We should work out our scientific strategies to solve the "pain point" of those key young researchers in mid-and-long-term and make all-out efforts to nurture researchers of world's topmost level. The last balance should be attained between the R&D incentives and "blue-collar innovation", a campaign to update and broaden the skills of front-line workers. We should attach great importance to kindling the industrial workers' enthusiasm for innovation. We should bring up the end supply of manufacturing and craft techniques, appearance design, and refined processing so as correct the products' deficiencies of low quality and rough workmanship and better meet the demands of modern markets.

We should enhance the application of technology in engineering. On the one hand, the construction of a common engineering technology platform needs to be accelerated. The basic guarantee for small tests and medium tests of engineering application should be given. On the other hand, the role of national science and technology program as an indicator should be brought into play and social capital and financial capital should be encouraged to participate in technology incubation. The government should devise special Sci-Tech financial planning for the industrialization of achievements and regulate and treat the social capital entering into the Sci-Tech with tolerance in a bid to bolster its enthusiasm for entering the market and reduce the risk of cost in the process of knowledge transformation.

We should proactively uphold the enterprises' status of main body in the innovation market. We should improve enterprises' abilities to allocate innovation resources by means of market and regard it as an opportunity to press ahead with the construction of national innovation system in an all-around way. The government should better the various technology transaction markets which take enterprises as main body in terms of the number, size and quality of the market. We should pay attention to government's function of safeguarding, and at the same time, promote the decisive role of the market mechanism in allocating innovation resources.

We should endeavor to construct an innovative ecological system featuring the integration of Production, Teaching and Research. In undertaking the supply reform of the technology, we should place considerable importance to the triple-helical structure[3] of the national innovation system, and encouraging industrial and knowledge sectors to widen their intersection of exchanges and communications. Efforts should be put in eliminating barriers to the flowing of innovation talents,

[3]The structure of Triple Helix refers to the concept of university-industry-government relationships. Initiated in the 1990s by Etzkowitz (1993) and Etzkowitz and Leydesdorff (1995), it encompasses the elements of precursor works by Lowe (1982) and Sábato and Mackenzi (1982), and interprets the shift from a dominating industry-government dyad in the Industrial Society to a growing triadic relationship between university-industry-government in the Knowledge Society (translator).

strengthening "tacit knowledge"[4] supply; the government should develop technical service agencies, provide patent service supply to meet the current demands, and make compensations in places lacking national innovation system. We should proactively develop various types of for-profit and non-profit intermediary service organizations, while expanding the scope of their market, expand the surviving space for the providers of the third party technology assessment service to better supervise the quality of the intermediary services.

6.3 The Intensification and Supply of Land Factors

As a crucial process, China's land reform represents a key challenge as it launches the economic transformation, presses ahead with the new urbanization and initiates a new round of institutional dividends. The government should build a unified and open market system with orderly competition. As is known to all, the establishment of an integrated construction-land market between urban and rural regions enables the market to play a decisive role in resource allocation. It can finally help the construction-land for rural collective profit-gaining and state-owned land get access to the market with the same price and the same rights. What's more, it can promote the land factors' effective circulation between industries and between urban and rural regions and bring up the efficiency of the new land supply in the process of urbanization.

6.3.1 Rural Land Reform and the Integration of Urban and Rural Land Markets

On the basis of the determining role of market in the resource allocation, the Third Plenary Session of the 18th Central Committee of Communist Party of China put forward the reforms for rural land system to be carried out in three aspects. First, on the premise of adhering to and improving an arable land protection system characterized by the strictest rules, we should allow farmers to possess, use, gain profits from and transfer their contracted lands and entitle them to the right to mortgage their rural land contractual management and security interests as guarantors. Second, on the premise of complying with the planning and usage regulation, we should permit market players to transfer, rent and become shareholders of construction-land for rural collective profit-gaining, and entitle them to the equal right and the same price as the state-owned land when entering the market. At the same time, the government should expend efforts to narrow down the land

[4]Tacit knowledge (as opposed to formal, codified or explicit knowledge) is the kind of knowledge that is difficult to transfer to another person by means of writing it down or verbalizing it.

acquisition scope, and standardize the land acquisition procedure. It is necessary to make available a reasonable, standard and multi-grantee mechanism for those farmers whose land has been acquired. We should improve the secondary market of land rent, transfer and mortgage, introduce a distribution mechanism that accounts for all the land added-value profits of the state, the collective ownership and the individual. In addition, we should raise the proportion of the personal earnings reasonably. Third, we should safeguard the usufruct of farmers' homestead. Conduct Reforms should be conducted to perfect the rural homestead system. To do this, we should select a number of regions for piloting the mortgage, guarantee and transfer of farmers' housing property in a cautious manner and seek methods for farmers to increase their property income. Thus, those three key areas of reform of the rural land system have covered the farmland, rural collective construction-land and rural homestead. The direction of the reform is to make sure that the ownership of rural collective land stays unchanged, and to give full guarantee to farmers' usufruct of land, which refers to their rights of possession, use and yields. The reform seeks to break down the original restraints on the transfer of rural collective land from institutions and is aimed to boost the rural society's vitality thoroughly, promote the endogenous growth in rural areas, and increase farmers' land revenue and narrow down the income gap between urban workers and rural farmers.

6.3.1.1 Transfer Market of Contractual Right of Land

At present, China is piloting land transfer in many regions. Under the general guidance of governments at all levels, rural land transfer has developed remarkably. Relevant statistics show that by the end of 2013, a total of 340 million mu of contracted land has been transferred nationwide. Compared with the figure by the end of 2008, it was 3.1 times larger, and meanwhile, the transfer proportion also reached 26%, an increase of 17.1%. There were over 2.87 million specialized households who managed more than 50 mu farmland, and there were also more than 0.87 million family farms. In sight of China's rural land transfer over the recent years, we have scored certain achievements in well-developed regions with relatively ripe conditions. In those places, the transfer has achieved large-scale, high efficiency, marketization in its transfer mechanism, and diversification in its transfer models. However, there are still some problems in the national rural land transfer. First, the irregular procedure of land transfer, such as insufficient service for land certificate replacement, disordered transfer and irregular transfer contracts etc. Second, imperfect transfer service system. The transfer lacks in a perfect pricing mechanism and a well-developed management service system. Besides, it is yet suffering from the lack of supports from financing credit. Third, the skewed implementation of transfer policy. As a consequence of such deviation, certain farm lands are not used for grain growing or for agricultural purposes. There are even some cases where transfer is made in violation of famers' wish or by compulsory measures. Fourth, the transfer of labor force is not stable. The problem of job placement for the surplus labor force persists. Fifth, lack of professionals in agricultural science and technology. The land transfer still suffers from the shortage of talents.

Confronted with the above-mentioned questions, the government needs to find causes and speed up the development of transfer market for the contractual right of rural land. To attain this goal, it is first of all, essential to perfect the intermediate organizations and improve the transaction information platform for the contractual right of land. Features of land such as scarcity, specificity and immovability often bring forth severe imbalance in status and asymmetry in information between both the buyers and sellers. Therefore, to address this burning question, it is necessary to set up intermediate organizations for the transfer of contractual right of rural land, formulate relative regulations and spell out clearly the legal status, rights and responsibilities for both parties. We also have to make sure that the intermediate organizations can provide necessary information and legal consulting as well as services such as price assessment, agency transactions and can serve as the intermediary of financing and investment. Secondly, we need to optimize the agricultural environment and drive up the demand of land management right. Through the formulation of preferential policy of scale operation of land transfer, we will be capable of improving the construction of agricultural public service network, such as agricultural technology promotion network, facility network of agricultural water conservancy, agriculture information service network, and rural public education network so as to create a favorable environment for agricultural management, and develop transfer market of land management right. More importantly, in order to inspire fundamentally the farmers' enthusiasm to protect arable land and to be engaged in farming businesses, the government needs to perfect the market system of agricultural product, adjust the corresponding compensation policy for agriculture and agricultural products, and build a reasonable pricing mechanism. Thirdly, we need to strengthen the government supervision and promote order and standardization in rural land transfer. In the process of promoting the standard transfer of contractual right of land, the government is supposed to play the role of "night-watchman" in order to ensure the negotiation on an equal footing and make sure the transfer process is completely fair and just and transfer contracts are legitimate. All these measure are proposed for safeguarding the land rights and interests of farmers, and for guiding, standardizing and regulating the land transfer market.

6.3.1.2 Market Entry of Construction-Land for Rural Collective Profit-Gaining

The evolution of China's policy on construction-land for rural collective profit-gaining can be summarized into two phases. In the first stage, it is forbidden to transfer the collective construction-land before it was allowed to be transferred with strict limits and on harsh conditions. In the second stage, the transfer of the collective construction-land was standardized, which was followed by the establishment of a unified market between urban and rural areas.

The first stage is marked by the policy transition from disapproving and imposing limitations to allowing conditioned transfer. *Circular of the State Council Concerning the Matters Relating the Development of the Real Estate Industry* promulgated in November 1992 stipulates that collectively-owned land can only be sold after it has been acquired to become state-owned. That is to say, the state did not approve the transfer of construction-land for rural collective profit-gaining at the time. The Revised *Law of Land Administration of the People's Republic of China* issued in August 1998 specifies that farmers' collectively-owned land shall not be transferred or leased for non-agricultural construction purposes except in circumstances where the transfer of land usufruct is incurred by bankruptcy, mergers and acquisitions of enterprises having obtained the land in accordance with law and the land use planning. In October 2004, the *State Council's Decision on Deepening Reform and Strict Land Management* stated that, on the premise of conforming to planning, the usufruct of the construction-land for rural collective profit-gaining in villages, towns, and designated towns can be transferred according to law. In October 2015, the official file entitled *Opinions Concerning the Pilot Work of Regulating the Link Between the Increase of Urban Construction-land and the Decrease of Construction-land of Rural Collective Ownership* advanced the policy of linking the increase of construction-land in urban areas with the decrease of construction-land in rural areas.

The second stage saw the change from standardization of transfer to the establishment of a unified land market. The *Decision of the Central Committee of the Communist Party of China on Several Major Issues Concerning Rural Reform and Development* promulgated in October 2008 put forward that the collective-owned land shares "the same price and right" with the state-owned land, and defined the objective to establish a unified market for construction land between rural and urban areas. In December 2012, in the *Opinions of the CPC Central Committee and State Council on Accelerating the Development of Modern Agriculture and Further Enhance the Vitality of Rural Development*, it was made clear that the pilot work of linking the increase of construction-land in urban areas with the decrease of construction-land in rural areas should be strictly regulated, and the transfer of the construction-land of rural collective profit-gaining should be standardized as well. Nevertheless, it further denied the access to the market the construction-land of rural collective ownership for non-management purposes. The *Decision of the Central Committee of the Communist Party of China on Some Major Issues Concerning Comprehensively Deepening the Reform* released in November 2013 provides that, on the premise of conforming to planning and usage control, it is permitted to transfer, rent and become a shareholder of the rural collective and operative construction-land. And the rural collective and operative construction land can enter the market with the same rights and price as the state-owned land so as to establish a unified market for rural and urban construction land. On 2nd December 2014, Leading Group for Comprehensively Deepening Reforms convened its 7th conference in which *the Opinions on the Acquisition of Rural Land, entry of the construction-land for rural collective profit-gaining into the market and the Pilot Work of Reform of the Homestead System* was deliberated. In order to further implement this *Opinions*, the Standing Committee of the National People's Congress examined the draft resolution on February 25, 2015, and intended to give mandate to the State Council to put into effect the land management law, the regulations of rural land acquisition, of the entry into market of the construction-land of rural collective profit-gaining, and of the management system of homestead under the management law of urban real estate in 33 pilot areas such as Daxing District across Beijing.

Therefore, in the next stage, we ought to endeavor to proactively conduct researches on the market-entering of rural construction-land, at the same time, to further specify the basic reform thought, which is to allow the rural collective construction-land recognized as land for management use to share the same rights with state-owned construction-land. On the conditions of conforming to the planning, utilization regulations and lawful acquisition, this kind of rural land specified above is allowed to be transferred, leased, become shareholder and enter into the market. Besides, we ought to perfect the transaction rules governing their entry into the market, supervision system and the reasonable distribution mechanism of land added- value revenue. To narrow down the land acquisition scope and release the market-entry space are critical to the market-entry of those rural lands. When it comes to the land acquisition, we need to distinguish between the "the general acquisition" and "policy acquisition". The former refers to the acquisition of those lands used for the development of public welfare undertakings, for which, the welfare items will have to be enumerated in details to the public, while the latter denotes the acquisition of land of public interest used for the "implementation of national economic policy", for which the specific compensation, land distribution and land premium are adopted by means of zonal expropriation. And the relevant authorities should provide a clear scope for Object of Transaction for the market-entry of construction-land of rural collective profit-gaining. As for the land in stock, those conforming to the planning and usage regulations can be transferred into market, and in the case where the lands located in far-flung areas are unable to gain access to the market immediately, its purchased developmental right could be remised to other regions' lands more suitable for development. The newly-acquired land should be at the time the land for agricultural purposes and should be transformed into construction-land for profit-gaining before they are allowed to be developed. As far as the incremental construction-land for profit-gaining is concerned, the government can either restore its original nature of non-profit-gaining or transform it into profit-gaining land according to the planning. These above-mentioned flexible policies are aimed at liquidizing and foregrounding the large amount of vacant rural collective construction-land, hence creating a broader space for its market-entry.

6.3.1.3 Compensated Use System and Voluntary Exit System of Farmers' Homestead

The basic idea for rural homestead system reform is to safeguard farmers' usufructuary right, create a new system of farmers' housing security, put in place a compensated use system and a voluntary exit system for famers' homestead and explore effective means of mortgaging, guaranteeing and transferring farmers' housing property right.

We should be prudent in determining the scope of the land transfer and lease, for our wish is to open up channels for increasing the farmers' property income and create an environment conducive to population flow and in situ urbanization rather than bringing about disruption to the rural social structure. Therefore, we need to explore various ways to realize housing security for farmers. In the course of farmers' citilization, we must take into consideration both the current situation and the future growth needs. To be specific, we can prioritize the policy of "household with a house held in hand" in areas where the land is in short supply while giving our support to the farmers' requirements for a better housing. We need to press ahead with the compensated use system of rural homestead in a steady manner and uphold farmers' wish. The scope of the compensated use should be expanded step by step so as to promote the economical and intensive use of homesteads and to promote the exchange of rural factors on a par with rural factors. Meanwhile, we ought to advocate the mortgage of farmers' housing property rights and the mortgage of farmers' usufruct of homestead, duly handle the relationships between welfare security function of homestead and commercial operations of financial institutions, explore various ways to provide guarantee, such as the collective economic organization guarantee, multi-household joint guarantee, the local government's guarantee etc. Those methods can both fulfil the farmers' basic housing needs, and outweigh as well the risk of incurred by mortgage right of homestead. Furthermore, it is essential for us to promote the coordinative utilization of vacant homesteads, to optimize and expand the range of surplus land-utilization index, to put in place a mechanism where farmers can share the profits reaped from development and promote the establishment of a unified market of construction-land for both urban and rural areas.

6.3.2 New Urbanization and Economical and Intensive Use of Land

Since the 1990s, the land has been playing an overwhelming role in China's economic growth, and has become the promoter of industrialization and urbanization. On one hand, its attribute as a resource endows the land with the capacity of bearing all of the human's economic and social activities; on the other hand, its attribute as a property, under China's unique political and institutional framework, makes it an important source of fiscal revenue for local governments. Besides, its capital attribute makes it a vital tool to utilize bank funds, and to make investment and financing for urban infrastructure and real estate. However, the current land system framework has exposed China's economic and social sustainable development in front of severe challenges. The rigid land system causes an inefficient use of the land factor, leading to a failure in establishing a supply mechanism up-to-date. To make it even worse, the utility efficiency of in-stock land is not high, and the problem of insufficient incremental supply of land remains pronounced. These problems are, to a great extent, due to the unclear relationships of property rights, a lack of developed land market and the immaturity of the land management system.

6.3.2.1 Land Urbanization Versus Population Urbanization

For more than 30 years after the reform and opening-up, China has experienced a rapid development of urbanization, with an average growth rate around 1%. During the process of this rapid urbanization, the land management policy of local governments, a special product of China's land system, has exercised great influences upon many aspects of urbanization. First, the local government's land profit-gaining policy, featuring land acquisition, land store and land disposal, has indirectly promoted the urbanization rate. The transaction cost in the market mechanism is brought down by virtue of the administrative power and government's overall planning and the land-acquisition. It has also helped shorten the process of agricultural land's transformation to non-agricultural land, and promoted the process of urbanization. Second, the financing method, characterized by land transfer and land mortgage, has provided fund support for the construction of urbanization. As the result of the primitive capital accumulation of urbanization development, the land transfer revenue generated by the liquidized land-rent contributed to the capital of urbanization. And the land mortgage financing has further brought into play the leveraging role of this sort of capital. What's more, many problems have arisen in the process of the local government's implementation of land profit-gaining policy. For example, extensive utilization of land, disordered urban spreading, uncoordinated planning between population urbanization and land urbanization and insufficient supply of total land amount. In addition, the construction of urbanization relies too heavily upon revenues from land sales. It in turn leads to the exorbitant housing price still skyrocketing and is inclined to exacerbate the social contradictions. These multifarious problems have severely hindered the further development of urbanization and continuous improvement of urbanization quality.

Population urbanization rate refers to the proportion of urban population in the total population, and is used to indicate population's aggregation degree towards urban areas. It is also an index that commonly employed to measure the urbanization level. At present, China's urbanization of population lags behind its industrialization, land urbanization, and its household register urbanization falls at the rear of its population urbanization. An analysis on population urbanization of different regions indicate that there is an obvious spatial difference in terms of

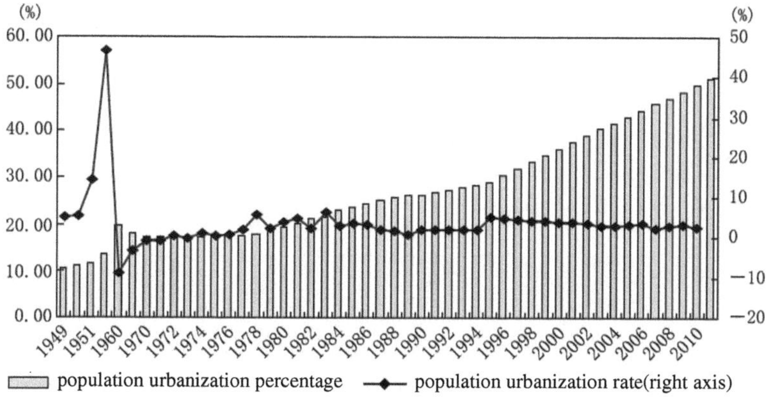

Fig. 6.9 Development trend of China's population urbanization from 1949 to 2011. *Source* Chinese Urban Statistical Yearbook

China's population urbanization, which is can be summarized as "high urbanization in eastern part but low in the west". In addition, the gap between land urbanization level of different regions, employment of the second and third industry, output value and GDP per capita are major reasons of such spatial difference. Seen from the nationwide perspective, China's urbanization level, which stood at about 10% in the 1950s, rose to 51.27% in 2011, an increase of more than four times. In terms of the speed, from 1951 to 1980, the urbanization speed keeps fluctuating considerably. Since 1984, the national urbanization level continued to go up, with the average annual growth reaching 4%, which means that altogether a total of 16.7 million rural people join the urban population per year (Fig. 6.9).

The other indicator of urbanization is urban spatial morphology. Many researchers opt to measure the urbanization level by looking at the ratio of urban area to the total area. In this chapter, the proportion of built-up area in total urban area and the utilization structure of urban built-up land are used to measure the land urbanization and structure. Since 1981, China's urban built-up area has expanded from 7438 to 43603.23 km^2, an increase of 3.75 times with an average annual growth rate of 6%. Seen from regional level, during the period from 1999 and 2011 the absolute expansion velocity of built-up area in 30 provinces (excluding Tibet) was exceedingly high, among which the top three provinces were Xinjiang, Yunnan, and Jiangxi, respectively attaining the rate of 29.32%, 27.9% and 26.98%. The province with the lowest rate is Heilongjiang, for which the average annual growth rate of 2012 reached yet as high as 6.38%. In sight of the relative value proportion of the built-up area's in total area, the average annual growth rate nationwide was 6.92%. Chongqing is the province with the fastest growth rate of 26.89%, and Gansu with the slowest, only −6.78% (Fig. 6.10).

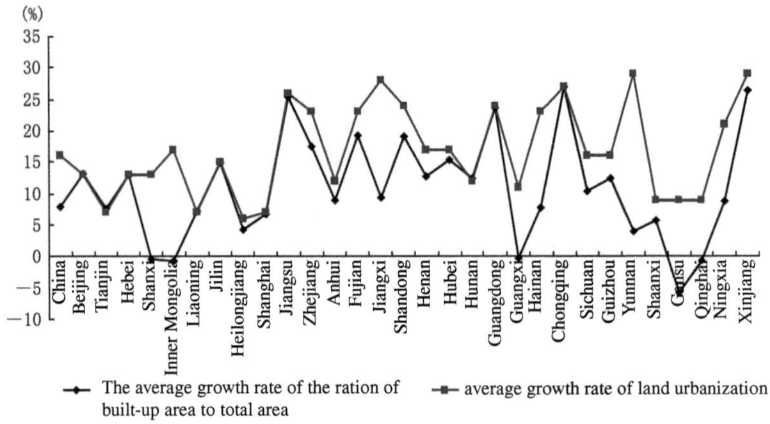

Fig. 6.10 Average growth rate of land urbanization in China's provinces from 1999 to 2011. *Source* Chinese Urban Construction Statistical Yearbook

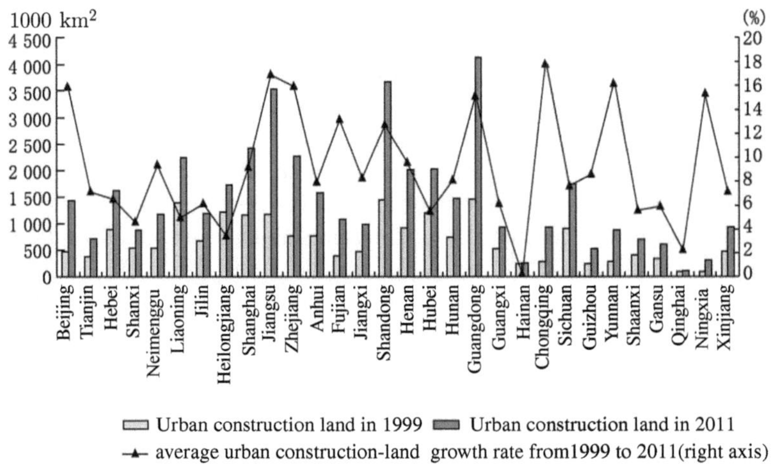

Fig. 6.11 The comparison of construction-land in China's provinces from 1999 to 2011. *Source* Chinese Urban Construction Statistical Yearbook

After 2000, with the implementation of national urban-rural integration system, urban construction land continued to expand in terms of scale. In 1999 alone, the size of urban construction land hit 20876.2 km^2. By 2011, the total amount of land used for urban construction doubled to 41806.25 km^2. In 1999, there were seven provinces and municipalities whose construction land area exceed 1000 km^2. Towards the end of 2011, the number climbed to 18. In terms of growth rate, the top five regions were Jiangsu, Zhejiang, Yunnan, Beijing, and Chongqing, for all of which the annual growth rate of construction-land was above 16%. And Hainan, though with the slowest growth rate, still kept the pace of increasing 1% on a yearly basis. The average growth nationwide in this period fell between 8 and 9% (Fig. 6.11).

6.3.2.2 Major Problems of Urban Land's Intensive Use

Either the land urbanization rate or the population urbanization varies from region to region and period to period. Between 1990 and 2006, the average annual growth rate of China's built-up area was 6.77%, while the average annual expansion rate of non-agricultural population was 4.56%, a disparity of nearly three percentage point in-between. The regional gap was even more articulated. The discrepancy between the land urbanization rate and the population urbanization rate for the eastern part of China was 1.8%, while 3% for the central part, and 5% for the western part, almost three times higher than eastern part. In other words, between 1990 and 2006, only the eastern regions achieved synergy between its urbanization of land and its urbanization of population, whereas in the central and western regions, the population urbanization lagged behind its land urbanization (Table 6.4).

From 1999 to 2011, the regional gap between population urbanization and land urbanization kept changing over the period of 1999–2011. In light of this single indicator, the non-agriculture transformation of population slowed down in the east regions, while speed up in the central and western regions, suggesting that the urbanization in eastern regions has entered its middle phase of development and the pace in the central and western regions is quickening. The overall rise of land urbanization implies that the built-up area has registered a fast expansion in three different parts of china. A further comparison and contrast shows that although both the level of non-agricultural population and the non-agricultural land nationwide were on the rise from 1999 to 2011, the yearly gap between these two indicators was becoming wider and wider. What's more, the regional gap in the east between the non-agricultural population and non-agricultural land was also growing to be 4.5%, as is the same case with the central region where the disparity reached 3.7%. In contrast, the western region, the gap reduced to 2.3 from 5%. On one hand, this evinces that China's population urbanization has registered a regional transition with the development of the east faster than that of the central and western regions. On the other, it demonstrates that non-agriculturalization of land in China is a trend nationwide created by the three parts of China vying against one another fiercely in

Table 6.4 The non-agricultural population growth and average annual expansion rate of built-up area from 1990 to 2006 (%)

Item	National average	Eastern average	Central average	Western average
Non-agricultural population growth rate	4.56	6.80	3.28	3.40
Expansion rate of constructed area	6.77	7.60	6.23	7.63
Differential	3.21	1.80	2.95	4.23

Source Chinese Urban Construction Statistical Yearbook

Table 6.5 The average annual growth rate of non-agricultural population and built-up area from 1999 to 2011 (%)

Item	National average	Eastern average	Central average	Western average
Non-agricultural population growth rate	6.80	6.79	4.07	6.54
Expansion rate of constructed area	9.31	10.31	6.79	9.84
Differential	3.51	4.52	3.72	2.30

Source Chinese Urban Construction Statistical Yearbook, Chinese Urban Statistical Yearbook

developing construction-land. This has obviously led to the current widening-gap between non-agricultural population and non-agricultural land (Table 6.5).

6.3.2.3 Connotative and New Urbanization Path to Improving Land Utilization Efficiency

From the above analysis, it can be concluded that in the course of rapid urbanization, the population urbanization falls behind the land urbanization. This problem is epitomized in the chaotic urban sprawl and inefficient and non-intensive utilization of urban land. Therefore, on the threshold of a new phase of development, we should not be satisfied with simply bringing up the proportion of urban population and expanding the urban area. Instead, we need to press ahead with the urbanization by putting the quality in the first place. Efforts should be made to materialize the real transformation from "country" to "city" in aspects such as the industrial structure, employment, living conditions and social welfare. Furthermore, the government should explore the connotative path of urbanization development, make concerted effort in industrialization, informatization, urbanization and agricultural modernization, and build a new pattern of development featuring urban-rural integration.

First of all, we ought to give impetus to the land in towns and cities by unlocking the land potential in old urban districts. We need to strengthen our planning for using urban land in stock and restrict the amount of new construction-land. For new projects, no new construction-land shall be endorsed if there is any yet in stock. Priority should be given to commercial housing, government-subsidized housing, and municipal utilities for low and medium income families in the re-utilization of the stock land. Besides, renovation should be carried out in old urban districts to speed up the adjustment of the industrial land structure there.

Second, we ought to press ahead with the reconstruction of "Villages Inside the Cities" and clear up the land for park-building and the land that lay unused. For those villages inside the built-up areas, encouragement should be given to all kinds of investors who wish to partake in their development and reconstruction. Necessary preferential policies should be available as incentives to prioritize it on our agenda. When it comes to the development zones and industrial parks, we need to improve their economical and intensive utilization degree and restrict their size and amount by strict planning and management. The right of formulating plans and approving shall be solely enforced by the planning administrative departments of the governments at county and municipal level rather than being decentralized. All the applications for setting up a development zone or expanding its acreage must be submitted to the governments at provincial level for deliberation and careful review. The range of land use should be checked and verified with feedbacks provided.

Third, we ought to advocate the new land resources and materials in an effort to use the land in an economical and intensive manner. In one word, we should tap the land underground and the space in the air. If funds and technologies permit, we should plan and utilize the urban underground space in a reasonable way. A review of the experiences over the world tells us that the exploitation of urban underground space is an effective means to enhance the land use efficiency and economize on land resources. The city has an enormous capacity underground which can furnish adequate back-up space and moderately increase the Floor Area Ratio of urban land and buildings; thus, on the condition of not affecting the overall landscape, we can relax the building's height-limit, and support the construction of the small and high-rise buildings while strictly forbidding the planning of villa.

Finally, we should push the reform related to land plan and land taxation in order to guide the economical and intensive utilization of land resource. As for the weak links of urban planning, we need to regulate it, improve its management, strengthen the land management and planning in the rural-urban fringe zone, and coordinate between various plans. We need to improve land tax structure by cutting down the current land value-added tax rate and the business tax rate levied in the transfer, raise the property-possession tax rate mildly and introduce tax on unused land. In one word, we need to adapt the present "high in transfer but low in possession" tax structure in an attempt to propel the land transfer, optimize the urban land resource allocation and bring up the efficiency in utilizing the land.

6.3.3 Breakthroughs of Reform of Distribution System of Land Added-Value Revenue

The Third Plenary Session of the 18th Central Committee pointed out in its *Decision* that we need to establish a distribution system of land-added value revenue to take into account the state's, collective and personal interests and improve personal interest appropriately. To surmount the problems such as imperfect distribution of land-added value revenue and inadequate consideration for the balance between the state's, collective and personal interests, we ought to work out a better method and a mechanism for distributing the revenue between the state and collectivity, and within the collective economic organizations.

6.3.3.1 Current Policy's Regulation on the Distribution of Land-Added Value Revenue

Regulation on the Land Transfer Cost and Revenue

Land transfer cost is mainly comprised of two parts: compensation cost of acquiring the land and development cost of the land.

Compensation cost consists of compensation fee of land acquisition and house relocation, subsidy to landless farmers and resettlement fee for enterprise employees etc. Compensation fee of land acquisition and house relocation encompasses the land compensation fee, subsidy for resettlement, compensation fee of ground attachments and compensation fee for green crops on the land etc., all paid by the governments at the county and municipal level during their attempts of land acquisition and house relocation. From 2008 to 2010, the yearly average proportion of compensation fee for land acquisition and relocation accounted for 36% of the total revenue of land transfer.

As for farmers who have their land acquired, the compensation is granted by the governments at county and municipal level with the purpose to protect their social welfare and maintain their original living standards. From 2008 to 2010, the yearly average proportion of compensation fee for those farmers occupied a 1.49% share of the total revenue of land transfer.

Resettlement is the fee paid by the governments at county and municipal level to the employees of bankrupt or restructured enterprises of state-ownership or collective ownership. From 2008 to 2010, the yearly average proportion of this item was about 7.9%.

Development cost refers to the expense incurred by leveling off the ground in the preliminary stage of construction. Paid by the governments at county or municipal level, this item represented a yearly average proportion of 9.03% from 2008 to 2010. The operational expenditure of land transfer is comprised of fees for land-surveying, assessment, transaction, advertising, venue rental, service of "Bid Invitation, Auction and Listing" and bid evaluation so on. From 2008 to 2010, the proportion of this item in the total transfer revenue arrived 0.62% on a yearly basis.

The span between 2008 and 2010 saw the land transfer revenue nationwide rise from 994.21 billion RMB Yuan to 2939.68 billion RMB Yuan, and development cost going up from 557.667 billion RMB Yuan to 1718.199 billion RMB Yuan, which accounted for 56.1% of the total revenue of land transfer (Table 6.6).

Relative Regulations on Land Transfer Expense

Land transfer revenue refers to the balance of the total land transfer income after deducting the cost. According to relevant laws and regulations, land transfer revenue is mainly used in the following eight aspects:

Table 6.6 Cost structure of national land transfer revenue over the years

Item	2008 (100 million RMB Yuan)	Ratio (%)	2009 (100 million RMB Yuan)	Ratio (%)	2010 (100 million RMB Yuan)	Ratio (%)	Average ratio (%)
Land transfer revenue	9942.1		14239.7		29396.98		
Fees of land acquisition and demolition	3662.13	36.83	4986.67	36.01	10677	36.32	36.06
Compensation to farmers who lost land	156.7	1.59	194.91	1.37	449.66	1.53	1.49
Land development in the early stage	903.38	9.09	1322.46	9.29	2561.15	7.71	9.03
Settlement fee of enterprise employees	782.41	6.87	1066.48	6.49	3336.63	11.35	7.90
Operative fee of land transfer	71.05	0.71	86.89	0.61	156.45	0.54	0.62
Subtotal cost	5576.67	56.09	7656.41	53.77	17181.99	57.45	56.10

Source Liu Shouying, Zhou Feizhou, Shao Ting land system reform and transformation model, China Development Press, 2012

Expense used for urban infrastructure development. There is no specific regulation on the proportion of capital expenditure on urban infrastructure construction. In 2010, the actual spending on the urban construction was 753.2 billion RMB Yuan, accounting for 62% of the national land transfer revenue.

Land use fee for newly constructed land. According to provisions, the land use fee is specially used for land development and land consolidation. For this fund, governments at provincial and municipal levels have their own charging standards. In 2010 alone, 98.373 billion RMB Yuan was spent altogether on this item, representing 8% of the total land transfer revenue.

Expense used for rural land development. Used for rural land development, it claims a proportion of no less than 15% of the total land transfer revenue. This part of spending in 2010 reached 18.787 billion RMB Yuan, equal to about 2% of the total land transfer revenue.

Expense used for urban and rural housing projects. Specially used for the construction of low-rent housing in urban and rural areas, it occupies a part no less than 10% of the total land transfer revenue. The actual sum of this item in 2010 reached 46.362 billion RMB Yuan, 4% of the total land transfer revenue.

Income fund of state-owned land. It is used specially for building land purchase reserve. The specific amount is decided by governments at county and municipal level. and usually represents a share between 3 and 5% of the total land transfer revenue. In 2010, it was 8%.

Table 6.7 National expenditure and revenue of land transfer revenue (0.1 billion)

Item	2008	2009	2010
Land transfer revenue	4563.08	6867.84	12216.99
Planned fees used for education	–	–	–
Planned fees used for construction of water conservancy	–	–	–
Planned fees used for income fund of state-owned land	307.91	440.63	1006.89
Planned used for rural land development	126.07	143	187.87
Expense for urban and rural housing projects	146.57	186.14	63.62
Expense for urban construction	3024.02	3340.99	7531.67
Expense for rural infrastructure development	337.3	433.1	1021.68
Additional fee	637.71	923.11	983.73
Total expenditure of land transfer revenue	4581.58	5466.93	11196.46
Surplus of land transfer revenue	−17.51	400.91	1017.53

Source Liu Shouying, Zhou Feizhou, Shao Ting Land System Reform and Transformation Model, China Development Press, 2012

Expense used for rural infrastructure construction. There is no regulation with regard to the exact percentage of this spending. This item in 2010 costs 7.36% of the total land transfer revenue.

Fees for education and construction of water conservancy and hydropower. According to regulations, these two kind of undertakings shall start to draw 10% of the total land transfer from 2010.

From the elaboration of the above items of expenditure, it can be concluded that the use of land transfer revenue has shifted. Originally spent on urban construction, it gradually started to be used for building rural infrastructure, agriculture facilities and improving people's livelihood. It signals that the distribution of the land added-value has become fairness and welfare-oriented (Table 6.7).

Management Policy of Revenue and Expenditure of the Land Transfer

Along with the deepening of the reform the compensable land utilization system, the land transfer revenue has witnessed a rapid growth, for which the state has strengthened its administration in respects of collecting and using the revenue.

In the aspect of access policy for the land transfer revenue, the *Land Administration Law of the People's Republic of China* issued in 1988 stipulated that "the land's usufruct of the state-ownership and of the farmers' collective ownership may be transferred in accordance with relevant laws" and "the state shall, according to the laws, introduce the system of compensable utilization to the state-owned land". In May 1990, the State Council came up with *Interim Regulations of PRC Concerning the Assignment and Transfer of the Usufruct e of the State-owned Land in the Urban Areas*, stating clearly that "the transfer of usufruct denotes that the state, which is the owner of the land, may transfer the right to use the land for a certain period of years to users who shall in return pay the state accordingly." In

1999, the Ministry of Finance and Ministry of Land and Resources jointly promulgated the *Regulations of Collecting and Using the Land Use Fee for the Newly-added Construction-Land,* which specifies that as the State Council or the provincial people's governments ratify the conversion or acquisition of the agricultural land, they can charge the average net income from the people's government at the country and municipal level having obtained the newly-added land for construction. In 2003, the Ministry of Land and Resources further published *Provisions for the Agreement-based Assignment of the Right to Use State-Owned Land*, which makes it clear that when the State transfers the usufruct to land users for a certain term by means of agreements, the land users shall in return pay fees to the State.

In the aspect of management policy for land transfer revenue, the State Council published the *Circular on Further Strengthening the administration of collection and administration of paid use of state owned land use right* in 1993, dictating that that the compensable utilization income of state-owned land gained by governments at all level must be included in the measurement of fiscal budget according to the current financial system. In 1995, the Ministry of Finance and State Land Administration jointly launched the *Circular on Strengthening the Collection and Administration of Land Use Right Leasing Fees*, requiring that fees collected by assigning the right to the use of the land be included in the fiscal budget and managed as a special fund, which shall be used for urban construction and land development. Henceforth, the total revenue of land transfer was brought into the administration of special local financial accounts whereas the net income shall be preserved in the local treasury. In 2006, the State Council promulgated the *Circular on standardizing the Revenue and Expenditure Administration of the Transfer of the State-owned Land Usufruct*, providing that the total revenue of state-owned land transfer shall come under budgetary control and its expenditure shall be planned through local fund. The practice of "separating the revenue with expenditure" is a strong proof that the land transfer revenue has been properly regulated and standardized. In 2009, the Ministry of Finance, Ministry of Land and Resources and the People's Bank of China jointly launched the *Circular of the State Council on Further Strengthening the Management of Revenue and Expenditure of Land Transfer*, reiterating and emphasizing that the revenue and expenditure shall be fully covered in the budgetary administration and the revenue and expenditure shall be separated and managed respectively. The revenue shall be fully preserved in the local treasury in an attempt to perfect the information sharing system of land transfer revenue. At the same time, the circular also required that the policies on budgetary lay-out, the statistical report compilation, and the accountability mechanism be put in place.

In the aspect of distribution policy of land transfer revenue, China has gone through three phased since 1989. The first stage lasted from 1989 till 1993, which was the stage of revenue-sharing between central finance and local finance. At the time, the balance of 40% of the state-owned land revenue was turned over to the central finance after the deduction of 20% as the fees for urban development and construction while the remainder shall be retained in local finance having obtained the income. The result of such policy implementation was the phase-down of central finance sharing ratio, which was 40% in 1989 but 5% in 1992. In the second stage, starting from 1994 to 1998, all land transfer revenue went into the local governments. In 1994, the tax-sharing fiscal system was carried out, stating clearly that land compensation income shall be enrolled as the local regular income and shall be in its totality at the disposal of the local governments. The total revenue shall come under the budgetary control of the special local financial accounts with the net income preserved in the local treasury. As for the revenue and expenditure, they could be administered either under or off the budget.

The third stage started from 1999 to this day. Different management methods are adopted for land transfer revenue in response to the newly-added or stock construction-land. In order to strictly control the behavior of occupying the cultivated land and encourage local government to efficiently use stock construction-land, the *Land Administration Law* (1998s revised version) has stipulated in its 55th provision that 30% of the land compensation fees of newly-added construction-land shall be handed over to the state, while the local finance shall retain the rest 70% to be used for the development of cultivated land. Actually, the real situation is that the ratio of local retention basically reached 80%.

6.3.3.2 Main Problems Facing the Distribution of Land-Added Revenue

The main problem facing land-added revenue is the distribution unfairness between urban and rural areas in the process of transforming agricultural land into the land for non-agricultural purposes. During this process, the land-added revenue is mainly levied by the government and the compensation shall be granted in line with the original purposes of the land. The maximum land compensation fees and resettlement fees shall not exceed 30 times of the average annual output value of the past 3 years. According to this principle, after being compensated, the farmers are not entitled to share the land-added revenue. Since the people's governments at the municipal and county levels are the implementers of land-acquisition and the sole providers of land in the primary land-market, they are entitled in the first place to obtain, use and dispose the land added-value. Under the current rules of state-owned construction-land, the land users have the right to occupy, use, benefit from, transfer and mortgage the land after possessing the usufruct according to the law. With the deepening of the urbanization, the land value keeps rising rapidly with the majority of the land added-value going to the land users in the foreseeable future. And the local governments will gain part of the income by levying tax on the transaction. The current distribution system fails to match the principle generating the land added-value during in the process of urbanization, and has caused a tremendous unfairness in distributing the land-benefits. The original collective owners obtain only a low level of compensation, and the compensation to farmers who have their land acquired needs to be standardized, more transparent and principle-orientated; the governments' lump-sum income is unreasonably high but the prospective benefit of added-value it can touch in the future is meagre; the lump-sum payment of the real estate investors and purchasers for the land transfer is exorbitant and the land users have in the future a lion's share in the benefits they could rear in the land added-value. These institutional factors have all led to the current unfair income distribution.

6.3.3.3 Redesigning Fair Compensation Principles as the Core of Land Acquisition System

The traditional land acquisition system suffers from a number of deficiencies such as an unreasonably broad scope of acquisition, the lop-sided operation of the government, low compensation standard and insufficient social welfare protection for the farmers having their land acquired. The dispute arising from the land acquisition is essentially a scramble of interested parties for land added-value. The compensation principles for land acquisition are directly pertinent to whether the distribution of the benefits of land added-value is fair or not. Therefore, the reform of the land acquisition system is supposed be based on the core of fair compensation principles. We should redefine the public interests and consider involving famers in the land-acquisition game. Efforts should be made as well to redesign the social welfare system to better support farmers.

Firstly, fair compensation principles shall be set up. According to the 47th provision in the *Land Administration Law*, as a result of land-acquisition, compensation shall be granted in line with the original purposes of the land acquired, which is affirmatively improper. Rather, through referring to the principle of "giving due consideration to both public and private interests" in the distribution of land added-value benefits, we can consider compensating the farmers according to the "well-off standard". All of the following should be taken into consideration as well: narrowing down the scope of land acquisition, redefining the public interests, making a list of exclusions for land-acquisition, building a reasonable, standard and pluralistic social welfare system. Besides, the compensation for land-acquisition shall be fair and reasonable, and the procedure should be standard as well. In addition, the scope-defining, compensation price-setting and procedure of land-acquisition should be lawful. What's more, the methods to support famers having their land acquired are pluralistic. Apart from monetary compensation, we have a number of alternatives such as compensation in kind, providing reemployment training for those famers, and approving the construction of the rural collective "household plot" for non-agricultural purposes.

Secondly, incentive and restraining mechanisms of government behavior shall be available. We have to admit that the GDP-based incentive mechanism has been highly conducive to promoting the local economic growth over a long period of time. However, with the adjustment of social structure and deepening of social reform, the negative impact of such a mechanism has started to present itself. Quite a number of local officials seeking eagerly to be promoted was seized by an urgent need to score "remarkable" achievements during his term of office. As a usual practice, they are rather active in pressing ahead with the land-acquisition on the pretext of public interest. The consequence is that a great number of vanity projects and prestige projects have mushroomed. Therefore, the achievement system for evaluating officials should be revised as soon as possible to encompass standards such as environmental protection, public welfare, social justice etc. so as to entitle people to more fruits of the societal development. We need to further legalize the administration's functioning mechanism by standardizing the governments' right to discretion from the perspective of entity and procedure. At the same time, we need to strengthen the administrative supervision function of National People's Congress at all levels, enhance the transparency of its administrative work and reduce the opportunistic behaviors on the part of the government agents by having recourse to penalties when necessary.

Thirdly, the system of land development right shall be in place. In designing the land development right system, we intend to address the ownership and distribution problems arising from the land added-value benefits generated by the conversion of land-use or the escalated development. Nonetheless, China has been default on establishing a lawful system of land development. In practice, the early form of land development rights has taken shape, for example, the construction-land in urban and rural areas has been linked and in Chongqing the "land ticket"[5] trading has emerged, by reclaiming the idle rural construction-land, the arable land is restored, which is to be swapped with urban construction-land on an equal footing. This so called "land ticket" can add to the increment of the state-owned construction-land, representing essentially the transaction of land development right. The philosophy of "giving due consideration to both public and private interests" means that China is intended the farmers and governments to be the future subjects of the land development right. The Land development right can be divided into land development rights of landless farmers, land development rights of farmers who have arable lands and land development rights of the government. This classification does not entail the presence of multiple independent development rights. Rather, it denotes a sharing between plural subjects of a single land development right, analogous to joint ownership or ownership-in-share or a division of the ownership in quantity. Giving due consideration to state, collectivity and individuals, it lays theoretical basis for the distribution system of land added-value income. As for the arable land, it is necessary to set up a permanent basic farmland protection system and a land development right system whereby we can make better protect the benefits of farmers in possession of arable land.

[5]Land ticket refers to the land index created by homestead, the land used for attached facilities, township enterprises, rural social undertakings after going through the government's strict checking-up.

Chapter 7
Supply Side Structural Reform and Exogenous Variables (Supply of New Institutions, Supply of New Structures, and Supply of New Policies)

The mainstream economics has long ignored the existence of institutional and structural factors, and economic growth is always seen as a process of input and output, in which resources allocation will be automatically optimized through market mechanisms so as to achieve continuous growth and overall improvement of welfare. However, with the rise of new institutional economics and the new structuralism, the effects of institutional innovation and structural adjustment to economic growth have drawn more and more attention. Especially for China, whose system has long been in a transition process from planned economy to market economy, there are a series of structural problems caused by the price distortions under the "plan", and therefore, the institutions and structures in economics have become important variables that cannot be ignored. Supply side structural reform implemented in China aims to improve the quality and benefits of the supply system, enhance the flexibility and adaptability of the supply structure to the changes in demand, and increase sustained economic growth momentum. To this end, it is necessary to speed up the factors upgrading, while increasing institutional and structural supply in a comprehensive manner, improving total factor productivity, and optimizing supply policy by developing effective measures according to the problems that constrain economic growth.

7.1 Institutions, Structures, Policies and Economic Growth

The rapid economic growth for the 30 years after China's reform and opening-up is largely the result of institutional innovation and structural adjustment, and the incremental reform outside the system greatly increases the supply side efficiency. The integration into the global economic system enhances China's position in the global value chain and sharpens China's overall economic competitiveness. With

L. Xiao, *New Supply Side Economics*, DOI 10.1007/978-981-10-4639-1_7

China's economy entering a new stage of "structural slowdown", the advantages of the traditional factors gradually weaken or disappear; therefore, we should pay more attention to institutional innovation and structural adjustment, mining the source of sustainable economic growth. From the perspective of both theory and practice, this section will analyze the relationship among institutions, structures, policies and economic growth in China's supply side structural reform.

7.1.1 Institutional Innovation and Economic Growth

American economist Douglass C. North, in his research on economic history in western countries, asks the questions that under the same capitalist system, why some countries develop fast while others slow, why some developing countries can accomplish their fast-track development, while other developed countries gradually fall into decline? North holds that institution plays a very important role in this process, and efficient economic organization is key to economic growth. What are decisive to economic growth are institutional factors instead of technical factors, and institutions can be defined as a set of established rules, procedures and ethics of behavior, which not only include formal institutions such as laws and rules, but also some informal institutions such as customs and conventions.

According to the new institutional economics, efficient institutions will reduce the uncertainty and the costs of transaction, stabilize the expectation of the economic subjects to the future, and prevent them from the opportunistic behavior to pursue maximal short-term benefits, thus promoting economic growth. First, institutional transaction structures help to identify the complicated social environment. As North has pointed out, the structure of a contract depends on the law system, the social conventions and the technical properties of the asset in the transaction. The more complete the law framework, the stronger connection between social rules and social conventions, the less uncertain the contract content. The transaction by the individual with bounded rationality in the complicated environment will be greatly simplified, and the reduction of transaction costs means the increase of economic benefits.

Second, institutions affect the personal choice through encouragement, constraint, punishment, etc. Thrainn Eggertsson maintains that contradictions exist everywhere. The rational pursuit of personal interests is the main reason of economic recession as well as the main source of economic growth and prosperity. Good or bad, the result depends on the man-made social institutional structures, in other words, social institutional structures decide the behavior of economic subjects, while the behavior of economic subjects under certain institutional structures decides the economic performance.

Finally, efficient institutions will stabilize the expectation of the economic subjects to the future, and prevent them from opportunistic behavior. When the transaction among individuals is a repeated game and its scale is fairly small, people tend to cooperate. However, with the increasingly complicated division of labor, when personalized transactions change into non-personalized transactions, this cooperation mechanism is hard to form. China is in its transformation period. Due to the uncertainties brought by frequent institutional changes, the economic subjects are stimulated to pursue maximal short-term benefits with opportunism. Although these behaviors are rational in terms of individual, they will lead to irrational consequences to the society.

Institutional economics is of great value to the analysis of contemporary China's economic reform. After the implementation of China's economic reform for over 30 years, the reform has entered the deep-water area, shifting its focus from incremental reform to inventory assets restructuring. At present, many problems arising in the development are related to the imperfect institutions, which mainly exist in the market, government and enterprise system. Generally speaking, the relationship among government, market and society is not completely straightened out. The phenomena such as offside, dislocation and absence of the government functions are still common, and there is still a gap between institutional innovation and demand of enterprises and market. Market access is still not open and transparent enough. Some provisions related to opening access lack operational details, and some hidden barriers to access still exist. The effectiveness of market supervision needs to improve, the methods of during-supervision and post-supervision are few, and the capacity to discover and deal with the violations is weak. The reform of state-owned assets and enterprises is facing a new situation. The unreasonable state-owned economic distribution persists, and the average efficiency and benefits of state enterprises are low. The reform of state enterprises in monopoly industries is in slow progress with many obstacles. Unreasonable interest structure is yet to break up, and the transfer of state owned property rights is facing many difficulties.

To solve those deep-seated problems, the key lies in institutional innovation to construct a mechanism conforming to the requirements of economic development under the "New Normal". The core issue is to deal with the relationship between the government and the market so that the market can play a decisive role in the resources allocation and the government can play a better role. China must actively and steadily promote market-oriented reform in width and in depth, greatly reduce direct resources allocation by the government, and promote the resources allocation in accordance with market rules, prices, and competition to achieve maximum benefits and efficiency. The role and function of the government is to maintain macroeconomic stability, strengthen and optimize public services, ensure fair competition, strengthen market supervision, and make up for market failure.

7.1.2 Structural Adjustment and Economic Growth

The general study of economic growth shows that economic growth is not only a process of total growth, but also a process of structural changes and structural growth, which has become the inherent power of sustained economic growth.

However, the understanding of structural adjustment in economics has experienced a process of evolution.

In the 1950s and 1960s, two schools of thought launched a heated debate: The structural school advocated government intervention or even government control of the entire economy, while the new liberal school advocated free trade, relying on comparative advantages to promote economic growth. The views of structural school were once applied in many developing countries. In those countries, through the implementation of the "import substitution strategy", the governments directly pooled their resources to overcome market failure and established modernized capital-intensive industries. But after a period of rapid growth, economic stagnation occurred, which led to an increasingly wider gap between those countries and the developed countries, making structuralism gradually fall into decline. Then the new liberalism theory began to prevail, attracting many followers. Since 1990s, the structuralism theory started to revive, and some mainstream economists applied the methods of new classical economics to structuralism, rethinking the relationship between government and market and forming a more convincing framework. Representative figures include Joseph, Bardhan, Faye Duchin etc.

In recent years, the new structural economics proposed by Justin Yifu Lin has drawn attention of many scholars. The analysis of new structural economics is based on the factor endowment and its structures at each time point, i.e., the economic structure is determined by the factor endowment and its structures at that time. Developing economies are usually relatively scarce in capital, but rich in labor and natural resources; developed economies are usually relatively abundant in capital, but scarce in labor. The industries with relatively abundant factor endowment constitute the advantageous industries of a country, or in other words, the most competitive industries. For an economy, factor endowment is given at one point, but it can change over time. New structural economics explains how the developing countries construct a dynamically competitive upgrading path of industry structures according to their own factor endowment, integrate the connections of different structures such as factor structures and industry structures into a unified analysis framework, and focus on the government's guiding role in industrial upgrading and diversification. Compared with the traditional structural economics, this theory is based on the logic to maximize the potential comparative advantages, integrating government and market into a unified analysis framework, and providing useful guidance on making dynamically competitive industrial policies.

When analyzing the relationship between structural adjustment and China's economic growth, we should closely combine theory with practice. From the perspective of economics, structural adjustment can promote economic growth mainly by transferring factors from less efficient sectors and regions to more efficient ones so as to enhance the efficiency of resources allocation and total factor productivity. Since the reform and opening-up, two important reasons for China's rapid economic development are the structural effects resulted from industrial structure evolution and the improvement of factor replacement efficiency. With the increasing rationalization of the industrial structure in China, the contribution rate of industrial structure changes and factor replacement efficiency to economic growth is decreasing. At the same time, China's low-end position in the global value chain has not been fundamentally changed. With the increasingly deepening division of labor in global manufacturing industry, although China's manufacturing industry has seen some features of upgrading, its high-end link and key technologies are still very weak. For a period of time in the future, to promote supply side structural reform, technological progress and industrial upgrading should be put in a more prominent position and more efforts should be made to drive innovation. We should also reshape the competitive advantage through technological progress, speed up independent innovation, and develop more leading industries that rely on first mover advantage.

Meanwhile, optimization of urban and rural structures and regional structures is also significant in China's economic growth. From the perspective of the supply side, urbanization leads to the agglomeration of innovation and capital, which makes the production factors and economic activities further concentrate in cities and city clusters, therefore, greater external effects and larger scale economies can effectively enhance innovation and vitality, promote more specified social labor division, drive the upgrading of traditional industries, and promote the development of emerging industries. Since the reform and opening-up, China's urbanization is continuously deepening, especially the eastern coastal regions, which take the lead in development, have formed a number of distinctive city clusters and numerous small and medium-sized cities and become the important growth pole and propeller of economic development. In the future, China needs to give full play to the urbanization's motivating effects to the supply side, coordinate the relationship among industrial development, employment and population concentration, coordinate the relationship between urban development and the carrying capacity of resources and environment, and coordinate the relationship between concentration of rural population in cities and the balanced development of urban and rural areas. Besides, China should pay more attention to efficient, inclusive and sustainable development so as to enhance the overall innovation capability and accelerate the industrial upgrading.

7.1.3 Policies Supply and Economic Growth

To promote China's supply side structural reform, we should take comprehensive measures both in the short term and in the long term. On the one hand, taking a long-term view, we should actively promote factor upgrading, structural adjustment and institutional innovation, expand effective supply and high-end supply, stimulate vitality and impetus of supply side, and improve the total factor productivity; on the other hand, to address the urgent problems at hand, we should step up to adjust or cut the inventory, prevent and resolve financial risks, promote economic structure optimization, and improve the quality and benefits. At present, China is facing overcapacity in large part of its economy, with economic benefits declining and losses increasing. Meanwhile, systematic financial risks become higher, especially when four risks appear together, i.e., local government debt, shadow banking, overcapacity, and excess inventory of real estate. If not timely and effectively dealt with, chain crisis may occur and bring a heavy blow to China's economy. In order to solve the current problems and create a sound environment to push forward the supply side structural reform in the medium and long term, we must absorb the overcapacity as quickly as possible, enhance the competitiveness of the real economy and enterprises, and eliminate the financial risks so as to realize stable and healthy economic development.

In the policy-making process, it is significant to combine short-term policy with deep roots. Take overcapacity as an example. In the market economy, that supply is moderately greater than demand is the normal state of competition. Only when the supply side maintains appropriate overcapacity will the enterprises feel the survival pressure, try to innovate and win more consumers. However, in China's current development, due to the existence of institutional mechanisms, overcapacity, to some extent, shows different characteristics compared with the developed countries. As a large developing country, China's economic development system is closely related to local governments' competition under the decentralization. In order to encourage governments to promote economic growth in the local areas, China adopts performance evaluation mechanism centering on the growth rate of GDP. The local governments use various policies to promote industries that can boost GDP growth, resulting in that the investment is not made based on the market but the policies, including financial subsidies, tax incentives, low land prices, bank credit and so on. Therefore, in order to make policies to absorb overcapacity, we should start with industrial policies to break up the governments' improper intervention of the industries, distinguish different overcapacity and adopt corresponding measures and policies, for example, those enterprises still prosperous after transformation and upgrading should be encouraged to reform, those unpromising "zombie" enterprises should be firmly phased out, and those enterprises that can be restructured should have business acquisitions and restructuring. Meanwhile, social security policy should be strengthened to prevent the emergence of massive unemployed population.

7.2 Market Reform and Supply of New Institutions

Under the New Normal, structural contradictions and problems in China can be boiled down to the bottleneck of institutional mechanisms, which should be addressed through comprehensive institutional reform. The core of the reform is to give full play to the decisive role of the market in the resources allocation, eliminate the supply constraints in the resources of labor, capital, technology, land, etc., fully release the vitality and potential of micro subjects in economy and society, and improve quality and benefits of the supply system. To be specific, the market reform mainly focuses on three levels: The governments properly perform their duties and better plays their role; the market operates efficiently to improve the efficiency of resources allocation; the enterprises, especially the state enterprises, compete independently as market players.

7.2.1 Government Performance and Power Boundary

7.2.1.1 The Transformation of Government Functions and Existing Problems

The transformation of government functions has always been the focus of China's administrative system reform. After years of implementation, streamlining administration and delegating power have accelerated, and public service, market supervision and social management have been strengthened. But overall, prominent problems still exist. The traditional system and the new system overlap with poor management and low efficiency. Demand of enterprises, market and government are not coordinated and consistent, so efficient and transparent administrative management system has not been formed. First, approaches to macro regulation still need to be improved. In recent years, China's macro regulation continues to improve by implementing such innovative approaches as the range-based regulation, targeted regulation and well-timed regulation, and adopting various regulation tools, and it is accelerating to create the system of macro regulation tools with The Chinese characteristics. However, generally speaking, a lot of macro regulation is still implemented through administrative means, not giving full paly to economic and legal means, the role of the market mechanisms also needs to be strengthened, and the macro regulation means need to be continuously innovated and improved. Second, the relationship among government, market and society has not been fully straightened out. The offside, dislocation and absence of the government functions are still common. The governments have not fully fulfilled their duties, or adapted to the new management concepts and methods. There is still a gap between institutional innovation and demand of enterprises and market. The decisive role of the market has not been fully embodied, and what should be left to the market mechanisms and enterprises has not been fully delegated to them. The pattern of multiple social subjects such as intermediary organizations participating administration has not been established, and the functions or responsibilities of intermediary organizations have not been fully fulfilled. Third, there are still many weak points in public services, social governance, market supervision, etc. There is still imbalance between public services and public demand. Some public welfare functions the government should fulfill need to be improved, and some prominent problems related to the interests of the people have not been completely resolved. Public services are not balanced, and the regional differences are sharp. Rural public services are not completely implemented, with public services level for the farmers being lower than that for urban residents. Social management cannot adapt to the changes of diversified social structure, which makes social governance innovation imperative. Market supervision cannot meet the new requirements. In some areas, there is no market supervision or inadequate market supervision, particularly the safety supervision, which cannot meet the expectations of the public.

7.2.1.2 The Paths to Deepening Government Reform and Functions Transformation

To press ahead supply side structural reform, we must effectively transform government functions, deepen the administrative system reform, develop new ways of administrative management, adhere to the combination of "take over, delegate or fulfill", and synchronize "control, adjust and reform". The role of government should be fully played through scientific macro regulation and efficient administrative governance. Meanwhile, the market should play a decisive role in the resources allocation, the environment of the supply side should be optimized and the supply efficiency should be enhanced so as to strengthen the sustainable momentum of economic growth.

The first duty of the government is to carry out scientific macro regulation and to create a stable macroeconomic environment. The focus of the government is to maintain economic balance, accelerate economic restructuring and productivity distribution optimization, curb inflation, prevent deflation, mitigate the impact of business cycle fluctuation, reduce systematic risks, stabilize market expectations, and promote the sustained and healthy economic development. To be specific, measures include adopting proactive fiscal policies, such as increasing financial deficit ratio step by step, expanding the scope of structural tax reductions, making more fiscal fund available, putting more dormant budgetary funds to good use, and optimizing spending structures; moderately flexible monetary policies should be implemented, such as developing multi-level financial system, promoting development of small loan companies, private lending and Internet finance in line with regulations, opening up inter-bank market, and making moderate progress in total social financing; the scope and intensity of the use of monetary policy tools should be continuously increased to reduce corresponding financing costs; exchange rate formation mechanism should be improved to create an enabling environment for monetary and financial structural reform. Therefore, more attention should be paid to the innovation and pertinence of macro regulation. On the one hand, we should innovate the methods of regulation by relying more on market and reform. We should focus on stabilizing the market expectation and strengthening the micro and targeted regulation, and focus on stimulating endogenous motivation, promoting structural optimization, increasing support for shutting down outdated production facilities, and pressing ahead the healthy development of strategic emerging industries. We should focus on increasing capital benefits, taking a combination of measures to put dormant budgetary funds to good use for ensuring people's livelihood and making up the weak points, and focus on preventing potential risks and orderly replacing dormant debts. On the other hand, we should step up to improve the macro regulation mechanism which can adapt to the development laws of the market economy and the open economy. We should strengthen the coordination among fiscal policy, monetary policy and other policies to form the mechanism which will coordinate international macroeconomic policies, and strengthen the perceptiveness and pertinence of the macro regulation. In responding to different stages, situations and characteristics, keeping pace with the times, we should explore, innovate, adjust and improve the regulation methods and policy tools, and enhance the policy's pertinence of the reality. We should maintain the continuity and stability of macroeconomic policies, adhere to the alignment of various regulation methods such as range-based, targeted, and well-timed regulation in a flexible way, and appropriately exercise pre-regulation and micro regulation to stabilize the market confidence and social expectations. We should establish and improve the coordination mechanism for important policies, and focus on the direction, efforts, rhythm and timing of policies, thus forming the concerted efforts of regulation. We should improve the policy analysis and evaluation mechanism, and strengthen comprehensive evaluation and coordination of policies, especially important policies, to enhance the effectiveness of the policy system of macro regulation.

Comprehensively and correctly performing the functions is the core requirement for government to better play its role. On the one hand, we should further streamline administration, delegate power and clarify boundaries of government functions. To be specific, we should further delegate power to market, clarify boundaries of government power so as to minimize the government's management of the micro items, and further delegate power to the local governments, making them manage the micro items of large quantity and wide range more conveniently and efficiently; meanwhile, we should strengthen the capacity of local governments, regulate the operation of administrative power, and further delegate power to the society, increasing the discourse power of the public to the government administrative operation, improving the mechanisms for the enterprises and the public to participate in the policy making, argumentation and evaluation, and attracting social intermediary organizations such as industry associations, chambers of commerce and market specialization services to participate in the public governance. On the other hand, we should accelerate the government reform and improve their ability to properly perform their duties. To be specific, we should deepen the reform of the administrative examination and approval system, aiming at furthest facilitating the enterprises as the main players in the market and pressing ahead the innovation of approval procedures; we should innovate during and post-supervision, delegate more power, improve regulation, and step up to establish the platform of government supervision through the use of big data, cloud computing, the Internet of Things and other means of information technologies; we should optimize the supply of public services, innovate the methods of providing public services, improve the resources allocation by the use of market and social mechanisms, attract social capital to participate in a wide range of public services, and improve their quality and quantity; we should promote and form green production and consumption, establish a complete system of ecological civilization, strengthen the constraints to low-end supply, and encourage green supply.

The main starting point of the government functions transformation is the institutional reform in the key areas. In particular, we should focus on promoting the reform of the financial system, deepening the division of responsibilities and expenditure of the central and local governments, establishing a public service oriented relation between the central and local finance, improving standardized and transparent modern budget system, and accelerating the reform of the tax system; we should focus on deepening investment system reform, properly defining the scope of government investment according to the economic and social development, keeping appropriate scale of government investment, making the decision-making process of the government-invested projects more scientific and democratic, implementing the autonomy of enterprises to invest, drawing up the long-term plans and annual plans for the government investment, coordinating and reasonably using various types of government investment funds; we should focus on deepening the reform of the financial sector, promoting the reform of the banking system and the capital market system, and strengthening the financial supervision institutions; we should focus on deepening the reform of opening-up system and mechanism in order to follow the trend of China's economy fully integrating into the world economy, establishing the international, legal and convenient business environment, expanding the opening-up of services in a planned way, improving the promotion system of services trade, pressing ahead cooperation of international production and equipment manufacturing, making progress in the mutual promotion of inside and outside opening-up so as to better integrate" and "bringing in" and "going out", allowing free and orderly movement of both international and domestic factors for efficient resources allocation and their deep embedding into the market, and developing a new open economic system of a higher level.

7.2.2 Market Mechanisms and Market Institutions

7.2.2.1 The Development of Market Mechanisms and the Existing Problems

Since the reform and opening-up, China's market system construction is gradually changing its focus from the construction of commodity market to that of factor market. The construction of market systems and mechanisms has made remarkable achievements, with its rules gradually completing and its functions and role significantly improving; however, there are still some prominent contradictions and weak links, in particular, the role of the market in the resources allocation has not been fully played, constraining the effective supply of factors and affecting the vitality of the market. First, market access is still not open and transparent enough. Government intervention in some micro economic activities still exists, and some of the administrative examination and approval procedures have not adapted to the requirements of business model innovation, which need to speed up their restructuring. Market access does not fully open, with hidden barriers of access still existing. Relevant statistics show that currently among the 80 sectors in the whole society, those allowing in foreign capital account for nearly 80%, while those allowing in private capital account for only 50%. Second, market regulation system needs to be improved. The relevant laws and regulations of the modern market need to be improved, and the construction of the basic system of some markets needs to be strengthened. Third, the market operation mechanism is not mature. Under the current situation, the pricing mechanism of resources and factors and the environmental charging mechanism, which reflect the supply and demand relationship, the scarcity of resources and the environmental damage costs, have not been established. Some markets need to speed up their reform and innovation in operation and management mechanisms. Regional market cooperation mechanism and integrated development mechanism are in slow progress, and there are still market barriers in government procurement, policy support, etc. Forth, market environment needs to be improved. At present, market supervision focuses on administrative management, lacking effective and comprehensive market supervision and institutional restriction. The methods of during-supervision and post-supervision are few, and the capacity to discover and deal with the violations is weak. The market order of fair competition has not fully formed, therefore, in some areas, the competition rules are not strictly followed and the procedures are not highly transparent, especially the procedures of bidding, procurement, and approval of the projects, which lack measures to maintain fair competition. The construction of credibility system is still in the starting stage, cross-sector and cross-field information sharing is inadequate, and the accuracy and the timeliness of the credibility information is yet to be improved.

7.2.2.2 The Paths to Deepening Market Mechanisms

The prerequisite of improving the market mechanisms is to establish fair, open and transparent market rules, whose core lies in expanding and improving the market access to allow market players into various industries and businesses legally with equal access; we should establish the access institution in line with the requirements of the market innovation, and formulate and adjust corresponding technical specifications and standard systems; during the administrative examination and approval, we should loosen the economic standards such as economic performance, the number of employees, the registered capital, etc., but stress on the resources conservation, environment friendliness, safety and security, etc.; we should further streamline administration and delegate power, speeding up to clear paid intermediary services before administrative approval such as technical examination, evaluation, verification, consulting, etc. While expanding the access, we should also complete the exit mechanism to shut down the market players that fall short of mandatory standards such as energy saving, environmental protection, safe production, food and drug quality, etc. Enterprise bankruptcy institution should also be improved to allow the market players access to be “in” and “out”.

A sound legal and regulatory system is the cornerstone of the effective operation of the market. On the one hand, in responding to the blanks of laws and regulations in the modern market system, we should step up to fill them in through establishing and improving laws and regulations regarding some emerging business. On the other hand, we should accelerate to adjust and improve relevant laws and regulations according to the new demand. We should execute the laws and regulations in respect to the current market development, and step up to sort out and adjust them to improve some laws, regulations and standards that cannot adapt to the development of modern market. In the light of the demand for legalized and internationalized business environment, we should eliminate or adjust various regulations and institutions that cannot adapt to the market economy systems and mechanisms.

To establish the operational mechanisms with efficient resources allocation is the key to further playing the role of the market. First, establish and improve the market price mechanism. To be specific, we should release the power of price management, promote the price reform in water, petroleum, natural gas, electricity, transportation, telecommunications and other areas, loosen the price control in competitive links, limit the scope of pricing by government in public utilities, public services and network utilities of natural monopoly, improve the transparency and accept social supervision; we should improve the market-based price mechanism, focusing on accelerating market-oriented price reform of factors and establishing standardized market price mechanism of factors in line with the international market, thus forming the price linkage between commodity market and factor market so that social resources will be allocated by market instead of the political means. Second, improve the market operation mechanism based on the market price. To be specific, we should establish a complete management system of various market operations and a unified market regulation system for the spot trading of bulk commodity, improve the operation and management rules in the markets of finance, land and technology, accelerate the construction of market operation management rules in the human resources, cultural services, third party professional services, and intermediary services; we should establish the operation mechanism of various markets, strengthen the market functions of currencies, stocks, bonds, foreign exchange, commodity futures, financial futures and gold, establish institutionalized and standardized mechanisms for land transaction, and establish the market-based technology transfer system and operation mechanism; we should improve the integrated development and cooperation mechanism for regional markets and focus on breaking up the regional blocks and trade monopoly so as to establish a big market of regional integration.

7.2.2.3 Creation of a Level-Playing Field

The creation of a level-playing field for all the market players is an important guarantee for the efficient operation of the market. First, to promote fair competition of the market, we need to strengthen the market supervision management and optimize the supervision methods. The key is to strengthen the during-supervision and post-supervision, deepen the standardized supervision, consolidate the classified supervision, and optimize the technological supervision. In the information age, we should particularly focus on the supervision by technological means, e.g. making full use of information network technology to realize real-time online monitoring, integrating record information management and harmful information filtering function to improve the network monitoring, establishing product traceability system through the Internet of Things, and forming traceable information chain. Second, as the market players, the enterprises should highlight their responsibilities, improve measures and mechanisms of self-management and internal governance structure. Meanwhile, we should also give full play to the self-discipline of industry associations and chambers of commerce, encouraging them to develop industry regulations, put forward or participate in the formulation of relevant national standards and industry standards, and supervise their members to comply with industry regulations, norms, and professional ethics. By strengthening social credibility and focusing on information publicity, information sharing and credibility constraints, we should accelerate to establish the information platform for main market players, establish credibility archives and exchange and sharing mechanism, and complete the "black list" of enterprises, thus creating an honest, self-disciplined, trustworthy social credibility environment and promoting the market players of all types to abide by contracts and keep good credibility. Third, step up efforts to promote fair competition and full competition. We should strengthen the law-based protection of all types of intellectual property rights, and encourage technological innovation; we should further break regional blocks and industry monopoly; we should severely crack down on counterfeit goods, false advertising, price fraud, commercial bribery and other unfair competitions. Most importantly, we should further create a fairly competitive environment for all types of economies, especially in the key links such as project approval, investment approval, project bidding, government procurement, and access to resources to ensure that the private enterprises can be equally treated with other types of enterprises. We can also support the private enterprises to participate in the regional major projects and government procurement, encouraging the qualified and credible enterprises with a sense of social responsibility and enterprising spirit to enter the market, including the enterprises of private capital, foreign capital and non-local capital.

7.2.3 *State-Owned Assets and Enterprises Governance and Market-Based Reform*

7.2.3.1 The Reform of State-Owned Assets and Enterprises and the Existing Problems

After the continuously deepening reform and innovation, China's micro economic structure with state-owned economy as the main body has been significantly improved, and the inefficient system of state enterprises has made a significant breakthrough. However, at present, the number of state-owned assets and enterprises is still large. The unreasonable state-owned economic distribution persists, and the average efficiency and benefits of state enterprises are low. The reform of state-owned assets and enterprises, which cannot fully adapt to the requirements of economic new normal, still has a long way to go. First, the state-owned assets management system does not adapt to the functions of state-owned capital. State-owned capital management is still mainly administrative with the combination of management of human resources, operation and assets, resulting in insufficient vitality of enterprises and the difficulties in adapting to rapid changes in the market both at home and abroad. Second, the reform of institutions in state enterprises needs to be deepened. At present, there are still a lot of the parent corporations at central and local levels which have not completed the corporation system reform, for example, among 112 central enterprises under the direct administration of the State Asset Supervision and Administration Commission of the State Council, 75 companies are still owned by the whole people. The phenomenon of state-owned share taking the main part is still common. According to the relevant statistics, the state-owned capital in state enterprises accounts for above 95% in the total paid-in capital, while the collective, private and foreign capital account for a very small proportion. The construction of a modern enterprise system lags behind, and some state enterprises are too large in scale and too long in their chains with confusion of government administration, enterprises and capital. Third, the state-owned capital flow and allocation mechanisms need to be improved. The reform of state enterprises in monopoly industries is in slow progress with insufficient motivation and many obstacles. With serious disharmony between monopoly industries and other industries in the national economy, unreasonable interests structure is yet to break up. There are many difficulties in the transfer of state-owned property rights, and the pricing in state-owned property rights transfer or restructuring is always a tough task. Problems left over by history are still prominent, because many state enterprises still bear the responsibility of social security for their retirees. The enterprises are solving social problems, and some of the old state enterprises, especially those of mineral resources, are faced with serious overstaffing.

7.2.3.2 The Paths to Deepening Market-Based Reform of State-Owned Assets and Enterprises

To press ahead the supply side structural reform, we should continue to promote the market-oriented reform of state enterprises, and accelerate the transformation of state-owned assets management, the cut of overcapacity and the reform of monopoly industries; we should accelerate the improvement of the modern enterprise system, strive to break up institutional obstacles so as to make the state enterprises become the real market players; we should effectively improve the performance of the state enterprises, step up their upgrading, increase their vitality and anti-risk ability, improve the supply efficiency of the state-owned capital, and promote the sustained and healthy development of economy and society.

To deepen the reform, the priority is to improve the management system of state-owned assets with its focus on capital management. To transform state-owned assets management into capital management, the key is to establish efficient state-owned capital operation platform, speed up the reorganization and the formation of market-based and specialized investment and operation companies for the state-owned capital so as to promote efficient flow and optimized allocation of state-owned assets, and enhance the vitality and competitiveness of the state enterprises. State-owned capital investment and operation companies should be strictly defined as players of capital operation, refrain from any business activities except investment management, and can only participate in business management in the invested companies as shareholders in accordance with the relevant provisions of the company law. As independent legal person, the enterprises can introduce strategic investors to operate and select operators independently. At the same time, an open and transparent market operation mechanism needs to be established. In accordance with the requirements of capital operation and equity management, state-owned operating platform should detail its functions, establish the organizational structure in line with its functions, explore the mode of strategic control supplemented by operational control, and manage the state-owned equity based on market operation.

The core requirement of deepening the reform is to promote the rational flow and the efficiency of state-owned assets. Under the New Normal, it is urgent to strengthen the exiting, restructuring, innovation and upgrading of the state enterprises. In the short term, it is necessary to make the "zombie" enterprises exit the market. In the long term, it is necessary to constantly press ahead the restructuring, innovation and upgrading of state enterprises with measures such as supporting them to develop strategic emerging industries and implement internationalized operation, and guiding them to create innovation and start-up platforms. Meanwhile, we should accelerate the reform of monopoly industries, release the competitive business of the natural monopoly industries, actively address the deep-rooted problem of "state-owned share taking the main part" in the state-owned listed enterprises of mining, iron and steel, chemicals, construction, public utilities and so on, implement relative concentration of ownership, and activate and strengthen endogenous motivation and vitality of the enterprises.

Deepening the reform also needs to improve the operational efficiency of state enterprises. In the long run, actively developing mixed ownership is a good way to improve the operation efficiency of state enterprises. We should continuously promote the joint-stock reform of state enterprises, encourage appropriate enterprise groups to be listed with the whole company or its core assets by various means, and guide the enterprise groups to integrate upstream and downstream industry chain through market means; we should actively implement the mixed ownership with employees holding the stock, and establish an open, transparent and standardized mechanism of incentive and constraint; we should give full play to the role of market in resources allocation to further promote the open restructuring for the state-owned listed companies or non-listed companies. At the same time, the development environment of state enterprises needs to be optimized, and the ability of sustainable development of enterprises needs to be enhanced. For example, we should improve the tax preferential policies relevant to the restructuring of state enterprises such as assets evaluation, alterant land registration and state-owned assets transfer, improve relevant policies about the exiting of the state enterprises, establish and improve mechanisms to allow for mistakes made in innovation and reform, and create an enabling environment for entrepreneurs.

7.3 Structural Adjustment and Supply of New Structures

Over the 30 years after the reform and opening-up, though the international status of China's economy has greatly improved and China has become the largest and the most influential emerging economy as well as a manufacturing power in the world, unreasonable economic structure has become increasingly prominent with uneven, uncoordinated, and unsustainable development, for example, the supply structure is not coordinated, there is no fundamental change to the extensive development, the efficiency of factors is low, and the costs of natural resources and environment are high. All these have become important reasons leading to the slowdown of economic growth and the decrease of benefits. To promote the supply side structural reform in the future, we should take economic structure adjustment as a priority. On the one hand, we need to cultivate new economic development momentum, expand effective and high-end supply and improve the quality and benefits of supply. On the other hand, we need to further adjust and eliminate the inventory, reduce ineffective and low-end supply, reform and enhance the traditional comparative advantage, thus we can fundamentally promote the competitiveness of the Chinese economy from the supply side.

7.3.1 Optimization and Adjustment of Industrial Supply Side Structures

7.3.1.1 Problems and Trend of Industrial Supply Side

In recent years, with the rapid development of China's economy, industrial structure has gradually advanced. Based on the long-term dominance of the second industry, the ratio of the tertiary industry has steadily increased. In 2013, the added value of the tertiary industry exceeded the second industry for the first time, and the tertiary industry has become the main driving force of China's economic growth. However, there are still a lot of prominent problems in China's industrial structure. One problem is that innovation capability in manufacturing industry is not strong enough, and its low-end position in the global value chain has not been fundamentally changed. In recent years, the proportion of China's high-tech products in exports gradually increases, but labor-intensive processing and assembly products account for more than 90% of the exported high-tech products.[1] Due to the rapid expansion of low-end production capacity, the average rate of capacity utilization in industries such as iron and steel, electrolytic aluminum, flat glass, etc. is less than 75% with serious overcapacity. The second problem is the development of modern service industry is lagging behind. In 2014, the wholesale and retail industry and the real estate industry accounted for 32.8% of the tertiary industry, with real estate industry alone taking up 12.4%. At the same time, producer services always account for around 58% of the tertiary industry output in recent years, and the proportion of R&D is not high. The third problem is the fairly low competitiveness in agriculture. Agricultural employment accounts for as high as 29.5%, but the proportion of agricultural added value is only 9.2%.[2] Agricultural production costs remain high with declining competitiveness. From 2013, domestic prices of the bulk agricultural products have exceeded the C.I.F. price of imported agricultural products after tax.

In the future, China's industrial structure optimization and upgrading will confront new situation and challenges, especially when a new round of global industrial revolution accelerates. Due to the rapid development of intelligent manufacturing and robotics, developed countries may realize the replacement of human by machine through the use of the highly efficient digital equipment, the comparative advantage of labor costs in developing countries will be somehow weakened, and the "Flying Geese Model" will disappear. At the same time, labor costs are rising. In 2012, the working-age population declined for the first time, a decrease of 3,450,000 over the previous year. After that there was a continuous decline for three consecutive years, leading to the fast rise of wage costs. Due to the rapid rise in labor and raw material costs, China's comparative advantage based on labor costs is significantly weakened. We are facing great challenges in the low-end manufacturing sectors from Vietnam, Malaysia and other Southeast Asian countries, so it is increasingly urgent to reshape our competitive advantage.

7.3.1.2 The Paths to Enhancing the Competitiveness from the Industrial Supply Side

First, promote the optimization and upgrading of the manufacturing industry. To build a manufacturing industry with international competitiveness is the fundamental support to enhance the inner vitality and power of the economy. The Chinese is facing double tasks in the information age: to catch up with the developed countries in industrial development and to strengthen points of weakness

---

[1]The data are provided by Research Institute of Industrial Economy and Technological Economy in National Development and Reform Commission, Development Report of The Chinese Industries, China Market Press, 2015, p. 134.

[2]The data are from Ye Xingqing, Promote the Agricultural Modernization with Structural Reform as the Entry Point, China Economic Times, January 7th, 2016.

in industrial foundation. Only through independent innovation can we fundamentally enhance the status and competitiveness of China in the global industrial chain. Based on our practice and conditions, aiming at the world top-level technologies, we should accelerate the development of a number of major scientific and technological innovation projects and industrial technology projects, thus creating a number of advanced high-tech industry clusters of information technology, intelligent manufacturing, new energy, new materials, biotechnology, etc. to control the commanding points of global industrial development.

Intelligent manufacturing is a top priority of China's manufacturing industry. In the face of a new round of global industrial revolution, China should accelerate the integration of new information technology and manufacturing technology, take intelligent manufacturing as the main direction, promote intelligence in production process, and cultivate new modes of production. We should strengthen the top-level design of intelligent manufacturing, accelerate the development of technological standards, establish intelligent manufacturing industry alliance, promote and coordinate intelligent equipment and product R&D, advance systemic integration, innovation and industrialization, and press ahead comprehensive application of industrial Internet, cloud computing and big data in the whole industry chain. We should accelerate the development of intelligent manufacturing equipment and products, and carry out R&D on high-end CNC machine tools, industrial robots, 3D printing equipment, etc. with functions such as deep perception, decision-making and automatic working to increase the capacity of precise manufacturing and agile manufacturing. We should further improve the application of the Internet in the manufacturing field, formulate the roadmap for the integration of the Internet and the manufacturing industry, develop new manufacturing modes based on Internet such as customization, crowdsourcing design, cloud manufacturing, etc., and promote the R&D, manufacturing and industrial organization based on the dynamic perception of consumer demands.

At the same time, it is very urgent to accelerate the transformation and upgrading of traditional industries. The challenges that the traditional industries are currently facing need to be analyzed case by case, for example, challenges in some industries such as clothing manufacturing are due to the rising costs of factors, or due to stricter supervision of energy-saving and environmental protection and the rise of resources prices, and challenges in some other industries such as display manufacturing are due to new technological upgrading which results in greater pressure. To meet those challenges, we should first encourage technological upgrading and business model innovation to increase the vitality of the traditional industry. In particular, we should strengthen the R&D of generic technology, and guide the enterprises to adopt advanced and applicable technologies, make more efforts in business model innovation, and apply Internet thinking and new business models so as to better adapt to and lead the consumer demands.

Second, foster new industries and new forms of business. With the in-depth integration of cloud computing, the Internet of Things, digital manufacturing, information technology and other industries, the trend of informationization will profoundly change people's production mode and life style. Through new technology, new models and new forms of business, the industry life cycle will probably be changed in a short period of time, even the whole industry in the world will be reshuffled. Affected by the change of consumer demands and technological progress, the integration of manufacturing industry and service industry is becoming increasingly obvious with a gradually blurred boundary between them. Under such a background, to promote supply side structural reform in China, we should actively cultivate new technologies, new business forms, and new models to create an enabling environment for public participation in starting businesses and making innovations, further stimulating the vitality of innovation. Especially for such a big country as China, with its huge market and great development potential, there are weak links in many industries and regional development, which, to a large extent, provides a broad space for the rapid development of the "Internet plus". We should give full play to the role of Internet platform in promoting industrial upgrading in traditional industries, encourage them to adopt Internet thinking, and accelerate the penetration of Internet into various economic and social fields so as to form an "Internet plus" ecological system with intelligence and coordination.

With the deep embedding of information technology in many industries, a series of growth points with broad prospects are continuously emerging, bringing great impact on supply system upgrading. China should aim at the global forefront of the industry development, focus on such fields as economic platform, sharing economy, big data, cloud computing, the Internet of Things, etc. based on the economic foundation and the demand, and actively cultivate emerging industries with competitiveness. For example, sharing economy, as a new business model, which optimizes the resources allocation by mobile Internet, big data and other technologies, has been widely used in house lease, transportation, catering, etc., and will penetrate into more areas, thus we should actively encourage its development. Take big data as another example. Big data are increasingly becoming fundamental and strategic resources in economic and social development. We should promote the collection and excavation of data resources, deepen the innovative application of big data in various industries, and promote the healthy development of the big data industry.

Third, promote high-end and refined service industry. In China's primary, secondary and tertiary industries, service industry has accounted for the highest proportion of GDP and absorbed the largest number of employees. But the development level and the competitiveness of the service industry are not high enough, which is related to China's current economic development, insufficient innovation ability, the long-term dominance of the primary industry, as well as the institutional mechanisms that cannot adapt to the demand of service industry. We should put the service industry upgrading in a prominent position of China's industrial structure adjustment, enhance the competitiveness of high-end service industry, and further play the supporting role of the service industry to enhance the efficiency of supply. On the one hand, we should promote the producer service industry towards professionalism and high end of the value chain. Taking the demands of industrial transformation and upgrading as the orientation, we should actively develop the producer service industry, guide the enterprises to separate and outsource their non-core business, enhance the division of services, and gradually transfer China's industries from productive manufacturing to service-embedded manufacturing. We should encourage service enterprises to develop towards the high end of the value chain, support enterprises to improve their innovative R&D and system integration capabilities, promote the use of patented technologies and innovative results, and strengthen their marketing and brand services. On the other hand, we should promote the consumer service industry towards refinement and high quality. In particular, we should increase the effective supply of services, encourage all types of market players to innovate service types and business models, and actively develop new service market in responding to the demand of various subjects and market segmentation. We should use such modern information technologies as the Internet, optimize service procedures, improve service quality, and build influential and reputable service brands to enhance the competitiveness.

Fourth, press ahead supply side reform in agriculture. Due to China's huge population and limited land resources, at a certain stage of industrialization and urbanization, labor and land costs of agricultural production will inevitably rise rapidly, resulting in that the production costs of agricultural products continuously go up, much higher than the costs in the United States and other countries, and the competitiveness in the world market significantly decreases. This trend will further aggravate in the future. With the in-depth development of economic globalization and deep embedding of domestic market into international market, we should optimize agricultural structure with new thinking and new mechanisms. In the past we motivated farmers to grow grains through government purchasing and increasing the minimum purchase prices, but now we should increase the benefit of growing grains by focusing more on promoting circulation of cultivated land, developing appropriate operation scale and accelerating scientific and technological progress to enhance the international competitiveness of agriculture.

With the further development of industrialization, more and more labor will transfer from the agricultural sector to other sectors, which provides conditions for improving the scale and efficiency of agricultural production. China should adapt to this trend, actively cultivating new agricultural entities such as the family farms and farmers' cooperatives, developing different forms of suitably scaled-up agricultural operations, promoting agricultural production by industrialized thinking, and substantially increasing the efficiency of agricultural productivity. In the premise of grain's self-sufficiency and absolute food security, we should accelerate the formation of regional agriculture distribution matching the resources, and allow the eastern coastal areas and mega cities to reduce their standards of agricultural production so as to purchase grains from areas with more comparative advantages such as the central and western regions and the grain producing provinces. At the same time, it is difficult to meet the growing demands for food if we only rely on the domestic land and water resources; therefore, China should start from its comparative advantage, coordinate the import and export of agricultural products, supplement the domestic market demand, promote structural adjustment, and protect the interests of the domestic industries and farmers. For the production of the staple food such as rice and wheat, we do not have comparative advantage, thus we should strive for better alignment between domestic production and imports. For example, the Southeast Asian countries such as Thailand, Laos, Kampuchea, Indonesia, and Malaysia have the prominent advantage of rice production, so China can import rice in a moderate scale from them to reduce the self-sufficiency rate. The land that has exited can be used to produce grains of high economic value with comparative advantage.

China should protect the food security and food safety, not only in quantity but also in quality. Quality should be given priority in the agricultural production, and the quality of the agricultural products should be continuously improved. On the one hand, environmental protection and source supervision of the land should be strengthened, strict management system of agricultural inputs should be implemented so as to cut off the channel through which pollutants pour into the farmland, and the creation of quality brands for agricultural products and food should be encouraged. On the other hand, quality and safety supervision should be improved, and agricultural products quality and food safety regulatory system from farm to dining table should be completed so as to establish a retrievable information sharing platform and a sound risk monitoring system, ensuring the safety of the food.

7.3.2 New Type of Urbanization and Well-Balanced Adjustment of Urban and Rural Structures

7.3.2.1 Problems in the Progress of Urbanization

Since the reform and opening-up, with the acceleration of industrialization, China's urbanization has experienced rapid development. From 1978 to 2015, calculated by the permanent urban residents, China's urbanization rate increased from 17.9 to 56.1%, with the urban resident population expanding from 172 to 771 million, an increase of 599 million. The acceleration of urbanization has contributed to the significant improvement in infrastructure and public services, attracted a large number of rural labor to transfer their employment to the cities, improved the allocation efficiency of the urban and rural production factors, and promoted rapid and sustained development. However, in spite of the rapid development of China's urbanization, there are still a lot of prominent problems which need to pay attention to:

First, urbanization lags behind industrialization. Despite the continuous improvement, compared with the industrialization level, China's urbanization level is still lagging behind, not only much lower than the developed countries, but also lower than the world average. According to the statistics, the rate of urbanization in developed countries is generally close to or higher than 80%. The neighboring countries with the similar per capita income of China like Malaysia and the Philippines have an urbanization rate of over 60%. But China's urbanization rate in 2015 calculated by permanent urban residents was only 56.1%. The low level of urbanization is neither good for the innovative cluster to play its role nor good for the industrial structure upgrading, which restricts the expansion of domestic demand and becomes a major reason for the uncoordinated regional economic development.

Second, the dualistic structure in the urbanization has not been broken. At present, migrant workers have become the main part of the industrial workers in China, but due to the influence of the division between urban and rural household registration system, 234 million migrant workers and their following families, who are counted as the permanent urban residents, fail to enjoy the basic public services for urban citizens in education, employment, health care, pension, insurance and housing, leading to new dualistic contradictions inside the cities. If this part of population without urban household registration are separated from the urban citizens, in terms of urban household, China's urbanization rate is only 35.33%, which is 19.44% lower than the rate calculated according to the permanent urban residents (data of 2014). In addition, the long-term implementation of the urban and rural land system is not reasonable. In accordance with the existing land management regulations, the rural collective construction land can only enter the land market through acquisition by the government. In this process, the local governments obtain a large amount of premium profit, but landless peasants cannot share the value-added profit from the land, which is neither conducive to reflecting the social justice nor conducive to the formation of a reasonable land price.

7.3.2.2 Promote Well-Balanced Urban and Rural Structures Through New Type of Urbanization

China's basic national conditions include a large population, limited resources, and a small ecological capacity, and China is undergoing a rapid process of industrial transformation and institutional change, which determines that urbanization progress must be based on its own reality, and focus on efficient, inclusive and sustainable development. To promote efficient urbanization, it is necessary to give full play to the decisive role of the market in the resources allocation and better play the role of the market to facilitate the optimal allocation of production factors between urban and rural areas and between different regions, maximize the external agglomerative effect, and enhance urban innovation ability and total factor productivity. To promote inclusive urbanization is to fully mobilize the enthusiasm of the government, the enterprises and the public so that all the people will share the benefits of urbanization. To promote sustainable urbanization is to deal with the relationship between economic development, resources conservation and environmental protection, and internalize the costs of resources and environment in the process of urbanization so as to achieve low-carbon green development.[3] To be specific, we should concentrate our efforts on the following key links:

[3]Refer to research group of the Development Research Center of the State Council, China's New Type of Urbanization: Paths, Model and Policies, China Development Press, 2014, p. 6.

Move faster to see that urban residency is granted to more people with rural household registration living in urban areas. With the deepening of industrialization and industrial upgrading, the transfer of labor from the agricultural sector to more efficient industrial and service sectors is an inevitable trend. To adapt to this trend, we should move faster to see that urban residency is granted to more people with rural household registration living in urban areas so that the agricultural population can fit in the city. To this end, the first step is to enhance the urban industrial support and employment bearing capacity, develop distinctive urban industrial system, strengthen professional cooperation based on division of labor among cities, increase industrial undertaking ability of small- and medium-sized cities, and form a stable support for employment. The urgent task at present is to accelerate the reform of the household registration system, and promote full coverage of the basic public services on all the permanent urban residents. Reform of the household registration system should be adapted to local conditions and pushed forward step by step. We should clarify the long-term goals, but we cannot press ahead too fast, otherwise it is difficult to bear for the big cities and the large cities in the short term. In accordance with national requirements of the new type of urbanization, fully relax restrictions on eligibility for residency in towns and small cities, relax restrictions on eligibility for residency in medium-sized cities in a planned way, reasonably determine the conditions on eligibility for residency in big cities, and strictly control the population scale in large cities. For those people with rural household living in cities who have an eligibility or intention for residency, we can adopt a residence certification system so as to ensure that the mobile population have the rights to enjoy basic public services.

Deepen the land system reform in urban and rural areas. Land system reform is a complicated but significant issue in China. Existing urban and rural land system is neither good for optimizing the allocation of land resources, nor adapted to the requirements of supply side structural reform and new type of urbanization, so we should intensify the reform prudently. With the principle of equal access and fair trade, under the premise of improving relevant land tax system, we should allow rural collective land and state-owned land an equal access to non-agricultural land market, establish a unified urban and rural land market and land price formation mechanism, and improve the secondary market of land lease, transfer and mortgage. We should reform the current land acquisition system, determine a reasonable profit allocation method among the government, the collective and the individual, and establish a fair and shared value-added profit allocation mechanism for urbanized land. We should protect farmers' homestead usufructuary right, reform and improve farmers' homestead system, steadily push forward the mortgage, guarantee and transfer of rural housing property, and expand the channel for farmers to increase their property income.

Innovate cost sharing, investment and financing mechanisms. The promotion of urbanization cannot be separated from a large number of capital investment, so we should give full play to the role of local government in providing public products, actively introduce social capital to participate in new-type urbanization, and share the benefits of reform and development. On the one hand, we should ascertain the way in which powers are shared between the central and local governments, ensuring the appropriate sharing of costs between them. For the more comprehensive issues such as basic pension, judicial system, and food and drug safety, the power should be placed on the central government, and expenditure of the central government should be moderately expanded. Besides, we should increase general transfer payments, as well as reduce and merge special transfer payments. On the other hand, innovate the financing mechanism of urban construction and public services. We should change the current financing mechanism in which the local governments rely too much on land transfer revenue; instead, we should actively introduce social capital into infrastructure and public services, and develop the model of public-private partnerships (PPP).

7.3.3 *Coordinated Adjustment Between New Growth Poles of City Clusters and Regional Structures*

From the perspective of economics, regional structural adjustment means the optimal allocation of factors among different regions, from the low profit regions to high profit regions. Through the agglomeration effect, a number of new growth poles form so as to improve the overall resources allocation efficiency and the economic development level. Therefore, the implementation of supply side structural reform should regard the regional structural optimization as a very important task, setting up a number of city clusters with competitiveness and influence to improve efficiency of the supply side and quality of the economic development.

7.3.3.1 Current Situation and Problems in Regional Structural Adjustment

China's economic development has chosen a non-balanced development path among different regions. After development of more than 30 years since the reform and opening-up, China's economic growth in the eastern region has achieved remarkable results. Three city clusters—Beijing and Tianjin, the Yangtze River Delta, and the Pearl River Delta—have become the important engine of China's economic growth, accommodating 18% of the population with 2.8% of the land and creating a total of 36% of China's GDP. At the same time, economic development in the central and western regions has continuously improved, playing a more and more important role in China's economics. However, there are still some prominent problems in regional economic structures, for example, the gap between regional economic developments is still wide, per capita income, per capita wealth and other important indicators between different regions continue to polarize, and public services are still far from reaching the equilibrium. We should pay particular attention to that in recent years, to a great extent, growth in central and western regions is due to national and regional preferential policies and large-scale investment; with the decline in the marginal benefit of investment, the problem of insufficient innovation ability in central and western regions will be more prominent.

Incomplete systems and mechanisms are important reasons to constrain coordinated regional development. At present, the market mechanisms for the free movement of factors in different regions still needs to be improved, the movement of labor force is still hindered by the household registration system and the public service system, and the roots for regional market separation have not been eliminated. Tax system still needs to be improved. Special transfer payments to regions with weak economic foundation and fragile ecological environment are numerous in types, but general transfer payments are too few, which cannot narrow the gap of basic public services in different regions. Regional cooperation and coordination mechanisms need to be improved, cross-regional integrated economic cooperation needs to be further deepened, and repeated construction and administration fragmentation still exist to a certain extent. All of those factors, to a large extent, restrict the coordinated development of the regional economy.

7.3.3.2 The Paths to Promoting Regional Structural Optimization

To bridge the gap in China's current regional economic development, it should be analyzed from the theoretical perspective and international experience. Through the cross-sectional analysis of the regional economic differences in 24 countries, Williamson (1965) finds that regional imbalance in developed countries is small, while the regional imbalance in the middle-income countries and underdeveloped countries is large. He further carries out the time sequence analysis of 10 countries and then finds that regional imbalance in most developed countries has experienced three stages, i.e., increase, stability and decline, thus he puts forward the "inverted U curve" about the differences in regional economic development. But regional balanced development is only a possibility, and the realization of this goal needs specific prerequisites, such as fully free movement of factors, specialized division of labor based on factor endowments in different regions, choice of reasonable economic development strategies etc. From China's current situation, to promote the supply side structural reform and the coordinated development of regional economy, we should start from the following aspects:

Free movement of production factors across different regions. According to the principle of comparative advantage, the movement of factors from the lower income areas to higher income areas will effectively reduce the regional gap of economic development, and ultimately achieve the equalization of factor income. The natural conditions and resources in different regions of China vary greatly, so do the income of labor, capital and techniques in different regions. Since the reform and opening-up, the production factors have been allocated through market across different regions, but there are still many restrictions on the systems and mechanisms. Employment population that has transferred from central and western

China's rural areas to eastern cities cannot enjoy full citizenship treatment, and the eastern capital, technology and talents, when entering the middle and western China, also encounter all sorts of obstacles. In the next stage, while stepping forward the reform of the household registration system and the popularity of urban public services, we should also take effective measures to attract capital, technology and talents to flow to the middle and western China in a planned way, especially to create a law-based business environment, improve the efficiency of government management, break local protection barriers, construct a unified market system, effectively protect the rights and interests of investors, intensify efforts in supporting the development of infrastructure, education, medical and other services, and increase the attraction of the middle and western areas to the talents and the capital.

Development of city clusters and adjustment and optimization of regional spatial distribution. The main challenges faced by the eastern city clusters are rapidly rising costs of factors, intensified resources and environment pressure and fiercer competition in the international market, thus they should accelerate the economic transformation and upgrading, improve the industry's core competitiveness and sustainable development ability, form new comparative advantage, and play their driving effects in China's economic development. The central and western regions should conform to the trend of global informationization and industrialization, undertake international and coastal industrial transfer in a planned way, rely on the advantages of resources to develop business operations with distinctive local features, speed up the new-type industrialization, and enhance the regional radiating and driving ability. In addition, we should promote the coordinated development in cities of different scales. While enhancing the radiation function of central cities, we should also accelerate the development of small and medium-sized cities so as to form a pattern of coordinated development of various types of cities.

Cultivation of new growth poles that facilitate the coordinated development of surrounding areas. From the experience of developed countries, the process of continuous rise of an economy is inseparable from the motivation of some world class city clusters with strong radiating effect. In order to realize the regional coordinated development in China, we must respect the laws of industrial agglomeration, and make use of its motivating effect to form strong growth poles and development engines. In the future, we should focus on promoting the implementation of three strategies: "the Belt and Road", the coordinated development of Beijing, Tianjin, and Hebei, and the Yangtze River Economic Belt, thus establishing a regional development network with multi centers that connects all the five directions to form world-renowned mega urban regions. In particular, we should strive to resolve regional market segmentation, disorderly competition and other outstanding issues, promote collaboratively major infrastructure construction, accelerate the elimination of invisible barriers among regions, and pay close attention to the establishment of a unified and complete market system so as to make it a new engine of economic growth in China.

7.4 Resolving of Risks and Supply of New Policies

At present, overcapacity in China's economy has become increasingly prominent, and business is in decline with less profits and more losses; at the same time, systematic financial risks have gradually increased, especially four risks that arise together, i.e., local government debt, shadow banking, overcapacity, and large inventory in real estate, which, if not timely and effectively dealt with, may result in chain crisis with serious impacts on China's economy. In order to resolve the current problems and create a sound environment to push forward the supply side structural reforms in the medium and long term, we must develop effective policies and realize stable and healthy economic development.

7.4.1 *Overcapacity and Policies*

In China's current development, due to the existence of institutional mechanisms, overcapacity, to some extent, is resulted from two factors: self-adjustment of the market cycle and "institutional overcapacity" brought by the over intervention of the governments. In order to stand out in the competition, local governments have full motivation to use a variety of policy tools to promote the development of the industries which can increase the GDP and revenue, thus leading to the distortion of resources allocation function in market mechanisms. Therefore, in recent years, although China has launched regulations against overcapacity many times, the effects are not obvious, trapped in a circle of "rectification—overcapacity again—rectification".

To thoroughly solve the problem, we must start from the root causes of institutional mechanisms to establish a long-term mechanism that can resolve the overcapacity. The key is to eliminate governments' unreasonable intervention in industries from the source, effectively reduce and correct total undertaking and direct intervention through administrative means, focus on creating a fairly competitive market environment and maintaining the market order, and avoid distortion of market signals due to excessive intervention. We should resolutely abolish the preferential policies for land, resources, taxes, tariffs, etc. adopted by the local governments in attracting business and investment, which will damage the fair competition. We should clearly define the market price mechanism for resources and factors, enhance the standards of energy consumption, material consumption, water consumption and environmental protection for industrial access, and play the basic role of the market in the resources allocation.

At present, outdated production capability in many industries are related to "zombie enterprises". These "zombie enterprises" always have a hopeless deficit and take up a lot of resources and market, which should exit the market as soon as possible. When they exit the market, based on local realities, we should take targeted measures such as mergers, reorganizations and bankruptcy liquidations, taking mergers and reorganization as the main measures in order to reduce the impact of a large number of laid-off workers. Therefore, it is necessary to implement and improve the policies of tax, finance, land, etc., which can promote the corporate mergers and acquisitions, such as the expansion of tax deduction, tax exemption and reduction ratio, etc. We should build mergers and acquisitions coordination and profit sharing mechanisms across different regions in order to make cross-regional horizontal tax allocation reasonable, and reduce the local governments' concern of revenue loss resulted from mergers. We should support social capital to participate in corporate mergers and acquisitions through equity participation, holding, asset acquisition and other ways, and encourage long-term capital such as insurance capital to innovate new products and investment methods. We should also support products upgrading and technological innovation of the restructured enterprises through financial products and service innovation.

Meanwhile, we should also see that the overcapacity in some industries mainly resulted from the changes of market and the lack of innovation. For those enterprises, as long as some new technologies and new concepts are introduced, it is entirely possible to rejuvenate them. Therefore, through technological renovation and business model innovation, we can transform the product structure and business structure to optimize the inventory capacity. Different industries can have different implementation methods, for example, for the textile industry, the priority is to renew and renovate equipment, increase the variety and added value of products, develop from the low-end processing and manufacturing to the high-end of value chain, and promote Internet-based customization model to produce personalized and flexible products in large varieties and small batch for the customers. For the iron, steel, shipbuilding and other industries, efforts should be made to break through and master a number of key technologies, apply more energy-saving, environmental friendly and efficient techniques and technologies, implement smart manufacturing initiative, and enhance the intelligent level of the enterprises in R&D, production and service.

To resolve the overcapacity under the background of economic globalization, we should coordinate domestic and international markets. In particular, we should seize the opportunity of "the Belt and Road" so as to speed up production output, especially in the industries of iron, steel, building materials and shipbuilding, where there is still much potential to make use of the international market. We should expand the scope of foreign engineering contracting, and actively undertake major infrastructure and large projects of industries and energy, promoting the export of domestic equipment and products. We should give full play to the technology, equipment and scale advantage of industries such as iron and steel, cement, electrolytic aluminum, glass plate, shipbuilding, etc. to carry out resources and value chain integration in the world; we should strengthen investment and cooperation with the neighboring countries and emerging market countries, carry out foreign investment of various forms, and establish overseas production bases.

7.4.2 Financial Risks and Policies

The systematic financial risks that China is facing are on the rise, especially in the fields of local government debt, shadow banking, overcapacity, and large inventory in real estate. Although currently the government debt including that of central government accounts for 60% of the GDP, lower than the safety line, in recent years there is a repayment peak, with the downturn in the real estate market and sharp decline in land transfer revenues, so the local governments are under increasing financial stress and debt pressure. Potential risks of shadow banking are increasing. The banks transform the on-balance sheet items into off-balance sheet items or other non-credit assets through bank financing, trust, investment, entrusted loans and other means, and a lot of problems arise in the development of Internet finance such as network lending (P2P) and crowdfunding, making the liquidity risks multiple. In addition, from the second half of 2012, the rate of non-performing loans in China's banking industry continues to rise, and this trend has not slowed down so far. In order to address these problems, we should start from institutional root to speed up the economic and financial reform, intensify our efforts to reduce prominent risks, cut the risk conduction chain, and curb the possibility of regional financial risks and greater crisis triggered by them.

Resolve debt risks of local governments. The trigger point of local government debt risks is the overdue breach or being unable to repay the debt. To prevent this from happening, we should strengthen the control on the debt scale, and establish systematic risk warning mechanism of local government debt. On the one hand, make more efforts to resolve the stock of debt. For the projects that have totally no debt-paying ability, it should be paid by the budget funds, if necessary, it can be paid by the income gained by government debt investment such as operational income, land transfer income and the state-owned assets transfer income. On the other hand, new debt should be strictly controlled. Local governments can only secure financing through bond issuance. Government financing functions will be taken back from financing platform companies, which cannot increase new government debt, and should be actively transformed into the general state enterprises.

Resolve debt risks arising from shadow banking. Deepening financial market reform, increasing effective financial supply, and striving for more efficient alignment between supply and demand of funds, are the fundamental ways to eliminate the shadow banking. We should accelerate the market-oriented interest rate reform so as to make the interest rate fully reflect the scarcity of funds and real market price. Meanwhile, we should accelerate the construction of a multi-level capital market, expand the access for folk capital into the banking industry, and strengthen the financial services for medium, small and micro enterprises. At the same time, in responding to the bank financial products, trust, network lending, non-governmental financing, etc., we should strengthen precise regulation, particularly to urge commercial banks to establish independent financial services organization and supervision system. The trust company shall not carry out non-standard financial capital pool and other business with the characteristics of shadow banking, small loan companies shall grant loans by its own funds, financial leasing companies shall not lend bank loans and related assets, and the organizations such as online payment platform, online financing platform, online credit platform shall not use the Internet technologies to do illegal financial business. Besides, regulatory departments should carry out accurate information statistics on the shadow banking, strengthen the statistics on of all kinds of social financing activities, and timely publicize the information so as to reduce the information asymmetry between financial institutions and investors.

Resolve risks arising from non-performing loans. The Chinese Bankers Survey Report (2015), jointly issued by The China Banking Association and PricewaterhouseCoopers, shows that 82.1% of the bank officials regarded the loans from industries with overcapacity as the main credit risk in 2015. With the slowdown in economic growth and the rise of corporate debt default rates, non-performing loans of banks may further increase. Commercial banks should pay close attention to the risk characteristics in key industries and key fields in order to avoid high-risk industries, establish the loan management framework with clear division of labor, and strictly reduce the risks of new loans. At the same time, we should pay close attention to the "normal" and "special mention" types of overdue loans and warning loans in the existing loans, and selectively adopt auction of mortgage assets, debt for equity swap, assets transfer, credit assets securitization, independent collection and other means to digest the inventory of non-performing loans. We should innovate the disposal methods of non-performing loans, promote their assets securitization, publish the projects of non-performing assets through online platform, and transfer them through fair market pricing and reasonable price bidding so as to improve disposal efficiency (Zheng 2015).

7.4.3 Enterprises Costs and Polices

At present, China's lack of vitality on the supply side, to a large extent, is related to the high costs and heavy burden of enterprises. Due to the constraints of many cost factors that they cannot overcome by themselves, it is difficult for enterprises to run with light packs, which results in the decreased profitability. These costs can be roughly divided into two parts: Some costs are decided by the market and difficult to be reduced by government intervention, including labor costs, raw material costs, capital equipment purchase costs, etc.; some costs have the potential to decrease, including the institutional transaction costs, taxes, social security costs, financial capital cost, power and logistics costs. To reduce the costs of real economy enterprises, we should focus on the latter, making concerted efforts from government reform, taxation, finance, social security, energy, logistics and other fields.

Reduce institutional transaction costs. The key is to speed up the reform of the governments, further transform the government functions, continue to streamline administration and delegate power, remove unnecessary regulations on enterprises, and stimulate market vitality and social creativity. We should further relax the control of access, increase efforts to streamline administration and delegate power, reduce the government's management of micro items to the maximum, and cancel the approval procedures for the economic activities which the market mechanisms can effectively regulate. The approval department should strictly regulate the approval behavior, strictly limit the discretion, optimize the approval procedures, and improve the efficiency. We should cut off existing unreasonable fees in China, rationally adjust the charging structure, and incorporate a part of the fees into tax system to achieve the "fee to tax", which will be collected by the tax department and budgeted by the financial department so as to cut off association of interests between administrative approval and charging items.

Make more efforts on structural tax cuts. Structural tax cuts are not comprehensive or large-scale tax cuts, instead, they are to cut the taxes for specific groups to achieve specific targets so that the tax structure will be more reasonable, and the transformation and upgrading as well as economic growth will be promoted. The pace of replacing business tax with VAT will be sped up to realize the integrity of VAT deduction chain so as to reduce and gradually eliminate repeated taxation, and promote the specialized division of labor and cooperation. We should reduce the enterprise income tax rate of high-tech enterprises and small, medium and micro enterprises, extend and expand the policies of cutting enterprise income tax by half, and promote growth of high-tech enterprises and small, medium and micro enterprises. On the basis of the current classified tax system, we should establish an individual income tax system both comprehensive and classified, integrating wage and salary income and remuneration for personal services into the collection scope, and including taxpayers' family burden into the deductible factors such as supported population and mortgage loans, and give full play to the individual income tax in the regulation of income distribution and promotion of social fairness. We should increase the export tax rebate rate, accelerate the progress of the export tax rebate, support the expansion of exports, and enhance the competitive advantage of China's export-oriented enterprises.

Reduce enterprises financing costs. There are many reasons for the high costs of enterprises financing, either real economic factors or financial issues, either long-term or short-term factors, and the basic ways to address this problem lie in deepening the reform of the financial system, accelerating the market-oriented interest rate reform, and developing small- and medium-sized financial institutions and private banks. In the short term, we should strengthen the management of shadow banking, trade business, financial services, etc., and clean up the unnecessary money "channels" and "bridge crossing" links so that funds source and application principles of all kinds of financial products can be directly aligned with the real economy. We should regulate the operation of financial institutions, and strictly prohibit various unreasonable charges and attached conditions of loan. On the premise of strengthening the supervision, we should actively encourage qualified private capital to initiate and establish small- and medium-sized banks and other financial institutions in accordance with the law, or invest in the existing banking and financial institutions, providing efficient financial services to the real economy, especially middle, small and micro enterprises. We should improve multi-level capital market system, optimize institutional arrangement of the main board, the SME board and the GEM board, expand the debt financing instruments of various non-financial corporate in small- and medium-sized enterprises, and expand the scale of collective debt and private debt.

Reduce enterprises' social security costs. Among five major social insurance, i.e., pension, birth, work-related injury, unemployment, and health, pension and health account for the largest proportion. Due to the balance which is currently common in work-related injury, unemployment, maternity insurance, etc., reducing the fees is relatively easy to operate, but with the pressure of income and expenditure balance increasing year by year, the fees of pension and health insurance, which account for two-thirds of social security fees, are more and more difficult to decrease. In the next step, we will research on how to streamline and merge the "five insurance and housing fund", combing maternity insurance and basic health insurance, moderately reducing the overall social insurance payment rate, expanding the fund sources of social insurance, and supporting social security with state-owned assets transfer and state enterprises' bonus. At the same time, we will improve the social insurance financing mechanism, giving full play to the role of government, enterprises and individuals to jointly share their appropriate responsibilities. We will also reduce the pressure on the balance of pension insurance by extending the retirement age and other approaches.

Chapter 8
Co-ordination of Supply Side Structural Reform and Demand Side Management

Demand management and supply management are both important means of macroeconomic management; however, the focus of macroeconomic management differs in different periods or stages of economic growth and economic development. Since the reform and opening-up, China has achieved sustained high-speed economic growth in the process of market-based reform. In the early and middle stage of the reform, the production efficiency improved, the supply increased, and the shortage eased mainly through reform, thereby the economic growth mainly resulted from the reform and management of the supply sectors; In the new century, as China's socialist market economy has been fundamentally established, demand is regulated and controlled mainly through monetary policies and fiscal policies so as to achieve the goal of steady and rapid growth, which mainly resulted from demand management. In China's economic growth of recent years, overall imbalance between total supply and demand is becoming increasingly conspicuous, and there are profound structural and institutional reasons behind it. Therefore, simple demand management has been unable to meet the needs of macroeconomic management, and we must resolve the deep-seated contradictions in the development by strengthening structural reform on the supply side.

8.1 Total Supply and Demand Analysis and Macro Regulation

Since the reform and opening-up, the rapid growth of China's economy ("Chinese miracle") is a common result of the expansion of total supply and total demand. At the present stage, due to the restricted expansion of the total supply and demand resulting from the internal changes, China's economic engine is sputtering, so the "Chinese miracle" is not sustainable. China needs to improve the internal structure of the total supply and demand in order to achieve sustainable economic growth,

L. Xiao, *New Supply Side Economics*, DOI 10.1007/978-981-10-4639-1_8

which is the theoretical basis of the major national policy at this stage—"adjust structure, transfer method, and promote growth".

8.1.1 Trend of Total Supply and Total Demand Since the Reform and Opening-Up

Since the reform and opening-up, China has seen years of sustained rapid economic growth, with an annual GDP growth rate of about 9.5% from 1979 to 2015. The long-term and high-speed economic development, known as the "Chinese miracle", is fairly rare in the world history. "Chinese miracle" is, ultimately, a common result of the expansion of total supply and total demand.

Why is there a rapid expansion in China's total supply and total demand since the reform and opening-up? With regard to the total supply, it can be analyzed by Solow's model; with regard to the total demand, it can be analyzed by the "Three Carriages" (investment, consumption and exports), which promote the GDP growth in China.

8.1.1.1 Expansion of the Total Supply Since the Reform and Opening-Up

According to Solow's model, $g_Y = \theta g_K + (1 - \theta)\, g_L + g_A$ (g for growth rate; θ for capital share), the expansion of the total supply can be divided into two parts: The increase of factor investment, i.e., expansion of K (capital) and L (Labor), and the progress of total factor productivity, i.e., expansion of A (general technological progress).

After the reform and opening-up, China's total factor investment increased rapidly. The increase of workforce can be boiled down to two reasons: One reason is that the incentive mechanism brought by China's market economy reform increases working participation rate and enthusiasm; the other reason is that women in China begin to leave their homes and start to work. Figure 8.1 shows the changes of China's total working population from 1979 to 2014: Since the reform and opening-up, the total working population increases rapidly, and this trend slows down in recent years.

Because of the traditional conventions, the incomplete social security system and the low efficiency of the capital market, China's savings rate has always been at a high level, which means a high rate of capital formation, namely, the rapid growth of the total investment in fixed assets. From Fig. 8.2 we can see that China's total investment in fixed assets shows an exponential growth. According to the relevant data from the National Bureau of Statistics, the total investment in fixed assets increased with an average annual growth rate of 9.9% from 1980 to 1998, and an average annual growth rate of 19.4% from 1999 to 2014, showing the trend of

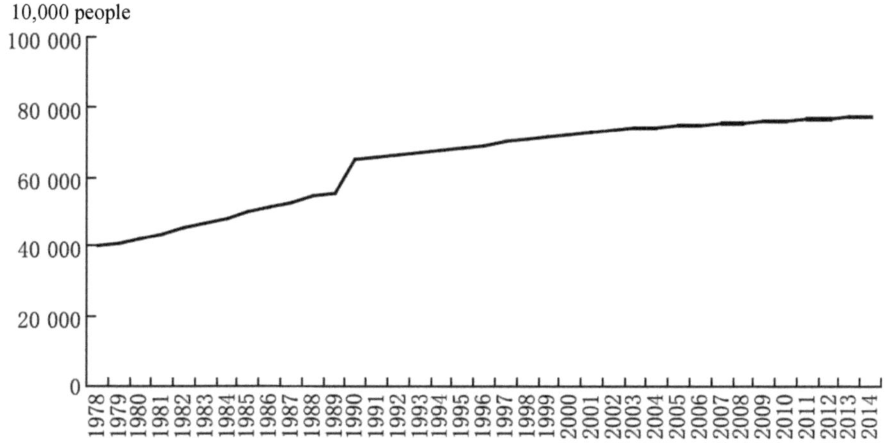

Fig. 8.1 Changes of China's total working population from 1979 to 2014. *Source* Website of National Bureau of Statistics

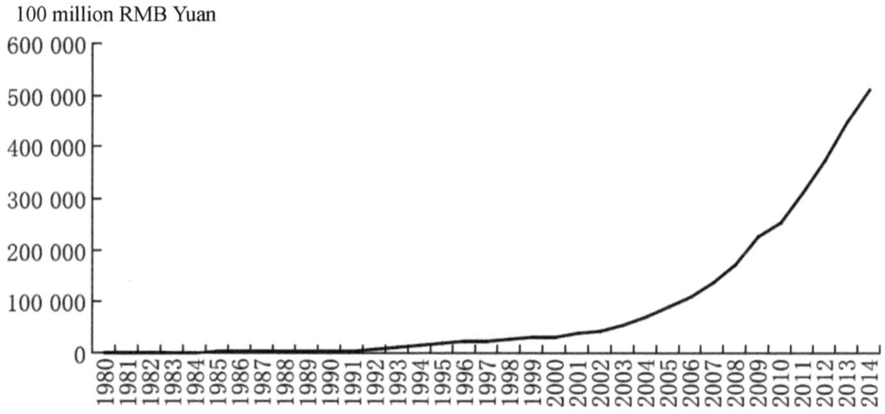

Fig. 8.2 Trend of China's total investment in fixed assets. *Source* Website of National Bureau of Statistics

accelerating. In addition, the increase of the total factor input in China is also related to the influx of foreign investment at that time. China's reform and opening-up met the information industry revolution in European and American countries. At that time, these countries needed to move out the old and traditional industries (mainly industrial sector) to achieve industrial upgrading. China, with its low factor price and a wide range of preferential policies of tax and investment, attracted foreign investment and achieved industrial reception.

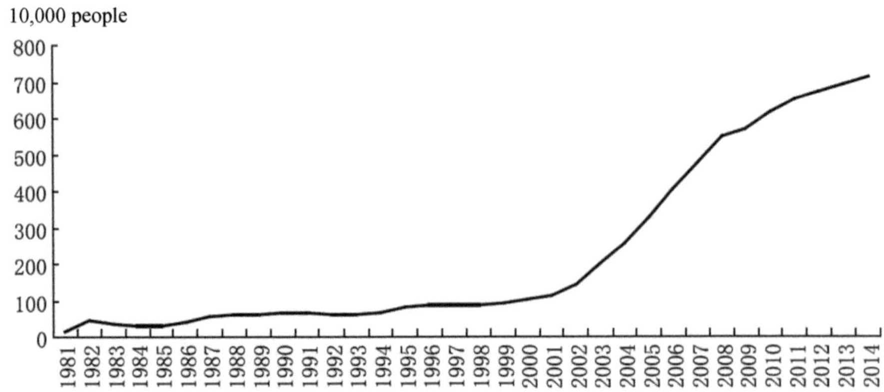

Fig. 8.3 Trend of the number of higher education graduates in China from 1981 to 2014. *Source* Website of National Bureau of Statistics

While the total investment of factors is increasing rapidly, the total factor productivity (TFP) has also made great progress in China. First, China's market-oriented reform, especially the state enterprises reform and the non-public sector's development, effectively enhances the efficiency of the resources allocation and improves the incentive mechanism. Secondly, China's rapid technological progress after the reform and opening-up is mainly the progress in the imported technologies. Technological progress can be achieved either through R&D, or through imitation and purchase. Due to the wide gap in technologies between China and the developed countries, China has the late-development advantage when choosing the methods of technological progress. After the reform and opening-up, China achieved rapid technological progress through imitation and purchase. Third, since the reform and opening-up, there has been a sharp rise in the quality of human capital in China. As can be seen from Fig. 8.3, since 1981, China has seen annual rapid growth in the number of higher education graduates, but in recent years there has been a slowdown in the trend. More and more highly educated people enter the production line, which is very significant for the efficiency improvement.

According to the calculation of some scholars, after the reform and opening-up, the contribution of factor inputs to economic growth accounted for around 64%, while that of total factor productivity accounted for only 36%, namely, only about 1/3 of China's economic growth was achieved through the improvement of labor productivity, which lags far behind 80% of the developed countries, and this, to some extent, reflects the extensiveness of China's economic growth.

8.1.1.2 Expansion of the Total Demand Since the Reform and Opening-Up

After the reform and opening-up, China's rapid expansion of the total supply brought about the increase of the total demand. In accordance with the expenditure method, the total demand will be analyzed from investment, consumption and (net) export.

After the reform and opening-up, due to the correlation between performance assessment and GDP, the local governments have a strong incentive to attract investment, and to this end, the governments need to provide preferential policies for investment, which include: artificial suppression on the price of production factors, for example, reducing the price of industrial land, labor and other factors; relaxing the administrative examination and approval procedures for the resources-dependent or environmentally unfriendly industries; and adopting relevant preferential tax policies, such as investment tax credit and reduction of the taxes. These preferential policies greatly reduce the costs of enterprises, resulting in greater competitive advantage of price for the enterprises' products, thus promoting the volume of investment. In addition, after the reform and opening-up, China's fiscal revenue increased rapidly, with an average annual growth rate of about 15% from 1980 to 2014, much higher than the GDP growth (9.5%) of the same period, and the high revenue, to a certain extent, determined the high level of government investment. Finally, China's high savings rate over a long period of time also made it feasible to achieve high level of investment. It can be seen from Fig. 8.4 that after

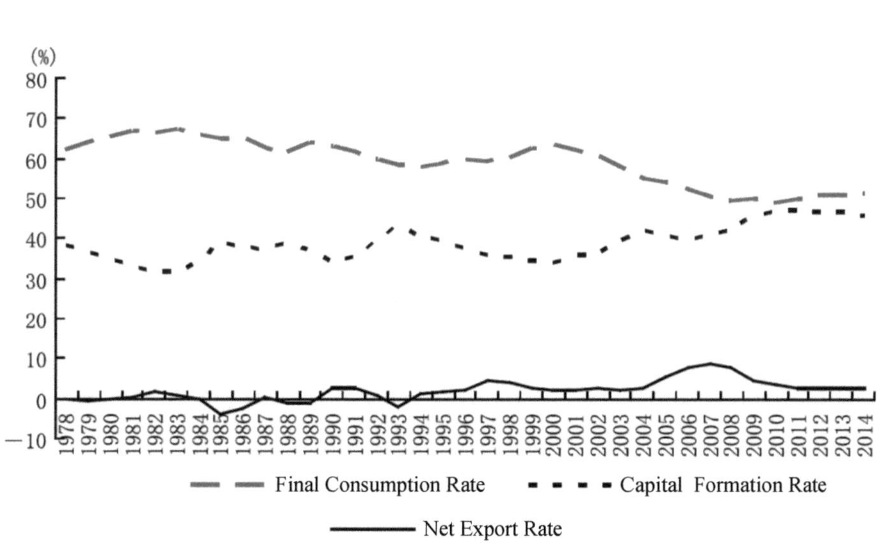

Fig. 8.4 Changes of China's consumption rate, investment rate and net export from 1978 to 2014. *Source* Website of National Bureau of Statistics

the reform and opening-up, the proportion of investment in GDP shows a stable upward trend.

The artificial suppression on the labor price resulted in the low income of labor and low level of consumption. As is shown in Fig. 8.4, to a certain extent, the long-term distortion in labor price was making China's final consumption rate present a downward trend. Although the income was low, after the reform and opening-up, the income of urban and rural residents in China still somewhat increased, and the low price of the products resulting from the low costs increased the consumption ability of the Chinese residents, therefore, in the short term, the distorted factor price is still bearable for the economy.

After the reform and opening-up, China's export trade increased rapidly, for which there are three important reasons. First of all, through the distortion of factor price, the products in China with their low costs had great price advantage compared with those of other countries, which made the export of the Chinese products relatively easy. Secondly, government regulation of the RMB exchange rate gave Chinese products the price advantage in quite a long period of time. As is shown in Fig. 8.5, the RMB exchange rate against the dollar had been on the rise from 1985 to 1994, i.e., the RMB had been devaluating; the RMB exchange rate against the dollar remained basically unchanged from 1995 to 2005; from the beginning of 2006, the RMB began to appreciate slowly. Finally, during the information revolution, industrial upgrading was implemented in the western countries, and a lot of low-end industries were transferred abroad; however, there was a considerable demand of the low-end industrial products from these countries, which provided much space for the export of the Chinese products. Figure 8.6 shows the changes of China's total export, from which we can see that except the impact of the economic crisis in 2008, China's export, in general, shows a trend of rapid growth.

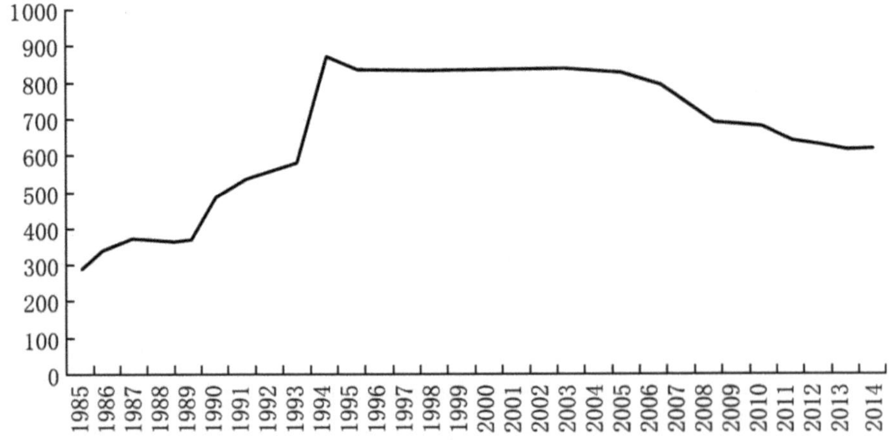

Fig. 8.5 Trend of RMB exchange rate against dollar from 1985 to 2014. *Source* Website of National Bureau of Statistics

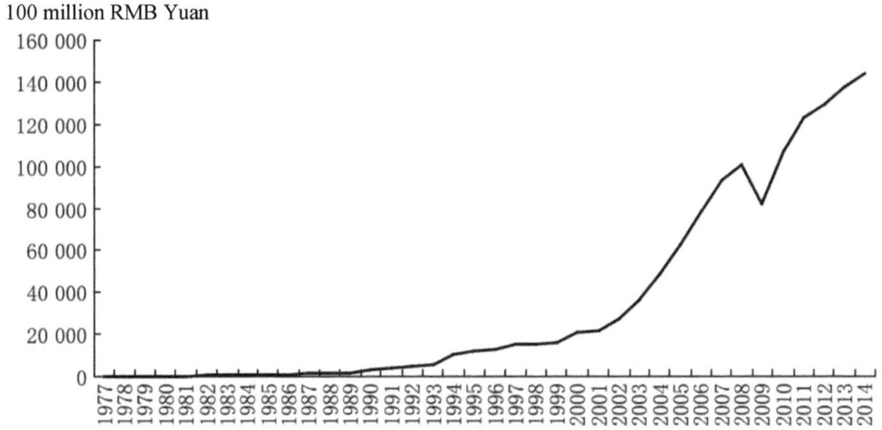

Fig. 8.6 Trend of total export from 1977 to 2014. *Source* Website of National Bureau of Statistics

8.1.1.3 Analysis of the Total Supply and Demand Since the Reform and Opening-Up

The path of "Chinese miracle" can be described by AD-AS model, as is illustrated in Fig. 8.7. In the beginning, the total supply of China's economy is AS1 and the total demand is AD1 with the economy on the balance point of Y1; due to the rapid growth of China's total supply and demand, the total supply moves right to AS2 and the total demand moves right to AD2 with the economy moving to the balance point of Y2, thus realizing rapid economic growth.

At present, the internal structure of China's total supply and demand has undergone great changes, which makes the expansion of AS and AD lack vitality, for example, AS2 and AD2 can only slightly expand to AS3 and AD3 with the economic balance point of Y3, clearly showing that the economic growth rate from

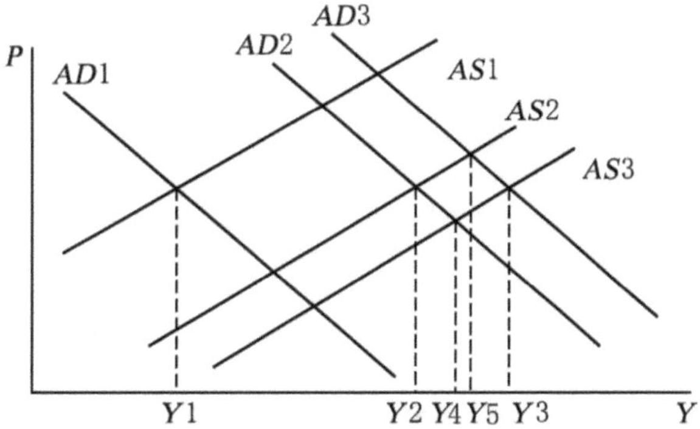

Fig. 8.7 Analysis of total supply and demand with AD-AS model

Y2 to Y3 is much lower than before. The expansion of AS2 and AD2 even stagnates on one side or on both side, so the total economic output can only reach Y4 or Y5, or even stops at Y2. Therefore, if the total supply and demand is not improved, there will probably be a slowdown in economic growth or even economic stagnation.

8.1.2 Total Supply and Demand and Macro Regulation

In the new stage of economic development, China's economy faces three deep-seated contradictions: one is the structural contradiction, another is the systematic contradiction, and the third is the economic cycle contradiction. These three contradictions overlap with each other, depend on each other and affect each other, which greatly increase the difficulty of the resources allocation by the market and the governments' macroeconomic regulation and control. Among these three deep-seated contradictions, the economic cycle contradiction arises in recent years, while the structural contradiction and institutional contradiction are deep-rooted and "hard to crack".

8.1.2.1 Complex New Changes of Total Supply and Demand in China's Economy

From a comprehensive perspective, China's economic structure can be divided into six parts. (1) Demand structure: economic operation first requires demand, which is not only the starting point but also the end of social reproduction. (2) Supply structure: the supply side is provided by the industries and can be regarded as industrial structure. Agriculture, industry, and service industry, all fall into the scope of the supply structure. (3) Factor investment structure: it is a problem of what the economic development of a country should depend on. The Harrod Domar model, or the Solow-Swan model of new classical economic growth theory, or the endogenous growth theory, all of them are centered on the factor input structure. (4) Emission structure, i.e., the resources and environment structure: Theoretically speaking, it is developed from the perspective of input and output. In addition to the three major traditional categories of factor input, it also includes input of energy and resources as well as emission of waste water and waste gas. (5) Urban and rural structure. (6) Regional structure: Among the above six structures, demand structure and supply structure are two big problems that China is facing in the new stage of economic development, including the insufficient consumption demand, especially the low consumption rate of residents, and the coexistence of excess supply and insufficient supply; therefore, the new strategy of coordinating supply side reform and demand management is put forward.

8.1.2.2 Problems in Demand Structure: Insufficient Demand and Low Consumption Rate of Residents

The traditional demand management theories pay much attention on the investment in the "Three Carriages" (investment, consumption and exports), and China has always been implementing the "investment-driven" development strategies, leading to the high investment rate and the declining proportion of consumption in the entire national by tightly squeezing the consumption. From the historical point of view, since the reform and opening-up, final consumption rate once fluctuated in the range of 60–70% for a long time, but declined year after year after entering the 21st century, from 62.3% in 2000 to 48.2% in 2010, with a drop of 14.1%, reaching the lowest level since the reform and opening-up. In 2011, although the rate rose to 49.1%, and then to 51.4% in 2014, compared with the other regions of the world, China's final consumption rate was about 30% lower than the world average.

Then let's look at the internal structure of consumer demands. For the final consumption rate, the most prominent problem is the low consumption rate of residents. According to the data from the World Development Indicators, in 2012 China's consumption rate was quite low compared with other countries in the world. The world average was 60.4%, but China was only 34.6%. According to the data from the National Bureau of Statistics, in 2014 China's consumption rate was 37.9%, a little higher compared with that of 2012. This number, however, compared with the world average (60.4%), was still 20% lower. At the same time, it can be seen from Fig. 8.8 that the consumption growth rate of rural residents has always been lower than that of urban residents, which is related to the unreasonable income distribution structure and social security system.

8.1.2.3 Problems in Supply Structure: Coexistence of Overcapacity and Insufficient Effective Supply

At present, China's supply structure is fairly complicated, not only with excess supply like overcapacity and housing inventory, but also with insufficient supply, especially the lack of innovative supply and public services supply. Therefore, China is now facing the coexistence of excess capacity and insufficient supply, which is reflected in the following five aspects.

The first prominent problem is the overcapacity. The overcapacity is not only a problem of supply but also a problem on the industrial level. It exists not only in the traditional industries such as steel, ferroalloy, coke, calcium carbide, chemicals, shipbuilding, cement, electrolytic aluminum and textiles, but also in the emerging industries such as solar photovoltaic and mobile phones. All of those industries are facing the pressure of overcapacity in varying degrees. The overcapacity in some industries has exceeded the warning line,[1] leading to the sharp decline of

[1]In order to understand and deal with overcapacity theoretically, we need to determine the standard of overcapacity. Some people regard the capacity utilization rate of 81–82% as a cut-off point;

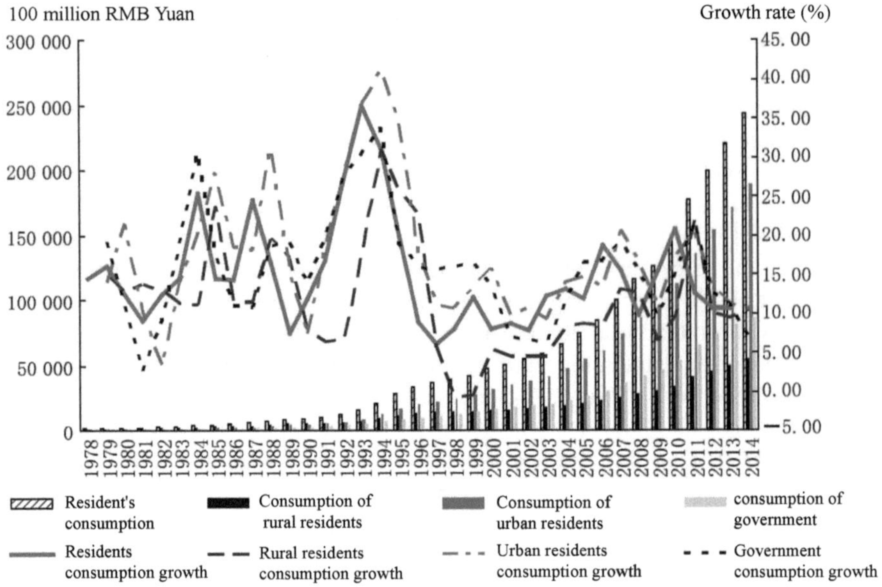

Fig. 8.8 Changes in the consumer demands structure since the reform and opening-up. *Source* Website of National Bureau of Statistics

enterprises' benefits. If we do not solve the structural contradiction of overcapacity, the price of industrial goods will probably continue to drop, the economy will be difficult to keep sustained growth, and the enterprises efficiency cannot be improved. According to the reality of China's utilization rate of overall industrial capacity shown in Fig. 8.9, the capacity utilization rate in recent years keeps at the level of 79%, less than 80%. There has been overcapacity in accordance with the internationally recognized standards. For the capacity utilization rate of some traditional industries, that of iron and steel is 72%, cement 73%, electrolytic aluminum 72%, flat glass 73%, showing serious overcapacity. Meanwhile, overcapacity has gradually extended from traditional industries to emerging industries. The capacity utilization rate of national automobile industry was estimated to drop to below 60% in 2015, and that of photovoltaic industry was as low as 39.8% in 2012. Most of the domestic production capacity was formed in the golden period of the world economy, i.e., the period with strong external demand and domestic high-speed growth, and the capacity expanded in order to cope with the international financial crisis, therefore, only relying on stimulating domestic demand is difficult to

(Footnote 1 continued)

while some people regard the capacity utilization rate of 78% as the cut-off point referring to the standard of the National Development and Reform Commission.

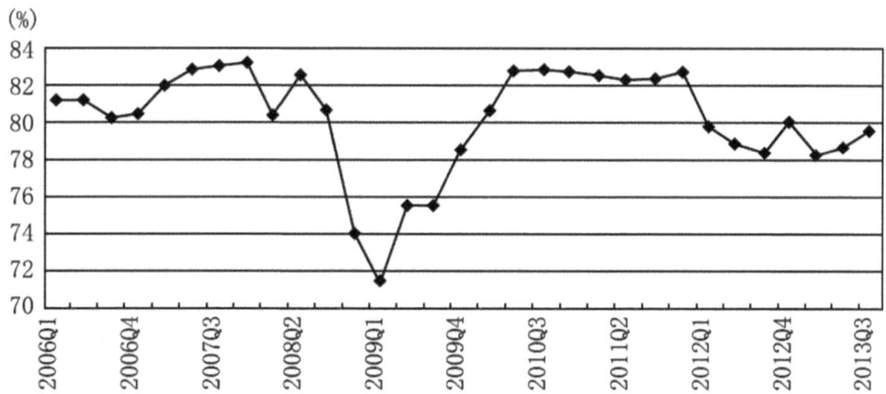

Fig. 8.9 China's utilization rate of overall industrial capacity. *Source* Chang Xiuze, On the new strategy of combining demand management with supply management—an academic report made in Peking University in December, 2015

completely deal with the overcapacity, which must be fundamentally addressed by advancing structural reform.

The second prominent problem is the high housing inventory. At present, from a national perspective, the per capita housing area of urban residents has been close to the level of developed countries, and the era of short supply has gone. At present, real estate is facing a middle and long-term inflection point, and differentiation of real estate in different cities, different regions, and of different types will increase. Except in several large cities like Beijing, Shanghai, Guangzhou and Shenzhen and some areas supported by the population, real estate in a considerable number of the cities is confronting high inventory. From the data of commodity housing area for sale (vacant) released by National Bureau of Statistics (Fig. 8.10), we can see that before 2007 China's real estate inventory was limited, and the growth was quite slow, but after 2007 the growth was quite sharp, especially after 2011, the growth was extremely fast and reached the peak in 2015.

The internal structure (see Fig. 8.11) shows that the growth of apartments for sale and the growth of all the commodity housing for sale demonstrate the same trend, i.e., they began to expand quickly from 2007. Villas and luxury apartments for sale (vacant) also expanded, but to a lesser extent, while office buildings and commercial business space for sale (vacant) almost saw no growth at all.

It shows that in recent years, the rapid rise of the commodity housing inventory mainly attributes to the overstock of commodity housing, and partly to the overstock of the villas and luxury apartments. Meanwhile, the situation varies in different regions, the area of commodity housing inventory in the eastern and central regions being generally higher than that in the western regions. The real estate inventory rate is particularly higher in the northeast urban areas because of the

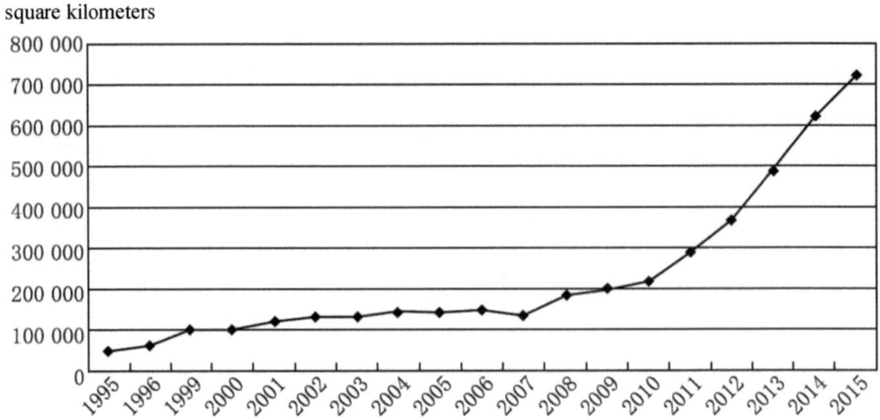

Fig. 8.10 Changes in areas of commodity housing for sale (vacant) from 1995 to 2015. *Source* Chang Xiuze, on the new strategy of combining demand management with supply management – an academic report made in Peking University in December, 2015

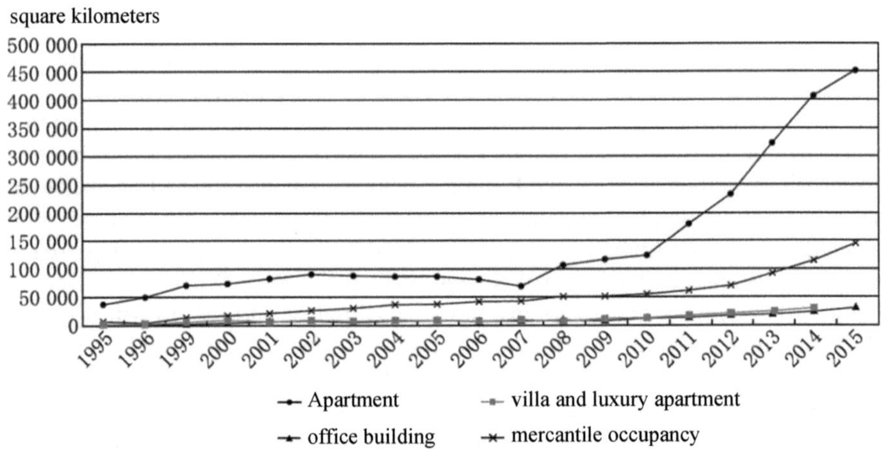

Fig. 8.11 Changes in areas of commodity housing of different types for sale (vacant) from 1995 to 2015. *Source* Chang Xiuze, on the new strategy of combining demand management with supply management—an academic report made in Peking University in December, 2015

severe economic situation, the lack of large and sustainable inflow of population, and the weak demand.

The third prominent problem is the high costs of production and operation of enterprises, including the costs of labor, capital, resources, rent, taxes, etc. With the transition from unlimited supply to the increasingly balanced supply and demand of labor, and then to the structural shortage, labor costs, including wage costs and social security costs, will increase accordingly. In fact, in recent years, China's labor costs have been showing a rising trend, and the high tax is a heavy burden that affects the development of enterprises. In the face of these high costs, we should follow the laws of the market (such as the rise of labor costs), and make use of the government regulation and control (such as government tax cuts) to effectively alleviate burdens on the enterprises.

The fourth prominent problem is the high leverage and increasing debt risk. According to the latest data from China's National Balance Sheet of 2015, at the end of 2014, the overall debt scale in China was about 150.03 trillion RMB Yuan, and the total social leverage rate was 235.7%, among which at the end of 2014 the debt scale of the real sector (excluding financial institutions) was 138.33 trillion RMB Yuan, and the leverage rate was 217.3%. Since the financial crisis, the proportion of the total debt of different sectors in GDP rose from 170% in 2008 to 235.7% in 2014, an increase of 65.7% in 6 years. If excluding financial institutions, and only considering real sectors, the leverage rate increased from 157% in 2008 to 217.3% in 2014, up 60.3% in 6 years. This fairly obvious upward trend indicates an increasing risk of economic systematic debt (Fig. 8.12).

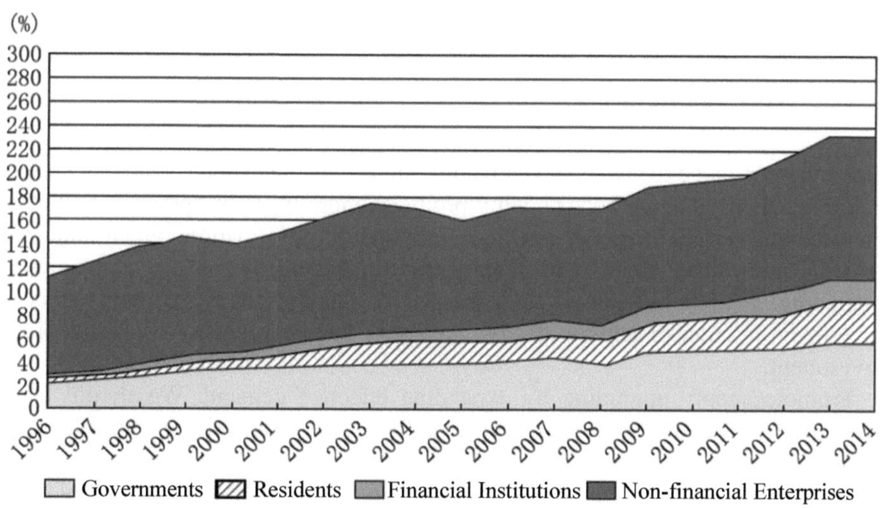

Fig. 8.12 Changes in social overall leverage rate from 1996 to 2014. *Source* China's National Balance Sheet of 2015, p. 550

The fifth prominent problem is insufficient supply in public services and innovative fields. Public services, especially the services related to people's livelihood, are seriously insufficient. There are still many insufficiencies in education, healthcare, low-cost housing, social security, environmental protection, infrastructure and other areas. For the innovative supply, there is a more serious shortage, whether it is new industry, a new product or a new type of operation.

It can be concluded from the above analysis that China is in the primary stage of socialism with distinctive characteristics, meanwhile it is facing the problems of insufficient consumer demands, relatively excess supply, and serious shortage of innovative supply. A new solution is needed to address the new problem of supply and demand in China's economy: a new strategy to combine the demand management and supply management.

8.2 Coordination of Supply Side Reform and Demand Side Management

Under the New Normal, when implementing the supply side structural reform, we should also carry out the demand side management in order to stabilize and expand the total demand. Therefore, we must continue to intensify our efforts to promote structural reform from both supply and demand, expand demand by innovating supply, and advance supply upgrading by expanding effective demand, achieving the mutual promotion of steady growth and structural adjustment.

8.2.1 Integration of Supply Side Reform and Demand Side Management

Drive the demand expansion by innovating the supply. We should guide and create consumer demands with better quality products, more types of operation and more convenient services, support new consumption in information, green industry, tourism and other areas, and release potential demand in the consumption upgrading. We should, based on a long-term view, actively promote effective investment in order to achieve steady increase of the comprehensive benefits of the investment.

Promote supply upgrading by expanding effective demand. We should make good use of structural tax cuts and other policies, press ahead the action plans such as the "Mass Entrepreneurship and Innovation", "Made in China 2025" and "Internet plus", promote the development of service industry and advanced manufacturing industry, support small and micro businesses, give play to the multiplier effect of institutional innovation and technical progress on the supply upgrading, and expand the effective supply.

Integrate the policies of supply side with the policies of demand side. Macro management policies for total supply include economic structural adjustment policies, industrial policies, employment policies, wage policies, and other policies involving the production supply. Demand policies are the macroeconomic policy tools to achieve some policy objectives by adjusting total demand, including monetary policies, fiscal policies, price policies and other policies related to market demand. To press ahead supply side reform is not to give up expansion of the domestic demand on the demand side, instead, it is to combine them together, i.e., integrate the policies of supply side with the policies of demand side, and make concerted efforts on both supply side and demand side to promote structural reform.

8.2.2 Policy Objectives of the Coordination of Supply Side Reform and Demand Side Management

China's economic development is confronted with double tasks: one is how to reverse the downward economic growth in the short term, and the other is how to achieve and maintain medium and high growth rate and move towards medium and high level in the long term. Therefore, the reform goals for both supply side and demand side are to maintain stable economic growth in the short term, and to steadily increase economic growth quality and efficiency in the medium and long term. Supply side structural reform and demand side management should be coordinated to achieve mutual promotion. Demand management should keep the economy running in a reasonable range through a moderate expansion of total demand so as to create a favorable macro environment for the supply side reform, while supply side reform should create conditions for sustainable and healthy economic development in the long run by increasing effective supply capacity, creating new supply, improving the quality, expanding consumer demands, and enhancing endogenous motivation and vitality of the economy.

The short-term objective is to prevent the total economic output "quantity" from suffering "a cliff-like drop" through the integration of the supply side reform with demand side management. At present, although demand management of stabilizing economic growth is fairly moderate due to the constraint of demand side, we should clarify the importance of demand management, and attach equal importance to both consumption and investment before the new round of the economic growth in order to prevent the total economic output from suffering "a cliff-like drop". Meanwhile, on the supply side, we should adhere to the short-term policy centered on "easing supply constraints", alleviate the pressure on enterprises, and mobilize the enthusiasm of producers and workers by taking such measures as reducing procedures of administrative examination and approval, increasing financial support, reducing the market monopoly, and implementing inclusive tax cuts.

The medium-term objective is to promote the "quality" of national economy through structural adjustment coordinated by the supply side reform and demand side management. In the medium term, to adjust the existing economic structure and development mode with supply side reform as the starting point is the main approach to promote the "qualitative" transformation of the national economic development. Structural policies mainly include the development and adjustment policies covering the industry structures, productivity distribution structures, urban and rural economic structures, etc.

The long-term objective is to get rid of the shackles of institutional mechanisms through the supply and demand side reforms so as to achieve efficient and sustainable economic growth. The long-term macroeconomic regulation and control must emphasize the dominant position of market, emphasize the decisive role of market in resources allocation, and prevent the macro regulation and control policies from developing into the government's direct intervention in the enterprise behaviors. To implement the long-term and effective macro regulation and control, we need deepen the reform to promote the cultivation of market economy system, and take the market economy system as the foundation of macro regulation and control policies.

8.3 Supply Side Reform, Consumption Upgrading, Effective Investment and Foreign Trade Transformation

Supply side structural reform needs synchronized and effective collaboration between both sides of supply and demand. We will stimulate supply innovation and effectively coordinate new demand and new supply through improving the consumption environment, accelerating the reform of consumer market and consumption system, promoting the consumption upgrading, and releasing new consumer demands. We will stimulate and create larger supply space for products or services through reforming investment and financing system, improving the efficiency of investment, and strengthening the weak points in society. We will also promote the production and investment of new supply products through optimizing and upgrading the structure of foreign trade.

8.3.1 Supply Side Reform and Consumption Upgrading

China has entered an important stage with sustained growth in consumer demands, accelerated upgrading of consumption structure, and effective stimulation of consumption to the economic growth. The new consumption mainly involves traditional consumption upgrading and emerging consumer boom, and the new investment and new supply can be found in the fields of related industries, scientific and technological innovation, construction of infrastructure and public services. There is enormous development potential in them.

8.3.1.1 Consumption Upgrading and Economic Growth

In the process of modernization, there is regular correlation among the industrialization and urbanization level, industrial structure and consumption upgrading in a country. In the middle and late period of industrialization, consumption gradually becomes the most important motivation of economic growth. Consumption upgrading is closely related to income, population structure, scientific and technological progress and other factors. According to the experience of different countries, when the per capita GDP exceeds 10,000 Geary-Khamis dollars and when the highest proportion of age is around 46, a country's consumption will enter a rapid upgrading period and spending peak; each round of technological revolution will bring about a new round of consumption upgrading. According to China's reality, China's per capita GDP was about 11,000 Geary-Khamis dollars in 2014, China will confront a 45 to 49-year-old population peak in the next decade, and public participation in starting businesses and making innovations is booming. All the factors determine that China will usher in an important period of strategic opportunity for rapid growth in consumption, accelerated structural upgrading and effective stimulation of consumption to the economic growth.

In recent years, the contribution of China's consumer demands to economic growth significantly increases. From 2011 to 2014, the annual contribution rate of final consumption to economic growth was 54.8%, 7.8% higher than the contribution rate of investment. Consumption upgrading with its new focus and new model of consumption in the fields of culture, tourism and information, and industrial development brought by it, are the important impetus to support stable economic development under the pressure of economic downturn. In 2014, the national film box office reached 29.6 billion RMB Yuan, a year-on-year growth of 36.2%; the information consumption reached 2.8 trillion RMB Yuan, a year-on-year growth of 25%. The E-Business developed very fast, and on November 11th, 2015, the platforms of Alibaba Group alone had harvested 91.2 billion RMB Yuan within a single day (Fig. 8.13).

In the new stage of economic development, we should focus on both supply reform and demand management. On the one hand, we should follow the laws of consumption upgrading, adhere to the principle of "Consumer First", and promote industrial upgrading by consumption upgrading; on the other hand, through the accelerated development of the new technologies, new models and new industries, China's manufacturing should adapt to the market to meet consumers' demand, and guide the market to promote consumption. Eventually a virtuous cycle will be formed in which consumption will guide investment, stimulate innovation and prosperity, and improve the livelihood of the people.

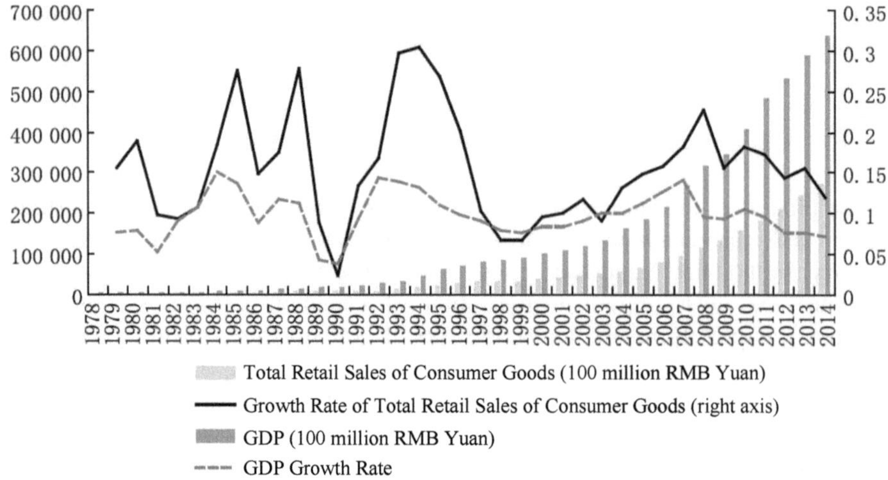

Fig. 8.13 Changes in total retail sales of social consumer goods and economic growth in China. *Source* Website of National Bureau of Statistics

8.3.1.2 Paths to Consumption Upgrading Through Supply Side Reform

In the supply side reform, we should grasp and adapt to the trend of consumption upgrading, drive industrial upgrading by consumption upgrading, and meet and create new consumer demands through institutional, technological, and product innovation. Promoting the consumption upgrading through supply side reform is not only the requirement to better meet consumer demands and improve the quality of people's lives, but also an important way to speed up industrial restructuring and upgrading, and improve economic performance; meanwhile, it is an inevitable choice to create a virtuous cycle of economic system, and build a stable and effective mechanism. Therefore, we should get rid of the structural and institutional obstacles such as the unstandardized competition order in the market, unfavorable consumption environment, etc., fully stimulate the vitality and creativity of the market, and transform potential demand into growth momentum so as to ensure the long-term health of the economy.

Transform and upgrade traditional industries. We will accelerate the transformation and upgrading of the light industry, textile industry, food processing industry, etc., aim at the international standards and the market segments demand, and improve consumer product quality in an all-round way by improving product effectiveness, performance, applicability, reliability and design. We will implement technological transformation and upgrading initiatives, encourage the traditional industrial facilities and equipment to realize intelligent transformation, and promote digital, refined and flexible production mode; we will promote the green transformation of traditional manufacturing industry, encourage ecological design, and strengthen green lifecycle management of the product. We will support manufacturing industry to shift from product-oriented to service-oriented, and guide manufacturing enterprises to extend the industrial chain and increase service links. To strengthen industrial foundation, the key is to make breakthroughs in the bottlenecks such as the core parts (components), advanced basic process, key basic materials, industrial and technological foundation, etc. We will strengthen the infrastructure construction of measurement technology, enhance its ability of transfer and traceability, and improve the industrial measurement service. We will improve the application mechanism for the first (set of) significant technological equipment, and support enterprises to develop, promote and apply significant innovative products.

Cultivate and develop strategic emerging industries. We will follow the new round of technological and industrial revolution trends, speed up to build a modern industrial technology system, attach great importance to the subversive technology innovation and application, promote product innovation by technological innovation in order to better meet the intelligent, personalized, fashionable consumer demands, and guide, create and develop new demand. We will cultivate and develop strategic emerging industries such as environmental protection, information technology, and new energy vehicles. We will accelerate the development of new areas such as printing, robotics, genetic engineering and other industries to explore new areas of consumption, support the development of emerging consumer goods with broad market prospects such as wearable devices, smart home, digital media, etc., and improve the supporting policies for strategic emerging industries.

Make major headway in developing service industry. With the demand of industrial transformation and upgrading as the orientation, we will focus on the development of industrial design, energy saving and environmental protection services, inspection testing and certification, e-commerce, modern logistics, marketing and after-sales service and other industries, actively cultivate new service industries, and promote professionalization of product-oriented industry to extend toward the high end of the value chain so as to support the upgrading of the manufacturing industry. We will follow the trend that the way of living and consumption is changing toward development-type, modernization-type and service-type, focus on the residents and family services, health care and elderly care services, and other services that are close to people's life with great demand and strong motivation effects, strive to enrich the content of services, innovate the ways of services, promote the life service industry to be more convenient and refined with higher quality, and support appropriate enterprises in service industry to carry out cross-industry integrated operation and group-based network management.

Encourage business startups and innovations by the general public to flourish. We will strengthen the policy system integration, improve the entrepreneurial innovation service chain, accelerate the construction of sound ecological environment for entrepreneurship, and encourage and support the development of various types of market players. Relying on the areas with intensive innovation resources such as National Innovative City, National Independent Innovation Demonstration Zone, strategic emerging industries agglomeration areas, etc., we will construct supporting system for collaborative development among industry chain, innovation chain and service chain in order to create a number of influential entrepreneurship and innovation centers in the world. We will accelerate the construction of technological services platforms for sharing large-scale experimental equipment as well as data resources, biological resources, knowledge and patent information services. New models such as crowd innovation, crowdsourcing, crowd support, and crowdfunding will be developed, and new incubators for innovation workshop and virtual innovation community will be encouraged so as to actively create an open service carrier combining the incubator with venture capital, online or offline, in order to provide support for new products, new types of operation and new models. We will improve the mechanism for knowledge, technology, management, skills and other innovative elements to participate in the distribution according to the contribution, develop intellectual property market, strictly implement intellectual property protection, intensify the punishment to the infringement, and establish cross-border rescue mechanism for intellectual property rights.

Encourage and guide the enterprises to accelerate the upgrading of products and services. We will guide the enterprises to proactively adapt to the changes in market demand, and support them to improve product quality, maintain a good reputation, create a well-known brand, and enhance the core competitiveness. We will support enterprises to apply new technologies, new processes and new materials, accelerate the product upgrading, and extend the industrial chain. We will also support them to use new platforms and new models to enhance consumer convenience and increase market share. We will encourage enterprises to strengthen their abilities of market analysis, product design and R&D, marketing development, etc., to participate in global competition. We will optimize the industrial structure, foster a number of enterprise groups and specialized small and medium enterprises with strong core competitiveness. We will stimulate and protect the spirit of entrepreneurship, encouraging innovation and the pursuit of excellence.

Encourage enterprises to strengthen quality brand building. We will implement the strategy of "Manufacturing Quality Power" to vigorously promote the quality of China's products and the construction of China's brands. We will implement management system of product quality commitment and quality service commitment, and carry out special operations to enhance the quality of key areas in service industry, such as education, tourism, culture, products, "Three Guarantees" for product quality, network consumption, etc. We will implement Brand Value Promotion Project, cultivate more high-quality goods, enrich the connotation of brand culture, and actively foster the development of geographical trademarks and famous brands. We will protect and pass on China's time-honored brands, revitalize the traditional Chinese handicraft, and improve the mechanism for brand rights protection and dispute settlement. We will guide enterprises to improve the brand management system, encourage the professional organizations to cultivate and operate brands, and establish a number of enterprises that can demonstrate the good image of "Chinese Manufacturing Brands" and "Chinese Service Brands".

8.3.2 Supply Side Reform and Effective Investment

At present, with increased downward pressure on the economy, "to maintain stable economic growth" is still the focus of China's economic work. "Maintaining stable growth" is inseparable from "maintaining stable investment", therefore, we should pay more attention to seek balance between demand management and supply management, and advance the reform measures. In the short term, we will intensify the proactive fiscal policies and continue to implement loose monetary policies; in the long term, we will improve the investment structure and efficiency. In the future development, investment will still be complicated, and we need to identify the best bonding point of steady growth, structural adjustment, appropriate expansion of effective demand and promotion of the supply side reform, improve investment efficiency, maintain effective investment momentum, focus on addressing weak links, and give full play to the key role of investment in economic growth.

8.3.2.1 The Bonding Point of Supply Side Reform and Effective Investment

"Effective investment" refers to the investment that can quickly form production capacity, increase the total supply of social products, and promote economic growth. In the stage of economic transformation and upgrading, economic growth has a higher requirement for effective investment. "Effective" is actually a combination of benefits and efficiency, not only to ensure high quality, but also to achieve high efficiency. Improving the effectiveness of investment is closely related to China's accelerating supply side reform. Supply side reform focuses on improving the quality of supply, including the improvement of technology, the increase of high-tech content, etc. At present, the quantity in China's supply side is in serious surplus, but the quality is obviously unsatisfactory. In terms of improving the effectiveness of investment, strictly controlling excess capacity is an important aspect. Therefore, the bonding point of supply side reform and effective investment is to accelerate resolving the excess capacity and the real estate inventory, and address weak links in people's livelihood by improving the efficiency and effectiveness of investment.

In order to avoid repeating the old practice of supporting high growth rate by high investment and high consumption, we should choose the right direction of investment, optimize the investment structure, and improve the investment efficiency. We will adjust the investment structure based on the development model transformation, and guide social funds to flow to the following areas: First, the projects that can promote industrial structure optimization and upgrading, including new energy, new materials, electric vehicles, new generation of mobile Internet, biotechnology, advanced manufacturing, marine economy and other strategic emerging industries. Second, production-oriented services, including R&D, design, finance, logistics, information, consulting, accounting, auditing, law, culture, creativity and other industries. Third, infrastructure and public services that are in short supply, including intercity high-speed railway, subway, parking lot, elderly care, healthcare, medical treatment, vocational education, pre-school education, etc. Fourth, the environmental protection industries, including industrial chimney desulfurization, denitrification, dust and sewage treatment, garbage disposal, promotion of low-emission car engine and high-grade fuel, environmental greening and other industries. Fifth, new regional economic growth poles, including those growth poles, growth zones and growth points formed in the "Three Major Strategies" and the "Four Plates".

8.3.2.2 Properly Deal with the Relationship Between Government Investment and Private Investment

To improve the effectiveness of investment, in the short term we will intensify the proactive fiscal policies and continue to implement loose monetary policies, and in the long term we will improve the investment structure and efficiency. At the same time, it is necessary to properly deal with the relationship between government investment and private investment.

Improving infrastructure and public services should be the focus of government investment. Whether in the period of rapid economic growth or gear-shifting, market failures can be effectively made up through government's macro regulation, and the government investment is vital to economic stability and sustainable growth. At present, the starting point of the government investment should be the improvement of infrastructure and public services. Based on the construction and investment in key areas, we will speed up "the Belt and Road" initiative, promote the interoperability among infrastructure such as transportation, energy, information, etc., strengthen the coordinated development of Beijing, Tianjin, and Hebei, and actively promote regional integration of major infrastructure.

Take the advantage of the crowding-in effect of government investment on private investment, and encourage and guide the private investment to grow. On the one hand, the government will effectively improve the investment environment, reduce the private investment costs, and stimulate the private investment enthusiasm by the production-based public costs formed through investment in the infrastructure; on the other hand, the fields of public investment, such as scientific research, education, infrastructure, etc. tend to have strong relevance and ductility. The development of those fields will drive the development of related production factors and industries, and provide and create new profitable investment opportunities, thereby increasing private investment.

Try to expand private investment into different fields through a variety of models, activate the large-scale investment led by governments in the past, and make the private investment as the focus. We will further improve the institutional mechanisms for investment and financing, create an investment environment with equal rights, equal opportunities, equal rules, and equal competition, fully mobilize the enthusiasm of various types of investors, especially private investors, experiment different models of introducing private capital in different fields, including BOT, TOT, BOO, PPP, equity funds, asset securitization, etc., establish and improve relevant legal system, and ensure that these models can be effectively put into practice.

8.3.2.3 Optimize the Internal Investment Structure of the Three Major Industries

As China's economy steps into the New Normal, optimizing the industrial investment structure has become a new requirement for development, and the methods of adjustment and optimization will determine the effectiveness and sustainability of government investment under the new situation.

Continue to increase investment in the first industry so as to consolidate the status of agriculture as the foundation of the national economy. China is a large agricultural country but with single structure, therefore, we will ensure grain production capacity, and on this basis expand investment in the breadth by vigorously developing the forestry, husbandry and fishery. First, enrich the internal structure of agriculture. We will increase investment in agriculture, make strategic adjustment to structure of agriculture and rural areas, and improve the overall efficiency of agricultural economy. In addition, we can further explore the domestic and foreign markets so that the agricultural products with competitive advantage will go abroad and increase their market share. We will make full use of the resources, rely on scientific and technological progress, and increase investment in husbandry, forestry and fishery. For the adjustment to the internal investment structure of agriculture, on the one hand we can improve the efficiency of agricultural production, and promote agriculture from labor-intensive industry to capital-intensive industry; on the other hand, the improvement of agricultural investment efficiency will be conducive to attracting private investment from diversified investors and further promoting agricultural development. Second, relax the restrictions on the investment of agricultural individual economy. We will further relax restrictions on the investment from non-state-owned economy, especially individual and private economy, lower the access threshold with the principles of national treatment and fair competition, encourage private investment projects, and implement the corresponding preferential policies on private investment and foreign investment during the process of tax credit, tax deduction and cost amortization.

Reduce the proportion of investment in the second industry, and optimize the internal investment structure. We will accelerate the development of pillar industries, and promote the development of related industries. At present, the focus of the second industry investment in China should be the five pillar industries determined by the Chinese government, i.e., machinery, electronics, petrochemicals, automobile and construction. We will focus on solving the problems of repeated distribution, repeated construction and uneconomical enterprise scale in the five pillar industries. We will establish and improve corresponding investment and financing mechanisms to accelerate the development of pillar industries, and speed up the transformation of traditional industries with high technologies. As for the investment and industry policies, China should encourage technical input into traditional industries, control the launch of new projects, formulate different policies for technical transformation projects, and prevent low-level and non-economical-scale projects from launching by the interests mechanism so as to concentrate limited funds on key technological transformation projects with wide influence and high efficiency. We will form a virtuous cycle of investment to attract more private investment into technological transformation projects, and further improve industrial productivity through full competition. We will relax restrictions on market access, attract foreign investment to flow to capital intensive industries and those with high capital output ratio, improve the comprehensive level of technologies and equipment in the industrial sectors, and attract foreign investment to transform and upgrade the technical level and product quality of traditional industries.

Promote the development of the tertiary industry, especially the sectors with high technology content and wide employment channels. We will increase investment in high-tech industries led by information technology. Technological innovation is an important driving force for the evolution of product structure; without technological innovation, it is difficult to make progress in industrial structure. The important reason for the low level of China's industrial structure and weak international competitiveness lies in the lack of technical innovation. In economically developed countries, the proportion of technical progress in economic growth has reached 50–70%, with many countries reaching as high as 60–80%, but China's technical progress accounts for less than 30% in economic growth. Therefore, it is necessary to focus on the development of high-tech industry, give priority to high-tech industry investment, and vigorously promote the informationization of national economy and society to push ahead industrialization, all of which are the important measures to optimize and upgrade industrial structure and achieve leapfrog development. We will increase the investment in information technology, biological engineering, new materials and other high-tech industries, and reduce the degree of monopoly of the tertiary industry. The development of various industries is achieved through increasing investment and improving efficiency. One of the main reasons for the slow development of the tertiary industry in China is that many sectors in the tertiary industry are monopolistic. The existence of monopoly has not only hindered the growth of the third industry, but also led to the low efficiency of the tertiary industry. In terms of the fund sources, we should vigorously encourage private investment into the tertiary industry, which requires creating an enabling environment for private investment, including good legal environment, fair competition regulations, convenient business registration procedures, etc., so as to allocate more resources to the tertiary industry.

8.3.3 Supply Side Reform and Foreign Trade Transformation

For a long time, the changes of external demand directly affect the development of foreign trade China. Affected by the slowdown of world economic growth, the shrinking of international demand, the falling price of bulk commodity, and the slowdown of domestic investment demand as a result of structural adjustment, China's foreign trade has encountered many difficulties with increasing downward pressure on exports. In the face of those difficulties, we should intensify our efforts to maintain stable growth and make structural adjustments in foreign trade. For the foreign trade enterprises accustomed to achieving development with low prices, supply side reform of foreign trade is to reform the backward productivity and revitalize the supply side, improving the efficiency and structure of supply so as to stimulate consumption and promote economic growth. In other words, it is to transform from the "massive imports and exports" to "quality imports and exports", i.e. through the transfer of mode and adjustment of structure, to cultivate new competitive advantage of foreign trade. From the middle and long term, China's foreign trade is in a key transition stage from the growing period of "increasing speed and quantity" to the mature period of "improving performance and quality", so cultivating comprehensive competition advantage and consolidating foundation of sustainable development are the key tasks in the current period. Therefore, we should accelerate the supply side structural reform of foreign trade, stabilize China's foreign trade and realize its transformation and upgrading through consolidating advantages of traditional trade and fostering new development momentum.

8.3.3.1 Accelerate the Transformation and Development of Traditional Trade

Traditional trade mainly refers to the foreign trade based on general trade and processing trade. Since the reform and opening-up, processing trade, as an important part of China's foreign trade and open economy, has played an important role in promoting industrial upgrading and stabilizing employment. Since 1981, China's traditional trade has developed with an average annual growth rate of about 18%, among which the average annual growth rate of general trade was 14.4%, and that of processing trade was 23.3%. In terms of the growth rate, processing trade grew faster than the general trade before 2005, and its import and export volume rose from \$2.635 billion in 1981 to \$690.4 billion in 2005. After 2007, affected by the external environment, the total import and export volume of general trade and processing trade declined, with the total import and export volume of traditional trade reaching \$3.35 trillion in 2012 (Fig. 8.14 and Table 8.1).

At present, global industry competition pattern is undergoing in-depth adjustment, and China's economy steps into the New Normal. The processing trade

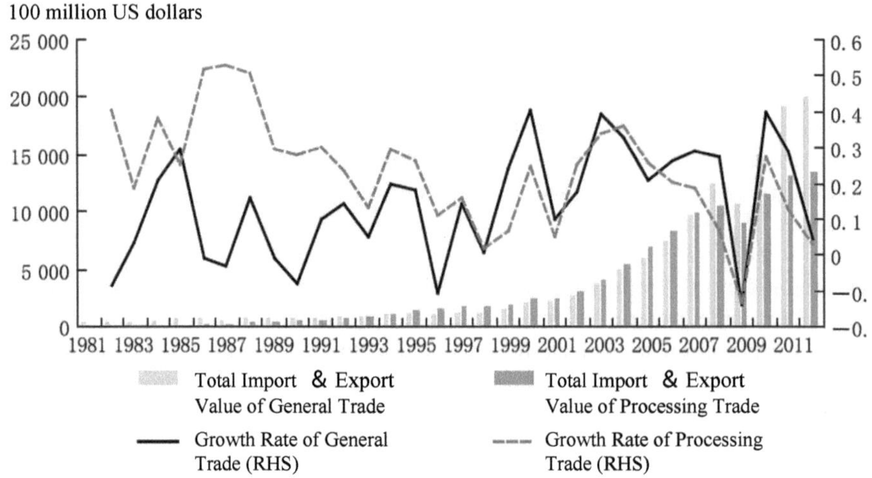

Fig. 8.14 Development of China's traditional trade from 1981 to 2011. *Source* China Trade and External Economic Statistical Yearbook

undertakes less international industries but transfers abroad more industries and orders with rising costs of production and weakening traditional competitive advantage. In order to meet the new challenges, it is necessary to accelerate the innovative development of processing trade through supply side reform and then improve the quality and efficiency of the traditional trade.

Extend the industrial chain, and enhance the status of processing trade in the global value chain. By strengthening cooperation in the industrial chain, we will encourage enterprises to actively integrate into the global industry with a more open attitude in order to better utilize the markets and resources both at home and abroad and improve the status of processing trade in the global value chain. We will promote industrial integration and upgrading, attract more investment, especially the investment in advanced manufacturing industry and the emerging industry, further expand the opening of the service industry, and encourage foreign enterprises to set up procurement, allocation and settlement centers and develop headquarter economy in China. We will continue to support the coastal areas to develop electronic information industry and other advantageous industries, and encourage enterprises to establish, upgrade, and transform. We will encourage the labor-intensive industry to take the priority to realize the gradient transfer to the inland and border areas and achieve the integrated cluster development. Through foreign investment and cooperation, we will utilize the overseas economic and trade cooperation platforms, encourage enterprises to go global together, and extend the industry chain to other countries. We will enhance the innovation ability of the enterprises, push the processing trade enterprises to develop from original

Table 8.1 China's Import and Export of General Trade and Processing Trade from 1981 to 2012 (Hundred Million US Dollars)

Year	Conventional Trade		Processing Trade		Other Trading Forms	
	Exports	Imports	Exports	Imports	Exports	Imports
1981	208	203.66	11.31	15.04	0.79	1.5
1982	206.69	170.17	15.77	21.28	0.74	1.45
1983	201.6	187.68	20.01	24.01	0.69	2.21
1984	231.62	238.49	29.29	31.47	0.49	4.14
1985	237.3	372.72	33.16	42.74	3.04	7.04
1986	250.95	352.07	51.41	63.9	7.04	13.13
1987	296.43	287.72	81.38	95.02	16.59	49.36
1988	325.96	352.08	128.33	137.46	20.91	63.16
1989	315.52	356.14	188.04	156.78	21.84	78.48
1990	354.6	262	254.2	187.6	12.1	83.9
1991	381.2	295.4	324.3	250.3	13.6	92.2
1992	436.8	336.2	396.07	315.14	16.53	154.56
1993	432	380.45	442.36	363.6	43.04	295.55
1994	615.6	355.2	569.8	475.7	24.7	325.2
1995	713.61	433.81	737.18	583.59	37.01	303.4
1996	628.24	393.63	843.27	622.75	38.99	371.92
1997	779.74	390.3	996.02	702.06	52.14	331.34
1998	742.35	436.8	1044.54	685.99	50.22	279.58
1999	791.35	670.4	1108.82	735.78	49.14	250.81
2000	1051.81	1000.79	1376.52	925.58	63.7	324.57
2001	1118.81	1134.56	1474.34	939.74	67.83	361.23
2002	1361.87	1291.11	1799.27	1222	94.82	438.59
2003	1820.34	1877	2418.49	1629.35	143.45	621.22
2004	2436.06	2481.45	3279.7	2216.95	217.5	913.89
2005	3150.63	2796.33	4164.67	2740.12	304.23	1063.08
2006	4162.33	3330.74	5103.55	3214.72	423.81	1369.15
2007	5393.55	4286.64	6175.6	3684.74	623.2	1590.2
2008	6628.62	5720.93	6751.14	3783.77	927.17	1820.92
2009	5298.12	5344.7	5868.62	3222.91	849.37	1491.62
2010	7206.12	7692.76	7402.79	4174.82	1168.63	2094.86
2011	9170.34	10076.21	8352.84	4697.56	1460.64	2661.07
2012	9878.99	10223.86	8626.77	4812.75	1981.38	3147.43

Source China Trade and External Economic Statistical Yearbook

equipment manufacturer (OEM) to original design manufacturer (ODM) or original brand manufacturer (OBM).

Play the demonstration role of the coastal areas, promote the transformation and upgrading, and improve the industrial performance. On the one hand, we will stabilize the industries with traditional advantages, and continue to develop the textile and garment, footwear, furniture, plastic products, toys and other traditional labor-intensive processing trade to consolidate the traditional advantages. We will support enterprises to strengthen their technical R&D and equipment transformation, increase technological content and added value, and enhance their core competitiveness. On the other hand, we will make major headway in developing the advanced manufacturing industry and the emerging industry, and encourage the development of advanced manufacturing industries such as electronic information, mobile communication, motor vehicles and parts, integrated circuits, medical equipment, aerospace and other industries with strong ability of radiation and technology spillovers. We will promote the development of new industrial clusters, such as biological medicine, new energy, new materials, energy saving, environmental protection, etc., and meanwhile actively support the development of productive service industry. We will press ahead the transformation of the manufacturing industry from production-oriented to service-oriented by promoting the deep integration of processing trade with service trade and encouraging the processing trade enterprises to undertake R&D and design, testing and maintenance, logistics and distribution, financial settlement, distribution, warehousing and other service-outsourcing business.

Support the inland and border areas to undertake gradient transfer of industries, and promote coordinated regional development. We will promote cluster development of processing trade industry in accordance with the layout of the country's key industries. We will step up to establish the coordination mechanism for the transfer of inter-provincial processing trade and industry in order to solve such problems as asymmetric information and incomplete supporting services, etc. We will intensify our support to the key undertaking places for the gradient transfer of processing trade, and make differentiated policies to develop the gradient transfer. Based on the premise that polluting industries and backward production capacity are prohibited to transfer, taking the layout of national key industries into consideration, we will study and formulate policies and measures to support the inland and border areas to undertake the gradient transfer of the processing trade.

Guide enterprises to carry out international capacity cooperation in a planned way, and co-ordinate international and domestic markets and resources. Through planning foreign cooperation of processing trade, we will reasonably arrange key countries and key industries of overseas cooperation, and guide the industries such as building materials, chemical industry, nonferrous metals, light industry, textiles, food, etc. to carry out overseas cooperation. We will transform the way of "going global" in the processing trade, support enterprises to achieve chain transfer and cluster development by relying on foreign trade and economic cooperation zones, industrial parks, special economic zones and other cooperative parks. We will support enterprises to expand foreign investment, promote export of equipment, technology and service standard, deeply integrate into the global industrial chain, value chain and logistics chain, establish a number of overseas production bases of bulk commodity, and foster a number of multinational corporations. We will improve international cooperation mechanism in processing trade, enhance the existing bilateral and multilateral cooperation mechanism, and strengthen the cooperation with key countries in the "going global" initiative in investment protection, finance, taxation, customs, quality inspection, personnel exchanges and other aspects so as to provide support for the enterprises. We will build platforms for foreign cooperation, organize domestic processing trade enterprises and key national industries to exchange and cooperate, and carry out industrial cooperation.

Improve the level of cross-border e-commerce development, and foster new advantages of open economy. Developing cross-border e-commerce and pressing ahead supply side reform are conducive to the promotion of China's manufacturing industry transformation and upgrading, conducive to "high quality and low price" and "quality imports and exports" of international trade, and conducive to the construction of cross-border e-commerce demonstration areas. They can also expand the scope and content of supply, and improve product quality and brand competitive advantage, which will effectively enhance the status of Chinese enterprises in the global value chain, helping China to participate in the reconstruction of global pattern of economy and trade. Under the background of supply side reform, we should gradually establish policy system and supervision system that can adapt to the characteristics of cross-border e-commerce development, constantly optimize its environment, promote new types of operation such as direct import, bonded stocking, flash purchase, etc., and promote its development level and international competitiveness.

8.3.3.2 Realize the Innovative Development of Service Trade

Since the reform and opening-up, China's service trade has made great progress. The total volume of foreign trade in services has increased rapidly. The annual growth rate of China's trade in services has reached 15.96% since 1998, exceeding the annual growth rate of China's GDP. At the same time, China's trade in services has long been in deficit. Since 2000, China's trade in services has been in deficit, with the balance of trade deficit in the first 10 years remaining almost unchanged and in the latest 6 years increasing rapidly. China's economic structure is transforming from secondary-industry-based to tertiary-industry-based, so how the service industry and foreign trade in services will cooperate to promote China's economic development has become an important task for China (Table 8.2).

In the current context, accelerating the development of service trade is an important support to promote the transformation and upgrading of foreign trade, an important starting point for promoting supply side reform and cultivating new momentum, as well as an important carrier of public participation in starting businesses and making innovations, which is of great significance to promoting exports and employment and realizing the transformation of foreign trade from "quantity imports and exports" to "quality imports and exports".

Develop trade in services with "the Belt and Road". We will increase international trade in services by utilizing the bright development prospects of the countries along the Silk Road. "the Belt and Road" initiative covers a wide range of countries, which have formed an economic belt with bright development prospects

Table 8.2 Development of China's Foreign Trade in Services from 1998 to 2014 (Hundred Million US Dollars)

	1998	1999	2000	2001	2002	2003	2004	2005	2006
Total Export Value	239	262	301	329	394	464	621	739	914
YoY	−2.40%	9.60%	14.90%	9.30%	19.80%	17.80%	33.80%	19.00%	23.70%
Total Import Value	265	310	359	390	461	549	716	832	1003
YoY	−4.30%	17.00%	15.80%	8.60%	18.20%	19.10%	30.40%	16.20%	20.60%
Balance of Trade	−26	−48	−58	−61	−67	−85	−95	−93	−89
	2007	2008	2009	2010	2011	2012	2013	2014	
Total Export Value	1216	1465	1286	1702	1821	1905	2106	2222	
YoY	33.00%	20.50%	−12.20%	32.40%	7.00%	4.60%	10.60%	7.60%	
Total Import Value	1293	1580	1581	1922	2370	2801	3290	3821	
YoY	28.90%	22.20%	0.10%	21.50%	23.30%	18.20%	17.50%	15.80%	
Balance of Trade	−77	−115	−295	−220	−549	−896	−1184	−1599	

Source Commerce Data Center in Ministry of Commerce, http://data.mofcom.gov.cn/channel/trade/trade.shtml.

of service trade, and this will become a powerful driving force for the development of international service trade. As an economy in Asia with service trade taking the dominant position, China must take this opportunity to develop modern service trade with the characteristics of the Silk Road on the basis of expanding the scale of traditional trade. We will build high-standard free trade areas by utilizing the bilateral free trade agreements reached by the countries along the Road, implement high-standard opening policy, and promote mutual opening and communication of the countries and regions along the Road in the financial, cultural, educational, medical and insurance services. Relying on the bilateral free trade agreements, China should actively seek extensive regional economic cooperation with those countries for more and wider service trade exchange, optimize industrial distribution of all service sectors, make coordinated development of the service industry, and build a more transparent, more standardized, and more equitable environment for economic cooperation of service trade by signing high-standard free trade agreements and establishing high-standard free trade areas.

Speed up to explore institutional mechanism that can adapt to the development of service trade. At present, in order to give full play to the enthusiasm and creativity of the local governments, the central government has selected Shanghai, Tianjin, Hainan, Shenzhen, Hangzhou, Wuhan, and Guangzhou as the pilot places for innovative development of service trade. We will further facilitate and liberalize service trade, focus on building a regulated, internationalized and convenient business environment, and push the institutional innovation of service trade towards a new level. Through exploring and improving the service trade management system, we will establish the promotion, support and supervision system aligned with the general rules of international service trade, and explore institutional mechanism that can adapt to the innovative development of service trade. Through exploring and expanding the two-way opening of service industry, considering the local industrial characteristics, we will steadily promote the opening up of industries such as finance, education, culture, health, child and elderly care, architecture and design, accounting, auditing, trade and logistics. Through cultivating market players of service trade, we will strengthen cooperation of different departments, integrate public resources, increase the support of enterprises in key areas of service exports, and promote the expansion of service exports. We will actively explore new development model of service trade under the background of informationization, promote innovative model of service trade by relying on big data, the Internet of Things, mobile Internet, cloud computing and other new technologies, build new network platforms of service trade, promote the development of technology trade, finance, and traditional Chinese medicine services, and actively undertake offshore outsourcing services in order to enhance the ability to deliver cross-border services.

8.3.3.3 Promote Development of Offshore Trade

Offshore trade is a new trade model, which has been developing very fast in the past 20 years. Offshore trade mainly concentrates in regions or cities with tax preferential policies, low transportation costs, and stable trade environment, through which many port cities in the world have successfully realized structural transformation. China (Shanghai) Pilot Free Trade Zone was formally approved in August, 2013 by the State Council as the first specially supervised zone by the customs in China compatible with the international practice. The establishment of Shanghai Pilot Free Trade Zone has created a great opportunity for the development of offshore trade. As is pointed out by the "Framework Plan for China (Shanghai) Pilot Free Trade Zone", it is necessary to develop new trade models, promote pilot offshore business (international trade settlement center), and support enterprises in the pilot area to conduct offshore business. As a new trade form, offshore business is one of the important tasks in the development and construction of Shanghai Free Trade Zone. Attracting more international trade intermediaries to concentrate in Shanghai Free Trade Zone and actively promoting the offshore business are conducive to enhancing China's position in the global trade value chain, thus gaining more distinct advantages in trade.

Accelerate the establishment of an offshore trade center with Shanghai Free Trade Zone as the core. We will break the constraints of foreign exchange management, improve the operation of offshore business, implement preferential tax policies to reduce the operation burden of offshore trading companies, create an offshore financial center to provide financial support for offshore business, promote the offshore business of RMB to support offshore trade, and establish a sound service system to remove concern of offshore trade. At the same time, we will speed up to explore and promote the policy innovation of offshore business. It is of great significance for China to attract offshore business settlement centers to concentrate since the offshore business is able to bring a lot of trade settlement business and tax benefits, promote the balanced development of China's trade in goods and in services, and promote the functional transformation of China's trade center cities. Therefore, we should speed up the innovation of foreign exchange supervision and tax policies to create a favorable policy environment for the development of offshore business. On the one hand, taking RMB settlement of cross-border trade as an opportunity, we will promote the development of offshore business in a planned way, increase the number of pilot enterprises with special account on cross-border business, and improve the design model of special account. On the other hand, we will introduce plans for international trade intermediaries into the free trade zone, encouraging them to do offshore business, and attract more enterprises of "going global" to set up their settlement center in Shanghai and other trade center cities in China.

Chapter 9
Supply Side Structural Reform and Sustained Growth of Economy

The core of the supply side structural reform is to realize effective supply of resources, improvement of quality and efficient allocation, gain stronger momentum, release the potential, and achieve the efficient and sustained economic growth. In the previous chapters, we have systematically illustrated the connotation of supply side structural reform, and taking it as the core content, explained China's new supply economics and its theoretical framework, analysis methodology, strategic paths, practical measures, etc. To aim at the objectives of supply side structural reform, we also need to elaborate on the relationship between the supply side structural reform and the economic growth. This chapter, through analyzing the process and stages of China's economic operation, carries out an empirical study on the total supply and demand structure, economic fluctuation, supply side structural reform and China's economic growth potential, etc., and on this basis, systematically analyzes the growth trend of China's economy in the medium and long term.

9.1 Analysis of Economic Transformation, Total Supply and Demand Structure and Economic Fluctuation

In the early academic studies on the economic operation, economic fluctuation is usually referred as "economic cycle" or "business cycle". The economists commonly hold that economic operation will inevitably experience four consecutive stages: recovery, expansion, recession and contraction, thus forming a cycle. For the reasons of economic fluctuation, the economists have analyzed from different perspectives and formed various theories. The representative theories include: the traditional economic cycle theory represented by Keynes, Samuelson and Hicks; the Monetarist economic cycle theory represented by Friedman; the neoclassical economic cycle theory represented by Lucas; the real business cycle theory represented by Kydland, Prescott, Long and Plosser; and the new Keynesian economic cycle

L. Xiao, *New Supply Side Economics*, DOI 10.1007/978-981-10-4639-1_9

theory represented by Dornbush, Blanchard, Mankiw and Stiglitz. These theories analyze the internal reasons for economic fluctuation from such perspectives as effective demand, money supply and people's economic projections. Based on the existing theoretical perspectives, this chapter will analyze the relationship between structural changes and economic fluctuation from the perspective of total supply and demand structures according to the theoretical logics of new supply side economics.

9.1.1 Total Supply and Demand Structures and Economic Operation

Supply and demand are two dimensions of observing the economic operation, which are related and coexist. Total social demand refers to the purchasing power on goods and services formed by the monetary expenditure used in investment and consumptions in a country or a region over a certain period of time, which includes domestic demand and foreign demand. According to the Keynesian economics, total social demand is determined by the "Three Carriages" (investment, consumption and exports). Total social supply refers to the total amount of goods or services available for purchase provided by social production in a nation or a region over a certain period of time, which includes domestic supply and import supply. The capacity of total supply in a society is mainly determined by the factor investment such as capital, labor, technology, etc. on the supply side.

Total supply and demand structures are closely related to the economic operation. In the economic operation, the balance between total supply and total demand is only a coincidence, while the consecutive spiral increase of total supply and total demand is the normal of economic operation. Therefore, the change or imbalance of the total supply and demand structures will directly lead to economic fluctuation and its range change. The influence of the imbalance between total supply and total demand to the economic operation is mainly reflected in three aspects:

First, imbalance between total supply and total demand, i.e., the total social product is in short supply or in short demand. Under the market mechanism, when the total social product is in short demand, the insufficient total demand will make it difficult for the market to let out all the product, leading to overstock, and the production will contract, lacking economic growth momentum, so the economic operation will fluctuate downward; when total social product is in short supply, the insufficient total supply will lead to rising prices and increased investment in production capacity, and the production will expand, so the economic operation will fluctuate upward. From the development process of the major countries in the world, we can see that in the period with relatively excess supply, the government, in order to avoid deflation, usually issues policies of stimulating consumption, increasing investment and encouraging merge and restructuring to curb the sharp fluctuation of economic operation; in the period with relatively short supply, the government, in order to avoid fast increase of prices and overheated investment, usually adopts macro policies such as increasing supply and ratio allocation, to stabilize economic fluctuation.

Second, imbalance of demand momentum structure. The demand momentum structure refers to the organic combination of all the factors and proportions that can expand the demand. According to the Keynesian economics, total social demand structure mainly includes investment, consumption and export. However, the demand of a country is always affected by such factors as economic institutions, policy system, consumer disposable income, consumption intention and macro regulation, and directly reflected by the variation of investment tendency, consumption tendency and net export. Meanwhile, since the "Three Carriages"—investment, consumption and exports—have different influences on the demand expansion, they also have different effects when promoting the short-term economic growth. For example, the variation of total investment, as the direct momentum to promote domestic demand, has a fairly significant influence on the variation of demand. Because of different effects of different momenta, when dealing with insufficient total demand, many countries choose to increase the total social demand by stimulating investment demand, which results in the imbalance of demand momentum structure and further leads to the imbalance of various proportions in the internal economic structure and greater fluctuation of economic operation.

Third, imbalance of supply momentum structure. The supply momentum structure refers to the combination of all the factors and proportions that can expand the supply. According to the economic growth theories, macroeconomics usually describes the production supply by the production functions. The macro production functions relate the economic output to factor investment and technologies. In the supply process of products and services, the production has realized the combination and allocation of such factors as labor, capital and technology, forming different industrial categories and departments, and their structures, to some extent, determine the internal momentum structure of total social supply. From the middle of 20th century, the economists have started to research on the relationship between economic operation and industrial structure changes. The representative economists include John Bates Clark, S. Kuzndets and H. Chenery. Chinese scholars start late in researching on the relationship between industrial structure and economic growth, and mainly focus on the relationship between China's industrial structure and economic fluctuation from different perspectives. A series of studies by scholars both at home and abroad show that when effectively utilizing technologies, the resources will transfer from low-efficient departments to highly-efficient departments, promoting the rapid economic growth and leading to economic fluctuation. Meanwhile, the influence of the rationalization and upgrading of industrial structure to economic fluctuation shows distinct characteristics in different stages, i.e., the upgrading of industrial structure is a main reason for economic fluctuation, and the rationalization of industrial structure helps to curb economic fluctuation.

To summarize, although there are various theoretical analyses on economic fluctuation, almost all the existing theories focus on the demand side or supply side of economic activities, and analyze the influence or effects of some aspects on the supply side or demand side on the economic operation and fluctuation, lacking systematic consideration of the relationship between total supply and demand structure changes and economic operation and fluctuation. The new supply side economics, put forward in this book, is theoretically based on promoting the effective supply of factors and resources, enhancing the optimization and adjustment of economic structures, releasing the economic growth momentum and vitality, and realizing the sustained economic growth. Therefore, the new supply side economics will return to the origin of market economy operation; and based on the decisive role of the relationship between supply and demand to the economic operation, the new supply side economics will discuss the economic operation and economic fluctuation from the perspective of total supply and demand structures.

9.1.2 Characteristics Analysis of China's Economic Fluctuation

Reviewing China's economic development, we can easily find that since the founding of New China, the long-term economic growth and short-term economic fluctuations reflected by China's GDP growth rate index demonstrate distinct characteristics of different stages and times (see Fig. 9.1). There is a correlation between China's economic fluctuation and China's economic system transformation, in other words, the socialist market economic system is continuously strengthened in the economic construction, and the role of the market in the resources allocation is gradually consolidated, but there is a closer correlation between economic fluctuation and China's total supply and demand structure. One important starting point of constructing the market economy with Chinese characteristics is to further release and

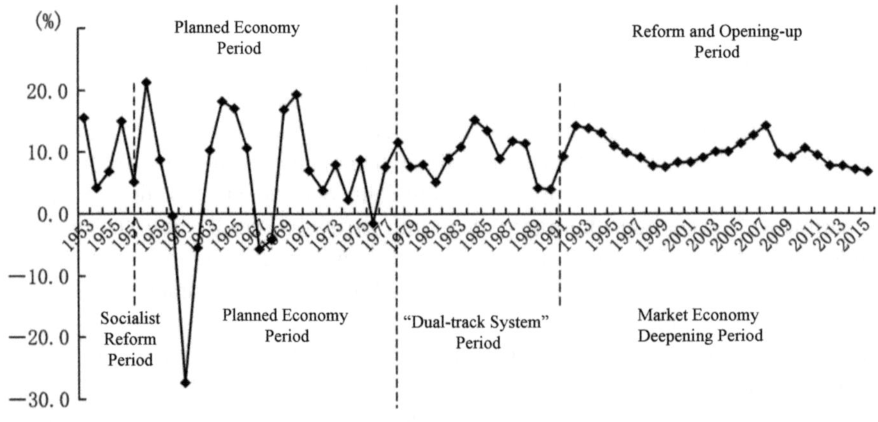

Fig. 9.1 The trend of China's actual GDP growth rate from 1953 to 2015. *Source* Wind Info

develop the productivity to realize the effective coordination of economic and social supply and demand. According to the similarities and differences of economic system, taking the year of 1978 as the cut-off point, we divide it into planned economy period (1949–1978) and post-reform-and-opening up period (1979–2015); Meanwhile, in order to better describe the characteristics of economic fluctuation in different stages of market economy, we divide China's economic growth into four stages, i.e., socialist reform period, planned economy period, "dual-track system" period and market economy deepening period.

9.1.2.1 Socialist Reform Period (1949–1956)

In this period, China had straightened out the economic chaos such as soaring prices and disordered market at the early stage of the founding of new China, carried out the cooperative transformation of individual agriculture, individual handicraft industry and capitalist industry, and implemented social reform of public and private partnership, gradually expanding the management power and scope of the state-owned economy and narrowing down the management power and scope of the private economy. During the socialist reform period, China's economy had rapidly transformed from a less developed market economy to a centrally planned economy. The overall economic operation remained stable, but the economic fluctuation showed the characteristic of high frequency. The economic growth index kept at around 109, but the economic fluctuation changed from 115.6 in 1952 to 104.2 in 1954, and then quickly rose to 115.0 in 1956.

9.1.2.2 Planned Economy Period (1957–1978)

In this period, China had been completely on the track of socialist planned economy. The government began to implement the system of balanced distribution of important materials in the country, and carry out the overall intervention and planning of industrial development to gradually establish a national planning and management system. During this period, the reckless "Great Leap Forward" movement and the people's commune movement also brought some impact on the economic construction and the people's life. Overall, in the planned economy period, China's economic fluctuation presented two characteristics: On the one hand, because China's economy was in the stage of recovery and development, the economy maintained a rapid growth for most part of this period. For example, in the years of 1958, 1964, 1965, 1969 and 1970, the economic growth rate topped 15%, of which the economic growth rate reached as high as 21.8% in 1958. On the other hand, due to the implementation of highly centralized production plans and the unified allocation of product supply, market allocation of resources and factor as well as market-based pricing were inhibited, so the economic fluctuation was more frequent and more volatile. If the growth rate was calculated according to the arithmetic average, the average level of the economic growth in this stage was 6.04%, but the highest economic growth rate was 21.3%, deviating by 15.26% from the average; the lowest economic growth rate was −27.3%, deviating by 33.34% from the average. Meanwhile, the economic fluctuation was more frequent, with wide fluctuation in economic growth rate about every three years. For example, the economic growth rate sharply dropped from the maximum value in 1958 to the extremely low value in 1961, from which rebounded to 18.3% in 1964, and then fell back to −5.7% in 1967.

9.1.2.3 "Dual-Track System" Period (1978–1991)

Taking the rural household contract responsibility system as the starting point, China began to implement the reform and opening-up and promote economic system reform, explore the mechanism of "the country regulating the market, and the market guiding the enterprises", thus ushering into the transition period from national ration system to commodity system. This stage was the exploration and trial period before the establishment of a comprehensive socialist market economy system, carrying out the economic development mode of "taking national regulation as the main and market allocation as the supplementary", and implementing the planned commodity economy based on public ownership. The market gradually played its pricing function, while in many areas the country was still implementing plans and rations. Overall, in this stage China's economy maintained a fairly high growth rate with much narrower economic fluctuation. If the growth rate was calculated according to the arithmetic average, the average level of the economic growth in this stage was 9.98%, among which the highest economic growth rate was 15.2% in 1984, deviating by 5.22% from the average; the lowest economic growth rate was 3.9% in 1990, deviating by 6.08% from the average. From the perspective of economic fluctuation cycle, this stage had only experienced two complete cycles, and the average time of each cycle span was 8 years or so with more gentle volatility.

9.1.2.4 Market Economy Deepening Period (From 1992 so Far)

Guided by Deng Xiaoping's South Talk, the 14th CPC Congress clearly put forward that the establishment of socialist market economic system was the target of China's economic system reform. As a result, China's economic system reform was further deepened, the market players gradually became mature, and the government's macro-control means were increasingly stable. In this stage, with the deepening of economic system reform oriented by Chinese socialist market economy, the market system gradually improved, and the market shifted its role from auxiliary to decisive in the process of resources allocation. Overall, in this period, China's economy maintained a high growth rate, the economic fluctuation further reduced, and the frequency of fluctuation significantly dropped. If the growth rate was calculated according to the arithmetic average, the average level of the economic growth in this stage was 9.43%, among which the highest economic growth rate was 14.2% in 2007, deviating by 4.77% from the average; the lowest economic

Table 9.1 Comparison of Average Annual Growth Rates and Fluctuation of China in Three Periods

	1953–1978	1979–1990	1991–2015
Variance of Annual Growth Rate	106.50	11.82	5.10
Arithmetic Average of the Growth Rate (%)	6.68	9.11	9.98

Note The smaller the variance, the better the stability.

growth rate was 6.9% in 2015, deviating by 2.53% from the average. From the perspective of economic fluctuation cycle,this stage has only experienced one complete cycle (Table 9.1).

From the stages of China's economic development and the cycles of economic fluctuation, we can see that along with the establishing of China's socialist market economy, the market plays an increasingly important role in the resources allocation, the market-based price mechanism of resources and factors gradually forms, releasing huge growth momentum and leading to the trend of rapid growth in China's economy, and the economic fluctuation amplitude and frequency gradually reduce.

9.1.3 Impetus Structure of Total Supply and Demand and Economic Fluctuation

In the process of China's economic development, with the establishment of socialist market economy with Chinese characteristics and the transformation of the government's macro regulation, the impetus structure of the total demand and the total supply is also changing. In the impetus structure of the total demand, investment, consumption and export play different roles in promoting economic growth in different development stages, which also leads to economic fluctuation. In the impetus structure of the total supply, the evolvement and changes of industrial structure also bring remarkable impacts on the economic growth and the economic fluctuation.

9.1.3.1 Impetus Structure of Total Demand and Economic Fluctuation

In retrospect, demand side management had played an important role in China's economic growth over the past 60 years, investment, consumption and export in the demand impetus played different roles in the economic growth, and therefore had different effects on economic growth and fluctuation. Generally speaking, since the founding of new China, no matter in the period of planned economy or socialist market economy, investment had played a prominent role in the demand impetus, effectively promoting the economic growth; comparatively speaking, consumption and export had provided a weaker support to the economic growth.

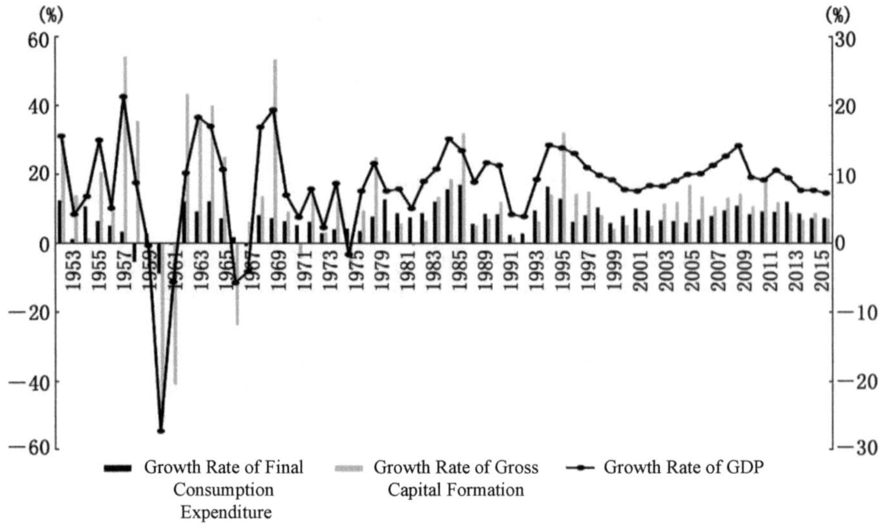

Fig. 9.2 The actual growth rates of China's GDP, consumption and capital. *Source* Wind Info

In the planned economy period (1949–1978), with the objective of accelerating the recovery and development of national economy, China implemented the strategy of "Heavy Industry First", and under the condition of capital shortage, engaged all the capital in the production at the expense of consumption, thus forming a development pattern of "high accumulation and low consumption". The contribution rate of investment to the economic growth was continuously increasing, and the economic growth rate showed a positive correlation with the investment growth rate. From Fig. 9.2 we can see that in this stage, the growth rate of gross capital formation was significantly higher than that of consumption expenditure; meanwhile, when the gross capital formation maintained a fairly high growth rate, so did the national economy. For example, in 1953, the growth rate of the gross capital formation reached 29.9%, the growth rate of final consumption expenditure was 12.5%, and the economic growth rate was 15.6%; in 1958, the growth rate of the gross capital formation reached 54.2%, the growth rate of final consumption expenditure was 3.4%, and the economic growth rate was 21.3%; in 1961, the growth rate of the gross capital formation reached −51.9%, the growth rate of final consumption expenditure was −8.7%, and the economic growth rate was −27.3%.

In the socialist market economy construction period (since 1979), China deepened its reform and opening-up by taking the advantages of labors and resources, accelerated the market-based reform in the field of resources and factors, and gradually released the inner vitality of resources supply; Meanwhile, China also strengthened the government's regulation on the economic operation, and further increased the impetus of the economy by expanding investment, promoting consumption and encouraging export. During this period, the contribution rate of investment to the economic growth maintained a high level, and the investment growth rate showed a positive correlation with the GDP growth rate, becoming an important impetus for economic growth. Especially after 2000, to deal with the impact of the international economic fluctuation on the domestic economic growth, Chinese government expanded the investment scale and increased the total investment, keeping the growth rate of investment at above 10% and thus ensuring the stable growth of the whole economy. From 2001 to 2010, the average growth rate of China's investment reached 13.48%, the average growth rate of China's consumption reached 8.13%, and the economic growth rate reached 10.51%. Meanwhile, the structure of the demand impetus such as investment, consumption and export had been optimized, the increase of consumption and investment had achieved relative balance, and their contribution rate to the economic growth was fairly stable (see Fig. 9.3).

Generally speaking, before the reform and opening-up, although consumption accounted for a large proportion in the national economy, in the process of accelerating economic recovery and development, investment in the demand impetus increased faster and provided stronger support to the economic growth. With the changes of the investment growth rate, China's economic growth also showed sharp fluctuations. After the reform and opening-up, with the establishment and improvement of the socialist market economy, domestic demand gradually expanded, making the structure of investment and consumption more reasonable, the economic growth more stable, and the economic fluctuation range much lower (see Table 9.2). The variance of the GDP growth rate dropped from 106.50 during the planned economy period to 11.82 in the early stage of the reform and opening-up, and then to 3.89 after 2002. It can be concluded that with the changes of the demand structures, the impact of the investment growth rate on the economic

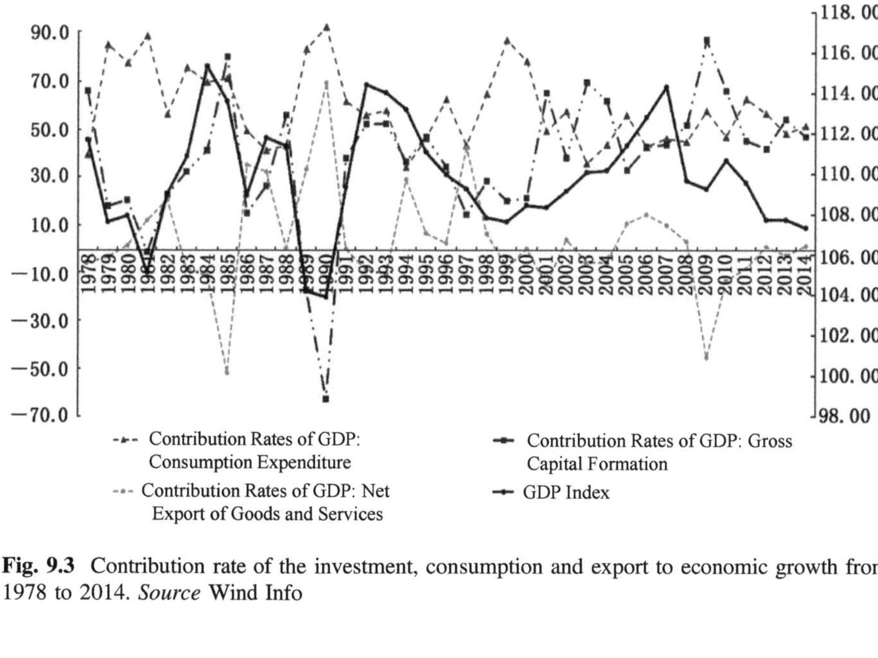

Fig. 9.3 Contribution rate of the investment, consumption and export to economic growth from 1978 to 2014. *Source* Wind Info

Table 9.2 Arithmetic Average of China's Consumption, Capital, GDP Growth Rate in Different Stages and Economic Fluctuation

	1953–1978	1979–1991	1992–2001	2002–2014	1953–2014
Growth Rate of Final Consumption	4.85	9.25	9.44	8.47	7.27
Growth Rate of Gross Capital Formation	12.32	3.70	11.55	11.92	11.35
Average Growth Rate of GDP	6.68	9.11	10.35	9.92	8.46
Variance of Growth Rate	106.50	11.82	6.64	3.89	50.20

Source Wind Info

fluctuation has gradually reduced, and the stability of the economic growth has continuously increased.

9.1.3.2 Impetus Structure of Total Supply and Economic Fluctuation

Impetus structure of supply refers to impetus structure of production, i.e., the industrial structure formed by resources supply, which is an important aspect for pressing ahead economic growth. Reviewing China's economic development history, we can find that with the evolvement of different economic development stages, the industrial structure has also undergone dramatic changes, exerting great impact on the economic development and operation.

In the planned economy period, China adopted the strategy of "Heavy Industry First", and on this basis implemented large-scale economic construction. In the subsequent period, the industrial economy maintained a high growth rate, which significantly exceeded the tertiary and the first industry. If the years of negative growth were excluded, the average growth rate of the industrial economy in this period reached 19.68%, much higher than 8.67%, the average growth rate of the tertiary industry. In such a context, the industrial economy had a fundamental influence on the national economic development, and the industrial fluctuation had a great impact on the economic fluctuation (see Fig. 9.4). For example, in 1956, the industrial economy grew by 34.5%, promoting the economic growth rate by 13%. This increase was higher than 13.3% of the tertiary industry and 4.7% of the first industry. At the same time, from the growth fluctuation of the three industries, we can see that the AVEDEV function value of the industrial growth fluctuation is 14.1, the AVEDEV function value of the tertiary industry and the first industry is 6.8 and 4.5 respectively, and the AVEDEV function value of the GDP growth is 7.38. Therefore, it can be concluded that the industrial growth fluctuation had brought greater impacts on the economic fluctuation.

After the reform and opening-up, with the continuous improvement of the socialist market economic system, the value of resources market gradually recovered, coupled with the gradual release of external demand and domestic demand,

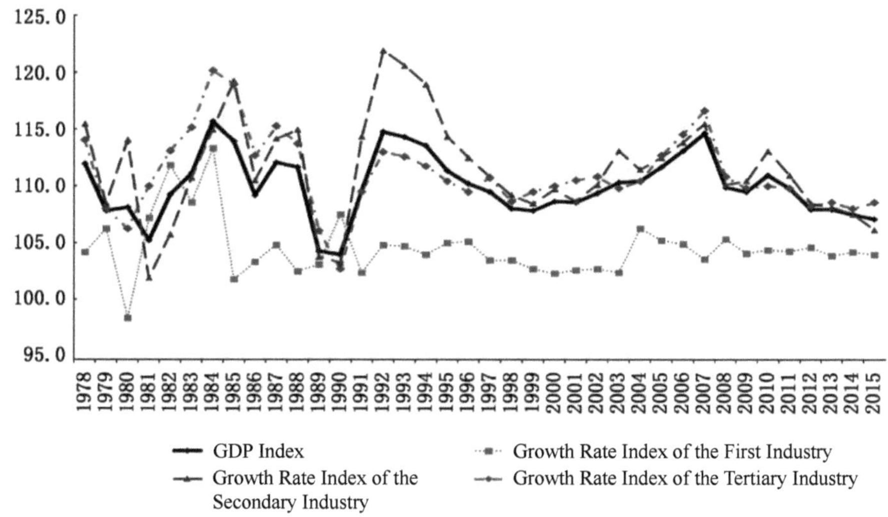

Fig. 9.4 Relationship between three-industry growth rate and GDP growth rate from 1953 to 1978. *Source* Wind Info

and China's three-industry structure continuously optimized (see Fig. 9.5). The proportion of the secondary industry in GDP gradually dropped from 47.6% in the early stage of the reform and opening-up to 40.5% in 2015, the proportion of the tertiary industry in GDP gradually increased from 24.5% in 1978 to 50.5% in 2015, and the proportion of the first industry in GDP gradually reduced from around 30% in 1978 to 9% in 2015. The proportion of the tertiary industry in GDP had exceeded the proportion of the secondary industry from the beginning of 2012, and China's economic operation began to show a trend of service economy-based development.

With the changes of the three-industry structure, the contribution rate of the three industries to economic growth also gradually changed (see Fig. 9.6). The contribution rate of the industrial economy to GDP growth gradually decreased from over 60% to below 40%. Meanwhile, the contribution rate of the tertiary industry to GDP growth gradually increased from below 20% to above 57%. The contribution rate of the first industry to GDP growth gradually dropped from 40% to around 5%. From 2014 on, the contribution rate of the tertiary industry to economic growth has exceeded that of the secondary industry for the first time.

Changes in industrial structure also mark the changes in impetus structure on the supply side. With the gradual development of the tertiary industry and the optimization of the three-industry structure, the stability of China's economic growth has also been enhanced (Fig. 9.7).

From 1978 to 1992, the market mechanism of labor, capital, technology and other factors had not been fully established in the process of exploring commodity economy in China, and there was a dual mechanism of market price allocation and national rationing price allocation. In the industrial structure led by the secondary

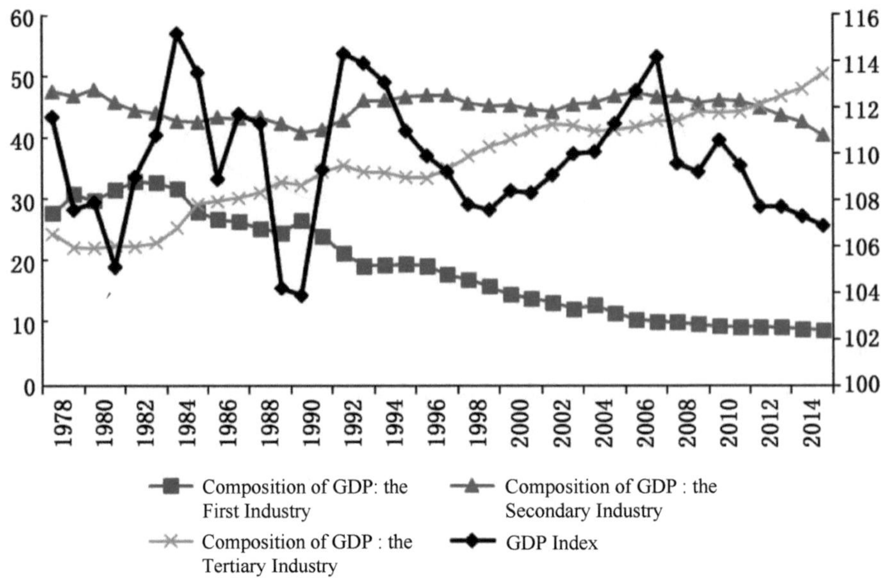

Fig. 9.5 Changes of three-industry structure from 1978 to 2015. *Source* Wind Info

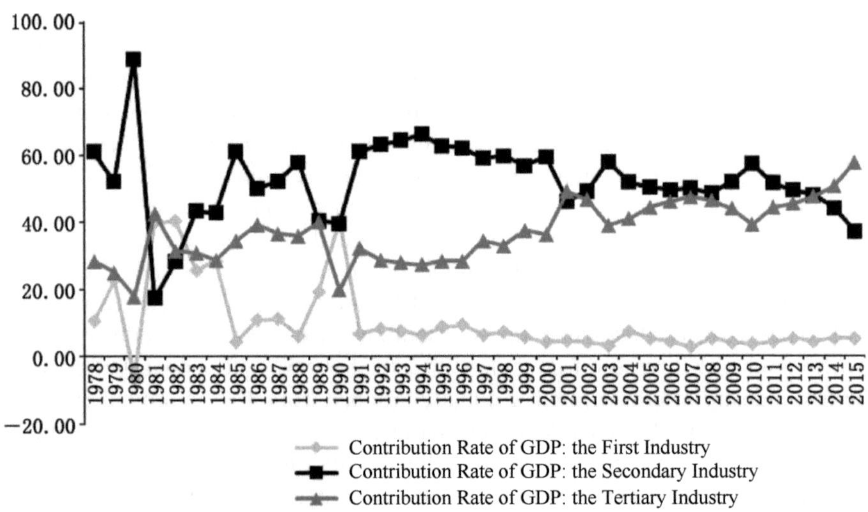

Fig. 9.6 Contribution rate of the three-industry growth to GDP growth from 1978 to 2015. *Source* Wind Info

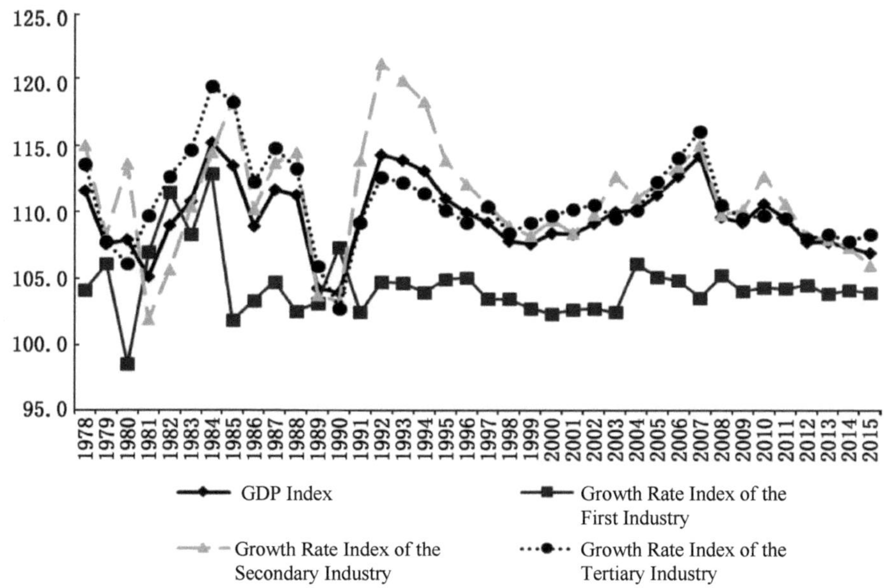

Fig. 9.7 Relationship between three-industry growth rate and GDP growth rate from 1978 to 2015. *Source* Wind Info

Table 9.3 Three-industry Growth Fluctuation and Economic Fluctuation from 1978 to 1992

	Growth Fluctuation of First Industry	Growth Fluctuation of Second Industry	Growth Fluctuation of Tertiary Industry	Growth Fluctuation of GDP
Variance	13.22	30.60	20.16	11.41
AVEDEV Value	4.11	10.88	6.41	5.86

industry, the sharp fluctuations of the three industries and their growth rates resulted in remarkable fluctuations in economic growth (see Table 9.3).

From 1993 to 2002, with the deepening reform of China's socialist market system, the role of the market in the resources allocation had been strengthening, and the service industry had been developing rapidly, steadily increasing its proportion in the national economy. In such a context, the internal structure of the three industries had been further optimized, the stability of China's economic operation had been enhanced, and the influence of the three-industry fluctuation on economic fluctuation had been weakened (see Table 9.4).

Table 9.4 Three-industry Growth Fluctuation and Economic Fluctuation from 1993 to 2002

	Growth Fluctuation of First Industry	Growth Fluctuation of Second Industry	Growth Fluctuation of Tertiary Industry	Growth Fluctuation of GDP
Variance	0.91	15.65	1.10	4.30
AVEDEV Value	0.84	3.29	0.81	1.72

Table 9.5 Three-industry Growth Fluctuation and Economic Fluctuation from 2003 to 2015

	Growth Fluctuation of First Industry	Growth Fluctuation of Second Industry	Growth Fluctuation of Tertiary Industry	Growth Fluctuation of GDP
Variance	0.75	6.50	5.69	4.21
AVEDEV Value	0.65	2.14	1.82	1.60

After 2003, the proportion of China's tertiary industry was close to the proportion of the secondary industry, and then exceeded it in 2012, leading to a fundamental change in the impetus structure on the supply side of economic development and an enhanced stability of the economic growth. As can be seen from Table 9.5, the fluctuation range of the GDP growth rate is smaller than that of 1993–2002, and the AVEDEV value is also smaller than that of 1993–2002.

Generally speaking, under the guidance of the strategies such as speeding up the transformation from an agricultural country to an industrialized country and speeding up industrial modernization, the industrial development quickly gains momentum and its contribution rate to the economic growth is fairly high. The fluctuation of industrial economy has a great impact on the fluctuation of economic growth. However, with the deepening of China's socialist market economic construction, the three-industry structure changes, so does the impetus structure on the supply side. The impact of supply on economic fluctuation is also gradually reduced, making the economic operation more stable.

9.1.4 Imbalance of Total Supply and Demand and Economic Fluctuation

The imbalance of the total supply and demand has a significant causal relationship with economic fluctuation and economic growth; whether in over supply or in short supply, the imbalance will definitely result in the deviation and distortion of the market prices and values, making it difficult for the market to let out all the products. Once this market condition continues, it is bound to further distort the market allocation of resources, and cause the reduction of economic efficiency of the whole society, which is presented as the economic fluctuation. Reviewing China's economic development, we can find that at different stages China's economy has shown different characteristics of imbalance between total supply and total demand, thus reflecting different economic fluctuations.

9.1.4.1 Shortage Economy Period and Economic Fluctuation

In the planned economy period, the total supply and demand relationship in China was mainly presented as shortage economy, and this shortage was not just reflected in the commodity market, but also a kind of overall shortage covering all the fields such as factor market, capital market and labor market. As a result of the implementation of national direct planning or allocation in the enterprise production, market circulation, supply of production materials, supply of consumer goods and so on, the production and the consumption lacked market regulation mechanism, and the overall supply and demand relationship was mainly presented as serious short supply. The government's plan or regulation of the production or allocation of goods was obviously lagging behind when promoting the balance between supply and demand, which intensified the economic fluctuation during the process of balancing supply and demand. This was reflected in the sharp economic fluctuation during the period of the planned economy.

9.1.4.2 "Dual-Track System" Period and Economic Fluctuation

Since the reform and opening-up in 1978, the role of the market mechanism in the allocation of resources and the adjustment of commodity production had been continuously strengthened, remarkably enhancing the balance between supply and demand. However, since there were both planning regulation and market regulation in this period, the structure of the total supply and demand was still unbalanced. Although the relationship between supply and demand gradually developed towards balance, there was still structural short supply.

From the relationship between the consumer price index and the GDP growth, we can see that China's price level was slowing rising from 1978 to 1993, with sharp price fluctuations (see Fig. 9.8). Over the same period, the growth rate of the total retail sales of social consumer goods also significantly changed (see Fig. 9.9), which showed that in the "dual-track" economy period transforming from the planned economy to the market economy, the total supply and the total demand were accelerating to achieve balance, but there was still a structural shortage. The rapid growth of social demand reflected the rapid growth of prices. At the same

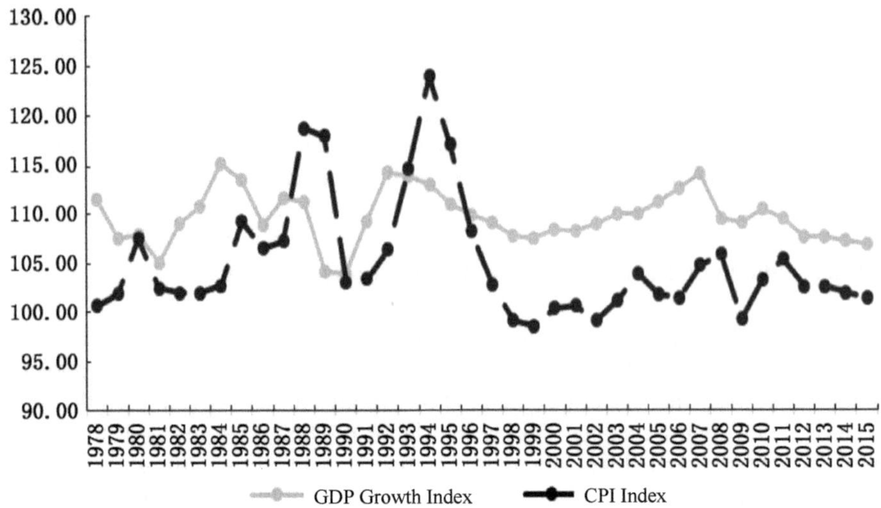

Fig. 9.8 Relationship between consumer price index and GDP growth index. *Source* Wind Info

time, since there was still a rationing method of the planned economy, the fluctuation of prices was slightly lower than the fluctuation of total social consumption growth (Table 9.6).

9.1.4.3 Market Economy Deepening Period and Economic Fluctuation

In 1992, the 14th CPC National Congress further clarified the direction of the socialist market economy reform. China had continuously deepened the market mechanism and system construction and the market fully played the fundamental and decisive role in the resources allocation, and the vitality of various market players had been constantly stimulated. At the same time, with the expansion of China's total demand, the supply capacity of various industries was continuously enhanced, and China had gradually achieved a balance between the structure of total supply and that of demand even with overcapacity in some areas. In such a context, China's social consumption growth had seen steady growth, but the price level was relatively stable (see Figs. 9.8 and 9.9). The stability of the total supply and demand structure significantly reduced the economic fluctuation. The variance of price fluctuation dramatically dropped from 46.62 in the "dual-track" economic period to 15.71, while the variance of GDP growth fluctuation dropped from 11.65 in the "dual-track" economic period to 3.2 (Table 9.7).

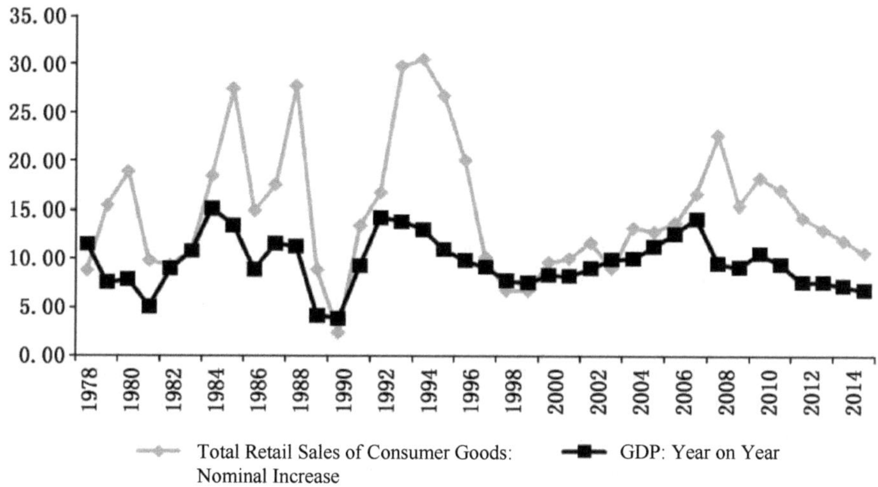

Fig. 9.9 Relationship between growth rate of total retail sales of social consuming goods and GDP growth rate. *Source* Wind Info

Table 9.6 Fluctuations of Price, Social Consumption Growth and Economic Growth from 1978 to 1994

	Fluctuation of Price	Fluctuation of Social Consumption Growth	Fluctuation of Economic Growth
Variance	46.62	64.04	11.65
AVEDEV Value	5.46	6.46	2.91

Table 9.7 Fluctuations of Price, Social Consumption Growth and Economic Growth from 1994 to 2015

	Fluctuation of Price	Fluctuation of Social Consumption Growth	Fluctuation of Economic Growth
Variance	15.71	24.45	3.20
AVEDEV Value	2.67	3.85	1.39

9.2 Supply Side Structural Reform and China's Economic Growth Potential Analysis

The analysis of economic growth in the modern sense was originated in the 1930s by two economists, Harrod and Domar. The first Harrod-Domar model, proposed by Harrod and Domar, with the first modern economic growth analysis, became the basis for the follow-up economic growth analysis models. Subsequently, the theory of economic growth had experienced two climaxes, i.e., in the 1950s Solow model was put forward by such scholars as Solow and Swann, which further deepened the theory of economic growth; in the 1980s Romer and other scholars put forward the New Growth Theory, which held that economic growth had a strong dependence on the exogenous variables such as population growth rate and technological progress. The New Growth Theory emphasized more on the promotion effects of technological progress, human resources accumulation and other factors on the economic growth. With the development and improvement of the economic growth theory, the role of labor, capital, technology, related industrial structure and institutional environment as an impetus to the economic growth has been continuously proved. The improvement of resources quality, the enhancement of efficiency, the optimization of structures and the innovation of system will have a great influence on economic growth. The promotion effects of the supply side structural reform on economic growth are not only reflected in increasing the effective supply of resources but also in pushing ahead the technological progress, institutional innovation and structural optimization. Therefore, the implementation of the supply side structural reform will effectively increase the potential of China's economic growth.

9.2.1 Input of Labor and Capital and Potential Growth Rate

According to the theory of economic growth, efficient supply of labor and capital is the basis of high-speed potential growth rate in the future. Labor and capital are the core factors that determine future potential growth rate.

9.2.1.1 Labor Input

The contribution of labor to economic growth is mainly reflected in the quantity and the quality of labor input. For a long time, China's economic growth, to a certain extent, relied on the continuous input of low-level and low-cost labor force. However, as China's population structure changes, the demographic dividend gradually weakens, and the quality upgrading of labor force will increase its impact on economic growth by playing a more important role.

At present, the number of Chinese labor force has been decreasing, and the potential impetus of labor quantity increase for economic growth will weaken. After 1984, China's employment growth rate has always been decreasing; by 2010, China's employment growth rate was only 0.36%, lower than the population growth rate, in other words, the annual retirement population was larger than the newly employed population. Although China has been implementing the "universal two-child policy" since the beginning of 2015, and the "delayed retirement" policy has been put on the agenda, as for the future labor quantity increase, the effects of these policies are difficult to appear in the short term. With the increasing aging trend in the future demographic structure, China's total labor force in the future may enter a process from negative growth to stable growth (Fig. 9.10).

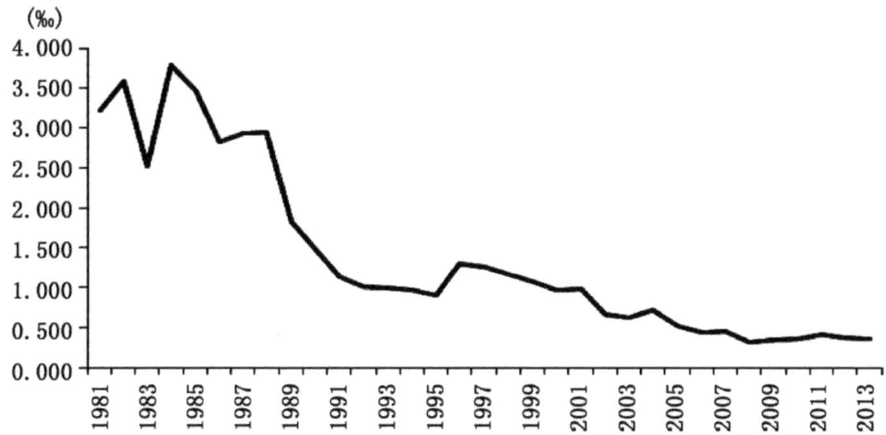

Fig. 9.10 Growth rate of employment population. *Source* Shanghai Municipal Government Decision-making and Consultation Project 2013-A-45

However, on the other hand, since the education reform of 1999, the number of college freshmen has rapidly expanded, and a large highly-educated population has improved the quality of China's labor force. The rapid development of education makes the high-end labor force replace the low-end labor force, leading to the unemployment of low-end labor force and rural surplus labor. In such a context, China's demographic dividend transforms into more competitive human capital dividend, in other words, the demographic dividend brought by the transfer of low-end labor will be transformed into medium and high-end human capital dividend. With the continuous upgrading of China's industrial structure, highly educated labor force will be effectively utilized, and the demographic dividend effect of the reallocation of labor resources will re-emerge. It is predicted that by 2025, China's per capita education will reach 11.4 years. Compared with 13.4 years achieved by the United States in 2010, China still has a great potential for human resources development in the future. Therefore, the change of demographic dividend will not bring a significant impact on China's economic growth in the coming decades. The promotion of labor force to the potential growth rate will maintain steady with a slight recovery (Fig. 9.11).

9.2.1.2 Input of Capital

In accordance with the economic growth model, capital input also plays an important role in economic growth. In the past decades, China's capital input maintained at a high level in economic growth, and China's capital output steadily increased. Since the reform and opening-up, the growth rate of China's fixed capital

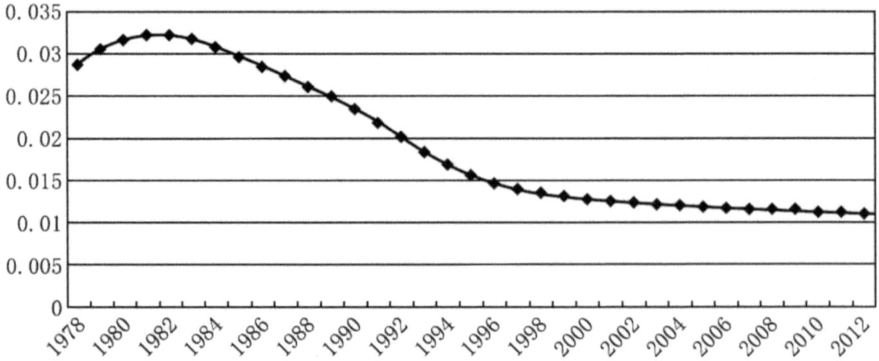

Fig. 9.11 Contribution rate of China's human capital to GDP growth rate since the reform and opening-up. *Source* Wang Yupeng, Analysis of China's economic growth factors, Review of Industrial Economics, 7th Edition, 2014

stock has always been higher than that of GDP, making a greater proportion of GDP transform into fixed capital investment. From the perspective of the public sector, the ever widening income gap and the imperfection of the social security system have weakened the average propensity to consume. From the perspective of the government, the process of capital deepening in China has been accelerated significantly under the expansionary policies since the financial crisis. From 1994 to 2007, the ratio of newly formed fixed assets in urban areas to fixed capital of the year was about 0.57 on average; from 2008 to 2013, the ratio was about 0.82. At present, the investment share of GDP is still close to 50%.

In the future, from the perspective of capital stock, although the scale of capital accumulation is still considerable when China is transforming from an agricultural country to an industrial country, with the increase of capital stock, the depreciation of capital will also increase. The capital stock changes resulted from the same amount of investment will continuously decrease and eventually tend to balance, and the impetus of investment to China's economy will gradually reduce. If the investment continues to be used to expand the scale, it may further lead to excess capacity, idle capital and other problems. In the future, investment will remain a key factor for China's economic growth, but its share will gradually decrease with a smaller contribution rate. From 2015 to 2020, the proportion of investment in GDP will remain at around 40%, vigorously supporting the economic growth (Fig. 9.12).

In conclusion, for a long time in the future, the dependence of potential economic growth on capital deepening will remain at a high level, while the contribution of human capital to potential economic growth will remain at the present level. However, there will be great changes in the structure of these two types of production factors. On the one hand, the "demographic dividend" supporting the potential growth will undergo fundamental transformation. The development trend

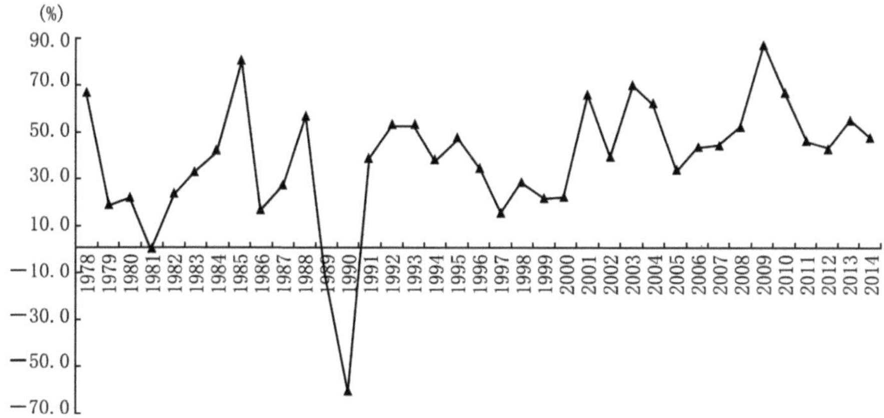

Fig. 9.12 Contribution rate of the total social capital formation to the economic growth since the reform and opening-up. *Source* Wind Info

of human capital from quantity to quality will be the lasting impetus for potential growth under the New Normal. On the other hand, promoted by the structural reform on the supply side, the act of driving economic growth by large-scale capital expansion will be difficult to sustain, and the proportion of investment in GDP will gradually reduce. In the future, we will pay more attention to the optimization of internal capital structure and the improvement of the investment efficiency so as to form effective impetus.

9.2.2 Technological Progress and Potential Growth Rate

Technological progress will contribute to raising the resources efficiency and the productivity level, thus exerting a great impetus to economic growth and promoting its quality. From the international experience, when the R&D input is close to 1% of GDP, a small amount of technological input tends to promote rapid economic growth; however, when the R&D investment accounts for more than 1% of GDP and increases significantly, its support to potential growth will dramatically reduce. It can also be seen from Fig. 9.13 that the proportion of China's R&D input to GDP increased from 0.5 to 1.4% in the decade from the early 1990s to the beginning of the 21st century, the total factor productivity growth index remained at a high level of 105 for a long time, and the economic growth indicators also maintained a stable and high-speed momentum. This shows that technological factors provided a great impetus to the potential growth in the initial stage of investment. However, when R&D input accounted for more than 1.5% in 2009, the technological input provided much weaker impetus to economic growth.

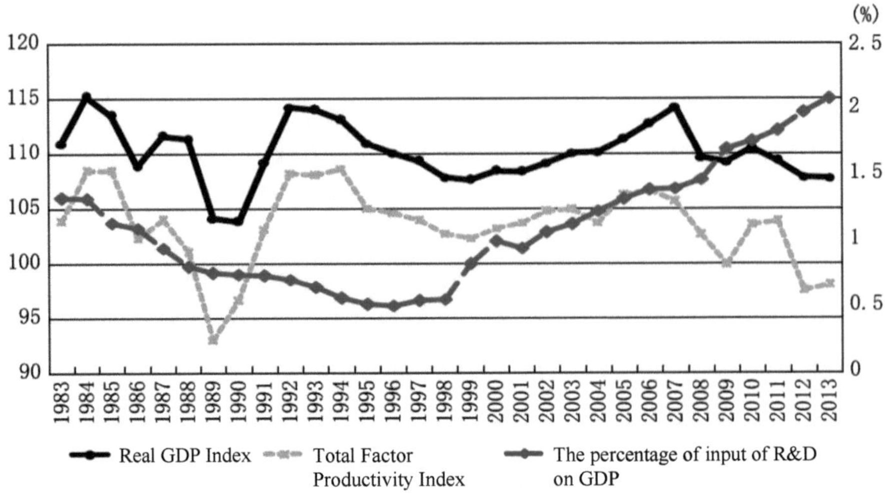

Fig. 9.13 Changes of China's GDP, total factor productivity index and R&D investment. *Source* Wind Info

Since the implementation of the "Twelfth Five-Year Plan", although the technological input has always been increasing, the total factor productivity does not rise but drop instead. On the one hand, it is because China has long been relying on the "imitation and innovation" of the introduced technologies to drive economic development; in the initial stage, it indeed greatly enhanced the domestic potential economic growth rate, but with innovative technology long confined to the low-end of value chain and the diminishing marginal benefit of technological input, the single dependence on increasing the technological input could hardly provide enough impetus to the future economic growth. On the other hand, it is because a large number of technological patents were not applied in the industrial production due to the restriction of the scientific and technological system; therefore, the technological input has not been transformed into real productivity, affecting the efficiency of technological factors transforming into potential growth rate.

In the future, in the supply side structural reform, China's economic growth will shift from factor-driven, investment-driven to innovation-driven, and relies more on technological progress and total factor productivity improvement. With the efficient use of Chinese R&D resources, China will shift from "following the others" to "running shoulder by shoulder with the others" in most areas of scientific and technological innovation so as to shorten the distance with developed countries. Some high-end technological innovation of China may be even "in the lead", and the total factor productivity will contribute increasingly more to China's economy.

9.2.3 Institutional Innovation and Potential Growth Rate

According to the general theory of economic growth, institutional factors are often regarded as the established "exogenous variables" of economic growth, in other words, as long as the factor input increases or the technologies improve, economic growth will naturally occur. Classical and neoclassical economic growth models assume there are no information costs, uncertainty, transaction costs and other institutional constraints, and hold that the "invisible hand", i.e., the market, guides the production factors to flow to the fields that can maximize the profits and achieve a balanced growth. However, in real life, the information is asymmetric with obvious externalities. For countries in transition, the impact of institutional innovation on economic growth should not be overlooked. Institutional innovation is an important part of total factor productivity. Take the British Industrial Revolution as an example. Some scholars regard it as a technological revolution, bit in fact it is an institutional innovation, and "the essence of the industrial revolution is to replace the medieval rules governing production and wealth distribution with competition" (North 1991). In the process of the reform and opening-up, China has continuously broken up the rigid planning system and established a market economy system, injecting vitality into economic growth and making great economic achievements. Therefore, institutional innovation, like production factors and technology innovation, is also the source of economic growth.

Compared with the input of additional production factors and technological progress, institutional innovation plays a more decisive role in economic growth. History shows that the more important source restricting the sustained, stable and coordinated growth of China's economy is not the shortage of capital, but the shortage of institutional supply. First, as the main players of the market, the enterprises' innovation motivation is closely related to the structure of their property rights. Since the reform of China's property rights system is rather lagging behind, they have inhibited the innovation vitality of the enterprises. Second, the costs of potential economic growth are mainly presented as the increasing social transaction costs, and the rising costs are related to the low-efficient economic organization process. Third, China's economic growth is obviously a kind of investment-driven growth, and the rising consumer prices result in unsustainable high-speed growth. The incomplete banking system further brings pressure to the mechanism, and the "separated management" of fiscal system leads to the increased number of local governments. Fourth, the mismatch between supply and demand structure, and the coexistence of economic shortage and overcapacity are partly due to the "institutional supply and demand imbalance" caused by administrative intervention.

In the supply side structural reform, new institutional supply will be an important external boost to economic growth, and therefore, deepening institutional reform will be the fundamental driving force to the future economic growth. First, constructing a system conducive to the initiative and enthusiasm of the market players will further release the vitality and potential of the market economy. Second, deepening the institutional innovation of labor, capital, technology and other factors will further promote the market-based pricing and value mining of the resources, thus promoting economic growth. Third, improving the institutional innovation of the market operation mechanism will ensure the effectiveness of capital allocation, and further enhance the market efficiency.

9.2.4 Optimization of Industrial Structure and Potential Growth Rate

Industrial structure is the external expression of both the total social production and the economic growth quality. Economic growth is often accompanied by changes in industrial structure, showing the characteristics of different stages. In the industrial era, the rapid growth of the secondary industry output resulted from investment made the potential economic growth maintain at a high level. At the later stage of industrialization, with the decreasing proportion of industrial output and the rising proportion of service industry, the economic growth rate had slowed down since the service sector had a relatively weak impetus on the economic growth. After World War II, in Japan, South Korea, Germany and other developed countries, the proportion of industrial added value had also gone through an up-and-down process, so had the economic growth rate. From the changes of the proportion of China's three industries, we can see that the proportion of the secondary industry in recent years maintains at 40–45%, while the tertiary industry is rising rapidly along with the decline in the proportion of the first industry (Fig. 9.14).

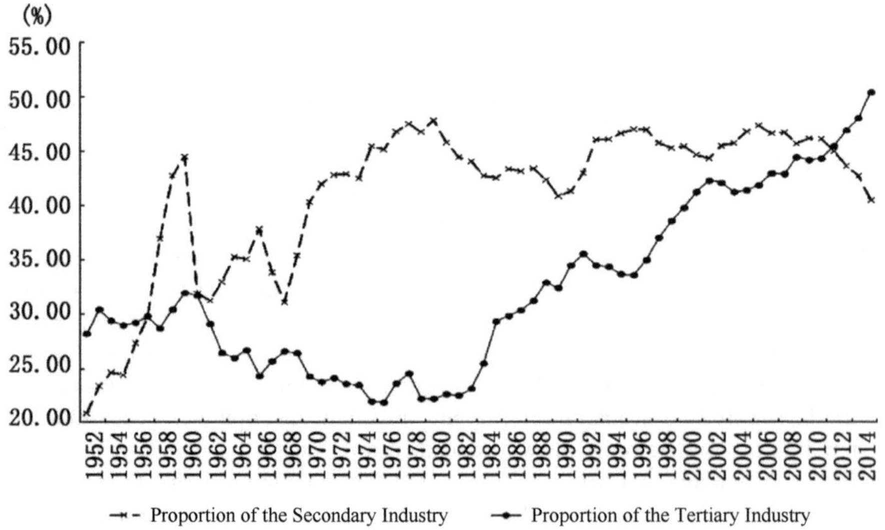

Fig. 9.14 Changes in proportion of the secondary industry and the tertiary industry in China's GDP since 1952. *Source* Wind Info

The industrial structure optimization degree determines the potential growth rate of China's economy. On the one hand, the distribution of labor in the three industries determines the level of social productivity. According to Yang Wenfeng (2014), the distribution of labor in different industrial structures will lead to different levels of productivity. After 1997, the total factor productivity (TFP) level of China's tertiary industry shows a stable upward trend, and the quality of economic growth continuously improves. Although the TFP level of China's secondary industry is smaller than that of the tertiary industry, it also changes from the type of factor-input to that of efficiency-improvement. In the future, with the changes of China's three-industry structure, with the rapid development of the tertiary industry and the steady development of the secondary industry, labor will be re-allocated in the three industries, which will further release the economic growth potential. According to the prediction by Li (2000), the labor force of the first industry in China will continue to shift outward in the future, reducing its employment proportion to 28.8%. The employment proportion of the secondary industry will slowly increase to 29.1%. Till 2030, the employment proportion of the three industries will be 26.5, 29.4 and 44.1% respectively (Table 9.8).

On the other hand, different "input-output" efficiencies of the three industries reflect the allocation of social resources, which are also important factors affecting potential growth rate. According to the changes of China's three industries' incremental capital-output ratio (ICOR) in recent years, the ICORs of the three industries have all been significantly improved, indicating that the coordinated development of the three industries in the long-term can promote potential economic growth; When analyzing from the input and output inside the three industries, we can find that the ICOR of the secondary industry is higher than that of the tertiary industry, which explains why during the transfer of the capital from the industrial economy to the service industry the potential growth rate will go down in the initial stage. However, with the deepening of China's supply side structural reform, the development of service industry and manufacturing industry toward high-end will further strengthen the potential economic growth impetus (Table 9.9).

Table 9.8 Prediction of the Labor Force Proportion in China's Three Industries from 2020 to 2035 (%)

year	The First Industry	The Secondary Industry	The Tertiary Industry
2020	32.6	28.3	39.0
2030	26.5	29.4	44.0
2035	23.9	29.8	46.3

Source Li Jingwen (2000)

Table 9.9 Changes of ICOR in China's Three Industries in Recent Years

Year	ICOR of The First Industry	ICOR of The Secondary Industry	ICOR of The Tertiary Industry
2003	0.63	1.95	4.66
2004	0.16	2.00	4.05
2005	0.84	2.31	4.07
2006	0.69	2.45	3.82
2007	0.32	2.30	2.82
2008	0.44	2.80	4.02
2009	2.20	9.49	6.39
2010	0.74	3.40	5.24
2011	0.98	4.00	5.06
2012	1.79	10.72	6.25
The First Three Quarters of 2013	2.53	11.60	5.42

Source Guan Xiaoming (2014)

9.3 Supply Side Structural Reform and Prediction of China's Economic Growth Trend

Structural problems have become main constraints to global economic growth. The increasingly serious structural problems, such as the imbalance between global supply and demand, the widening gap between developed and emerging economies, heavy debts in developed economies, etc., not only lead to various types of economic and social contradictions, but also restrict the economic restructuring and recovery in different countries. At present, the world has launched an in-depth discussion on the global structural issues, and concludes that promoting structural reform is the recipe for economic growth. In such a context, China's implementation of supply side structural reform will further enhance the potential, stimulate the vitality, and ensure the stable economic growth in a planned way. Many Chinese scholars have predicated and analyzed China's economic growth trend, but the existing predictions and analyses are mainly limited to the economic growth and operational situation, lacking the overall and structural predications and analyses. This section, based on existing research, after analyzing the global economic growth pattern brought by the global structural reform, will focus on the promotion of China's supply side structural reform to the economic growth, and further systematically predict the future trend of China's economic growth.

9.3.1 Global Structural Reform and World Economic Growth Prospects

At present, the far-reaching influence of global economic and financial crisis is still fermenting. There are significant differences in economic growth around the world, and the basis of global economic recovery is still unstable with insufficient impetus. Fundamentally speaking, the slowdown in global economic recovery is closely linked to cyclical factors and short-term downside risk, but the deeper causes stem from the long-term structural problems in the global economy. From the medium and long-term development of the world economy, we can find that the impetus brought about by the information technology and industrial revolution has been gradually disappearing since the 1990s, and the potential of the traditional economic system and development model has been declining. At the same time, the problem of unbalanced development is far from being solved, and the shortcomings of the existing economic governance mechanisms and structures are gradually emerging. These problems lead to that the global economy as a whole lacks impetus, and the effective demand is weak; the total factor productivity growth slows down in the major economies, and the potential level of output declines, which are mainly manifested as weak global economic growth, rising unemployment rate, increasing debt, sluggish trade and investment, stagnant real economy, high-level financial leverage, fluctuations in the international financial and commodity markets, and a series of other problems.

The G20 Financial Ministers Meeting of 2016 puts forward that to regain the economic growth momentum for the world economy, we must further promote structural reform with the focus centering around four aspects. First, promote international trade and investment. Through reducing barriers to market access, eliminating tax barriers to cross-border trade and investment, and increasing flexibility in the labor market, we will encourage the private sector investment, promote trade development and try to restore the growth momentum of the global economy. Second, vigorously promote the labor market reform. By breaking down labor market segmentation, we will reduce employment barriers and enhance labor mobility. Some countries should carry out necessary reform to the social security system, stimulate the employment by increasing the competition, and prevent the labor costs from rising too fast; meanwhile, increase investment in education, improve the quality of education and promote the balance between education and labor market demand. Third, further encourage innovation. We should continue to increase support for technological progress, including the improvement of technological innovation incentive and protection system and non-institutional arrangements to promote new technological revolution and new industrial revolution; meanwhile we should carry out necessary institutional innovation, not only including reforming and innovating on the national level such as the taxation system, industrial supervision, social security, property rights protection and intellectual property, but also including multilaterally reforming on the international level such as currency, trade and investment, finance, taxation, etc., so as to improve the global economic governance. Fourth, improve the financial sustainability. We should ensure the sustainability of the debt, gradually restore the fiscal policy space, and lay the foundation for sustained economic growth. In addition, countries in the world are also facing the medium and long-term challenges such as infrastructure, competition, financial reform, environmental sustainability, etc., which should also be taken as the key areas of structural reform for the next step.

With the steady progress of the global structural reform, the world will regain new momentum of economic growth. Based on Autoregressive Integrated Moving Average (ARIMA (1, 1, 1)) model, the World Bank's predication of the global economic growth over the next 30 years shows that the world economic growth rate will remain around 2.9% between 2016 and 2050, and the global real GDP will reach about 162 trillion dollars till 2050. PricewaterhouseCoopers, based on IMF (International Monetary Fund) data, uses the long-term economic model to predict the economic growth trend for the period between 2014 and 2050. The results show that between 2014 and 2050, the average annual growth rate of the global economy will be only slightly higher than 3%. By 2037, the global economy will be twice that size of 2014, reaching over 110 trillion dollars; by 2050, the global economy will be close to 3 times that size of 2014, reaching about 167 trillion dollars. It can be seen that all these prediction results of different models show that the global economic growth will not reach the average growth rate over the past 30 years due to the slowdown of the global population growth, more serious aging trend, resources and environment constraints and other factors. The global growth rate will tend to "retreat to the average."

While the global economic growth momentum is gradually being restored, the world economic growth will be more balanced. According to the predication by the PricewaterhouseCoopers model, calculated by purchasing power parity, the proportion of China's GDP in the world GDP will rise from 16.5% in 2014 to 20% in 2030 and the proportion of India's GDP in the world GDP will steadily rise from less than 7% in 2014. With the rapid development of the Asian countries represented by China and India, the status of the western developed countries will be weakened in the global economic growth. The proportion of GDP of two major economies, i.e., the United States and the European Union, in the world GDP will drop from 33% in 2014 to around 25%. In this context, the east–west economic growth will be more balanced, and the emerging economies will become the important force in the world economic pattern. Analysis results of PricewaterhouseCoopers model show that the rankings of the predicated GDP in most developing countries and emerging economies are expected to rise.

9.3.2 The Overall Trend of China's Medium and Long Term Economic Growth

From the international experience, after years of rapid growth, with the economy gradually growing mature, economic growth will slow down towards the world's average. The majority of authoritative institutions and well-known scholars generally believe that from now on to 2050, the high-speed growth stage of China's economy will come to an end, gradually returning to the average growth rate of the mature economies. From the development track of East Asian economies, after decades of rapid growth, the economic growth rate began to slow down, and the total factor productivity gradually got close to that of the United States. Japan, for example, saw rapid growth between 1950 and 1975, followed by a gradual decline in economic growth, but by 1975 its total factor productivity was about 83% of that of the United States. Korea had also experienced a period of rapid development from 1965 to 1990. By 1990, South Korea's total factor productivity was about 63% of that of the United States. During the same period, Taiwan's economic growth in China was also remarkable. By 1990, the total factor productivity of China's Taiwan had reached 90% of that of the United States. At present, China's total factor productivity, compared with that of the United States, is still very low. Even though China has had a high growth rate for more than 30 years, there is still much growth potential.

9.3.3 Predication of Medium- and Long-Term Growth Rates of China's Economy

The study of the World Bank holds that since the demographic dividend gradually disappears, and the promoting role of capital gradually weakens, by 2026 to 2030, China's GDP growth rate is estimated to drop to about 5%. PricewaterhouseCoopers believes that for the next 30 years, China will transform from an export-dependent economy to a consumption-driven economy with increasingly mature economic development, and the rising real labor costs and the rapid expansion of aging population will accelerate the process. It is estimated that China's economy will maintain an average annual growth rate of 6.3% between 2015 and 2020, but will significantly decelerate after 2020. By 2050, China's economic growth will slow down to around 3%, still higher than the main developed countries.

From the prediction model of the system dynamics, after the global financial crisis, China's economy gradually enters the adjustment phase with the growth rate slowing down. By 2020, the GDP growth rate may fall to 5.6%, and by 2030, it may fall to 2.3%. Then, with the advance of technology, the GDP growth will slightly rebound to 2.8% in 2040 and 3.1% in 2050.[1] Generally speaking, China's economic growth rate will gradually slow down in the future, and fluctuate at a low level (Fig. 9.15).

To sum up the predications and analyses of the global research institutions or scholars, the overall judgements for China's economic growth in the future are: growth rate will gradually slow down and return to the average level of mature economies.[2] "General Report on Shanghai's Development Strategy for the Next 30

[1]Qian Ying, "Trends, Cycles and Motivational Mechanisms of China's Future Economic Growth and Their Impacts on Shanghai's Development: A Study Based on System Dynamics Model", Shanghai Municipal Government Decision-making and Consultation Project 2014-A-26-B.

[2]Xiao Lin: "General Report on Shanghai's Development Strategy for the Next 30 Years", March, 2016.

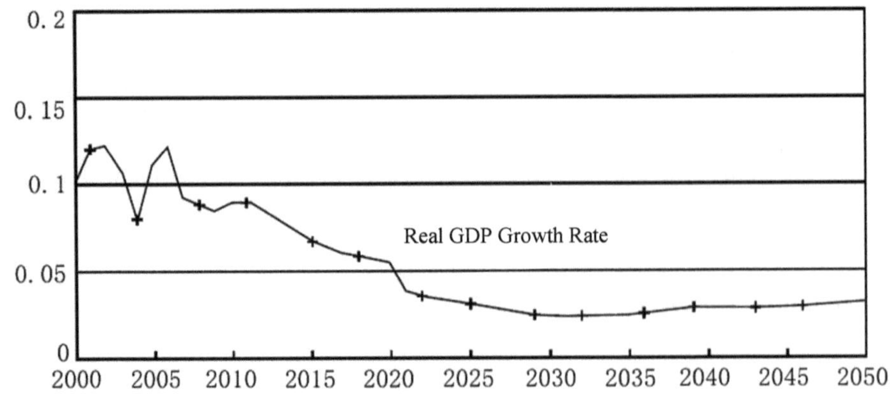

Fig. 9.15 The trend of China's future GDP growth rate

Table 9.10 Predication of China's Long Cycle Economic Growth Rate

Institutions years or Scholars	2015–2020	2020–2030	2030–2040	2040–2050
Development Research Center of the State Council	7.0%	5.4%	4.5%	3.4%
World Bank (2012)	7.4–10.1%	4.2–7.8%		
Goldman Sachs Group (2003)		4.1%		2.9%
PricewaterhouseCoopers (2013)	6.3%			3.0–4.0%
Shi Zhengfu (2013)	6.0%		4.0%	
Qian Ying	5.5%	2.4%	2.8%	3.1%
Yang Ruilong	6.2%	5.6%	5.3%	

Source Summary of relevant researches and reports

Years" presided over by Xiao Lin from Shanghai Municipal People's Government Development Research Center puts forward that China's economic growth rate will be 6.5–7% from 2015 to 2020, 5–6% from 2020 to 2030, 4–5% from 2030 to 2040, and 3–4% from 2040 to 2050 (Table 9.10).

9.3.4 Predication of Medium- and Long-Term Economic Aggregate of China's Economy

The World Bank holds that by 2030, the medium- and high-speed economic growth will promote China's economic aggregate to the top of the world. Calculated by market exchange rate, by 2030 China's economic aggregate will reach 26.7 trillion US dollars, exceeding the United States and becoming the largest real economy. From 2030 to 2050, although China's economy will enter the low-growth period, China will continue to occupy the leading position in terms of the economic

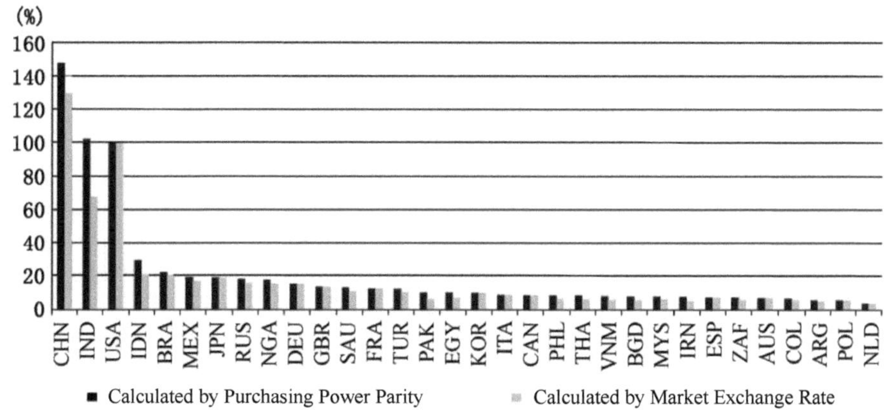

Fig. 9.16 Relative GDP of different economies in 2050 calculated by purchasing power parity and market exchange rate. *Source* PricewaterhouseCoopers: The World in 2050, 2015. *Comment* The ration is based on the United States

aggregate. In addition, the total population of China will form a turning point around 2028 to 2030, and tend to decline afterwards. In 2050, China's population will return to the level around the year of 2000, less than 1.3 billion, so the GDP per capita will have an obvious increase, which may reach about 40,000 US dollars. China will successfully skip over the middle-income trap, reaching the level of moderately developed countries (Fig. 9.16).

9.3.5 Prediction of China's Medium- and Long-Term Economic Growth Structure

In the future, China's economic structure will tend to be more reasonable and balanced. From the perspective of industrial structure, pushed by the new industrialization and urbanization, China's economic structure will be more optimized, and the three industries will gradually transform into the structure of "tertiary, secondary and first industries". It is estimated that by 2050, the proportion of China's service industry will account for about 65%, reaching the level of the United States in the 1980s, the proportion of industry will be about 30%, and the proportion of agriculture will be about 5%. In addition, with the technological progress and the gradual upgrading of total factor productivity, China's industrial level will also continuously improve. The labor transfer from the less productive agricultural economy to the more productive industrial economy will gradually come to an end. China's productivity growth will depend more on technological advance within industry, agriculture and services than inter-industry transfer. Therefore, through the industry's internal technological progress, China's industrial competitiveness will be significantly enhanced. From the perspective of regional

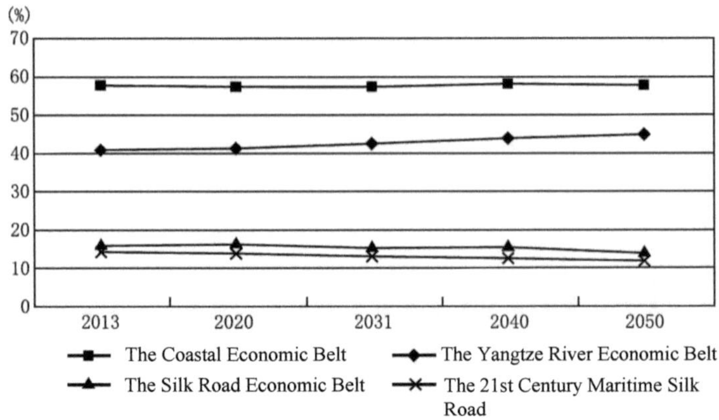

Fig. 9.17 Trends of GDP proportion in major economic belts (roads) from 2013 to 2050. *Source* Dou Jianming, Research on China's New-type urbanization and regional economic pattern changes and Shanghai's city function promotion, Shanghai Municipal Government Decision-making and Consultation Project 2014-A-39

structure, in the future the three major city clusters and the three major economic belts will lead China's regional economic development forward. Three city clusters, i.e., the Yangtze River Delta, the Pearl River Delta and Beijing-Tianjin-Hebei will become the world-class city clusters with strong international competitiveness and remain the growth poles leading China's economic development, especially the Yangtze River Delta region, which is expected to become a world-class super-economic zone. It is estimated that by 2050, the economic aggregate proportion of coastal economic belt will increase from 57.73% in 2013 to 58.75%. In addition, three major economic belts, i.e., the Silk Road Economic Belt, the 21st Century Maritime Silk Road and the Yangtze River Economic Belt established under the national strategies, will lead the overall coordination of China's regional development forward, especially with the rapid urbanization and improvement of high-speed rail network and highway network, population, capital and industry will flow along the three major economic zones from east to west. The Yangtze River Economic Zone will play a significant role in promoting the gradient development of the coastal area and the inland. The construction of "the Belt and Road" will push the open economy in the central and western regions to a new height, narrowing down the gap between the eastern, the central and the western regions in China (Fig. 9.17).

Postscript

Over the years, we have been committed to the research on innovation of China's economic theory and practice of reform and development. Especially in recent years, China has entered an economic new normal, with constantly weakening effects of demand management policies and macro regulation, so we are more concerned about the research on the supply side, such as the economic growth potential and economic growth trend, the coordination between the supply side and the demand side, the improvement of total factor productivity, the market-based reform and institutional innovation, the structural contradiction and economic structural adjustment, the proactive strategies of opening-up and construction of Shanghai Free Trade Zone, the innovation-driven development strategies and technological innovation centers construction, etc. We have formed a series of related research results, some of which have already been put into practice.

In November 2015, the central government of China explicitly put forward the economic initiative of supply-side structural reform for the first time, which is not only a major adjustment of economic development, but also a major innovation of economic theory. At the same time, entrusted by the National Development and Reform Commission, I presided over a national major policy advisory project: "Research on China's Structural Reform and Structural Policy under the New Normal". The members are mainly from the research team of Shanghai Municipal Government Development Research Center. I work as the head of the team, and the members include Dr. Li Feng, Dr. Wang Dan, Dr. Zhang Minghai, Dr. Yang Chang, Dr. Wang Pei, Shi Xiaochen and Song Qi. The research team has carried out an extensive and in-depth research on the theory and practice of supply side structural reform, formed more than 10 special research reports and one summary report, and made fruitful achievements.

This book is written based on my research results in recent years, of those projects presided over by me and the project entrusted by the National Development and Reform Commission, after further deepening and refining so as to make them more systematic and theoretical. Throughout the research process, many economics scholars have given us great attention and enthusiastic help. We have also consulted with some famous economists from Shanghai and Beijing, and adopted some of

L. Xiao, *New Supply Side Economics*, DOI 10.1007/978-981-10-4639-1 their opinions. I would like to express my high respect and sincere gratitude to all of those economists.

While researching on the supply side structural reform, we have also received support from lots of companies and enterprises. Many entrepreneurs have also proposed valuable suggestions about the supply side structural reform from the micro perspective of enterprises. In this regard, I would like to express my heartfelt appreciation to them. In addition, our research, especially the theoretical research, the global case studies and the literature review, has referred to lots of articles and books. Therefore, our thanks also go to the Information Institute of Shanghai Library, which has given us strong literature support.

"New Supply side Economics" is soon to be published, but China's New Supply side Economics theory is far from being mature. We welcome all the comments from the economists on our academic viewpoint and theoretical framework. We are determined to persevere and promote the innovation and development of China's economic theory.

The "postscript" should have drawn a period here, however, I cannot help but add several more lines since several days ago, I, as an alumnus, received an invitation to celebrate Shanghai Jiaotong University's 120th anniversary, which immediately brought the good time back to me. I have left my alma mater for more than 20 years. Time fleeting, the days have gradually been burdened with routine, and those innocent, vibrant or contemplative souls have been engraved with deep or shallow imprints in the hustle and bustle of life. The words are powerless to describe all the ups and downs of those years, but what remains unchanged is the spirit of my school forever cherished in my heart, and its motto which I will pursue all my life. My alma mater, my teachers, my classmates, and everyone else will always be kept in my memory, to whom I will be so grateful. The twilight I had walked through, the magnolia trees I had passed by, the dormitory I had boarded in, the cherry blossom I had lingered around, will always be the spring of my nostalgia.

As is indicated by the school motto, we should always keep in mind the principle of "Study Extensively, Enquire Accurately, Reflect Carefully, Discriminate Clearly, and Practice Earnestly". Innovation will lead us forward, while perseverance and diligence will help us conquer all.

The sun and the moon will witness all the transformation of the universe, and we are just passers-by.

April 1, 2016 in Shanghai Xiao Lin

References

Authority. 2016. Leading the new normal through supply-side structural reform. *People's Daily*, January 4th.

Ba, S.S. 2004. Market regulation: The new trend of macro control. *China Economic Times*, April 23rd.

Bangye, J. et al. 2010. *Japanese economic history (1600–2000).* Nanjing University Press.

Bartlett. 2011. *The New American economy: Failure of reaganomics and a new way forward.* China Financial Publishing House.

Bush, V. 2004. *Science: The endless frontier.* Commercial Press.

Cai, F. 2012. *Avoid the 'middle income trap', and explore the source of China's future growth.* Social Sciences Academic Press.

Cai, F. 2013. Turning China's economic growth into total factor productivity driven type. *Social Sciences in China* 1.

Cai, F., and Y. Lu. 2013. Potential growth rate of China's economy. *Review of Economic Research*, 24.

Cai, Z.Z. 1999. Quantitative analysis of the contribution of education to economic growth. *Economic Research Journal* 2.

Chang, X. 2001. Deregulation and regulation reconstruction: An analysis of the government behavior after challenges enter china's basic sectors. *Economic Theory and Business Management* 11.

Chang, X.Z. 2006. An analysis of three strategic problems in the reform of state-owned economy. *Study Monthly* 12a.

Chang, X.Z. 2015. An analysis of the economic development and reform tendency in the new stage of China—An academic report in Guangdong in February 2015. *Reform and Strategy* 5.

Chen, B.S. 2014. *American economy and government policy.* Social Sciences Academic Press.

Chen, Z., G.H. Wan, and M. Lu. 2010a. Inter-industry inequality: An increasingly important cause of urban income inequality—Based on the decomposition of regression equation. *Social Sciences in China* 3.

Chen, Z., G.H. Wan, and M. Lu. 2010b. Inter-industry inequality: An increasingly important cause of urban income inequality. *Social Sciences in China* 5.

Department of Economics, Chinese Academy of Governance. 2014. Research on the management of excess capacity. *Review of Economic Research* 14.

Department of Economics, Chinese Academy of Governance. 2016. *Structural supply-side reform in China.* People's Publishing House.

Development Research Center of the State Council. 2010. The influence of migrant workers' citizenization on expanding domestic demand and economic growth. *Economic Research Journal* 6.

Development Research Center of the State Council. 2011. Calculation of the time window of China's potential economic growth rate. *Development Research* 10.

L. Xiao, *New Supply Side Economics*, DOI 10.1007/978-981-10-4639-1

Development Research Center of the State Council. 2014. *China's new urbanization: Path, pattern, and policy.* China Development Press.

Dong, F.R. 1994a. The reform of banking system in China—Also on the reform of shareholding system. *Economic Research Journal* 1.

Dong, F.R. 1994b. *Research on the reform of economic system (a).* Economic Science Press.

Dong, F.R. 2002. Reasons on developing private economy, which must be made clear in theory. *Great Tide* 9.

Dong, M.J., Y.M. Liang, and Q.Z. Zhang. 2015. Industrial capacity utilization in China: Industry comparison, regional disparity and influencing factors. *Economic Research Journal* 1.

Dosi, Giovanni, Giorgio Fagiolo, and Andrea Roventini. 2010. Schumpeter meeting Keynes: A policy-friendly model of endogenous growth and business cycles. *Journal of Economic Dynamics & Control* (34).

Du, Y. 2015. Economic development in low Birth age: Structure, efficiency and human capital investment. *International Economic Review* 2.

Du, Y., F. Cai, X.B. Qu, and J. Cheng. 2014. Continuation of China's miracle: Reap dividends from the reform of the household registration system. *Economic Research Journal* 8.

Fan H.S. 1998. Ownership breakthroughs: New breakthroughs and new tasks. *Marxist & Reality* 1.

Fan, G., X.L. Wang, and G.R. Ma. 2011. The contribution of China's marketization to economic growth. *Economic Research Journal* 9.

Feng, T., and X.W. Luo. 2015. A study on the distortion of labor market and income gap: From the perspective of 'identity'. *Economic Management* 37.

Freeman, C. 2004. *The economics of industrial innovation.* Peking University Press.

Freedman, C. 2013. *Free choice.* China Machine Press.

Freeman, C. 2008. *Technology policy and economic performance: An empirical study of Japan's national innovation system.* Southeast University press.

Gai, Q.E., X. Zhu, M.W. Cheng, and Q.H. Shi. 2015. Factor market distortion, monopoly power and total factor productivity. *Economic Research Journal* 5.

Gan, C.H. 2011. The impact of chinese industrial structure change on economic growth and fluctuation. *Economic Research Journal* 5.

Gao, S.Q. 1993. The reason for proposing labor market. *Economic Daily*, November 19th.

Gao, S.Q. 1998. Ownership structure and economic system reform in China. *Social Sciences in China* 1.

Gao, S.Q. 2005. *People based economy.* Social Sciences Academic Press.

Ge, W. 1995. The theory of progressive opening: Export processing zones, multinational corporations and export oriented economic growth. *Management World* 7.

Gilder, G. 1987. *Wealth and poverty.* Shanghai Translation Publishing House.

Groenewegen P.D. 1973. A note on the origin of the phrase 'supply and demand'. *The Economic Journal* 83 (330).

Guan, X.M. 2014. Analysis of structural transformation and potential growth rate fluctuation in China. *Financial Theory and Practice* 4.

Guo, M. 2008. The evolution and countermeasures of labor relations in China. *Economic Perspectives* 12.

Guo, Q.W., and J.X. Jia. 2005. Estimation of total factor productivity in China: 1979–2004. *Economic Research Journal* 6.

Guo, Q.W., and J.X. Jia. 2006. Local government behavior, investment impulse and macroeconomic stability. *Management World* 5.

Guo, S.Q. 2001. Deepen the reform of investment and financing system and improve the transmission mechanism of monetary policy. *Journal of Financial Research* 2.

He, P.P., and G.M. Zhuang. 2014. Focus on green conflict—Thinking on the development of renewable energy. *Environmental Protection* 1.

He, W. 1998. How to understand the distribution based on production factor. *Economic Perspectives* 94.

Hu, Y.G., and X.Q. Guo. 2012. Endogenous growth, government's productive expenditure and chinese residents' consumption. *Economic Research Journal* 9.

Huang, Z.L. 2014. Views on China's economic rebalancing. *Review on Investment Studies* 9.

Hughes, Jonathan, and Louis Cain. 2013. American economic history, Chinese simplified language edition. Truth & Wisdom Press.

Ikeda Nobuo. 2012. *The lost twenty years: Real reason for the stagnation of Japanese economy.* China Machine Press.

Ikujiro, Nonaka. 2006. *The enterprise of knowledge creation. The impetus for continuous innovation in Japanese and American enterprises.* Intellectual Property Publishing House.

Institute of Industrial Economics of DRC. 2012. *China's economy: Labor supply and demand, inflation, and the business cycle.* Economic Science Press.

Institute of Industrial Economics of DRC. 2015. *China industry development report 2015.* China Market Press.

Institute of World Economy, Fudan University. 2006. *Institutional changes and structural adjustments.* Shanxi Economy Publishing House.

Ji, M., and Z.B Liu. 2014. The impact of China's demand structure evolution on economic growth and fluctuation. *Economic Science* 1.

Jia, K., and J.C. Su. 2015. The cognitive framework of 'three carriages' needs to connect with the structural dynamic mechanism construction of supply-side reform—On the deepening of macroeconomics. *Globalization* 3.

Jia, K., and Q.B. Feng. 2016. The supply-side reform in '13th five-year' period. *Journal of Chinese Academy of Governance* 6.

Jia, K. 2013. *New supply: China's innovation in economic theory.* China Economic Publishing House.

Jia, K. 2015. The core content of supply-side reform is to liberate productive forces. *China Economic Weekly* 49.

Jiang, X.J. 2008. Review and prospect of China's 30 years' opening-up. *Social Sciences in China* 6.

Jiang, Z. 2014. The industrialization level, local government efforts and land finance. *China Industrial Economics* 10.

Jin, B. 2010. On the reorientation of state-owned enterprise reform. *China Industrial Economics* 4.

Kornai, J. 1990. *Economics of shortage.* Economic Science Press.

Kuznets, S. 1999. *The economic growth of nations.* The Commercial Press.

Lai, D.S., and W.W. Ji. 2015. Human capital allocation and innovation. *Economic Perspectives* 3.

Li, J.W. 2000. Long term forecast of Chinese economy in 21st century 2000–2050. *Metallurgical Economics and Management 6.*

Li, K.Q. 2015. Putting innovation at the core of the national strategy. *China Government Procurement* 11.

Li, S.L., and J.S. Li. 2014. A study on the contribution of consumption, investment, import and export to economic growth—Based on the perspective of demand structure imbalance. *Business Economy* 9.

Li, X.Y. 2015. Efficiency analysis and policy advise on urban infrastructure investment in new urbanization process. *Macroeconomics* 10.

Li, Y., and J.F. Yin. 2005. High saving, high investment and economic growth of China in the process of labor transfer. *Economic Research Journal* 2.

Lin, Y. 1998. The initial formation of demand constrained economy and the sustainable economic growth in China. *Contemporary Finance & Economics* 6.

Lin, Y.F. 2012. New structural economics: Reflections on the theoretical framework of economic development and policy. *Peking University Press.*

Lin, Y.F., and M.X. Liu. 2004. Economic development strategy and China's industrialization. *Economic Research Journal* 7.

Lin, Y.F., and P.L. Liu. 2003. The influence of economic development strategy on capital accumulation and technology advance. *Social Sciences in China* 4.

Lin, Y.F., and X.F. Sun. 2008. Banking structure and economic growth. *Economic Research Journal* 9.
Lin, Y.F., and Y.J. Li. 2003. Export and China's economic growth: A demand driven analysis. *China Economic Quarterly* 7.
Lin, Y.F., F. Cai, and Z. Li. 1999. Comparative advantage and development strategy. *Social sciences in China* 5.
Lin, Y.F., H.M. Wu, and Xing Y.Q. 2010. 'Wave phenomenon' and the formation mechanism of excess capacity. *Economic Research Journal* 10.
Liu, Q.Z., and Q. He. 2013. Population aging, economic growth and fiscal policy. *New Industrial Economy* 2.
Liu, R. 2014. How to interpret the spirit of the land system reform in the third plenary session of the 18th central committee of the communist party of China. *Journal of China National School of Administration* 1.
Liu, R.M., and R.J. Zhao. 2005. Did national high-tech zones promote the development of regional economy? *Management World* 8.
Liu, S.B. 1998. *Subject property right theory.* Economic Science Press.
Liu, S.C. 2004. A comparative analysis of the five macroeconomic controls in China. *Price: Theory & Practice* 7.
Liu, S.J. 2015. Supply-side reform is not to say that demand is unimportant. *China Economic & Trade Herald* 34.
Liu, S.J., P.L. Liu, and J.W. He. 2015. China's future productivity growth potential and economic growth prospects. *Management World* 3.
Liu, S.Y. 2014. The characteristic, problem and reform of dual land system in China. *International Economic Review* 3.
Liu, W., and H. Zhang. 2008. The change of industrial structure and technological progress in China's economic growth. *Economic Research Journa*, 11.
Liu, W., and J. Su. 2007. The supply management and macro control in China at current stage. *Economic Research Journal* 2.
Liu, W., S.R. Li, and S.Y. Li. 2002. Monetary expansion, economic growth and institutional innovation of capital market. *Economic Research Journal* 1.
Liu, X., J. Yang, and F. Wang. 2012. The theoretical innovation of capital market development in the transition of economic growth: A summary of the symposium on 'economic growth transformation and capital market development'. *Economic Research Journal* 7.
Liu, X.H., P. Zhang, and X.J. Zhang. 2008. *Economic growth and structural change in the reform era.* Truth & Wisdom Press.
Liu, Y.G., and Y. Chen. 2015. China's immigration policy in the context of globalization: Comment and expectation. *World Regional Studies* 24.
Long, H.L. 2015. Land use transformation and land resource management. *Geographical Research* 9.
Lu, M., Z. Chen, and G.H. Wan. 2005. Suffering from poverty and inequality: The interaction among income inequality, investment, education and growth in China. *Economic Research Journal* 12.
Lv, N. 2009. *Research on the labor policy of thatcher administration.* Social Science Literature Press.
Ma, H.Q. *Study on Shanghai's economic growth potential and dynamic mechanism under the new normal.* The Shanghai Municipal People's Government Decision Consulting Research Project 2015-A-05A.
Ma, W.X. 2010. *Japan-US trade friction and Japan's industrial structure adjustment.* People's Publishing House.
Mao, R. 2014. *A study on the economic and social policies of the thatcher administration.* Shandong People's Publishing House.
Ni, H.R. 2013. Research on the taxation system of infrastructure construction capital supply in China's urbanization progress. *Taxation Research* 9.

North, D.C. 1991. *Structure and change in economic history*. SDX Joint Publishing Company.

North, D.C. 1992. *Structure and reform in economic history*. Commercial Press.

Pan, J.H., and H.K. Wei. 2013. *China urban development report 2013*. Social Sciences Academic Press.

Peng, S. 2007. *International comparison and reference of China's economic system reform*. People's Publishing House.

Propaganda Department of the Communist Party of China. 2014. *Series of important speeches by general secretary Xi Jinping*. People's Publishing House.

Qian, Y. China's future economic growth trend, cycle and dynamic mechanism and their impact on the development of Shanghai: A study based on systematic dynamics model. The Shanghai Municipal People's Government Decision Consulting Research Project 2014-A-26B.

Qian, Y., and R. Weingast. 1996. China's transition to market: Market preserving federalism, Chinese style. *Journal Policy Reform* 1.

Quan, H. Study on the economic growth potential and dynamic mechanism of Shanghai under the new normal. The Shanghai Municipal People's Government Decision Consulting Research Project 2015-A-05B.

Ren, Y.Y. 2009. *The economic development of Japan and East Asia in the postwar period*. Showwe Information Co. Ltd.

Ren, Z.P. 2014. China's potential economic growth rate and long-term growth prospects. *Development Research* 3.

Research Group of Economic Growth and Macro Stability in China. 2007. Financial development and economic growth: The transition from expansion of mobilization to market allocation. *Economic Research Journal* 4.

Research Group of Economic Growth and Macro Stability in China. 2010. Capital expansion and the technological progress of catching up economy. *Economic Research Journal* 5.

Research Group of Ministry of Finance. 2012. Macroeconomic situation and financial regulation: From the short to medium term analysis. *Review of Economic Research* 61.

Research Group of the Evaluation on Chinese R&D Environment. 2014. *A nationwide evaluation report on Chinese R&D environment*. China Science and Technology Press.

Roberts, P.C. 2011. *The supply-side revolution: An insider's account of policymaking in Washington*. Truth & Wisdom Press.

Sang, B.C, W. Zheng, and H. Tan. 2014. A comparative study on the service trade development of BRICs. *The Economist* 3.

Say, J.B. 1998. *Political economics*. The Commercial Press.

Shen, B.P., and W.P. Shen. 2014. System construction: A new source of economic growth in China. *Jiangsu Social Sciences* 6.

Shen, L.S., and Z.Y. Wu. 2003. The contribution of exports to China's GDP growth. *Economic Research Journal* 11.

Shi, J.X. 2015. The reconstruction of international trade investment rules and China's response. *Social Sciences in China* 9.

Song, Y.H. 2002. *Research on the new economy in America*. People's Publishing House.

Stiglitz, J. 1994. Endogenous growth and cycles. In *Innovation in technology, industries, and institutions, studies in schumpeterian perspectives*, ed. Shionoya, Y., and M. Perlman. Ann Arbor: The University of Michigan Press.

Su, J. 2015a. Comprehensive reform is the premise of China's long-term and healthy economic development. *China Opening Journal* 6.

Su, J. 2015b. The new economic normality and adjustment of China's population policy. *Population and Society* 31.

Su, Z., Y. Li, and S.D. Xu. 2013. China's investment structural optimization under 'structural' deceleration: An analysis based on the effect of the four trillion investment. *Public Finance Research* 1.

Sun, W.K., C.E. Bai, and P.C. Xie. 2011. The impact of household registration system reform on rural labor mobility in China. *Economic Research Journal* 1.

Teng, T. 2013. *Wealth of people: The centennial road of stronger China under the new supply doctrine*. Orient Publishing.

Teng, T. 2015. The launching of supply-side reform—Start a new rising cycle in China's economy by reform. *China Small and Medium Enterprises* 12.

Tian, D.H. 1998. *Housing policy: International experience and China's realistic choice.* Tsinghua University Press.

Tu, X.F. 2011. *Comparative public policy.* Beijing University of Aeronautics and Astronautics Press.

Wan, H.Y. and S. Li, 2013, "The Impact of Household Registration Discrimination on the Income Gap between Urban and Rural Areas", *Economic Research Journal,* 9.

Wan, J.Q., and T. Xu. 2004. The impact of exchange rate adjustment on China's employment. *Economic Research Journal* 2.

Wang S.Z. 2013. A review on adjustment and optimization of investment structure in China. *Review of Economic Research* 16.

Wang, C., and X. Li. 2014. The emergence and development of socialist economic theory with Chinese characteristics. *Economic Research Journal* 6.

Wang, D. 1994. The labor market under the condition of socialist market economy. *Research on Financial and Economic Issues* 1.

Wang, D.X., L.L. Li, and G.H. Ran. 2009. Financial capital formation and economic growth. *Economic Research Journal* 9.

Wang, H.R. 2015. Supply-side reform is just like traditional Chinese medicine. *China Economic Weekly* 47.

Wang, J.H. 2001. *Introduction to the economics of government regulation: Basic theory and its application in the practice of government regulation*. Commercial Press.

Wang, J.H. 2013. *Performance evaluation and regulatory policy for the privatization of China's urban public utilities*. China Social Science Press.

Wang, K.X., and L.Y. Yu. 2016. A review of the research on progressive retirement age policy. *Population & Economics.*

Wang, L.R. 2015. The way to improve the mechanism of rural land appreciation income distribution. *Agricultural Economics* 7.

Wang, L.Z. 2015. Path selection of rural land contract system reform in the new era. *Agricultural Economics* 2.

Wang, T., and X.F. Liu. 2016. The promotion system construction and policy suggestions on China's service trade in the background of 'one belt one road' strategy. *Modern Management Science* 1.

Wang, W. 2010. Savings and growth effects of family planning policy: Theory and China's empirical analysis. *Economic Research Journal* 10.

Wang, W.G., et al. 2010. Viewpoint on problems of China's economic and social development reform in '12th five-year' period. *Economic Research Journal* 12.

Wang, X.L. 2000. The sustainability of China's economic growth and institutional change. *Economic Research Journal* 7.

Wang, X.L. 2010. An economic analysis on the urbanization path and urban scale in China. *Economic Research Journal* 10.

Wang, Y.P. 2014. Analysis of China's economic growth factors: 1978–2012. *Industrial Economic Review* 7.

Wang, Z.H. 2013. *Economic history of the United Kingdom*. China Social Sciences Publishing House.

Wei, J. 2014. The structure imbalance of China's macro economy: Theoretical and empirical research. Doctoral Dissertation of Northwestern University.

Wei, X.H., and W.M. Hou. 2007. The selection and transformation modes of China's economic growth model. *Economic Research Journal* 7.

Wei, X.H. 2000. How to correctly understand the socialist economy. *Theory Front* 3.

Wei, X.H. 2008. A study on the shareholding system and the reconstruction of individual ownership. *Economics Information* 6.

Wei, Z. 2015. The way to resolve the outbreak of non-performing assets. *Oriental Business* 11.

Weng, Y.Y. A study on the sustainability of China's economic growth. Shanghai Municipal People's Government Decision Consulting Research Project, 2009-A-03B.

Williamson, J.G. 1965. Regional inequality and the process of national development: A description of the patterns. *Economic Development and Cultural Change*.

Wu, J.L. 2008. How to make China's rapid economic growth sustainable. *The Economic Observer*, February 21st.

Wu, J.L., et al. 1994. *The reform of large and medium sized enterprises to establish modern enterprise system*. Tianjin Peoples Publishing House.

Wu, Z.Q. 2002. The determination of consumption and investment in China's economic growth. *Social Science in China* 5.

Xi, J.F. 2005. The design of evaluation index system for social economic system: Methodology principle and its realization. *System Engineering Theory and Practice* 11.

Xi, J.P. 2014. *Xi Jinping: The governance of China*. Foreign Languages Press.

Xia, Q.J., S. Li, L.N. Song, and S. Appleton. 2012. The income distribution effect of the wage structure and the employment scale change of state-owned units: 1988—2007. *Economic Research Journal* 6.

Xiao, G.L. 2011. *The economic history of People's Republic of China 1949–2010*. Peking University Press.

Xiao, L., and D. Wang. 2016. Supply-side structural reform and China's economic growth potential. *Scientific Development* 4.

Xiao, L. 2008. *Public economics: A perspective on the boundary of "visible hand"*. Truth & Wisdom Press, Shanghai People's Publishing House.

Xiao, L. 2012. *Financial strategy and economic forum: Shanghai's road to international financial center*. Truth & Wisdom Press, Shanghai People's Publishing House.

Xiao, L. 2015a. The practice of structural reform in Shanghai under the new economy. *Scientific Development* 12.

Xiao, L. 2015b. *National experiment: The system design of China (Shanghai) pilot free trade zone revised edition*. Truth & Wisdom Press, Shanghai People's Publishing House.

Xiao, L. 2016a. New supply economics: The economic thoughts and theoretical innovation on supply-side structural reform. *Scientific Development* 5.

Xiao, L. 2016b. Planning the relatively definite future in uncertainty—The development strategy of Shanghai in 2050. *Scientific Development* 1.

Xiao, L. 2016c. Supply-side economics and supply-side structural reform from a global perspective. *Scientific Development* 4.

Xiao, L. 2016d. Supply-side structural reform and China's economic growth forecast. *Scientific Development* 5.

Xiao, L. 2016e. The political economy of socialism with Chinese characteristics and the theoretical logic of supply-side structural reform. *Scientific Development* 3.

Xiao, L., et al. 2016. The practice of new supply economics: The ideas and measures of supply-side structural reform in Shanghai. *Scientific Development* 4.

Xing, Y. 1994. Labor market in socialist market economy. *Finance & Trade Economics* 3.

Xu, C.G. 2011. Five problems brought by state monopoly on land ownership. *Party and Government Cadres Reference* 5.

Yang, L.J. 2009. *The second revolution—On reagan's economics*. Truth & Wisdom Press.

Yang, L.Y., and H.F. Pan. 2003. Human capital, basic research and economic growth. *Economic Research Journal* 4.

Yang, R.L. Changes in medium and long term economic growth factors and the impact on Shanghai's economic development. Decision Consulting Research Project of Shanghai Municipal People's Government, 2013-A-45.

Yang, R.L. 1993. Institutional innovation: The source of economic growth. *Reform of Economic System* 5.

Yang, R.L. 1998. The three-stage theory of institutional change mode in China—On the institutional innovation of local government. *Economic Research Journal* 1.

Yang, W.F. 2014. The measure of total factor productivity and the reasons for changes in decomposition of China's three industries. *Journal of Changchun Finance College* 2.

Yang, X.K. 2003. *Economics: New classical and neoclassical frameworks*. Social Sciences Academic Press.

Yang, Z., H.M. Liu, and B. Yu. 2013. Evaluation estimation of ecological value loss in the process of land resource conversion. *Population, Resources and Environment in China* 10.

Yang, Z.B., and C. Zhang. 2015. Research on measurement and influence factors of industrial excess production capacity of China. *Nankai Economic Studies* 6.

Ye, S.Y. 2015. Thoughts on supply-side structural reform. *Development Research* 12.

Yi, B.C., and G.H. Hua. 1996. *Supply-side economics*. Wuhan Press.

Yi, G., G. Fan, and Y. Li. 2003. Theoretical thinking on China's economic growth and total factor productivity. *Economic Research Journal* 8.

Yu, L.C., and W. Zhang. 2010. Research on the intensity and efficiency loss of China's administrative monopoly. *Economic Research Journal* 3.

Yu, X.M., S. Li, and T.L. Shi. 2010. Discussion on high income in monopoly industries. *Social Science in China* 5.

Zhan, S.H., and W.J. Jiang. 2014. Measurement and decomposition of total factor productivity in China. *Statistical Research* 3.

Zhang, C.W., and Y.F. Cai. 2012. General trends of labor supply and demand in China: Problems and policy options. *Population and Economy* 4.

Zhang, J. 1996. Why can the gradual reform in China achieve success? *The Economist* 5.

Zhang, J. 2002. China's capital formation and economic growth since the reform: Some findings and explanations. *World Economic Forum* 1.

Zhang, J. 2006. *The "double-track" economy: China's economic reforms 1978–1992*. Shanghai People's Publishing House.

Zhang, J. 2015. Abnormal state of China's economy: Short-term and long-term solution. *Journal of the Party School of CPC Hangzhou* 4.

Zhang, J., S.Y. Chen, and Jefferson. 2009. Structural reform and industrial growth in China. *Economic Research Journal* 7.

Zhang, J.K., and C.W. Zhao. 2014. *Analysis of the problem of overcapacity in China*. Tsinghua University Press.

Zhang, L. 2013. Calculation of potential GDP growth rate in China. Doctoral Dissertation of South China University of Technology.

Zhang, L., S. Li, et al. 2016. The discrimination in job obtainment by Hukou in labor market in China and its change trend. *Journal of Finance and Economics* 1.

Zhang, M.N, 2015. Supply-side reform releases new growth dividend in China. *View Financial Fortune* 12.

Zhang, P., and X.H. Liu. 2012. China's long-term economic growth: Path, efficiency and potential growth level. *Economic Research Journal* 11.

Zhang, W.C. 2014. *Economic explanation, volume 4: Institutional option*. CITIC Press.

Zhang, Y.C., and Y.G. Zhou. 1997. Asymmetric information, enterprise reform and the securities market. *Economic Research Journal* 5.

Zhang, Z.B. 2016. *China's supply-side structural reform*. People's Publishing House.

Zhang, Z.H. 2014. Study on the urban land use efficiency in China. *Quantitative Economics and Technology Research* 7.

Zhang, Z.L., Q.Y. Zhao, and C. Lin. 2015. Some problems needed to be solved in the profitable collective constructive land entering the market. *China Land* 12.

Zhao, C.W., Z.Y. Xu, and H.M. Zhu. 2015. New growth impetus of China's economy in post industrial era. *China Industrial Economic* 6.

Zhao, X.F., X.J. Huang, Y. Chen, and Z.G. Chen. 2010. Research progress of the urban land intensive use. *Journal of Natural Resources* 11.

Zhao, Z.Y. 2014. Innovation driven development: From the supply side to demand side. *China Soft Science* 8.

Zhou, S.L. 2000. The theoretical analysis of state-owned enterprises reform based on 20 years experience. *Journal of Graduate School of Chinese Academy of Social Sciences* 3.

Zhou, T.Y. 1997. *Efficiency and the supply of economics*. Economic Science Press.

Zhu, B. 2014. *Study on systematic risk in China's financial system*. Southwestern University of Finance and Economics Press.

Zhu, L. 2010. Research on the fairness and sustainability of China's social security system. *Chinese Journal of Population Science* 5.

Zuo, X.J. 2014. China's current land system and the integration of urban and rural areas: Problems and future policy. *Journal of Shanghai Jiaotong University* 4.

MIX
Papier aus verantwortungsvollen Quellen
Paper from responsible sources
FSC® C105338

If you have any concerns about our products,
you can contact us on
ProductSafety@springernature.com

In case Publisher is established outside the EU,
the EU authorized representative is:
Springer Nature Customer Service Center GmbH
Europaplatz 3, 69115 Heidelberg, Germany

Printed by Libri Plureos GmbH
in Hamburg, Germany